THE WORLD'S GREATEST
SEX AND SCANDALS

D0676199

CHANCELLOR
PRESS

This 2001 edition published by
Chancellor Press, an imprint of Bounty Books
a division of Octopus Publishing Group Ltd,
2–4 Heron Quays, London E14 4JP

The material in this book has previously appeared in:
The World's Greatest Political Scandals
(Bounty, Octopus Publishing Group Ltd, 1999)
The World's Greatest Hollywood Scandals
(Hamlyn, Octopus Publishing Group Ltd, 1994)
The World's Greatest Royal Scandals
(Bounty, Octopus Publishing Group Ltd, 1999)
The World's Greatest Rock'n'Roll Scandals
(Octopus Publishing Group Ltd, 1989)

ISBN 0 7537 0423 4

Printed in Great Britain by Mackays of Chatham

Reprinted 2001, 2002

Front cover picture acknowledgments:
Monica Lewinsky (Rufus F.Folkks/Corbis)
Marilyn Monroe and Christine Keeler
(Hulton Getty Picture Collection)

Contents

Royal
Scandals

A Fairy-tale Too Far

It was a fairy-tale wedding of the 20th century. Over 750 million people around the world watched as the heir to the British throne and shy virgin bride descended the steps of St Paul's Cathedral on 29 July 1981 to the cheers of the crowds. Just 11 years later, with the publication of Andrew Morton's *Diana: Her True Story*, the fairy-tale turned into a farce and the greatest royal scandal for more than half a century began to unfurl.

In many ways, one of the functions of the royal family seems to have been to amuse its subjects with periodic royal scandals. It keeps the public's minds off important things like war, pestilence, famine, crime, death and taxes. It forges a nation into one people who share common emotions as they witness the outrageous antics of the royals. And it gives them something to talk about. When Charles II frolicked with the orange-seller and actress, Nell Gwynne, people were shocked and scandalized. Yet they were also grateful that the newly restored king was not one of those dull old Puritans who had, a decade before, banned Christmas. Oranges were on sale openly on the street. The theatres were open again, so the public could see actresses, and most particularly, actresses' legs once more. And there were plenty more buxom young ladies like Nell who would give a gentleman a whole lot of fun for sixpence.

However, the scandal of Charles and Di's sham marriage and its shocking exposé was taking things a bit too far. For more than six years, it rocked the monarchy to its foundation. It led to the queen complaining of at least one *annus horribilis*. And she was forced to scale down the civil list and pay taxes.

It is not difficult to see how the scandal came about.

Prince Charles had been brought up steeped in history. In royal families, it is generally accepted that married people fool around, but stay together for the sake of propriety. In the British royal family particularly, it was the men who fooled around and their long-suffering wives were supposed to put up with it. The first king in the current dynasty, George I, arrived in England from Hanover in 1690 with two mistresses-dubbed the 'maypole' and the 'elephant', one being tall and thin, the other short and fat. He left his wife behind, imprisoned in the castle because she had the temerity to take a lover.

Charles's great-great-grandfather, Edward VII – the notorious Prince of Wales known to actresses and prostitutes across the world simply as Bertie – scandalized the nation with his salacious goings on while his dutiful wife, Queen Alexandra, not only put up with his infidelities, she was kind to his mistresses. She even allowed one of them to visit him on his deathbed.

Although, as a rake, Charles was nowhere near Bertie's league, he had sown a few wild oats. Several of his early entanglements made the newspapers. According to the Fleet Street scandal sheets, Charles lost his virginity to Lucia Santa Cruz, daughter of the Chilean ambassador, when he was a student at Cambridge in his early 20s. She was a post-graduate student, three years his senior. Later, it is said, the plucky Prince scaled the walls of the all-woman Newham College to share the bed of Sybilla Dorman, daughter of the Governor General of Malta. Soon after, he was photographed escorting Audrey Buxton to the May Ball at Trinity College.

He managed to keep most of his aristocratic escorts out of the newspapers. There was Lady Jane Wellesley, daughter of the Duke of Wellington; the daughter of the Duke of Northumberland, Lady Caroline and Lady Victoria Percy; the Duke of Westminster's daughter, Leonora, and her sister Jane, who became the Duchess of Roxburghe; the Duke

of Rutland's daughter, Lady Charlotte Manners, and her
cousin Elizabeth; the Marquis of Lothian's daughter, Lady
Cecil Kerr; the Duke of Grafton's daughter, Lady Henrietta
Fitzroy; Lord Astor's daughter, Angela; Lord Rupert
Nevill's daughter, Angela; Sir John Russell's daughter,
Georgiana and so on through Burke's Peerage. He kept
these amours quiet by entertaining the young ladies con-
cerned at Broadlands, the country estate of his Uncle
Dickie – Lord Mountbatten.

However, some slipped under the wire. There was a
good deal of fevered press speculation about Prince
Charles's relationship with Lady 'Kanga' Tryon and some
snobbish tut-tutting about his sipping at the lips of Sabrina
Guinness, daughter of the famous brewing family.

When he took up with the rich and stylish Davina
Sheffield, her jilted lover James Beard spilt the beans of
their cosy cohabitation in the Sunday papers. And when
Prince Charles started seeing Lord Manton's daughter.
Fiona Watson, the papers had a field day. The curvaceous
Fiona had once stripped off for the soft-porn magazine
Penthouse, so here was a royal scandal complete with juicy
pictures.

Then in 1972, Charles met the love of his life, Camilla
Shand. He was introduced to her at the up-market Mayfair
disco, Annabel's, by Andrew Parker-Bowles, the guards
officer whom he would later cuckold as her husband.

Camilla made no secret of her scandalous intent. She
introduced herself to the Prince as the great-granddaugh-
ter of Alice Keppel – the last mistress of Edward VII. Alice
had once famously remarked that her job was to 'curtsy
first and then hop into bed'.

Camilla and the Prince got on famously. They shared a
love of riding, the countryside, gardening and architecture. They also both had the same juvenile sense of
humour. However, duty intervened. As heir to the throne,
Charles had to do his bit in the armed forces. Reluctantly,

in 1973, he left Camilla on the dockside and shoved off in his ship HMS *Minerva*. It had already been made clear to Camilla that she was not the material queens were made of. Four weeks after she had kissed her sailor prince good-bye, she accepted the proposal of Andrew Parker-Bowles. Within months they were married, and the very next year Prince Charles became godfather to the couple's first child.

Prince Charles consoled himself with other women. After dining at his flat in Buckingham Palace, many women would stay the night. The prince's valet would often find items of ladies underwear concealed around the house. These would be laundered and returned in an Asprey's box, if the owner was known. Otherwise they would be given to members of the Palace staff, many of whom were gay.

The Palace managed to keep the details of these affairs out of the press. At the time, Prince Andrew told a girl-friend that Charles was trying to compete with Warren Beatty who, it is said, had laid every starlet in Hollywood. *The Daily Mail* even reported that Charles had a slush fund to buy the silence of women who objected to being used once and then cast aside.

During this period, Charles was seeing Sarah Spencer, Diana's older sister, who was deemed unsuitable as a wife because she was heavy smoker. Meanwhile, his younger brother, Prince Andrew, was having a brief dalliance with Di herself.

Charles was now 30 and the pressure was on for him to do what heirs to the throne are supposed to do – produce more heirs. The race was on to find him a suitable wife. Foreign princesses, including Marie-Astrid of Luxembourg, were vetted. But all those of a suitable age and disposition were Catholics. Under the *Act of Settlement* (1701), it is deemed unlawful for the heir to the throne to marry a Catholic.

So the Royal Family looked closer to home and their

eyes soon alighted on Diana. She was everything they could have wished for – English, upper class, naïve and, by her own admission, none too bright. More importantly, she was a virgin. At least this was the firm assertion of her uncle, Lord Fermoy, though no one asked how he was in a position to know.

Her virginity was also important under English constitutional law. Catherine Howard had been executed for treason, not just because she had fooled around after her marriage to Henry VIII but also because she had lost her maidenhead before it.

Randy Andy, apparently, had got nowhere with Diana. Neither had author and socialite, George Plumptree, with whom she had been going out for more than a year. Or, at least, they were not saying. The public swallowed this, not least because she looked the part. With her blushing good looks and her innocently averted gaze, she could have been tailor-made for the role. She was everyone's idea for the fresh, unsullied maiden who gets to marry Prince Charming.

But Charles was not Prince Charming. In fact, his coolness towards his delightful young bride was palpable. In the couple's first face-to-face interview with the press, he was asked whether he was in love with her. He replied, awkwardly: ' Yes, whatever than may mean.'

'I think an awful lot of people have got the wrong idea about love,' he had said in an interview four years earlier. 'It is rather more than just falling madly in love. It's basically a very strong friendship. I think you are very lucky if you find the right person attractive in both the physical sense and the mental sense. If I am deciding who I want to live with for 50 years, that's the last decision on which I would want my head to be ruled by my heart.'

He could have been talking about Camilla.

The problem was not just that Diana was not Camilla. She was not of royal blood, nurtured in regal seclusion.

She had not been brought up to play aristocratic games, to turn a blind eye to her husband's misdemeanours and conduct her own affairs, if she felt the need to have any, discreetly. She was a modern young woman who expected more. She wanted to be loved and she was not going to put up with her fiancé fooling around.

And fooling around he was. While they were courting, Charles was seeing Davina Sheffield and Anne Wallace, who in turn was seeing other men. He was also maintaining an interest in Camilla Parker-Bowles. Just weeks before the royal wedding, Diana found a bracelet in Charles's desk drawer. At first, she thought this expensive gift was for her. But on closer examination, she spotted the initials 'F' and 'G' engraved on it. In intimate conversation, Charles and Camilla had adopted the Goon Show nomenclature, 'Fred' and 'Gladys'.

Diana was heartbroken; Charles nonplussed. He could not see what Diana had to complain about. It seemed perfectly normal to him to carry on an active love life with other women, even though he was getting married. After all, his father, the Duke of Edinburgh, had been doing that very thing for all the long years of his marriage to the Queen. That is what royals did. Besides, the wedding plans were almost complete. Heads of state from around the world were on their way. The TV networks had cleared their schedules. The world was waiting. It was too late to back out now. The fairly-tale wedding had to go ahead.

The nightmare situation she had innocently walked into must have been apparent to Diana from the very first night, which the young couple spent at Broadlands. Instead of extending that first night of bliss long into the following day, Charles slept off the exertions of their long and tiring wedding day, then leapt from his marriage bed bright and early the next morning to go fishing.

Their honeymoon on the Royal Yacht *Britannia* was

more successful. Apparently, they went to bed early and rose late. Rumours spread that they had taken candid pictures of each other. Some said that these pictures fell into the hands of the press but, so far, no newspaper has dared to publish them.

However, instead of having intimate dinners à *deux*, evening meals were formal affairs, surrounded by staff. Even when they were alone, Charles would propound his great thoughts on such weighty topics as world affairs and mysticism. He was old beyond his years and she was just a normal 20-year-old airhead, whose interests did not extend beyond clothes, make-up, pop music and babies. Not only was she bored by him, she was hurt, too. During the cruise, pictures of Camilla fell out of his dairy. She also realized the significance of the entwined 'CC's on the cuflinks he wore. Fortunately, as a balm for his boorish behaviour, there were plenty of handsome young sailors to flirt with.

Back on dry land, Diana flirted openly with the President of Portugal, the dashing Mario Soares. And there were others. But the story circulated in the press that this was just the high spirits of a sexy young woman and the marriage was solid. This was far from the case.

Within a year of their marriage, Charles made it clear to Diana that he had no intention of giving up his friendship with Mrs Parker-Bowles. As heir to the throne, having a *maîtresse en titre* was not only right and fitting, it was practically his duty. Diana did her duty, too, and produced Prince William in 1982.

Soon after giving birth, Diana overhead Charles on the phone saying: 'Whatever happens I will go on loving you.'

These are the words every young mum would love to hear from her husband, but not when he is saying them to his mistress.

With the birth of a second son, Prince Harry, securing the succession, Diana's duty was now done. Publicly, she was seen as a loving mum and she loyally turned up at Charles's side at state occasions. Otherwise her life was her own. Soon the press got wind of the fact that, like his mother and father, they slept in separate bedrooms.

Once, while Charles was away, Diana went to an all-night party. Afterwards, she spent the weekend with Philip Dunne. Then she was seen at a David Bowie concert with Major David Waterhouse.

The gossip columns were soon reporting that Diana had an unusual number of close male 'friends'. Names were bandied around. There were Mervyn Chapling, Roy Scott, a friend of hers from the days before she was married, and Nicholas Haslam, hi-fi dealer to the aristocracy. Once the affair with Haslam was over, it was reported later, she became a phone pest.

The name that provoked the most heated rumours was Captain James Hewitt. He had taught Prince William to ride and eased Diana back into the saddle. Hewitt's long-term girlfriend stormed out of the relationship, claiming that he was besotted with the princess. During the Gulf War, Hewitt was posted to the Middle East and he and Diana exchanged torrid love letters.

Next, there was the upper-class car dealer and scion of the gin family, James Gilbey. They had been friends in her single days and, trying to put the best possible construction on the Princess's increasingly reckless social life, it was generally assumed that she was using him merely as a shoulder to cry on.

But Diana was now being tailed by journalists. At 8 p.m. one evening in 1989, they saw Diana's bodyguard, Sergeant David Sharp, drop her off at Gilbey's flat. They waited. No one left or entered the flat for five hours.

At 1 a.m. she emerged, slightly dishevelled. Sergeant Sharp drove up. Furtively, Diana got in the car and they sped away. When journalists asked what the two of them had been doing for five long hours, Gilbey gallantly said that they had been playing bridge. But you need four people to play bridge.

By now the press was feverishly speculating that there was something wrong with the royal marriage. Buckingham Palace managed to keep the lid on it. Then Andrew Morton's sensational book, *Diana: Her True Story*, blew the whole thing out of the water.

Although everybody – including Morton – stoutly denied it at the time, it was plain that the book had been produced with Diana's active co-operation. After her death, it became clear that she had actively colluded with Morton on the book. It was her mouthpiece. The book exposed the marriage as a sham from the very beginning. The Royal Family had employed her simply as a baby machine. In fact they had isolated and excluded her to the point that she fell prey to the eating disorder, bulimia nervosa. And Charles's cold and unfeeling behaviour had driven her to attempt suicide.

Andrew Morton's book was quickly followed by *Fall of the House of Windsor* by Nigel Blundell and Susan Blackhall. It maintained that it was Diana's petulant tantrums that had alienated the Royal Family. Charles, it said, had been driven into the arms of another woman by his young wife's unreasonable behaviour. It also mentioned the existence of the notorious 'Squidgygate tapes'.

On New Year's Eve 1989 and 4 January 1990, secretarial agency manager Jane Norgrove and retired bank manager Cyril Reenan had recorded mobile phone conversations between two people who were obviously physically intimate with each other. One purported to be James Gilbey; the other the Princess of Wales.

They had been touted around Fleet Street for two years. In 1992, they surfaced in the USA. It was only then that the British press ran them. At first derided as fakes, they pretty soon proved to be the real McCoy. In them, Diana cursed 'the f***ing family'. Now the Royal Family had a full-scale scandal on their hands.

The tapes were known as the Squidgygate tapes because throughout Gilbey refers to Diana as 'Squidgy'. They went like this:

GILBEY: You know, all I want to do is to get in my car and drive around the country talking to you.

DIANA: Thanks (laughs).

GILBEY: That's all I want to do, darling. I just want to see you and be with you. That's what's going to be such bliss, being back in London.

DIANA: I know.

GILBEY: Kiss me, darling. (Blows kisses down the phone.)

DIANA: (Blows kisses back and laughs.)

GILBEY: Squidgy, laugh some more. I love it when I hear you laughing. It makes me really happy when you laugh. Do you know I am happy when you are happy?

DIANA: I know you are.

GILBEY: And I cry when you cry.

DIANA: I know. So sweet. The rate we are going, we won't need any dinner on Tuesday.

GILBEY: No. I won't need any dinner actually. Just seeing you will be all I need.....

(Pause)

DIANA: Did you get my hint about Tuesday night? I think you missed it. Think what I said.

GILBEY: No.

DIANA: I think you have missed it.

GILBEY: No, you said: 'At this rate, we won't want anything to eat.'

DIANA: Yes.

GILBEY: Yes, I know. I got there, Tuesday night. Don't worry, I got there. I can tell you the feeling's entirely mutual.

Next they talked about making babies.

DIANA: You didn't say anything about babies, did you?
GILBEY: No.
DIANA: No.
GILBEY: Why darling?
DIANA: (laughs) I thought you did.
GILBEY: Did you?
DIANA: Yes.
GILBEY: Did you, darling? You have got them on the brain.
DIANA: Well yeah, maybe I….
(Pause)
DIANA: I don't want to get pregnant.
GILBEY: Darling, it's not going to happen.
DIANA: (Sighs)
GILBEY: All right?
DIANA: Yeah.
GILBEY: Don't worry about that. It's not going to happen, darling. You won't get pregnant.

The tapes continued in the same vein.

GILBEY: Oh Squidgy, I love you, love you, love you.
DIANA: You are the nicest person in the whole world.
GILBEY: Pardon?
DIANA: You're just the nicest person in the whole world.
GILBEY: Well, darling, you are to me too.
DIANA: You don't mind it, darling, when I want to talk to you so much?
DIANA: No. I love it. Never had it before.
GILBEY: Darling, it's so nice being able to help you.
DIANA: You do. You'll never know how much.
GILBEY: Oh, I will, darling. I just feel so close to you, so wrapped up in you.

13

DIANA: Yes please. Yes please.

GILBEY: Oh, Squidgy.

DIANA: Mmm.

GILBEY: Kiss me please. (Blows more kisses.) Do you know what I'm going to be imagining I am doing tonight at about 12 o'clock. Just holding you so close to me. It'll have to be delayed action for 48 hours.

DIANA: (Titters.)

GILBEY: Fast forward.

DIANA: Fast forward.

These were plainly two people deeply in love who could not wait to get their hands on each other. But they had to be careful.

DIANA: I shall tell people I'm going for acupuncture and my back is being done.

GILBEY: (Giggles) Squeegee, cover them footsteps.

DIANA: I jolly well do.

If all that was not damning enough, there was a portion of the transcript that was so hot that the newspapers did not dare publish it. Of course, journalists and other insiders knew what was said and this helped fuel the scandal. The omitted section was about masturbation.

GILBEY: Squeegee, kiss me. (Sounds of kisses being exchanged.)

GILBEY: Oh God, it's wonderful, isn't it? This sort of feeling. Don't you like it?

DIANA: I love it.

GILBEY: Umm.

DIANA: I love it.

GILBEY: Isn't it absolutely wonderful? I haven't had it for years. I feel about 21 again.

DIANA: Well, you're not. You're 33.

GILBEY: Darling, MM. Tell me some more. It's just like sort of mmmmm.

DIANA: Playing with yourself.

14

GILBEY: What?

DIANA: Nothing.

GILBEY: No, I'm not actually.

DIANA: I said it's just like, just like….

GILBEY: Playing with yourself.

DIANA: Yes.

GILBEY: Not quite as nice. Not quite as nice. No, I haven't played with myself, actually. Not for a full 48 hours. (They both laugh.) Not for a full 48 hours.

Although no one could doubt their authenticity, there was still a mystery that surrounded the tapes. From the tapes it is plain that James Gilbey was talking on the mobile phone in his car. As he drove, the phone would automatically be passed from station in the cellular network. So an amateur radio enthusiast tuning into the call would catch only part of the conversation before it jumped frequency between stations. It was quickly concluded that the recording has been made using a bug in the land line at Diana's end, then rebroadcast on a fixed station in the hope that someone would pick it up.

Who could have done such a thing? Suspicion fell on the security forces – MI5, Special Branch, the Royal Security Squad or the government listening station in Cheltenham, GCHQ. Plainly, orders to tape the phone of the future Queen of England would have to come from the highest authority. Diana's supporters suspected Charles. They said that he used the security forces to gather evidence he could use in a divorce, but had leaked the information to get his own back for Diana's collusion in *Diana Her True Story*.

With the press on his tail, James Gilbey went into hiding. But Diana pressed home her advantage. She demanded an immediate divorce, a sizeable financial settlement, unfettered access to her sons, the retention of her royal titles and a court of her own.

The Palace fought back. It leaked stories that Charles

and Diana had had a romantic reconciliation at the annual Ghillies' Ball at Balmoral. ITN aired an hour-long documentary, assuring the world that divorce was off the agenda.

But Charles's faction could not sit still. They said that the Prince loathed Diana, and that he considered her co-operation in *Diana: Her True Story* an act of betrayal. They said that he called her 'Diana the Martyr' and that the Squidgygate tapes had given her a dose of her own medicine.

The Palace insisted that the couple made one last attempt to bluff it out. Together they made a state visit to South Korea. It was a glittering occasion with plenty of photo opportunities for the world's press. But it was plain from their body language that the royal couple detested each other.

With the two parties still clearly at each other's throats, something has to be done. It fell to the luckless Prime Minister John Major to make a statement to the House of Commons.

'It is announced from Buckingham Palace that, with regret, the Prince and Princess of Wales have decided to separate,' he told the packed chamber. 'Their Royal Highnesses have no plans to divorce and their constitutional positions are unaffected. Their decision has been reached amicably, and they will both continue to participate to carry out full and separate programmes of public engagements and will, from time to time, attend family occasions and national events together. The Queen and the Duke of Edinburgh, though saddened, understand and sympathise with the difficulties that have led to this decision. Her Majesty and His Royal Highness particularly hope that the intrusion into the privacy of the Prince and Princess may now cease. They believe that a degree of privacy and understanding is essential if their Royal Highnesses are to provide a happy and secure upbringing for their children, while continuing to give whole-hearted commitment to their public duties.'

Fat chance.

Mr Major added that the succession was unaffected and that when he became King, Charles would still become head of the Church of England. Some doubted that. Even senior churchmen shook their heads at Charles running around with a married woman and made it clear that if he attempted to marry Camilla they would press for the church to be disestablished.

The Sun proclaimed that John Major's announcement was a 'Victory for Di'. But she felt that she had been out-manoeuvred by the Palace, which was seeking to sideline her. The game was far from over though.

That there should be one tape could be considered a misfortune, but that there were two smacked of careless-ness. But two there were.

The second came to light in Australia. It purported to be a telephone conversation between Prince Charles and Camilla recorded on the night of 18 December 1989 – two weeks before the notorious Squidgygate tapes. Its authen-ticity has never been questioned because its content was so sensational.

A man claiming to be a radio ham sold the tapes to at least one national newspaper, but it was thought too tawdry to use. However, in January 1993 an Australian magazine called *New Ideas* got hold of a copy of the tran-script and broke the story Down Under. Within minutes of publication, copies were being faxed around the world. Now there was no reason for Fleet Street to hold back.

The conversation is said to have taken place between Camilla, who was at her family home in Wiltshire, while Charles was lying on his bed with a mobile phone in the Cheshire country home of the Duke of Westminster, where he was a guest. The reading begins when the conversation is already in progress.

CHARLES: ...he was a bit anxious actually.

CAMILLA: Was he?

CHARLES: He thought he might have gone a bit far.

CAMILLA: Ah well.

CHARLES: Anyway you know, that's the sort of thing one has to be aware of and sort of feel one's way along with, if you know what I mean.

CAMILLA: Mmm. You're awfully good at feeling your way along.

CHARLES: Oh stop! I want to feel my way along you, all over you and up and down and in and out....

CAMILLA: Oh.

CHARLES: Particularly in and out.

CAMILLA: Oh, that's just what I need at the moment.

CHARLES: Is it?

CAMILLA: I know it would revive me. I can't bear a Sunday night without you.

CHARLES: Oh God.

CAMILLA: It's like that programme 'Start the Week'. I can't start the week without you.

CHARLES: I fill your tank.

CAMILLA: Yes, you do.

CHARLES: Then you can cope.

CAMILLA: Then I'm all right.

CHARLES: What about me? The trouble is I need you several times a week. All the time.

CAMILLA: Oh God, I'll just live inside your trousers or something. It would be much easier. (She laughs.) What are you going to turn into, a pair of knickers? It would be much easier. (They both laugh.) Oh, you're going to come back as a pair of knickers.

CHARLES: Or, God forbid, a Tampax. Just my luck. (He laughs.)

CAMILLA: You're a complete idiot. (She laughs.) Oh, what a wonderful idea.

CHARLES: My luck to be chucked down a lavatory and

go on and on forever swirling around the top, never going down...

CAMILLA: Oh, darling.

CHARLES: ...until the next one comes through.

CAMILLA: Oh, perhaps you could come back as a box.

CHARLES: What sort of box?

CAMILLA: A box of Tampax so you could just keep going.

CHARLES: That's true.

CAMILLA: Repeating yourself. (She laughs.) Oh, darling. Oh, I just want you now.

CHARLES: Do you?

CAMILLA: Mmm.

CHARLES: So do I.

CAMILLA: Desperately, desperately, desperately. I thought of you so much at Yearly.

CHARLES: Did you?

CAMILLA: Simply mean that we couldn't be there together.

CHARLES: Desperately. If you could be here – I long to ask Nancy sometimes.

CAMILLA: Why don't you?

CHARLES: I daren't.

CAMILLA: Because I think she's so in love with you.

CHARLES: Mmm.

And on it goes. She tells him that she loves him 11 times; he tells her twice. She calls him 'darling' 18 times; he calls her 'darling' seven times. Her husband is referred to simply as 'A' or him. At one stage, she says: 'He won't be here Thursday, pray God.'

That assignation arranged, she begs him to get some sleep and to call her in the morning. Then they say goodnight to each other no fewer than 19 times. The final sequence goes like this:

CAMILLA: ...night, night.

CHARLES: Night, darling, God bless.

CAMILLA: I do love you and I am so proud of you.

CHARLES: Oh, I am so proud of you.

CAMILLA: Don't be silly, I've never achieved anything.

CHARLES: Yes, you have.

CAMILLA: No, I haven't.

CHARLES: Your great achievement is to love me.

CAMILLA: Oh darling. Easier than falling off a chair.

CHARLES: You suffer all these indignities and tortures and calumnies.

CAMILLA: Oh darling, don't be so silly. I'd suffer anything for you. That's love. It's the strength of love. Night, night.

CHARLES: Night, darling. Sounds as though you're dragging and enormous piece of string behind you, with hundreds of tin pots and cans attached to it. I think it must be your telephone. Night, night, before the battery goes. (He blows a kiss.) Night.

CAMILLA: Love you.

CHARLES: Don't want to say goodbye.

CAMILLA: Neither do I, but you must get some sleep. Bye.

CHARLES: Bye, darling.

CAMILLA: Love you.

CHARLES: Bye.

CAMILLA: Hopefully talk to you in the morning.

CHARLES: Please.

CAMILLA: Bye. I do love you.

CHARLES: Night.

CAMILLA: Night.

CHARLES: Night.

CAMILLA: Love you forever.

CHARLES: Night.

CAMILLA: Goodbye. Bye my darling.

CHARLES: Night.

CAMILLA: Night, night.

CHARLES: Night.

CAMILLA: Bye, bye.
CHARLES: Going.
CAMILLA: Bye.
CHARLES: Going.
CAMILLA: Gone.
CHARLES: Night.
CAMILLA: Bye. Press the button.
CHARLES: Going to press the tit.
CAMILLA: All right darling. I wish you were pressing mine.
CHARLES: God, I wish I was. Harder and harder.
CAMILLA: Oh darling.
CHARLES: Night.
CAMILLA: Love you.
CAMILLA: (Camilla yawns.) Love you. Press the tit.
CHARLES: Adore you. Night.
CAMILLA: Night. (Camilla blows a kiss.)
CHARLES: Night.
CAMILLA: Goodnight my darling. Love you...

And finally Charles hangs ups.
Not only were people appalled at the Tampax exchange, they realized that they could not figure out Prince Charles at all. Here was a man who was married to one of the most beautiful women in the world, who was obviously besotted by a woman who, not to put too fine a point on it, needed ironing. She was a little older than Charles and a good few years older than his glamorous young wife.

If Charles had been cut in the mould of his great-great-grandfather Bertie, the public would have forgiven him for fooling around. If he had been seen out on the town with a supermodel on each arm, he would have got away with it. But no one could understand how he could cast aside a supermodel for a woman who, frankly, looked like one of the horses she liked so much to ride.

The sad truth was that Charles was no playboy prince,

no lovable rogue with a heart of gold. He was like his mother, deeply middle class. He was a one-woman man. Unfortunately, that one woman was not Diana.

Again, people began to wonder where the Tampax tape had come from. The author and former MI6 officer, James Rushbridger, pointed the finger at GCHQ. A year later he was found hanged in his West Country home.

Next out of the woodwork was James Hewitt. In 1994, a 'novelized' version of the torrid love affair between Hewitt and Diana called *Princess in Love* was published by Anna Pasternak, a distant relative of the author of *Dr Zhivago* and former girlfriend of Hewitt.

Open warfare between Charles and Di continued on TV. Diana appeared on *Panorama*, where she admitted committing adultery and begged to be the people's 'Queen of Hearts'. She said she wanted to be a British goodwill ambassador to the world – despite the fact that, as consort to the heir to the throne, by admitting adultery she was also technically admitting treason. No one from Scotland Yard was sent to investigate.

Charles responded with an authorized biography and an extended TV interview with a sycophantic Jonathan Dimbleby. He, too, admitted adultery and having three separate affairs with the winsome Mrs Camilla Parker-Bowles. The battle of the documentaries was a draw. They both limped from the battlefield, licking their self-inflicted wounds.

Diana then threw herself into a charm offensive. She was seen very publicly doing good works. There were plenty of photo opportunities showing her with sick children. And, in front of the world's TV cameras, pages completely.

Diana then won a £15-million divorce settlement, but was forced to drop the tittle 'HRH' in the process. Even a publicized affair with England ruby captain, Will Carling, which lost him his wife, failed to dent her popularity.

Then she shot herself in the foot. She began a serious affair with Dodi Fayed, son of Harrods' boss Mohamed Fayed. This was a dangerous move. Mohamed Fayed's business methods had long been a source of criticism and he had been refused a British passport. Although Dodi Fayed himself listed his profession as 'movie producer', he was better known for his activities on the casting couch than for those behind the lens. The newspapers referred to him more accurately as 'millionaire playboy'.

Dodi wooed Diana on his yacht on the Côte d'Azur. Their love blossomed in front of the telephoto lenses of the paparazzi, for the delectation of tabloid readers worldwide. Meanwhile, Charles seized the opportunity to walk out with the freshly divorced Camilla, laying on her 50th birthday bash. It seemed the scandal would never end. But end it did, tragically.

Mohamed Fayed revelled in the publicity that his son's royal affair afforded him. He bought the house in Paris where the last British royals to be ousted by scandal, Edward and Mrs Simpson, had spent their exile. It was rumoured that this was where his son and the exiled Princess of Wales would set up home, too.

But it was not to be. On the night of 30 August 1997, Dodi and Di enjoyed a romantic dinner at the Ritz Hotel in Paris where he proposed – although a Hollywood starlet was quick to say that Dodi was already engaged to her and produced a ring to prove it. The couple left the Ritz late that evening, apparently on their way to view their putative matrimonial home. On the way, the car they were being driven in smashed into a pillar in an underpass, killing them both.

Criticism of Di ended at that moment. Fears that the mother of the heir to the throne – and hence a future head of the Church of England – might marry a Muslim were put aside. No further mention was made of the fact that Di's marriage to Dodi Fayed would be opposed by the establishment because he was, shall we say, tainted.

The press, perhaps guilty over its own role in the hounding of Di, now shot the line that the fairy-tale princess had died in the arms of her handsome young sheikh. When the Royal Family maintained their usual regal decorum, they were pilloried for being cold, old-fashioned and out of touch. The fresh, young, modernizing Prime Minister Tony Blair had to step in.

Nevertheless, the tabloid-reading public blamed the paparazzi for hounding Di to her death. Echoing public sentiment, the press were vilified from the pulpit by Diana's brother, the adulterous Earl Spencer, whose own messy divorce was already attracting the newspapers' scrutiny.

Slowly, Prince Charles turned the situation to his advantage. With Di dead, Charles now had no rival on the global stage. He was now 'keeper of the flame' – and the royal children. Even when Camilla emerged as stepmother-in-waiting, no one said a thing. Everything was going swimmingly.

But then, in an ill-judged move, biographer and journalist Polly Toynbee did an Andrew Morton, publishing *The Prince's Story*. The book told the story of the royal marriage from the Prince's side, seemingly with the collusion of, if not Charles himself, certainly those in his camp. When it came to the key issue – adultery – his defence was simply 'she did it first'. Suddenly, the longest running royal scandal of the 20th century showed that, even though its central, most glittering character had been written out, it still had legs.

Edward and Mrs Simpson

During their recent crises, the Royal Family's behaviour has been guided by one over-arching memory – that of the greatest scandal to hit the British throne this century, the Abdication Crisis of 1936.

For the British people it came like a bolt from the blue. As Prince of Wales, Edward had been popular. He had visited the front during World War I and genuinely seemed to sympathize with the plight of the unemployed during the Great Depression. For several years, he had been having a torrid affair with an American divorcee. He wanted to marry her and thought he would be able to when he came to the throne in January 1936.

The press barons were pillars of the establishment and, although foreign newspapers were full of the royal romance, nothing about the relationship was published in Britain. Sooner or later, the matter had to come to a head. The American papers were predicting that Edward would marry Mrs Wallis Simpson before his coronation in May 1937, so that she could be crowned Queen at the ceremony. But they had counted without the redoubtable Prime Minister, Stanley Baldwin, who was implacably against the match.

Over the years the waters have become muddied. Some say that the government opposed the marriage because Wallis Simpson was an American. Others think it was because she was a divorcee – twice over. Still others say it was because she was a commoner. And there are those who believe that Edward had already exhibited pro-Fascist sympathies and that the proposed marriage was simply an excuse to oust him.

The crisis was sparked by someone who knew nothing about the affair. The Bishop of Bradford, ironically named

Dr Alfred Blunt, spoke out at the diocesan conference in 1936, condemning the King's playboy life style. Indeed, before he met Mrs Simpson, he had been a bit of playboy and along the way it is said, sired two illegitimate children.

His first sexual experience was in a brothel in Calais during World War I where he said he found the prostitutes 'perfectly filthy and revolting'. That did not stop him going back for more in Amiens, or taking up with a courtesan in Paris.

On his return to England, he began walking out with Lady Sybil Cadogan, but was soon in love with Mrs Marian Coke, a married woman 12 years his senior. He seemed to have a thing about married women. One of his long-time lovers was Freda Dudley Ward, the wife of a Liberal MP. They met during a zeppelin raid when she ran into a house for cover where he was having dinner.

The affair lasted several years but then, as now, there were plenty other women, married and single, prepared to ease the libido of the heir to the throne. But in those days they did not kiss-and-tell in the newspapers. Besides, the owners of Fleet Street were peers of the realm and would not allow such things to be printed.

The Prince of Wales had a particular fascination for Americans. He visited America several times and set his cap at Audrey James, the daughter of an American industrialist. She rejected his advances when she was single but, once married, she had an affair with him that she recalled as 'merry but brief'.

Next came Lady Thelma Furness, the daughter of an American diplomat. Not only was she married, she was also a divorcee. At 16, she had eloped with a man twice her age. The marriage did not last. Once shot of her first husband, she snared Viscount Furness who was famous for his consumption of brandy and women.

Lady Furness accompanied Edward on a visit to Kenya in 1928 where, she said, she felt 'as if we were the only two people in the world'. In her diary she recorded: 'This was our Eden, and we were alone in it. His arms about me were the only reality; his words of love my only bridge to life. Borne along on the mounting tide of his ardour, I felt myself inexorably swept from the accustomed moorings of caution. Every night I felt more completely possessed by our love.'

Compare this with the Camillagate tapes, or Squidgygate.

The affair came to an end when she had a fling with Aly Khan, who had been trained in the art of delaying ejaculation in the brothel of Cairo when he was 18. He was so good at this that in aristocratic circles it was said that like Father Christmas, he only came once a year.

With competition like this, the Prince of Wales could not stand up. Thelma openly complained that Edward was a poor sexual performer and not very well endowed, scandalizing society by openly calling the heir to the throne 'the little man'. His deficiencies in the genital department had already been noted when he was at Osborne Naval College, where the other pupils called his private parts 'Sardine' rather than 'Whales'.

Ill-equipped to satisfy women, he may well have experimented with men. The gay writer, Lytton Strachey, tried to pick him up once in the Tate Gallery, only to flee when he realized who his intended was. Later, Strachey wrote about it, ruing what might have been.

When Dr Blunt spoke out, Edward had in fact been faithful to Mrs Simpson for several years. But Blunt's remarks at the diocesan conference breached the dam. The press pact was already under strain. Soon after Edward came to the throne, he began to put his marriage plans into action. First, he had to arrange a speedy divorce for Mrs Simpson. Her husband Ernest was found in the bedroom of a Thames-side hotel with a professional co-respondent, who rejoiced in the name of Buttercup Kennedy. When

Lord Beaverbrook, the Canadian-born owner of the *Express* newspaper group, heard that the divorce proceedings were to be heard at Ipswich on 27 October 1936, he called Mrs Simpson's solicitor and warned him that he intended to report the proceedings in the *London Evening Standard*. The solicitor told Beaverbrook that Mrs Simpson had no intention of marrying the King and that the notoriety their friendship had brought her was making her ill.

Beaverbrook bought it and, together with Lord Rothermere, owner of the *Daily Mail*, persuaded the rest of the papers to continue their code of silence on the matter. However, pressmen did turn up for the divorce hearing and were locked in the courtroom while Mrs Simpson made her escape. Two enterprising photographers tried to photograph her as she sped away in a car driven by the King's chauffeur, only to have their cameras smashed by the police. Nevertheless, while details of the divorce proceedings did appear in the papers, they were published without comment.

The American newspapers had a field day, of course. One ran the memorable headline 'King's Moll Reno'ed', after the Nevada's quickie-divorce capital, and they began calling Wallis Simpson 'Queen Wally'.

Parliament was getting restive, too. On 17 November 1936, Labour MP Ellen Wilkinson asked the President of the Board of Trade why two or three pages had been ripped from distinguished American magazines.

'What is it that the British public are not allowed to know? She asked.

It was not until 3 December, when Dr Blunt made his remarks, that she got an answer, Although Dr Blunt later denied that he knew anything about the affair of Edward and Mrs Simpson, the newspapers assumed that he did. He was a senior churchman, an insider. The establishment, the press thought, were breaking ranks.

Now the whole thing was out in the open and the

national debate raged.

'Why shouldn't the King marry his cutie?' asked Winston Churchill.

'Because England does not want Queen Cutie,' replied Noël Coward.

Stones were thrown through the windows of Mrs Simpson's London home. Letters and telegrams of abuse came in by the sack full. Terrified, she fled to the south of French, leaving Edward to face the furore alone.

Queen Mary, Edward's mother, was against the marriage instinctively. But Baldwin's opposition was more reasoned. The abdication of the King could cause a royal scandal, yet his marriage would cause a bigger one. The British Secret Service had already compiled a weighty dossier on Mrs Simpson's activities. It did not make pretty reading, especially if the papers got their hands on it.

Of Virginian stock, she had been born in Baltimore. Her first husband, navy flier Lieutenant Earl Winfield 'Win' Spencer had been a alcoholic and a sadist, who liked to tie her to the bed and beat her. He had numerous extramarital affairs with both men and women.

Wallis, for her part, had launched herself on the diplomatic scene in Washington, bedding the Italian ambassador and a senior Argentine diplomat, who was said to dance the best tango in DC.

In a belated honeymoon, Win took her on a trip to the Far East where together, and separately, they visited the brothels of Shanghai and Hong Kong. Wallis particularly liked watching girls performing lesbian acts and would sometimes join in threesomes without her husband.

It was in these famous 'singing houses' that Wallis learnt the ancient art of Fang Chung. The Chinese have been studying the erotic art since the fifth century BC. Ancient Chinese Emperors would employ a mature woman as a sexual advisor to pick new wives and concubines for him, and to advise him to how to satisfy the hundreds and sometimes thousands off wives and concubines he had. These women distilled their knowledge of sex and produced books.

Fang Chung is a method of relaxing a sexual partner. It involves massaging hot oil into their nipples, stomach and inner thighs. Only when the recipient is totally relaxed are the genitals caressed. Aficionados of Fang Chung are said to be able to arouse even the most passionless of men by concentrating on the nerve centres and delicate brushing of the skin, and they learn to delay ejaculation almost indefinitely by firm pressure on the perineum.

Despite all Wallis's undoubted accomplishments in the erotic arts, Win decided that he was gay after all and moved in with a handsome young artist. This left Wallis free to practise her new-found techniques on a string of other men. These included a young American called Robbie, the Italian naval attaché Count Galeazzo Ciano, soon to be Mussolini's foreign minister, and American millionaire Herman Rogers. Together with Roger's wife Katherine, they set up a *ménage à trois*. Wallis suffered a botched abortion that left her unable to bear children.

She met her second husband Ernest Simpson, a British subject, in New York. He, too,was married, but they quickly divorced their respective spouses and moved to London. Married life changed nothing. They were members of a fast set that included the Mountbattens and Lady Thelma Furness. Wallis went on a women-only holiday to the south of France with Consuela Thaw and Gloria Vanderbilt, who was having a lesbian love affair with Nada, wife of the Marquis of Milton Haven and lover of Edwina Mountbatten at the time. Consuela and Wallis shared a bedroom. And they went out together on the pull.

After Wallis was introduced to the Price of Wales by Lady Furness, the two of them would often make up a foursome with Wallis's husband and Mary Raffray, Ernest Simpson's mistress. In 1934, Edward holidayed with Mrs

Simpson in Biarritz. Mr Simpson could not join the party, so Wallis was chaperoned by her aunt Bessie.

In February 1935, Edward was photographed with Mrs Simpson leaving a lingerie shop in Kitzbühel, where they were enjoying a skiing holiday together. In May, the gossip came home to London when Edward danced with Mrs Simpson at his parent's Silver Jubilee ball. In June, he told the British Legion that they should extend the hand of friendship to Germany. This was taken to indicate that he was pro-Nazi. Meanwhile, Wallis found a way to express her pro-German sympathies more directly. It was rumoured that she was having a brief fling with Hitler's ambassador to the court of St James, Joachim von Ribbentrop. But that did not stop her holidaying with Edward in the south of France and then on Corsica.

On 27 May 1936, the King invited Mr and Mrs Baldwin to dinner along with the Mountbattens and the notorious swingers, the Duff Coopers – to meet Wallis. Baldwin was impressed with Wallis. He was also impressed by how the King loved her. But he knew that a woman with Wallis Simpson's track record could not become Queen of England.

The British press respected the King's privacy when he set off on a cruise in the Adriatic with Mrs Simpson that summer, but the rest of the world's press and the news-reels followed every move. Many noted that her husband was nowhere to be seen. The Foreign Office was outraged when he paid an unauthorized visit to the Greek dictator, Ionnis Metaxas, who drove them through cheering crowds. Mrs Simpson was received like a queen. The couple also visited Kemal Ataturk, Turkey's dictator, and invited him on a state visit to Britain. All this was done without the knowledge of the British government or Parliament.

Baldwin bided his time and slowly public opinion turned against the King. He was due to open a hospital extension in Aberdeen, but cancelled and sent his brother instead, on the grounds that the court was still in mourning. However, Edward had already been seen at Ascot and had been on a Mediterranean cruise. Some noticed that the King was actually hosting a house party at Balmoral at the time and, according to the Court Circular, Mrs Simpson was on the guest list.

Not only was the King losing the support of the people, the Dominions were turning against him. They were following the King's romance in the American papers and were sending letters of protest to the government and prominent members of the establishment in London.

Baldwin put pressure on the King to halt Mrs Simpson's divorce proceedings. Edward refused on the grounds that it would be wrong to interfere in Mrs Simpson's affairs as she was 'just a friend'. From Edward's point of view, there could be no delay. As Mrs Simpson would have to wait six months after the decree nisi was issued before she got a decree absolute and could marry again, and if she was to be by his side at his coronation in May, the divorce had to go ahead as planned.

Even friends counselled caution. He did not have to confront the matter now. Once he was crowned, he could introduce Mrs Simpson slowly and then, with the people on his side, marry her. He rejected this, saying that it would be like 'being crowned with a lie on my lips'.

Once Wallis Simpson was granted her divorce, nothing could prevent a constitutional crisis. In mid-November, Baldwin called a cabinet meeting to discuss what could be done. The government firmly rejected any marriage to Mrs Simpson.

Edward still believed that the situation could be saved. He set out for Wales where thousands of unemployed miners turned out to cheer and sing hymns of praise, in Welsh, to the man they still considered to be their champion.

Soon after, the press pact was broken and things moved fast. Edward withdrew to his country house, Fort

Belvedere, near Virginia Water in Surrey, and spent hours on the phone to Wallis who was in Cannes. They had already discussed the possibility of a morganatic marriage, which denied her and her heirs any position in the succession.

Edward put the proposal to Baldwin. Under the 1931 Statute of Westminster, to make any alteration to the succession required not only the approval of the British Parliament, but also the parliaments of all the Dominions. Under the King's instructions, Baldwin put it to them. They rejected it.

In Britain, it was not just the government that was against the marriage, but the opposition was against it, too. Baldwin told the King that if he went ahead and married against the government's advice, he would resign and force an election over the matter.

With the press now free to discuss the matter, the King could get some sense of public opinion. *The Daily Mirror* issued a challenge on its front page.

'God save the King,' it said. 'Tell us the facts Mr Baldwin ... The nation insists on knowing the King's full demands and conditions.... The nation will give you its verdict.'

Others were not so equivocal. They mistrusted Mrs Simpson's hold over the King and her Nazi sympathies. It was rumoured that Mrs Simpson was blackmailing him; that Edward had punched his brother the Duke of Gloucester on the nose for criticizing the liaison; that the next in line to the throne, the Duke of York, was an epileptic; that American newspaper tycoon William Randolph Hearst had offered £250,000 for Mrs Simpson to file her divorce petition in America and name the King as co respondent; and that the King was a closet Fascist. This last was not without foundation. He had refused to meet the exiled King of Abyssinia, ousted by the Italian invasion, when asked to do so by the Foreign Secretary.

Although there were, on balance, more papers against the marriage than for it, the embattled couple did not think that the situation was irretrievably lost. Mrs Simpson suggested that the King take a leaf out of the American president's book and go on the radio for a cosy 'fireside chat'. She felt sure that when his people heard the story of their romance from the King himself, they would back him.

Edward agreed, but he showed a draft to Baldwin, who pointed out that such an appeal to the people over the heads of the government was unconstitutional. Baldwin insisted that whatever the King did he should not divide the British people. The King offered to abdicate.

Wallis Simpson issued a press release, offering to withdraw from the situation. She even sent a message to the Prime Minister, offering to drop her divorce petition. But it was too late. The King had been outmanoeuvred by Baldwin. Even his one parliamentary champion, Winston Churchill, gave up after being shouted down in the House of Commons.

'Our cock won't fight,' said Beaverbrook.

On Thursday 10 December 1936, just seven days after the scandal had broken in the press, Edward signed the Instrument of Abdication, renouncing the crown of Great Britain and Ireland. He also resigned as head of state of the Dominions and as Emperor of India, and all the other titles and positions those posts entailed. He did, however, keep the £1 million settled on him by his grandmother, Queen Alexandra.

Alice Keppel, the last mistress of Edward VII, was dining at the Ritz when she heard the news.

'We did things much better in my day,' she said.

The following day, Edward was driven to Windsor where he broadcast to the Empire, explaining that he could no longer go on being King without the woman he loved. The whole world listened. People wept openly. Even tough New York cab drivers pulled over, amazed that the

King of England would renounce everything for the love of a woman. This, everyone agreed, must be the greatest love story ever told.

Well, not exactly. Cynics have suggested that the tricks that Wallis picked up in the singing houses of China were deployed to such good effect that the thought of living without her was unbearable. She was also adept at fellatio and, it is said, had an operation to have her vagina tightened to help stimulate her undersized genitals.

Prominent socialite, Lady Ottoline Morrell, claimed Edward was also taking injections to make him more virile that were driving him quite mad. There was also talk of him being a foot fetishist, which Wallis ruthlessly exploited. She also acted as his dominatrix. One day in front of friends, she turned to Edward and ordered: 'Take off my dirty shoes and get me my shoes and bring me another pair.' To everyone's amazement, he did.

There was talk of elaborate nanny-child scenes enacted between them. Freda Dudley Ward also commented on this side of his nature.

'He made himself the slave of whomsoever he loved and became totally dependent on her,' she said. 'It was his nature; he was like a masochist. He liked being humbled, degraded. He begged for it.'

After the broadcast, Edward sailed into exile on board a Royal Navy destroyer. This was ironic as the prevailing joke was that Edward had resigned as Admiral of the Fleet, only to sign on as third mate on a Baltimore tramp.

In June 1937, Edward and Mrs Simpson married in France. No members of the Royal Family attended the ceremony and most of their friends stayed away. He was created Duke of Windsor. Although he retained his HRH, the Duchess was refused one. 'A damnable wedding present,' he called it.

But that was not the end of the scandal. In the run up to the War, Edward and Wallis paid a social call on Adolf

Hitler. That Edward was sympathetic was beyond doubt. He encouraged friends to contribute to the Nazi cause and liked to speak German in private.

In 1937, he told a cheering crowd in Leipzig: 'What I have seen in Germany is a miracle.'

At the outbreak of hostilities he joined up but he was considered a security risk. When France fell, he sought refuge in Fascist Spain with friends who were openly pro-German. There was even talk that, should Britain fall, Edward would be restored to the throne as Hitler's vassal.

To get him out of harm's way, the government dispatched Edward to the Bahamas as Governor. Edward and Wallis became embroiled in illicit currency deals, making money out of the war. This all went disastrously wrong when one of Edward's friends, Sir Harry Oakes, who was also involved, was murdered. A relative of Oakes's was framed but, in court, was acquitted. No one has ever got to the bottom of the Oakes scandal.

Low-level scandal continued to follow the Duke and Duchess of Windsor for the rest of their lives. By the 1950s, there were rumours that Wallis had grown tired of Edward's cloying love and was seen everywhere with Woolworth heir, Jimmy Donahue.

Donahue was exclusively homosexual, but the rumour had it that Wallis was trying to convert him. Others said that it was the Duke who was sleeping with Donahue, although it was widely known that he despised all homosexuals.

Noël Coward, who moved in the same circles as the Windsors after the abdication, explained the situation.

'I like Jimmy,' he said. 'He's an insane camp but he is fun. I like the Duchess; she is the fag hag to end all fag hags, but that's what makes her likeable. The Duke... well, although he pretends not to hate me, he does because I'm queer and he's queer. However, unlike him I don't pretend not to be. Here she's got a royal queen to sleep with and a rich one to hump.'

The Duke and Duchess lived out the rest of their lives in Paris. The Duke never set foot in England again. But when he died in 1972, at the age of 77, his body was flown home. He was laid in state for two days in St George's Chapel, Windsor. Nearly 58,000 people filed past his body.

The Duchess accompanied the body and stayed, for the first time, in Buckingham Palace. After the chapel was closed to the public she was driven to Windsor, where she was greeted by Princes Charles and her old friend, Lord Mountbatten.

The Duchess of Windsor died herself 14 years later, in 1986. At the foot of her bed was a poem written by the Duke in his own handwriting. It read:

'My friend, with thee to live alone,
Me thinks were better to own
A crown, a sceptre and a throne.'

Mrs Brown

Although in our troubled times, politicians like to hark back to Victorian values, it was estimated in 1850 that there were 80,000 prostitutes in London alone, many of them underage girls sold into vice by parents who could not afford to keep them. And, although Queen Victoria is seen as a paragon of virtue, scandal was never far from her door.

Her father Edward, Duke of Kent, was so dissolute that his father, King George III, exiled him to Gibraltar. There he took a French mistress named Julie St Laurent and sadistically disciplined the regiment put under him. Posted to Montreal, he sentenced one soldier to 999 lashes. His unit rebelled. After a second rebellion in Gibraltar, he hanged three and brutally flogged dozens more.

Returning to London with his long-standing mistress,

he ran up such enormous debts that they had to flee to Brussels. When his debts pursued him, he married Princess Victoria of Leinigen to put himself back his father's good books. The King paid off his debts. His Madame St Laurent only found out about the match when it was reported in the Continental newspapers. They had been together for 25 years.

And the Duke of Kent was by no means the worst of them. His younger brother, Ernest, the Duke of Cumberland, was said to have committed incest with his sister, Princess Sophia, in a mirror-lined room in St James's Palace. He was accused of attempting to rape the wife of the Lord Chancellor in her own drawing room, and Lord Graves slit his throat when he heard that the Prince was having an affair with his 50-year-old wife. The scandal sheets also said that he had killed a servant in a fit of rage, that his wife had bumped off her two previous husbands, and that the two of them planned to poison Victoria to put Ernest on the throne.

Princess Sophia gave birth to an illegitimate child, sired by an equerry at the Palace who was 33 years her senior. Her sister, Princess Augusta, fell in love with the King's equerry, Major-General Sir Brent Spencer. She never dared ask the King whether she could marry him. When she plucked up the courage to ask the Prince Regent, he forbade it. This did not prevent them being lovers and they may have married in secret. Princess Amelia also fell for one of the King's equerries, a middle-aged philanderer named Charles Fitzroy who was descended from one of Charles II's bastards. They never married but she considered herself to be his wife and left everything she had to him when she died. Then there was Princess Elizabeth, who was rumoured to be pregnant while unmarried at the age of 16. She did not marry until she was 47.

George III's youngest son, Prince Augustus Frederick, married Lady Augusta Murray secretly in Rome, in direct contravention of the Royal Marriage Act. When she fell pregnant, they married again publicly in St George's Hanover Square. He used the name Mr Frederick Augustus. The marriage was ruled invalid and Prince Augustus was exiled. His wife's passport was seized to prevent her following him. However, using forged papers, she escaped and caught up with him in Berlin. For 10 years, they lived happily there until the lure of £12,000 and Duchy of Sussex persuaded him to abandon her and return to England. He then sued for the custody of their children and married again, bigamously, to Lady Cecilia Buggin, the widow of a city grocer. Condoning the match, Queen Victoria created her Duchess of Inverness.

The Duke of Kent died less than two years after marrying. But in that period, Princess Victoria of Leinigen produced a daughter who would become Queen Victoria. The young Victoria knew of her father's murky past and sometimes referred to his former mistress as 'the old French lady' or 'the discovery of St Lawrence'. The misbehaviour of her uncles and aunts was simply overlooked, although she remained on friendly terms with her cousin, King Leopold of the Belgians, who was partial to feather boas and high-heeled shoes.

The scandalous behaviour of her widowed mother brought more shame to the young Victoria. She took her lover the Irish upstart, Sir John Conroy, and made no effort to hide her physical familiarity with him in front of her impressionable young daughter. Together they tried to dominate the Princess, but when Victoria became Queen she banned Conroy from court.

Victoria became convinced that Conroy was using one of the Ladies of the Bedchamber, Lady Flora Hastings, as a spy. After Lady Hastings travelled back from Scotland with Conroy in 1838, her belly swelled and Victoria was convinced that she was pregnant by 'that Monster and Demon incarnate'.

Flora consulted the royal physician, Sir James Clark, a poor diagnostician, who quickly concluded that she was indeed pregnant. The other Ladies of the Bedchamber broadcast the fact. But when she was given a thorough examination, she was found still to be a virgin. The scandal had reached such proportions, however, that Flora's uncle Hamilton FitzGerald had to publish an open letter in *The Examiner*.

Once the public realized that Lady Flora was not pregnant but gravely ill, Queen Victoria's scandalous treatment of her made her very unpopular and she was hissed at by the crowds at Ascot. In 1839, this turned into a full-scale political scandal called the 'Bedchamber Crisis'.

When Victoria's prime ministerial favourite, Lord Melbourne – a two-time divorcee who once complimented Victoria on her 'full and fine bust' – fell from power, he was replaced by Sir Robert Peel, who insisted that she dismiss her gossiping Ladies of the Bedchamber. Victoria refused. In the street, mobs hurled abuse at her. They called her 'Mrs Melbourne', suggesting that the former Prime Minister was more than just an advisor. Eventually she had to give way.

When Lady Hastings died on 5 July 1839, it was found that the cause of the swelling was a tumour on her liver. The *Morning Post* described the Queen's behaviour in the affair as 'the most revolting virulence and indecency'.

Victoria's husband, the strait-laced Prince Albert, was not free from the whiff of scandal either. His mother had outraged the good people of Saxe-Coburg-Gotha by having an affair with the court's Jewish chamberlain, who may have been Albert's real father. His parents divorced when he was five. His mother married an army officer and Albert never saw her again, while his father, in proper Hanoverian style, consoled himself with a series of mistresses.

Albert's brother took after his father and died of

syphilis, but the young Albert prided himself on being a pillar of moral rectitude. He went to an all-male university and forswore contact with women.

As soon as she saw him, Victoria was bowled over by his looks.

'Albert's beauty is most striking,' she remarked.

'At their third meeting, she asked him to marry her, while remarking that she was quite unworthy of him. He eventually consented, but warned that he would not be 'corrupted' by her.

Albert was good to his word. The first night of the honeymoon was strangely short, the diarist Charles Grenville noted.

'I told Lord Palmerston that this is not the way to provide us with a Prince of Wales,' he wrote.

Queen Victoria was a woman of robust sexual appetites, however, and she knew how to get the best out of Albert. She hung their bedroom at Osborne House with painting of male nudes.

She hated getting pregnant, partly because Albert believed that sex was for procreation and not recreation. He would abstain for the nine months of the pregnancy and at least another three months after she had given birth. So she would have to go without sex for over a year. They had nine children in all. When Albert said that there should be no more, Victoria said: 'Can we have no more fun in bed?'

It was Albert who set the prudish standard that have become synonymous with the Victorian era. The Queen's maids were forbidden to entertain gentleman callers in the maid's parlour. Even their brothers were ushered into a special waiting room where their behaviour could be watched.

No lady with the slightest blemish on her character was allowed at court. One 70-year-old lady, who had eloped with her childhood sweetheart in her youth, was banned –

even though the couple had led a blameless life ever since.

This lofty standard made scandals out of behaviour that would have passed unnoticed before. When one night, the Foreign Secretary Lord Palmerston blundered into the bedroom of Lady Blunt, a Lady of Bedchamber, and tried to seduce her, Albert proclaimed that any man capable of such 'fiendish' behaviour should be debarred from high office. The public took a different view. Palmerston later won a landslide election after it was rumoured he had sired an illegitimate child at the age of 80.

When Prince Albert died in 1861, Queen Victoria was only 42. She went into prolonged mourning, ordering that his room at Buckingham Palace, Balmoral, Osborne and Windsor were to remain as they were on the day of his death. They were photographed so that when they were cleaned everything could be put back in exactly the same place.

She ordered that a picture of Albert be placed at the foot of her bed, wherever she slept. His nightshirt was to be laid beside her at bedtime and, in the morning, his hot shaving water was to be brought as if he were still alive.

Her withdrawal from public life was complete. This was a dangerous move with republicanism on the rise. People began to wonder what she was being paid for and mobs called for her to be overthrown. Even loyal newspapers, such as *The Times*, called her the 'Great Absentee', while the *Pall Mall Gazette* called her 'the invisible monarch'

The Queen was quite clear about what she missed about Albert.

'What a dreadful thing this going to bed is,' she lamented. 'What a contract to that tender lover's love. All alone.'

She brooded alone at Osborne, the home they had built together, and those around the Queen fear that she might become unhinged. She had to snap out of it. They sent for her carriage and favourite pony from Balmoral. They arrived in harness, led by her Scottish ghillie, John Brown, in bonnet and kilt. He was a giant of a man with a great shock of red hair. It is said that when she saw him she smiled – for the first time since Albert had died.

She hired him as her 'personal highland servant' and he was told to take orders from no one but herself. This piqued the Queen's equerry, General Sir Charles Grey, who was short with Brown. The Queen offered him an obscure posting in a remote part of India.

John Brown's salary was fixed at £120 a year – five times what he was earning at Balmoral. He addressed the Queen merely as 'woman' and told her off if she was dressed too lightly for the cold weather.

With John Brown's help, the Queen began to fulfil her public duties again. In 1866, she attended the state opening of Parliament for the first time since Albert's death. And he was with her when she reviewed the troops at Aldershot.

Punch magazine began calling her 'Mrs Brown' and published a spoof Court Circular detailing their activities. In September 1866, the Swiss newspaper *Gazette de Lausanne* ran a story from the special correspondent in London, saying that Queen Victoria was pregnant and that she and Brown had married secretly.

The republican movement seized on these rumours to its own ends. A pamphlet saying that the Queen had hatched a morganatic marriage with Brown circulated. Cartoons showed him eyeing the empty throne. Brown was even blamed for the Queen's withdrawal from public life. It was said that she would rather spend tome at Balmoral with her ghillie than attend to affair of state.

Fearing hostile demonstrations, the government asked her not to appear in public with Brown. She refused to leave him at home, but the execution of Emperor Maximilian of Mexico – a remote relative by marriage – was used as an excuse to plunge the court back into mourning and cancel the Queen's public engagements. By this time, republican pamphleteers were claiming that she was diverting government money into her own private account.

Returning from a thanksgiving service for the Prince of Wales's recovery from typhoid at St Paul's Cathedral in February 1872, the Queen was confronted by a gunman who pointed a pistol in her face. Brown, who was on the box of the Queen's carriage, jumped down and barged the man aside. He made a dash for it. Brown pursued and caught him. Instantly Brown was a hero.

The would-be assassin was found to be deranged and the pistol did not work, but that did not matter. The tide of scandal had turned. The Queen had a special award – the Devoted Service Medal – struck and John Brown was awarded an annuity of £25 a year.

When John Brown died in 1883, at the age of 56, he lay in state in Windsor Castle for six days and his obituary in the Court Circular was longer than Disreali's. His room at Windsor was given the same treatment as Albert's, until Edward VII came to the throne and turned it into a billiard room. Edward also had the statue of John Brown removed from the hallway at Balmoral.

Queen Victoria had already published a book dedicated to Brown. It was called *More Leaves from the Journal of a Life in the Highlands*. She began *The Life of John Brown*, but the Dean of Windsor read the manuscript and found it so scandalous that he threatened to resign if she published it. Eventually she gave in.

After John Brown's death, Victoria turned to her beturbaned Indian secretary, Munshi Hafir Adbul Karim, whom she called Munshi. Although he was still in his 20s, she gave him a cottage at Windsor and he had staff of his own.

The government was concerned about their relationship and there were rumours that he was a spy. She was also told that it was deemed inappropriate to be on such intimate terms with a black man. She pointed out that since he was her subject, she could not do what she liked with him.

After the death of Queen Victoria, when Munshi himself died, Edward VII had his papers burnt and all trace of him expunged.

The Badness of King George

That George IV – and for that matter William IV – turned out as badly as they did is little wonder. They came from bad stock. The poet Walter Savager Landor wrote savagely of the Hanoverian kings:

'I sing of the George four,
For Providence could stand no more.
Some say that far the worst
Of all was George the First.
But yet by some 'tis reckoned
That worse still was George the Second.
And what mortal ever heard
Any good of George the Third?
When George the Fourth from earth descended,
Thank God the line of George ended.'

When the lesbian Queen Anne died childless she left behind her something of a problem. Her half-brother James Edward, the Old Pretender, was enjoying the debauchery of the Italian courts, but he was a catholic. Britain was staunchly protestant and had ended the scandalous reign of James II when he had declared for Rome. So George, the Protestant Elector of Hanover, was invited to Britain to reign as George I.

He arrived with two hideous mistresses, Ehrengard Melusine von Schulenburg and Baroness von Kielmannsegg. England had seen nothing like it. Ehrengard was enormously tall while the Baroness, who was actually George's half-sister was enormously fat.

Horace Walpole recalled being terrified of her huge bulk as a child. 'The mob of London were highly diverted at the importation of so uncommon a seraglio,' he wrote. They called them 'the maypole and the elephant'.

To be fair, George had had to leave his attractive mistress, Countess von Platen, behind in Hanover, where she had borne him a child, while her husband milked the exchequer. But she was a catholic. He also left behind his wife, Sophia Dorothea of Zell.

Like his father before him, George was a debauched man. He even shared a mistress with his father. Although his 16-year-old wife was a renowned beauty, he spent his time fooling around with all and sundry. After 12 years of neglect, his wife thought she deserved a little fun, too. So she took a lover, the handsome Swedish soldier, Count Philip von Königsmark.

When George found out about it, he had Konigsmark murdered and his body buried under the floor of her room. He divorced her on the grounds of desertion – she intended to elope with her lover, he said. Divorce on the grounds of adultery would have cast doubt on the succession. Sophia was then imprisoned in the castle at Ahlden for the remaining 32 years of her life.

Ehrengard von Schulenburg bore George three children and acted as hostess at royal functions. She was, said Walpole: 'As much Queen of England as any woman was.'

With two such odd creatures as 'the maypole and the elephant' holding sway in the royal household, all kinds of other women flocked to court to try their luck. Even mistresses of the three previous kings turned out. On spotting Louise de Kerualle, Duchess of Portsmouth, a mistress of William III across George's drawing room, James II's mistress Catherine Sedley exclaimed: 'Who would have thought that three whores should have met here?'

The biggest scandal of George's reign was not sexual, but financial. It was the 'South Sea Bubble'. The inspiration for the scam came from France, where a Scottish gambler called John Law had persuaded the Duc d'Orléans, then Regent, to open a bank that issued notes in lieu of gold. Against six million francs in gold, he issued 60 million francs in notes and believed that he had discovered the recipe for unlimited wealth, until a run on the bank finished him off four years later.

In Britain, the South Sea Company, which had been set up to transport slaves to the new plantations in South America, took note. Its director, John Blunt, realized that more money could be made in trading stock than in trading slaves.

First, he had to build confidence in the company. So, in 1718, he persuaded George I to become its governor. In January 1720, with the King's backing, parliament passed a bill allowing the South Sea Company to take over the national debt, which stood at £50 million. Privatizing the national debt meant that the government would pay only four per cent, rather than five on its borrowing. Those who held treasury bounds, essentially the government's creditors, would be paid the same modest interest, but they would also be given a chance to convert their holdings into their shares in the new company, which promised fabulous wealth to come.

Initially, an investor holding £10,000 in bonds would get you 50 shares, leaving another 50 to sell on to another buyer. You could do this again and again, provided the share price continued to rise.

To start with it worked well. Shares rose to £400. George I himself bought in, which boosted confidence in the company. But he was a shrewd player. He quickly sold his £20,000 worth of shares, realizing a profit of £86,000. And he maintained market confidence by giving John Blunt a knighthood.

Blunt became over confident. He flouted the rules laid down by Parliament by issuing a further 20,000 shares only 12 weeks after the company was floated. A month later he issued another 10,000 but the share price kept on climbing. Money was coming in so fast that no one bothered to do anything with it. It seemed pointless to invest in any other enterprise when you had a money-making machine that generated wealth a such a rate.

Naturally, other shysters followed Blunt's example, launching all manner of harebrained schemes on the gullible public. One company's prospectus offered merely the chance to invest in an 'undertaking of great advantage but no one to know what it is'. The dividend it promised was £50 for every £1 invested. On its first day of trading, the company's director took in £2,000 and disappeared.

Blunt had the temerity to sue four rivals, on the grounds that they were trading without a royal charter, which Blunt had secured from King George. He won, but it was a Pyrrhic victory. Defeated in the courts, his rivals had to liquidate their assets. They did this by selling their shares in the South Sea Company. Major investors pulling out shook confidence. Share prices began to go down rather than up. The bubble burst and the whole enterprise collapsed. Shares plummeted from £900 to £190 when dealing was suspended. The Duke of Chandos lost £30,000 in a couple of hours.

The King's part in this could not be hidden. Von Schulenburg and Kielmannsegg had also made a fortune during the rise of the 'South Sea Bubble'. One day, they found their carriage surrounded by an angry mob.

"Good pipple, what for you abuse us?' Von Schulenburg cried out in imperfect English. 'We hef come here for your own goodz.'

'And our chattels,' yelled someone from the mob.

The King made plans to mobilize his troops in Hanover, but the riots he feared never materialized. As many people had made money out of the 'South Sea Bubble' as had lost it. Plainly, the rich had lost most since they had more to lose, but the redistribution of wealth the collapse produced has actually stimulated the economy.

George's English mistresses – which included among their number Lady Montagu, the Duchess of Shrewbury and the Duchess of Bolton – took bribes from those who sought favours from the King. At court one day, the Duchess of Marlborough spotted that Lady Montagu was sporting expensive new earrings and remarked: 'What an impudent creature to come with her bribe in her ear.'

'Madam,' replied Lady Montagu. 'How should people know where wine is sold unless a sign is hung out?'

Anne Brett, the Countess of Macclesfield's daughter, was given an apartment in St James's Palace. It was rumoured that George was going to create her a Countess in her own right. There was also much gossip about the King's interest in Lord Hervey's young wife. Despite these dalliances, George made little secret of the fact that he had come from England only for the gold.

When he heard that his wife finally died in November 1726, George showed his delicacy of feeling by going to the theatre. He left her body unburied for six months, until a French fortune-teller warned him that if he did not let his wife rest in peace in her grave, he would occupy it before her. A superstitious man, he headed off back to Hanover to attend to her burial, where he died of a stroke in 1727.

George I's son, George II, was little better. Although he was very much in love with his wife, Queen Caroline, he felt it was his kingly duty to take as many mistresses as he could manage. It helped the smooth running of the court and his mistresses were used to convey messages by the competing political factions.

One of his early mistresses, Molly Lepell, was a noted beauty and Lord Chesterfield celebrated the affair in verse:

> "Were I king of Great Britain
> To choose a minister well

> And support the throne I sat on
> I'd have under me Molly Lepell.
>
> Heaven keep our good king from rising
> But that rising who's fitter to quell
> Than some lady with beauty surprising
> And who should that be but Lepell.'

George was extremely crude in his advances to women and made no secret that he paid them well for their services. One evening at a ball, while ogling Mary Bellenden, one of his wife's ladies-in-waiting, he began counting the gold coins in his purse.

Like his father, George II went back to Hanover for a bit of rest and recreation every two years. His mistress there was Madame d'Elitz, a divorcee who reputedly had a thousand lovers. These included his father, George I, and his son, Frederick.

'There is nothing new under the son,' wrote one courtier, 'nor the grandson either.'

Queen Caroline was usually sanguine about her husband's affairs, but when he returned from Hanover with a portrait of the lovely Madame Walmoden, which he hung at the end of their bed, she was livid. She had already been treated to a graphic account of her seduction in a letter thoughtfully penned by the King himself. He was nothing if not a sharing husband.

He compounded the sin by asking her to arrange a visit by the notoriously promiscuous Princess of Modena as he felt 'the great inclination imaginable to pay his addresses to the daughter of the late Regent of France'.

As the Queen was rarely jealous, particularly when her husband found a 'sensible' woman to divert himself with. She told the Archbishop of York that although she 'was sorry for the scandal it gave others...for herself she minded it no more than his going to the closed stool.'

The King's trips to Hanover made him unpopular in Britain, particularly as the British taxpayer was expected to maintain his 'Hanover bawdy house in magnificence and enrich his German pimps and whores'. Even when the Scots rebelled in 1745, George insisted on going to see Madame Walmoden.

The outrage was such that a thin and spindly horse was let loose in London with a sign around its neck saying: 'I am the King's Hanoverian Equipage going to fetch his Majesty and his whore to England.'

A note was pinned to the door of St James's Palace, which read: 'Lost or strayed out of this house, a man who has left a wife and six children on the parish; whoever will give tidings of him to the churchwardens of St James's Parish, so he may be got again, shall receive four shillings and sixpence. N.B. This reward will not be increased, nobody judging him to deserve a Crown.' A crown was five shillings.

This worried the Queen, who wrote to the King in Hanover begging him to return urgently. His reply was full of further graphic details of his erotic encounters with Madame Walmoden and instructions to have Henrietta Howard's old apartments readied for her.

In fact, he returned alone. By this time the Queen was ill. While a surgeon was operating on her, her bowels burst.

'Here lies, wrapped in forth thousand towels,
The only proof that Caroline had bowels,' wrote Pope.

On her deathbed, Queen Caroline asked the King not to take another wife.

'No,' said George tearfully, 'I shall have mistresses.'

On that comforting note, Queen Caroline expired.

With the death of the Queen, Lady Deloraine moved in. This caused a political crisis.

Walpole wished that 'His Majesty had taken someone

less mischievous than that lying bitch'. When the Duke of Newcastle suggested that they use the King's daughter, Princess Emily, as their intermediary, Walpole was scandalized.

'Does the Princess design to commit incest?' he asked. 'Will she go to bed with the father? Does he desire that she should? If no, do not tell me the King intends to take a vow of chastity or that those that lie with him won't have the best interest in him.'

Walpole's solution was to send for Madame Walmoden. He said he was 'for the wife against the mistress', but now he was 'for the mistress against the daughter.'

When Madame Walmoden arrived, she was created Lady Yarmouth and she supported herself by selling her influence with the King. Elevation to the peerage, for example, cost £15,000 a time. Although this may appear scandalous in itself, the fact that she cost the state nothing to maintain was widely praised and she was compared to Madame de Pompadour, the extravagant mistress of Louis XV, who was costing the French taxpayer millions.

'While Madame de Pompadour shares the absolute power of Louis XV,' wrote a French count. 'Lady Yarmouth shares the absolute impotence of George II.'

George's son Frederick, the Prince of Wales, was not popular. He was criticized for his choice of mistresses, which included the Hanoverian mistress of his father and grandfather, Madame d'Elitz, and a chemist's daughter in Kingston.

'Like the rest of his race,' Walpole wrote, 'beauty was not a necessary ingredient.'

Frederick's own father, George II, described him as 'a monster and the greatest villain ever known'. His mother, Queen Caroline, claimed that he was impotent and had employed another man to father his children.

The great public scandal around Frederick concerned Anne Vane, a 'fat and ill-shaped dwarf' who, according to the Queen, had 'lain with half the town'. When she took up with the Prince of Wales, she was simultaneously sleeping with his best friend, Lord Hervey, and deliberately engineered a row between them to prevent them finding out.

When she fell pregnant, Frederick thought the child was his and set her up in a house in Soho Square. Hervey moved in with her and threatened to expose her unless she used her charms to persuade the Prince to take him back into his favours. Anne eventually confessed all, used Frederick's fling with a chambermaid as an excuse to dump him and ran off with Hervey.

The balladeers of the time had a field day satirizing these shenanigans. After marrying a 17-year-old beauty, Augusta of Saxe-Gotha, he confined his attentions to the elderly mother of 10, Lady Archibald Hamilton.

When he died suddenly, few mourned the loss. A contemporary epitaph caught the mood:

> 'Here lies poor Fred who was alive and is dead,
> Had it been his father, I had much rather,
> Had it been his sister, nobody would have missed her,
> Had it been his brother, still better than another,
> Had it been the whole generation, so much better for the nation,
> But since it's Fred who was alive and is dead,
> There is no more to be said.'

With Fred dead, his son took over when George II died, and reigned as George III. He was the first of the Hanoverian Kings to speak English. This led him to dabble in politics, resulting in the loss of the American colonies.

His first act as King was to send Lady Yarmouth packing. She returned to Hanover with a strong-box containing £10,000, a bequest from George II. George III then put aside his love of beautiful women and dutifully married a plain princess from Mecklenburg-Strelitz. They had 15 children and George was much praised for his 'resolute fidelity to a hideous Queen'.

Then he set about cleaning up the Royal Family. It was an uphill battle. His uncle, the Duke of Cumberland – the infamous 'Butcher of Culloden' – had a penchant for actresses. There was scandal when he brought one to Windsor in a carriage, but sent her away on foot because she would not consummate his amorous demands.

George's brother, the Duke of York, a libertine, made a scandalous marriage with Mrs Clements, the widow of George's tutor and the illegitimate daughter of Walpole's brother. It ended in an even more scandalous divorce.

Prince Henry, Duke of Gloucester, liked to flaunt his mistresses by driving them around Hyde Park in an open coach. Just in case anyone should mistake him for any other 18th-century blade, he made sure that his royal coat of arms was prominently displayed. Even worse, he had a particular taste for married women. This reached its scandalous zenith when Lord Grosvenor sued the Duke for committing adultery with his wife. Grosvenor won £10,000, which George III was forced to pay. He had only just coughed up when the Duke of York married his mistress, a young widow named Anne Horton, without the King's permission. George declared that his brother had the morals of a 'Newgate attorney' and resolved to have nothing further to do with him.

In an attempt to control the morals of the royal children, George III introduced the Royal Marriage Act in 1772. It stipulated that members of the Royal Family under the age of 25 could not marry without the sovereign's permission. In practice, one minister said in the House of Commons, it was the 'Act for the Encouragement of Adultery and Fornication'. It meant that the Prince Regent, for example, could marry without his father's permission, then put his wife aside when it suited him, claiming that the marriage had no validity in law.

The royal children were kept in baby clothes into their teenage years. Of George III's six daughters, three were never allowed to marry. Another two only married when in their 40s, Princess Charlotte married at 31, but her husband was the Prince of Wurttemberg who was obese. Napoleon remarked that he was so fat that the only reason for his existence was to demonstrate how far skin could stretch without breaking.

The strain of keeping his own sexual nature under control eventually proved too much for King George. In 1788, he went mad. His insanity manifested itself in him making scandalous suggestions to the respectable dowager Elizabeth, Countess of Pembroke. She was doubly mortified when the Archbishop of Canterbury asked her not to take advantage of a sick man's passions.

Renowned for his rustic passion, George III was nicknamed 'Farmer George'. His growing madness became widely known when it was reported that he had got out of his coach in Windsor Great Park to shake hands with an oak tree, believing it to be Frederick the Great. He recovered briefly, but in 1801 he relapsed. His final bout of madness overcame him in 1811. The Keeper of the Queen's Robes, Fanny Burney, wrote : 'He is persuaded that he is always conversing with angels.'

The poet Shelley's obituary was:

> 'An old, mad, despised and dying King;
> Princes, the dregs of their full race, who flow
> Through public scorn – mud from a muddy spring
> Rulers who neither see nor feel nor know
> But leechlike to their fainting country cling
> Till they drop, blind in blood, without a blow.'

The Lesbian Queens

In 1708, Queen Anne caused a scandal, not because she was a lesbian, but because she threw over her aristocratic lady love, Sarah Churchill, Duchess of Marlborough and forebear of Britain's great wartime Prime Minister, Winston Churchill, for a common chambermaid called Abigail Hill.

A scurrilous ballad of the time went :

> 'When as Queen Anne of great renown
> Great Britain's sceptre swayed,
> Besides the Church, she dearly loved
> A dirty chambermaid.
>
> Of Abigail that was her name,
> She stitch'd and starch'd full well,
> But how she pierc'd this mortal heart
> No mortal man can tell.
>
> However, for sweet service done
> And causes of great weight
> Her royal mistress made her, Oh!
> A minister of State.
>
> Her secretary she was not
> Because she could not write,
> But had the conduct and the care
> Of some dark deeds at night."

Although, for political reasons, Anne had been married off to Prince George of Denmark, she was a life-long lesbian. George made the best of the situation and impregnated Anne 17 times. None of their offspring survived infancy and the disappointment drove her to drink. She became known to her subjects as 'Brandy Nan' and grew so fat that she had to be carried to her coronation in a sedan chair.

Anne and her older sister Mary, who also became Queen, were the daughters of James II and were brought up in an all-female household at Richmond Palace. At the age of 12, Mary had a crush on 20-year-old Frances Apsley, whom she referred to as 'my dear husband'. Their correspondence left nothing to the imagination. Mary wrote to Frances saying:

'I may, if I can tell you how much I love you but I hope that is not doubted. I have given you proofs enough. If not, I will die to satisfy you dear, dear, husband. If all my hairs were lives, I would lose them all twenty times over to serve or satisfy you. I love you with a flame more lasting than the vestals' fire. Thou art my life, my soul, my all that Heaven can give. Death's life with you, without you that I love you with more zeal than any lover can. I love you with a love that never was known by man. I have for you excess of friendship more of love than ever the constantest lover had for his mistress. You are loved more than can be expressed by your ever obedient wife, very affectionate friend, humble servant, to kiss the ground where you go, to be your dog on a string, your fish in a net, your bird in a cage, your humble trout....'

Although Anne had maintained a similarly heated exchange with Cecily Cornwallis, she moved in on Frances, too. But soon she tired of her and moved on to Sarah Jennings, who later married John Churchill.

At 15, Mary was heartbroken when she was sent to Holland to marry William of Orange. It was not a bad match. William was gay. A former pageboy named William Bentinck, whom he had slept with as a youth, had risen to be his closest adviser. William was also a soldier so he was frequently away, and Mary found herself surrounded by pleasing Dutch women. However, the couple were royals and had to do their duty. When he was in Holland, he would visit her chamber, Mary said, 'about supper time...[so] that I not tire him with multiplicity of questions, but rather strive to recreate him.'

When William finally got her pregnant, Mary wrote home to Frances admitting: 'I have played the whore a little; because the sea parts us; you may believe that it is a bastard.'

Like her sister Ann, Mary had several miscarriages and failed to produce a living heir.

To everyone's surprise, William took a mistress, Elizabeth Villiers, one of Anne and Mary's childhood play-mates at Richmond. She was no beauty, especially when compared with the comely Mary, but William threw him-self at her from the first time he saw her.

Elizabeth had been one of Mary's ladies-in-waiting when she had come to Holland in 1677. To discourage her mistress's husband, Elizabeth encouraged the attention of Captain Wauchop, a Scottish mercenary. It did no good. Soon she was entertaining William in secret. By 1679, the affair was the talk of Paris. When Mary heard the gossip, she waited outside Elizabeth's apartments and caught her husband creeping out at two o'clock in the morning. There was a blazing row, but William was sanguine.

'What has given you so much pain is merely an amuse-ment,' he said.

William Bentinck was put out, too. For William to take a wife, out of duty, was one thing; to take a mistress for pleasure quite another.

Mary took the matter in hand. She sent Elizabeth to England with a letter for the King. However, Elizabeth opened it on the way. In the letter, Mary had asked her father to detain Elizabeth. Instead of delivering it, Elizabeth went straight back to Holland.

She was met by Mary and Bentinck, who both told her she had to leave. But William heard of Elizabeth's return and forced Mary to take her back. She consoled herself with more long, passionate letters to Frances Apsley.

When James II was deposed, William and Mary went to England to take the throne. Elizabeth went, too. She settled in a house near Kensington Palace and was given a 90,000-acre-estate in Ireland.

Supporters of James II tried to use William's scandalous entanglement with Elizabeth Villiers to their political advantage. They spread rumours that she was pregnant. William quelled the scandal by ordering the clergy to speak out against sin. He still maintained Elizabeth, however, until Mary's death in 1694. In a deathbed letter, Mary begged William to put away his mistress. In grief and remorse, he gave Elizabeth £30,000 a year and married her off to the Earl of Orkney.

William then resorted to his way again, taking as his favourite the pageboy, Arnold Jooset Van Keppel. William Bentinck was once more put out.

Even while her husband was alive, Anne kept Sarah Jennings as her Lady of the Bedchamber and their passionate correspondence continued. Sarah married the soldier, John Churchill, who was frequently away at the wars. When he did return, however, she recorded that he 'pleasured her with his boots on.'

This marriage played a key role in history. During the Glorious Revolution of 1688, it was John Churchill who delivered Anne and her husband, Prince George, safely into the camp of William and Mary, thereby ending effective resistance in England.

Although John Churchill was rewarded with the title, Duke of Marlborough, Mary tried to prevent Anne bringing her lover Sarah Churchill to court. To get her own back, Anne took Frances Apsley, now Lady Bathurst, into her household.

When Anne became Queen, Sarah sought to control the court while her husband brought glory to England on the battlefield. But she could not control the new Queen's passions and quickly found herself supplanted by Abigail Hill, who used to visit the Queen for two or three hours at night when the Prince was asleep.

A fierce struggle broke out between Sarah and Abigail for the heart of the Queen. When this became public knowledge, a visiting French count was greatly amused by the way the British, who were so sophisticated in some ways, were shocked by 'that refinement of love of early Greece.'

It was suggested in the House of Commons that Abigail, who was now Mrs Masham, be fired from the royal household. But Abigail insisted that it was Sarah who should go. She got her way, but Sarah Churchill then threatened to publish her memoirs, including extracts from the Queen's letters. However, discrepancies in the accounts of the royal household were discovered and Sarah was blackmailed into silence.

Her position at court was taken by the redheaded Duchess of Somerset, who immediately caused fresh scandal when her young lover. Charles Konigsmark, killed her husband. Jonathan Swift, a long-time supporter of Abigail's, wrote clumsily:

'Their cunnings mark [Konigsmark] thou for I have been told
  They assassin when young and poison when old
  O root out these carrots [redheads], O thou whose name
  Is backwards and forwards always the same [Anna].
  And keep close to thee always that name
  Which backwards and forwards is almost the same [Masham].'

It was not until 1742, 28 years after Anne's death, that Sarah Churchill's memoirs were finally published. They caused a sensation.

Gay Times

There have been more than a few scandalous queens on the throne of England – queens in the homosexual sense that is.

William the Conqueror's son, William Rufus, made little secret of his sexual preferences, and scandalized the nation with the camp goings on at court. Here is a description from one disapproving cleric: 'Then was there flowing hair and extravagant dress, and was invented the fashion of shoes with curved points; then the model for young men was to rival women in delicacy of person to mind their gait, to walk with loose gesture, and half naked. Enervated and effeminate, they unwillingly remained what nature made them, the assailers of others' chastity, prodigal of their own.'

William II died young in a mysterious hunting accident. Despite allegations that it may not have been an accident, there was little scandal surrounding his death. The people of England thought they were well rid of him.

The great hero, Richard the Lionheart, was also gay. He was warned by a prominent clergyman to leave off his unnatural practices and spend time with his lovely Spanish wife. But he left his marriage unconsummated and went dashing off to the Middle East with his rough crusaders

His heterosexual brother, King John, took over but made so free with the wives and daughters of his barons that they made him sign the Magna Carta. His wife, Isabella of Angoulême, caused scandal when she took lovers of her own. John had them slaughtered and their bodies draped over her bed as a warning.

The most notorious homosexual to sit on the throne was Edward II, largely because of the nature of his death. While Edward was still Prince of Wales, his father banished his lover, Piers de Gaveston. When Edward took the throne, de Gaveston returned to become Earl of Cornwall and Keeper of the Realm. Naturally, Edward had to get married. He picked as his bride the 12-year-old Isabella of France and, so that Piers would not feel left out, Edward arranged for his marriage to Edward's young niece. At the royal wedding breakfast, Edward and de Gaveston made so free with their affections to one another that Isabella's uncles left in disgust.

Despite his marriage, Edward banned women from his court. Within nine months of his accession, the barons were demanding that de Gaveston be exiled again. Edward was too weak politically to resist. De Gaveston was banished, but Edward accompanied him to his ship and they kissed and caressed on the dockside.

De Gaveston tried to return two years later, but was banished again. The next time he returned secretly, but when he appeared openly at Edward's side during the Christmas festivities of 1311, the barons rebelled.

Edward and de Gaveston fled to Scotland where Edward begged Robert the Bruce for sanctuary. He refused. De Gaveston was captured and put to death. Edward went home to his wife, who seems to have offered some solace. Just five months after de Gaveston's death, she gave birth to the future Edward III.

Over the next nine years, Queen Isabella gave him three more children. Then Edward fell in love with Hugh Despenser, whose father had long been a court favourite. This sparked another rebellion. Isabella fled to France where she took a lover, Lord Roger Mortimer.

Edward demanded that Isabella return to his side. She refused to come back until he dropped his boyfriend. When he refused, Isabella claimed that her husband was dead and went into mourning. Mortimer then led a masterly military campaign against Edward. The elder Despenser was captured and put to death. Edward and

Hugh tried to escape to Ireland, but the wind blew their boat back on the Welsh coast. Hugh suffered the same fate as his father, while Edward was forced to abdicate in favour of his son and was imprisoned. Later, Edward was found dead in his cell. A red hot poker had been shoved up 'those parts in which he had been wont to take his vicious pleasure'.

When Edward III came to the throne at the age of 16, he avenged his father and had Mortimer put to death as a traitor. But the new King did not follow in his father's footsteps. He had four children by his wife and three by his mistress, Alice Perrers.

The most flamboyant homosexual to sit on the throne of England was James I, who was also James VI of Scotland. His very birth was shrouded in scandal. His mother was Mary Queen of Scots. At the age of six she had been betrothed to the Dauphin and sent to France to be brought up in the debauched court of Francois I. There she was tutored by the Queen, Catharine de Medici, whose main educational goal seems to have been the corruption of her own children.

Mary married at the age of 16, but two years later the Dauphin died. She returned to Scotland, pursued by her lover, the poet Pierre de Chatelard. John Knox was outraged by the way that Mary would lean on Chatelard's shoulder and kiss his neck. Chatelard was executed after twice being caught in Mary's bedroom.

Elizabeth I of England tried to unload one of her own lovers, Robert Dudley, on her, but Mary secretly married Henry Stewart, Lord Darnley, who was said to be beautiful, beardless and, it was said, 'more like a woman than a man'. Although Mary liked his looks, she soon found that he was a syphilitic adulterer and a drunk.

Just four months after her wedding, Mary was caught 'playing cards' in a private room with the musician David Rizzio. Darnley and a group of armed men burst in. They grabbed Rizzio, who clung to Mary's skirts for protection. He was dragged from the room and hacked to death on the stairs.

There was uproar in Edinburgh and Mary and Darnley fled. Six months later, she gave birth to James. Darnley was soon plotting to kidnap the child and seize the throne. One night, in Mary's absence, there was a terrific explosion and Darnley's half-naked body was found in the garden. He had been strangled.

Suspicion fell on Lord Bothwell, who was tried but acquitted. Three months later, when Mary was on her way from Stirling Castel to Edinburgh, she was kidnapped and raped by Bothwell. However, once he had divorced his first wife, she married him But in 1567, Mary was deposed in favour of her one-year-old son, who became King under the regency of James Stuart, Earl of Moray, one of the many illegitimate sons of James V.

Mary fled to England where she was imprisoned by her cousin, Queen Elizabeth I. Bothwell fled to Denmark where he died in prison in 1578. In 1586, Mary was implicated in a plot against Elizabeth I, tried and beheaded – despite the half-hearted protests of her son – at Fotheringhay Castle the following year.

Mary's son James VI of Scotland, was brought up strictly. He was kept well away from nubile young girls and confined to an all-male court – with predictable results. The Earl of Holland had to spurn the young King's advances by turning aside and spitting after the King had sladdered in his mouth'.

James was just 13 when his colourful cousin, Esmé Stuart, turned up at court. Esmé was 30 and had just returned from the court of the flagrantly homosexual Henry III of France. Esmé immediately prostrated himself in front of the teenage monarch. The effect was electric.

'No sooner did the young King see him,' said an eye-witness, 'but in that he was so near allied in blood, of so renowned a family, eminent ornaments of body and mind, took him up and embraced him in a most amorous manner, conferred on him presently a rich inheritance; and that he might be employed in state affairs, elected him one of his honourable privy council, gentleman of the bedchamber and governor of Dumbarton Castle.'

He was also created Duke of Lennox. James's Regent, the Earl of Moray, had already been murdered. James had his new Regent, the Earl of Morton, arrested and executed, and Lennox became his closest adviser.

The courtiers who had accompanied Stuart from France were notorious for their drunkeness and their swearing, and the Scottish clergy complained that 'the Duke of Lennox went about to draw the King into carnal lust'. English diplomats also reported on the growing romance between the two young men. But what most concerned everyone was that Lennox had a Catholic wife whom he had left behind in France.

With English support, Scotland's Protestant lords kidnapped James and forced Lennox into exile. Lennox wrote that he would rather die than lose the King's love. James expressed his grief in passionate poetry, comparing Lennox with a little bird pursued by hunters, which he hoped he could save by hiding between his legs.

With Lennox gone, James consoled himself with a string of lovers. He was seen to 'hang around' these young men's necks and kissed them quite openly. This was pretty brave, if not foolhardy, in a country where sodomy was a capital offence. In 1570, during James's reign, two men convicted of sodomy in Edinburgh were burnt at the stake.

James's homosexuality became a political problem when the rumour spread that James, like Elizabeth I of England, was of 'barren stock'. Something had to be done. He needed a queen. He began writing love letters and sonnets to 15-year-old Princess Anne of Denmark. She sent him a portrait, which he hung at the end of his bed and looked at every night.

The marriage was arranged, but the ship on which she made the crossing was blown back to Denmark. James sailed to Copenhagen to get her. For political reasons, he wrote; 'God is my witness I could not have abstained longer.'

It took him four years to get her pregnant. Then they fell out over the upbringing of their son. To make his point, James wrote *A Satire Against Woman*. In it, he expressed his true feelings, Here is a sample:

> 'Even so all women are of nature vain
> And cannot keep a secret unrevealed
> And where as once they do conceive disdain
> They are unable to be reconcealed.
> Fulfilled with talk and clatters but respect
> And often times of small or no effect.'

James continued to do his duty. The Queen gave birth to two more sons and four daughters. But James's preference for his own sex persisted. In 1603, when, on the death of Elizabeth I, James acceded to the throne of England, he went south with a smooth-faced young man named James Hay, who was officially Master of the Royal Wardrobe.

Hay fell out of favour after making free with England's treasury and was married off to the daughter of a peer. On the morning after his wedding, he and his bride found the King clambering into the bed with them.

Hay was replaced by Philip Herbet, who was similarly married off when James grew tired of him. Next came Robert Carr, a handsome young Scottish pageboy who was thrown from a horse at a jousting competition. The King rushed over to check whether he was injured and immediately put him in the care of the royal physicians. During Carr's convalescence, the King visited him every day and even tried to teach him Latin. Some said that his time would be better spent teaching the young Scot to speak English.

When he was fully recovered, Carr became a Gentleman of the Bedchamber and the two of them were inseparable. Their relationship was not 'carried' on with discretion sufficient to cover less scandalous behaviour'. They were seen kissing and fondling openly at the theatre, leaving little doubt as to what they got up to when they were on their own. Not that it mattered so much now that they were south of the border. In England, the attitude to homosexuality was less Draconian. In the 45 years of Elizabeth's rule and the 23 years of James's, only six men in the Home Counties were indicted for sodomy, and only one was convicted, even though London itself was awash with the vice. Nevertheless, it was still considered shocking for the King to flaunt his sexual preferences so openly.

The scandal grew when James created Carr Lord Rochester. The ambitious young man then sought further advancement by wooing Lady Essex. But her husband, who had been away for four years, suddenly turned up. Carr pressed the King to grant Lady Essex a divorce, while she defended her honour with potions she had bought from a magician. They seem to have worked. In 1613, her marriage was annulled on the ground of impotence.

Rochester and Lady Essex were then married. At the ceremony, the bride wore her hair loose over her shoulders to symbolise, disingenuously her virginity. As a wedding present, James created Rochester Earl of Somerset.

But that was not the end of the matter. Lady Essex was even less of a virgin than she pretended. She had a former lover called Thomas Overbury, who opposed Rochester's relentless ambition. Rochester used his influence with the King to have Overbury arrested and imprisoned in the Tower, but when he was found dead, poisoned, James had no choice but to have his former lover, Rochester, and his wife arrested.

There was rioting when the newly weds went on trial. Copious evidence implicated Rochester, at least, in the crime. They were both sentenced to death, but James, for old times' sake, commuted the sentence to imprisonment at his pleasure. They served seven years in the Tower. Rochester never saw the King again.

By this time, James was well provided for by young men eager to advance themselves. One political faction even sought to win the King's favour by employing the Countess of Suffolk to find young men for him. She spent her time curling their hair and perfuming their breaths, ready just for the royal pleasure.

The Queen had disliked Rochester. She had sought to curb his influence by pushing forward a candidate of her own. This was George Villiers, whom Bishop Goodman described as the handsomest man in England. Few disagreed, although some pointed out that he was somewhat effeminate.

He was also the protégé of James's former lover, Philip Herbert, but it was the Queen who secured him his position as Gentleman of the Bedchamber. James was soon hopelessly in love.

James called Villiers Steenie, after St Stephen who, according to the Bible, had a face that glowed like 'the fact of an angel', He referred to him in his letters as both 'wife' and 'husband' and told the Privy Council that he loved him more than any other man. Villiers was rewarded with the title Earl of Buckingham and an advantageous marriage. There was no doubt in anyone's mind that James loved Buckingham in the way that he had loved Rochester.

'The love the King showed was as amorously conveyed as if he had mistaken their sex and thought them ladies; which I have seen Somerset and Buckingham labour to resemble, in the effeminateness of their dress,' wrote one eyewitness.

When James died, it was rumoured that Buckingham

had poisoned him, after growing tired of the ageing King's sexual demands. He certainly had plenty of opportunity as he had nursed the King through his final illness. James's death did Buckingham no harm either. He was already tight with James's heir, his son who became Charles I. Charles was submissive, narcissistic and effeminate. As a youth, he was jealous of his father's lover, but by the time James died he, too, was calling Buckingham 'Steenie'. In letters, he addressed him as 'sweetheart' and the two were constant companions. Francis Bacon remarked how nice it was that Buckingham could 'ease the heart of both father and son'.

Before James's death, rumours spread that 'Baby Charles' was 'sterile'. The problem had to be solved once more by a rapid marriage. James sent Charles off to Madrid to woo the King of Spain's daughter, the Infanta Maria.

Buckingham was sent along to keep Charles out of trouble. While they were away, James wrote to them saying: 'I wear Steenie's picture on a blue ribbon under my waistcoat, next to my heart.'

Instead of keeping Charles out of trouble, Buckingham precipitated it. He put out the nose of their go-between, Count Olivares, by arranging an assignation with his wife. The Countess sent a prostitute in her place, but negotiations were blocked. Charles, who mistakenly believed that he had made a good impression on the Infanta, took matters into his own hands. He climbed over the palace wall at the Casa Del Campo and caught her without her chaperone. The Infanta responded to this bold advance with a loud scream. She ran and told her father that she would rather become a nun than marry the future King of England. The situation turned so nasty that Charles and Buckingham had to be rescued by the Royal Navy. But back in London, James, Charles and Buckingham closeted themselves in the King's private chambers and, for four hours, peels of laughter could be heard echoing down the hallways.

James dispatched envoys, including his former lover, James Hay, now Earl of Carlisle, to woo other princesses. But Charles I solved the problem himself when his father died and he came to the throne. He married 15-year-old Henrietta Maria of France by proxy.

When she arrived in England the couple were cordial enough, but things did not seem to be going so well in the bedroom. Soon, the court was worried that there might be no heirs.

Buckingham tried to solve the problem. He tried to pass the benefit of his advice to the Queen via Henrietta Maria's Lady of the Bedchamber, Madame St Georges. But she refused to interfere in such delicate matters and was sacked.

The solution to the problem arrived via a more round-about route. Buckingham had been having an affair with the beautiful and experienced Lady Carlisle, wife of James Hay. He had even prevailed on the King to send Hay away on a diplomatic mission so that he could seduce her.

When Buckingham's wife found out, he tried to pass Lady Carlisle on to the King. He refused the offer, but made her a Lady of the Bedchamber. Lady Carlisle then proceeded to impart everything she knew about the ways of love to the young Queen. Within weeks, Henrietta Maria was pregnant. She and Charles had nine healthy children, and several more stillborn.

Of course, the great scandal of Charles I's reign was not sexual, it was his high-handed attitude to parliament, which tried to curb his excesses. He alienated them when he purchased a collection of paintings he could ill afford. And when they opposed him, he tried to have five Members of the House of Commons arrested. The Civil War ensued. After five years, his forces were defeated by the Puritans under Oliver Cromwell.

Charles was imprisoned on the Isle of Wight, where he

was comforted by Jane Whorwood. The wife of the royalist leader of the City of London, she had come to him with
half of the £1,000 he had raised for the royalist cause.
Charles kept her as a courtier in lieu of the other half.

During his imprisonment Charles wrote at least 16 letters to her. On 26 July 1648, six months before he died, the
doomed King wrote to 'Sweet Jane Whorwood' to meet
him in his room as if by accident. He outwitted his guard
on numerous occasions to see her and, in his last letter to
her, he spoke of the 'great contentment' she had brought to
him.

Sentenced as 'a tyrant, a traitor, a murderer and a public
enemy', Charles died on the scaffold outside the banqueting hall in Whitehall. Unrepentant to the end, he warned
the axeman that he would 'forgive no subject of mine who
comes to shed my blood.'

Virgin Sovereign

Elizabeth I was the Virgin Queen, or so she said. In 1559,
she asked Sir John Mason to tell the House of Commons to
erect 'a marble stone which shall declare that a Queen
lived and died a virgin'. No such stone was ever erected.
The reason was that throughout Elizabeth's reign there
were a series of royal sex scandals that she only just managed to keep in check.

When she was just 16 there were rumours that she had
been made pregnant by her guardian, the ambitious
Thomas Seymour, husband of her father's widow
Catherine Parr, who had once caught them in a passionate
embrace.

When she came to the throne, Elizabeth showed little
interest in men. Perhaps her father's philandering had put
her off. Naturally, she was besieged with offers from for-

eign princes, eager to wear the English crown. Even Philip of Spain, widower of Elizabeth's half-sister Mary who was hardly cold in her grave, rushed forward with a proposal. But he was a Catholic. Elizabeth, the daughter of Henry VIII and Anne Boleyn, was a confirmed Protestant. England was now a Protestant Kingdom and she was determined to keep it that way.

A year after she was crowned, Elizabeth began taking a romantic interest in Lord Robert Dudley. They had been born on the same day in September 1533 and had been imprisoned in the Tower together during much of Mary's reign.

In 1559, the eve that Elizabeth declared that she would live and die a virgin, the Spanish ambassador reported that 'Her Majesty visits him in his chamber both day and night'.

The problem was that Dudley had a wife. She stayed out of the way in Berkshire and it was rumoured that she had a 'malady of the breast'. Apparently, she was not long for this world and, when she died, Elizabeth intended to marry Lord Robert.

Dudley's wife did die, but not of a malady of the breast. She was found at the foot of the stairs in their Berkshire home. Dudley was immediately suspected of murdering her. The Queen herself was implicated and she had no alternative but to send him away.

But he did not give up on the match. Slowly, she tried to rehabilitate him. Four years later, he was back in court and she created him Earl of Leicester. This was hardly calculated to dampen down the gossip.

'I am spoken of as if I am an immodest woman,' Elizabeth complained to the Spanish ambassador. 'I have favoured him because of his excellent disposition and his many merits, but I am young and he is young, and therefore we have both been slandered. God knows, they do us grievous wrong.'

With Leicester still out of the running, other men threw their hats into the ring. Sir Christopher Hatton, a handsome young lawyer from Northampton, wrote to the Queen with a great passion. Those closer to home were soon unmasked as womanizers. One of them was Sir Walter Raleigh, who was front runner for a while, until he got Elizabeth Throckmorton, one of the Ladies of the Bedchamber, pregnant.

Leicester, too, developed a reputation as a ladies' man. Enemies spread the word that he would pay as much as £300 to sleep with the Queen's ladies-in-waiting. He bedded Lady Frances Howard, but broke off with her to seduce the Queen's beautiful cousin, Lady Douglas Sheffield. Her husband died mysteriously – poisoned by Leicester it was said – and she presented him with a son. To get her own back, the Queen entertained the advances of the Duke of Anjou, the King of France's brother and half her age. He was a devout Catholic and practising bisexual.

When that fell though, she began entertaining Anjou's younger brother, the Duke of Alencon. Finally, Leicester broke it off with Lady Sheffield and Elizabeth dropped Alencon. It was only later that one of Alencon's envoys pointed out that Leicester had dropped Lady Sheffield to take up with Lettice, Countess of Essex, another of the Queen's cousins and reputed to be the most beautiful woman at court.

Elizabeth sent Leicester off on a military campaign in Ireland and chastized Lettice for her disloyalty. But when Leicester returned, the affair continued. Then Lettice's husband died. Again, Leciester was suspected, and it was said that he was the real father of her children.

They married secretly in 1578, weeks before the birth of their first legitimate child. Driven half-crazy with jealously, the Queen dragged Lady Sheffield in front of the Royal Councillors and tried to force her to admit that Leicester had secretly been married to her – making him a bigamist.

However, Lady Sheffield had since made a favourable match with Sir Edward Stafford and saw no reason to jeopardize her new marriage.

In 1579, Elizabeth invited the Duke of Alencon to England and fawned over him. She even allowed Leicester back into court so that he could witness their love-making. When Alencon fell ill, Elizabeth acted as nursemaid to her 'little frog', as she called him. The Puritan preacher, John Stubbs, thought this quite scandalous. He condemned Alencon as a serpent, come to seduce our English Eve and destroy the paradise that was England.

This did nothing to dampen Elizabeth's ardour and in 1581, when Alencon visited England again, she announced that she was going to marry him. But her ladies-in-waiting kicked up such a fuss that, the following day, she told him the wedding was off.

When Leicester died in 1588, Elizabeth was reconciled with her cousin, Lettice. When she returned to court, she brought with her her son, the Earl of Essex. He stepped into his stepfather's shoes and began to woo the Queen. It was a bold, if cynical move. Essex was young and handsome; the Queen was in her 50s. A bright auburn wig hid her thinning hair. Thick white make-up hid her wrinkles. Only by maintaining an unsmiling face could she hide her rotting teeth.

Essex knew the extent of the damage. Excitedly returning from an expedition one morning, he had impetuously pushed past the guards and barged into her chamber, before she had had time to put on her wig and make-up. He also had to contend with a court that was filled with young and scandalous distractions. Elizabeth sent her lady-in-waiting, Anne Vasavour, to the Tower after she gave birth to the illegitimate son of the Earl of Oxford. Later, Anne married, then had another illegitimate son by Sir Henry Lee. When he died, Anne married again, only to be fined £200 for bigamy.

When another lady-in-waiting, Mary Futton, was brought to court, her father asked Sir William Knollys to protect his innocent daughter. Sir William seduced the girl himself and promised to marry her when his wife died. In the meantime, Mary began an affair with the Earl of Pembroke. To meet her lover, Mary would steal away from court in men's clothing. The scandal broke when Mary fell pregnant. Pembroke refused to marry her and was sent to Fleet jail. Mary was sent home to the country in disgrace.

Essex himself secretly married the widow of Sir Philip Sidney. When Elizabeth found out about it, she was forgiving and allowed Lady Essex to be presented at court. But neither his wife's presence nor the censure of the Queen stopped him from bedding other ladies-in-waiting. His indiscreet affair with Elizabeth Brydges, daughter of Lord Chandos, was so scandalous that the Queen banished her from court. But she did not act quickly enough in the case of Elizabeth Southwell, who bore Essex's child.

The Queen was so jealous when Lady Mary Howard started throwing herself at Essex that she borrowed one of her dresses and wore it herself. It did nothing for the ageing Queen. When Essex was less than impressed, she confiscated the dress and condemned Lady Mary and all the other 'flouting wenches' of the court.

Essex's scandalous behaviour then developed a political dimension. He was charged with spreading sedition in Ireland, but Elizabeth merely had him censured in private, rather than put on trial for treason. This taught him nothing. With a small band of followers, he rode into London, intent on seizing the Queen. Forewarned, the Palace of Westminster was barricaded. Essex's following quickly dwindled. He was arrested and this time he was tried for treason and sentenced to death.

Even then he might have got away with it. The Queen

had once given him a ring that, she had said, would absolve him from any crime. From his cell in the Tower, he sent it to her. But on the way, it fell into the hands of his old enemy, Lady Nottingham, who only passed it on to the Queen after Essex had been beheaded.

Of course, we cannot be sure that the relationship between Elizabeth and Essex was ever consummated. But we can be sure that the Virgin Queen was no virgin. She once said that she was 'of barren stock'. If she had not had sex with a number of men, how could she have known?

Elizabeth's half-sister, Mary, fared little better in love, but the main scandal in her reign was her propensity to burn Protestants, especially bishops. This earned her the epithet 'Bloody Mary'. Also, through her bad choice of a mate, she lost Calais, England's last possession in France.

Mary's reign began in scandal. The daughter of Catherine of Aragon, Henry VIII's first wife, she suffered the shame of seeing her mother divorced and her father repudiating the Catholic faith she had been brought up in. With the death of Henry VIII, her half-brother Edward VI, the son of Jane Seymour, took the throne. He died at the age of 16 – hardly enough time to get involved in any serious scandal. Not that he didn't try. After his betrothal in 1552 to Princess Elizabeth of France, he held a pageant in Greenwich called The Triumph of Cupid. He also fooled around with the 35-year-old Mary of Guise, the Regent of Scotland, and Mary, Queen of Scots.

With his death, Lady Jane Grey took over in a constitutional coup. She was only fifth in line to the throne. Like Elizabeth I, she had been brought up in Thomas Seymour's house and seems to have had a crush on the older man. When she blossomed into a young woman, he put about the rumour that he was going to marry her, possibly to discourage other suitors.

However, the ambitious Duke of Northumberland was not to be put off. He was Edward VI's chief adviser and the most powerful man in the land. He could do almost anything he pleased. But Edward was a sickly child and if he died, Northumberland's power would die with him. So he decided to marry Lady Jane Grey off to his witless son, Lord Guildford Dudley, and put the two of them on the throne. That way he would retain his influence.

There was a problem though. When Jane was told that she was to marry Dudley, she refused point blank. She protested that she was already promised to Lord Hertford. Her parents bullied and beat her until she agreed. Lord Hertford was placated by marriage to Jane's sister. In fact, Northumberland had arranged a series of marriages in order to secure his dynastic hold on the reigns of power. Katherine Dudley married Lord Hastings. Jane's 13-year-old sister, Katherine, married Lord Herbert and eight-year-old Mary was betrothed to her cousin, Arthur Grey. They were to be married as soon as she reached puberty.

Even so, nothing went smoothly. Although Jane's wedding was lavish, the bridegroom came down with food poisoning and was unable to consummate the marriage. By the time he had recovered, Edward was on his deathbed. Northumberland persuaded the young King to alter the succession in favour of Lady Jane and ordered that she be publicly 'abedded' by Dudley. Once this was done, Lady Jane went to take a rest cure at the Palace in Chelsea.

When Edward died, Lady Jane was proclaimed Queen. Her reign lasted just nine days. Mary swept to power. Jane and Dudley were arrested and tried for treason. She was sentenced to public burning; he to hanging, drawing and quartering.

Mary showed every sign of being merciful. But when she announced her intention to marry the Catholic King Philip II of Spain, the Protestants under Sir Thomas Wyatt rebelled. Although the rebellion was swiftly put down, Mary realized that Jane and Dudley posed a threat as long as they lived.

From his cell, Dudley asked to see his young wife one last time. She refused, although she did see his headless body as it was carried back from Tower Hill. Jane was then examined to see if she was pregnant before being taken to the block on Tower Green.

After observing the Fortunes of her father's six wives, one might have thought that Mary would have had reservations about marriage. Indeed, when she first came to the throne, she surrounded herself with pretty young women and she resolutely stood in the way of any marriage plans they might have. One of them, Jane Dormer, slept in Mary's chamber and was often seen wearing the Queen's jewels.

But Mary had one major political ambition – to return Protestant England to the Catholic Church. To do that, she accepted the proposal of Philip of Spain.

This was no love match. When Philip arrived in Southampton in July 1554, he kissed all her ladies-in-waiting. Mary herself was 10 years his senior and plainly not to his taste. To Philip and his courtiers, English women were very loose and Philip made his intentions towards the Queen's maids very plain. However, when it came to Mary herself, his ardour was less than flaming. But, for the sake of the throne and the church, they went through the motions.

By September 1554 it was announced that Mary was pregnant. Spanish ladies flocked to attend her at Hampton Court. They waited and they waited. By Easter 1555, it was circulated that the date of conception had been miscalculated. By May, rumours suggested that she was not pregnant at all. The doctors and courtiers stuck valiantly to the official line throughout June and July. It was only in August that Mary was forced to admit that it was only air – not an heir – in her belly.

In disgust, Philip sailed back to Spain. Mary put a brave

face on things in public but, in private, broke down and wept. She wrote to him often, begging him to return to her. He did in March 1557. But he wanted her, not as a bed mate, but an ally. Spain was at war with France. Philip wanted England to join in. The result was the loss of Calais. Mary said that when she died, Calais would be found written on her heart.

Philip left England again in January 1558. Again, it was announced that Mary was pregnant. Indeed, her belly was swollen, but swelling was caused by the dropsy that killed her later that year.

The Six Wives of Henry VIII

There have been few more scandalous monarchs than Henry VIII. He changed the religion of a kingdom in order to divorce his first wife and had two subsequent wives executed. With six wives he had the reputation of being a great stud. In fact, with two of them he was almost certainly impotent. He only married so much in an effort to secure an heir. At the time it was seen as a political imperative to avoid plunging England back into the 30 years of internecine feuding that had preceded his father's reign, which have come to be known as the Wars of the Roses.

Henry Tudor, Henry VIII's father, had won the Wars of the Roses by defeating Richard III at the Battle of Bosworth Field and was crowned Henry VII. A Lancastrian, Henry VII ended any further struggle by marrying the daughter of the other great rival dynasty, Elizabeth of York.

As a prince, Henry VIII was brought up chastenly. A studious lad, he wrote the religious tract called *Assertio septem sacramentorum adversus Martin Lutherum*, a reply to Martin Luther's 95 theses nailed to the church door in Wittenberg that started the Protestant Reformation. As a result, Henry was awarded the title *Fidei Defensor*, or 'Defender of the Faith', by the Pope.

The first scandal of his reign centred on the marriage of his brother, the 15-year-old Arthur, to the 16-year-old Spanish princess, Catherine of Aragon. Arthur had died soon after and Henry was encouraged by his father to take an interest in Catherine. A marriage between the heir to the English throne and Spain was important for English foreign policy, so Henry VII pushed for a dispensation from the Pope to allow Henry to marry his brother's widow – which was technically incest – on the grounds that her marriage to Arthur had never been consummated.

Henry VIII came to the throne at 18 and, two months later, he married Catherine. Although she was six years older than him, he genuinely loved her. They enjoyed hunting, hawking and making music together, and the grooms who escorted him from his bedchamber to the Queen's reported that he made the trip regularly.

For five years, he was faithful. In that time, Catherine produced a number of stillborn children, a son who lived just two months and a daughter, Mary. Then Henry's attention began to wander. At first, his attention alighted on Lady Anne Hastings. He used one of the Grooms of the Bedchamber, Sir Henry Crompton, as his go-between. But Sir Henry promptly seduced Lady Anne himself.

When they were interrupted by Lady Anne's husband, Sir George Hastings, Crompton claimed that he was making love to Lady Anne not for his own sake, but for that of the King. In the resulting scandal, Lady Anne was sent to a nunnery by her irate husband, and Henry banished her brother, the Duke of Buckingham, and Sir George's sister, Elizabeth, from court for spreading gossip. This did not prevent the news from reaching the ears of the Queen and the Spanish ambassador.

While the Queen remained vexed, Henry moved on to Jane Popincourt, the Flemish-born mistress of the Duc de

Longueville, a French noble long held hostage in the English court. Her reputation was notorious. Louis XII personally crossed her name off the list of maids-of-honour who were coming to France with Henry's sister, Mary, saying that he would rather see Popincourt burn at the stake than attend his young bride.

Henry returned de Longueville to France to clear the way for his affair. And, when he tired of Jane, he gave her £100 to follow her lover. He had already transferred his affections to 18-year-old Elizabeth 'Bessie' Blount.

The daughter of a Shropshire knight, Bessie had come to court at the age of 13 when her dancing had brought her to the King's attention at a masque. The Queen was so taken by their performance that she had them repeat their *pas de deux* in her chamber by candlelight.

At 18, Bessie became Henry's mistress and in 1519, she presented him with a healthy living son, Henry Fitzroy. Bessie was quickly married off to Gilbert Talboys, one of the wards of the Chancey. The happy couple were given Rokeby Manor in Warwickshire as a wedding present.

Later, Henry considered marrying his illegitimate son to Mary to secure the line – albeit incestuously – but Henry Fitzroy died of tuberculosis while still a teenager.

The next woman to bear Henry a child was Mary Boleyn, Anne's older sister. Both Mary and Anne had been maids-of-honour in the licentious French court, but Mary, it seems, had out performed the local talent. An Italian diplomat described her as the 'greatest and most infamous whore', while the King of France himself called her a 'hackney'.

Back in England, Mary was Catherine of Aragon's lady-in-waiting when Henry seduced her. Her compliant husband was rewarded with a knighthood. Henry named a ship in his new navy after her, but he dropped her without a penny when he grew tired of her.

Mary's father, Thomas Boleyn was an ambitious man.

It was said that he had even offered his own wife to Henry, who refused her, saying: 'Never with the mother.' Mary's younger sister, Anne, was more to Henry's taste. But Anne wanted nothing to do with him and proclaimed her intention to marry one James Butler.

However, fate – perhaps in the form of Thomas Boleyn – took a hand. Anne was picked to be one of eight ladies to take part in a masque at Cardinal Wolsey's London home, York Place. They were to represent Virtue and had to defend their castle against eight masked men, representing Desire, by dousing them with rose water and pelting them with fruit.

The outcome was predictable. After a few minutes of mock combat, Virtue succumbed. The ladies then danced with their assailants. When the gentlemen unmasked themselves, Anne found her suitor was none other than the King.

But Anne was not to be won over so easily. She took up with a married man, the poet Sir Thomas Wyatt, to protect herself from Henry's advances. Then she received a proposal from the Earl of Northumberland's heir, Sir Henry perky. But, knowing the King's interest, Cardinal Wolsey put a stop to that match.

Henry stopped sleeping with the Queen and, in a series of passionate love letters, promised to make Anne his sole mistress 'rejecting all others'. This came as a bit of a shock to the court as Anne was no great beauty. She had an unsightly mole on her neck which she hid with high collars, and she wore long sleeves to hide the tiny sixth finger that she had on each hand. But it was her pert young bosom that took the King's fancy – 'those pritty duckys I trust shortly to kysse,' he wrote. 'Ducky' is a medieval word for breast.

Anne still did not succumb. She did not want to suffer the short shrift that Henry had meted out to her sister Mary. But Henry was growing desperate to have a son and he thought Anne might provide him with one. He needed a legitimate heir, however, so he would have to marry her.

Henry began to contend that the dispensation the Pope had given Catherine to marry him had been obtained under false pretences. That was why God had cursed their union and it had failed to give him the son he craved. Henry persuaded the Dowager Duchess of Norfolk to testify that Catherine had indeed slept with his older brother, Arthur. The marriage had therefore been consummated, making her marriage to Henry incestuous and illegal.

Unfortunately for Henry, the Pope was being held hostage by Catherine's nephew, Charles V, at the time and did not see it that way. All Cardinal Wolsey's attempts to seek an annulment failed. Anne, who was still sore at Wolsey for preventing her marriage to Sir Henry Perky, demanded his dismissal. Wolsey retired to York and died on his way back to London, summoned there to face a charge of treason.

Sir Thomas More took over as Chancellor, but he was against the divorce and wanted to fight what he saw as the Lutheran heresy. He was replaced by the ambitious Thomas Cromwell, who saw that the way to give Henry the divorce he wanted was for him to reject the authority of Rome and make himself head of the English Church.

After holding out for six years, Anne finally succumbed. By January 1533, she was pregnant. On 25 January, Henry and Anne were married secretly. In May, a new Archbishop of Canterbury, Thomas Cramner, presided over an ecclesiastical inquiry into Henry's first marriage, and on 23 May a special Act of Parliament declared it null and void. At Whitsun, Anne was crowned Queen, and in September, she gave birth – to Princess Elizabeth. The Pope's response was excommunication. It bothered no one.

Disappointed at the birth of a daughter, Henry began indulging himself with other lovers. Anne herself complained to her sister-in-law, Lady Rochford, that Henry was neither skilful at love-making nor very virile. Nevertheless, she kept entertaining him in her bed in the hope that she would produce the male heir he so desperately wanted. Anne fell pregnant three more times – although she miscarried on each occasion. Anne blamed one of her miscarriages on Henry's dalliance with a pretty maid.

Anne turned for advice to her Lady of the Bedchamber, the sly Lady Rochford – whom Henry banished from court. In desperation, Anne tried to interest Henry in her own cousin, Madge Shelton. When Henry found out that Anne was trying to manipulate his love life, he dismissed Madge from court, too – after bedding her first, of course.

But Henry was slowing down. He suffered occasionally from bouts of impotence. To his doctors, he complained: 'I am forty-one years old, at which age the lust of a man is not as quick as in lusty youth.' This was in the days before Viagra.

Even so, Anne became pregnant again. Henry, then 44, was delighted. But the prospect of being a father again did not stop him from turning his attentions to Anne's maid-of-honour, the beautiful and nubile Jane Seymour.

In January 1536, Catherine of Aragon died and Henry held a joust to celebrate. During the action, Henry was thrown from his horse. He was stretchered from the tournament field and for two hours he lay unconscious. Anne suddenly realized how precarious her position was. If the King died without a son, England would be thrown back into civil war and she would be the first for the chop. Her anxiety triggered premature labour. She gave birth to a son – dead.

Rumours quickly spread that the foetus was deformed, a sure sign that she had been involved with witchcraft. When Henry revived, he denied paternity. In his eyes, the deformed foetus proved that his second marriage, too, was cursed by incest. After all, Anne's sister, Mary, had been his lover before their marriage.

With Catherine now dead, Anne was in a very vulnerable position. Henry could now simply declare that his first marriage had been legitimate after all. That would reconcile him with the Catholic Church, rid him of Anne and allow him to find a new wife.

Anne was also isolated. Those courtiers who had maintained a loyalty to Catherine called her 'the concubine' and 'the goggle-eyed whore'. In an attempt to find allies, Anne flirted. Enemies spread rumours that she had lovers. This played into Henry's hands. He encouraged the scandal by boasting that his wife had slept with a hundred other men.

'You never saw a prince, nor a man, who made a greater show of his cuckold's horns,' one observer said.

On 2 May 1536, Anne was arrested for adultery, incest and plotting to kill the King. Sir Henry Norris, a Gentleman of the Privy Chamber, the grooms Sir Francis Weston and William Brereton, along with a handsome young musician named Mark Smeaton were also arrested. The first three denied having sex with Anne, but Smeaton confessed, after torture. The four of them were found guilty of treason and paid a terrible price. They were hanged at Tyburn, cut down while still alive, castrated, disembowelled and, finally, had their limbs cut off. It was a gruesome way to go.

Anne's brother, Lord Rochford, was also arrested. The two of them were tried together in the Great Hall in the Tower of London. Their chief accuser was Rochford's wife, good old Lady Rochford, who alleged that her husband had always been in his sister's room. Other maids gave their own accounts of the 'pastimes of the Queen's chamber'. Lady Rochford also testified that there had been an 'undue familiarity' between brother and sister. The implication was that since Anne had been unable to produce the male heir Henry craved with Henry himself, she had tried to conceive one with other lovers. Her own brother lent a hand, as it were, because his position depended on being the brother-in-law of the current King and the uncle of a future monarch.

As evidence of incest this was less than convincing, but there was no crossing the King. The judge, who was Anne's own uncle, the Duke of Norfolk, shed a tear when he delivered the guilty verdict. For treason, the death sentence was mandatory. But whether they were to be burnt or beheaded was a matter for the King's pleasure.

Henry was merciful. Rochford was beheaded on Tower Hill. Perhaps in deference to the great love he had once had for Anne, Henry spared her the axe. He paid £24 to bring an expert swordsman over from Calais to dispatch his love on Tower Green.

Curiously, two days before Anne was executed, Henry divorced her. He had their marriage annulled on the grounds that she had previously been contracted to marry Sir Henry Perky. The annulment technically nullified the charge of adultery. And with no adultery there was no treason – and, thus, no reason to execute her. No one mentioned this to Henry. He was too busy having fun.

While Anne was preparing to die, Henry began a round of parties where he pursued any woman he found remotely attractive. He was now 45 and not in the best of health, but he compared his new-found freedom with a man who had disposed of 'a thin old vicious hack in the hope of getting soon a fine horse to ride'.

It did not take him long to find his new mount. On 13 May 1536, just 11 days after the death of Anne Boleyn, he married her pretty maid-of-honour, Jane Seymour. Although Jane had been in Henry's debauched court for several years, she was still reputed to be a virgin – a neat trick in a court where it was held a 'sin to be a maid'. As Queen, Jane imposed her modest demeanour on others. She forbade Anne Basset to wear 'French apparel' and insisted that she use 'chests', material that covered the plunging necklines.

Already, the rumour was that the King was impotent, but something about Jane must have inspired him. In February 1537, it was announced that the Queen was pregnant and on 12 October she gave birth to his long-awaited son, Edward.

Twelve days later, she died.

Henry was heartbroken. But now he had sired a Prince of Wales, he was eager to sire a Duke of York, too a younger brother for the sickly Edward.

There was a problem though. Since there was now no Queen at court, most of the eligible young ladies-in-waiting were home in the country.

The English ambassador to the Netherlands, John Hutton, was commanded to draw up a list of eligible women. These ranged from a 14-year-old lady-in-waiting to the Queen of France to a well-preserved 40-year-old widow. Hutton's recommendation, however, was the 16-year-old Duchess Christina of Milan. Henry was now 48.

However, Henry was interested in the current crop of French princesses and suggested a beauty pageant of five girls in Calais. The French ambassador said that if the princesses were to be paraded like ponies, why did His Majesty not go one step further – mount them in turn so he could pick out the best ride? The idea was dropped.

The artist Hans Holbein was sent to Italy to paint a portrait of Christina of Milan. Henry was impressed. The young lady was also experienced in the ways of love. At 13 she had been married to the Duke of Milan, who had died a year later. The wedding arrangements were set in hand, but the wily Lord Chancellor Thomas Cromwell was against the marriage. Politically, an alliance with Protestant Germany would be more advantageous.

Holbein was sent off again, this time to Germany, to paint a portrait of Anne of Cleves. The English envoy who went with him protested that Anne and her sister, Amelia, were so well covered that Holbein could see neither their figures nor their faces.

'Why, would you have them naked?' replied the Chancellor of Cleves.

Knowing which way the political wind was blowing, Holbein turned in an exceedingly flattering portrait of Anne. Henry did not find it displeasing and, bowing to the political exigencies, agreed to marry her.

It was noted that the King was very lusty at the time and, despite a gouty leg, he rode on horseback from Greenwich to Rochester to greet his bride. But when he set eyes on her, he was appalled by her ugliness and quickly dubbed her his 'Flanders Mare'. To make matters worse, she spoke no English.

After their first night together, Henry told Cromwell: 'I liked her before not well, but now I like her much worse.'

She was 'not as reported', he said. He breasts were slack and droopy – he liked small pert ones like Anne Boleyn's – and other parts of her body were 'in such a state one suspected her virginity'. She was apparently in such bad nick that Henry complained that never in her company could he be 'provoked or steered to know her carnally.'

Eight days later, he complained to his doctors that even though he had slept with his new wife each night she was 'still as good a maid…as ever her mother bore her.' And it was not his fault, he claimed. During the nights he had had a number of nocturnal emissions.

Anne was blissfully unaware of the problem. When Lady Rutland made discreet enquiries about the physical side of their marriage, Anne said: 'When he comes to bed, he kisses me and taketh me by the hand and biddeth me "Farewell, darling". Is that not enough?'

Lady Rutland tried to explain that a little more was expected of Anne if England was to have its Duke of York. But Anne would not listen. She regarded such talk as shameful.

Failing to get much stimulation from his new wife, Henry's amorous attentions quickly turned to Anne of Cleves's 18-year-old maid-of-honour, Catherine Howard, a cousin of Anne Boleyn. She was neither modest nor pious. She had been brought up in the crowded house of the Doweger Duchess of Norfolk in Horsham in Sussex, with numerous young relatives. There they had midnight feasts that often ended in communal sex.

Catherine took her first lover at 14. His name was Henry Manox and he was a young music teacher hired to teach her, ironically, the virginal. She later claimed that full sex had not taken place but he was persuasive and, she said: 'I suffered him at Sunday times to handle and touch the secret parts of my body which neither became me with honesty to permit nor him to require.'

But when the family moved to Norfolk House in Lambeth, she met another young man named Frances Dereham. He set about seducing her and they were soon calling each other 'husband' and 'wife'.

'Frances Derham,' said Catherine later, 'by many persuasions procured me to his vicious purpose and obtained first to lie upon my bed with his doublet and hose, and after in the bed; and, finally, he lay with me naked and used me in such sort as a man doth his wife many and sundry times, but how often I know not.'

They were not alone. Dereham would come to the maiden's chamber at night with Edward Waldegrave, where they would stay until dawn with their respective loves – Catherine and Joan Bulmer. According to Joan, Dereham and Catherine would 'kiss and hang by their bellies as if they were two sparrows'. Love tokens were exchanged and, in the dark, Joan heard a great deal of 'puffing and blowing'.

Catherine, despite her young years, was advanced. Joan said she knew 'how a woman might meddle with a man and yet conceive no child unless she would herself.'

Another member of the household, Katherine Tylney,

later admitted that on occasions she had joined Dereham and Catherine in what *The Sun* today would call a 'three-in-the-bed love romp'.

Catherine's behaviour was widely known, but her colourful past was quickly hushed up when Henry took an interest. He described Catherine as 'a blushing rose without a thorn' and a 'perfect jewel of womanhood'. He took her as his mistress, but the powerful Howard family had greater ambitions. They were Catholics and wanted to rid the realm of its Protestant Queen.

The diplomatic need for Henry's German marriage had passed. Thomas Cromwell now backed the King's desire to sire more children. He began to arrange for Henry a divorce from his 'Flanders Mare'.

A convocation of clerics was set up to investigate the validity of the marriage. Anne's blushes were not spared when she was asked to repeat her conversations with Lady Rutland in front of the committee. Henry's doctors were also called to give evidence. After the scandal of two very public divorce cases centring on incest, the people of England were treated to hilarious testimony concerning the King's inability to get it up. But this was just a foretaste of the even more juicy scandal that was to follow.

The clerics quickly found that 'there had been no carnal copulation between Your Majesty and the said Lady Anne, nor with that just impediment interceding could it be possible'. The King's inability to perform, they ruled, resulted from a troubled conscience concerning the fact that Anne of Cleves had previously been promised elsewhere. The marriage was quickly annulled.

Anne remained in England and hit the bottle. She took other, more virile, lovers. Rumour had it that she became pregnant twice and gave birth to an illegitimate child.

There was another impediment to Henry's marriage plans, however. Since Catherine was Anne Boleyn's cousin, marriage to Catherine was technically incest. The

Archbishop of Canterbury, Thomas Cramner, quickly arranged a dispensation and the marriage went ahead. Catherine was already pregnant, but who was the father? Henry was fat, 50 and sick, and his waist had swelled out to a massive 54 inches. Nineteen-year-old Catherine had already shown her preference for younger, slimmer men.

Henry's court was soon packed with Catherine's adolescent playmates, including Joan Bulmer and Katherine Tylney. But, unfortunately, one of them had been overlooked. Her name was Mary Lassels. She had been one of the gentlewomen in the service of the Duchess of Norfolk, who had shared Catherine's communal bedroom at Norfolk House and had witnessed Catherine's youthful indiscretions. Egged on by her brother, a Protestant who sought to end the influence of the Catholic Howard family, Mary split the beans to the Archibishop of Canterbury, Thomas Cramner.

Under torture, both Francis Dereham and Henry Manox admitted their sexual encounters, with Catherine. Although he denied that he had known Catherine 'carnally', Manox admitted making advances to her in the small sacristy behind the altar in the Duchess's chapel. Both had ceased any sexual involvement with Catherine before she was married. However, it was revealed that Thomas Culpepper, a Gentleman of the King's Privy Chamber, had succeeded Henry in Catherine's affections.

Culpepper was one of Henry's favourites. According to the French ambassador, as a youth, Culpepper had shared the King's bed. Plainly, the Frenchman added mischievously, he 'wished to share the Queen's bed too'.

It was not the first time that Culpepper claimed that Catherine's attendant, Lady Jane Rochford – who had given such eloquent testimony against Anne Boleyn – had 'provoked' him into a liaison. But even under torture, he continued to deny that he had ever enjoyed full carnal knowledge of the Queen. When questioned, Catherine also accused Lady Rochford of encouraging her to flirt and, like Culpepper, denied actual intercourse. Meanwhile, Lady Rochford condemned them both as adulterous, while simultaneously maintaining that she had no knowledge of the affair. Soon, the dungeons of the Tower of London were so full that the royal apartments had to be turned into a jail to accommodate the new influx of prisoners.

The trial was a juicy affair. It was Katherine Tylney's evidence that tipped the scales. She said that the Queen often strayed out of her chambers at night and ran up the stairs to Culpepper's room, where they stayed until two in the morning.

Dereham and Culpepper were both convicted of treason at the Guildhall and sentenced to be hanged, drawn and quartered. Culpepper's had been the lesser crime. Dereham, on the other hand, had besmirched his bride by taking her precious virginity. He had to pay the full barbaric forfeit. Afterwards, both their heads were fixed on poles on London Bridge, where they were still to be seen, stripped of their flesh, four years later.

Catherine was stripped of her royal titles for a 'carnal copulation' with Dereham. She was indighted for having led 'a voluptuous and vicious life'.

Camelot, It's Not

Even before the prodigious Henry VIII, the English royals have been mired in scandal. Just think about King Arthur. The tranquillity of the fabled Camelot was destroyed when one of the Knights of the Round Table, Sir Lancelot, had an illicit affair with Arthur's wife, Guinevere.

But there was a worse scandal to come. King Arthur was killed by Mordred, the son of his incestuous union with his sister, the enchantress Morgan le Fay.

King Ida, who reigned from AD 547 to 559, had 12 bastard sons. Ethelfrith, who died in 616, had five and Oswiu, who died in 670, just the one. Apparently, illegitimate daughters did not count in those days. That was changed in 786, when it was proposed that all children 'begotten by adultery or incest' should be allowed to succeed to the throne.

This admonition was obviously taken to heart by King Ethelbald, whose scandalous reign was condemned by St Boniface in 746 for being 'governed by lust'. It did no good. Ethelbald, King of the West Saxons from 858 to 860, married his own stepmother in order to maintain the alliance his father had forged with the Franks.

Ethelred the Unready, who reigned from 978 to 1016, was illegitimate. His mother, the concubine Aelgifu, is supposedly the mother of two other kings. There may, however, be some confusion over names. Ethelred's son, King Canute, who reigned from 1016 to 1035, was also supposed to be the son of Aelgifu. And, while trying to hold back the sea, Canute took time off to dally with a mistress named Aelgifu. Now she is not necessarily the same woman as the one who slept with his father and grandfather – though if we look at the case of Madam d'Elitz who bedded George I, George II and Frederick, Prince of Wales, we see that such things can happen in royal circles. But if it was the same Aelgifu, then she was clearly going for the record, because King Canute's son, Harold Harefoot, who reigned from 1035 to 1040, also had a mistress called Aelgifu!

Mindful of such things, Edward the Confessor was a pious man. This brought him – as well as a frustrated wife – canonization. He was succeeded by Harold of Wessex, who was trounced by a more scandalous candidate to the throne at the Battle of Hastings in 1066. Although the victor is known reverently in England as William the

Conqueror, in France he is known as William the Bastard.

His father, Robert of Normandy, was a noted bisexual who one day spotted a strapping peasant girl called Helve, washing her clothes in a stream. He seized her and took her back to his castle. During her captivity, she bore him two children. Then when he released her, she married Baron Heliun, the Vicomte of Conteville

Robert of Normandy died leaving no legitimate heir, so William went to war with the other Dukes of Normandy to claim his birthright. This meant, by the time he came up against Harold, he was a seasoned campaigner.

Henry I, who reigned from 1100 to 1135, had 20 illegitimate children, but only one legitimate son, who died while trying to save his illegitimate half-sister, Maud, from drowning. Another illegitimate half-sister, Matilda, took his place on the throne.

Henry II's reign, 1154-1189, was marked by the murder of Thomas à Becket in Canterbury Cathedral. It is thought that Henry ordered the murder, although he claimed that when he said the immortal words, 'Who will rid me of this turbulent priest' – he was just thinking out loud.

However, Henry II was also involved in a sex scandal when he fell for the 'Fair Rosamund'. His wife, Eleanor of Aquitaine, was outraged at this, although she had a chequered past of her own. Her first husband had been Louis VII of France, but she had divorced him when she discovered that his love for his knights during their excursions on the crusades was not always platonic. Eleanor urged their two sons, Richard and John, to rise up against Henry, but they were defeated and Eleanor spent the rest of her days in jail.

Towards the end of his life, Edward III, who reigned form 1327 to 1377, took a mistress. This must have been something as a shock to the nation since Edward had an enduring marriage to Philippa of Hainault, whom he had wed in 1328 when he was 16 and she was 14.

His mistress was one Alice Perrers, a tiler's daughter from Essex. When the King became senile, she seized the opportunity to make herself a wealthy woman. She had already amassed more wealth than the Queen, when Parliament stepped in and banished her. Nevertheless, she managed to slip back into the country to throw herself weeping on the dead Edward's corpse – only to steal the rings from his fingers.

Richard II, who reigned from 1377 to 1399, married twice but had no children. He was gay and the opulence of his court led to the Peasants' Revolt in 1381. He foolishly legitimized the bastard sons of John of Gaunt, who turned against him, starting the Wars of the Roses. Richard was deposed, arrested and murdered in jail.

His successor, John of Gaunt's son Henry IV, the 'usurper' who reigned from 1399 to 1413, was a scandalous lecher. He was married twice, and it was said 'no woman was there anywhere... but he would importunely pursue his appetite and have her'. His son, Henry V, was the great warrior king who beat the French at the Battle of Agincourt in 1415. He was also said to have 'fervently followed the service of Venus as well as of Mars'.

Henry V's son, Henry VI, was more prudish, however. When a troupe of half-naked dancing girls were laid on to entertain him, he ran from the room crying 'Fy, fy, for shame'. This may have been because he was impotent. When his wife, Margaret of Anjou, announced that she was pregnant, he fainted. The court gossip was that the child's father was the Duke of Somerset, and the scandal surrounding his parentage helped Edward IV to seize the throne.

According to contemporary reports, Edward was 'licentious in the extreme'. He was not a very choosy lover. It was said: 'He pursued with no discrimination the married and the unmarried, the noble and the lowly.' However, he handed his women on to other courtiers once he had finished with them often against their will. This was considered 'most insolent', but in his favour it was said that 'He took none by force ' – not for want of trying. He tried to rape the widowed Elizabeth Woodville at knife point. She still refused him, saying she wold rather die than give in. So he married her and they had seven children. Meanwhile, he took three new mistresses, who were said to be the 'merriest', the 'wiliest' and the 'holiest' in the land. The merriest, Jane Shore, was a great beauty.

'Nothing about her body you would have change,' wrote the saintly Thomas More. She herself was far from saintly. Her first marriage was annulled on the grounds of her husband's impotence and, when Edward died, she took up with his stepson, the Earl of Dorset.

Twelve-year-old Edward V succeeded his father in April 1483. His uncle, Richard, Duke of Gloucester, who was already thought to have been responsible for the deaths of Henry VI, his son Prince Edward and his own brother the Duke of Clarence, took the boy from his family to the Tower of London, which was then a royal palace. Edward's brother, Richard, Duke of York, was brought to join him. The two children disappeared, presumed murdered by Gloucester who seized the throne as Richard III. In 1674, when alterations were being made to the Tower, the skeletons of the two children were found. They were taken to Westminster Abbey where they were buried. Shakespeare painted Richard as one of the blackest villains of all time. But then Shakespeare was writing in Tudor times.

Still, mired in scandalous allegations surrounding the disappearance of the princes in the Tower was not the most auspicious way to begin a reign. But worse was to follow. One of the first victims of his regime was Lord Hastings. He was reputedly killed in the arms of the lovely Jane Shore who was still around. She was tried for immorality. This was somewhat hypocritical as Richard had fathered seven illegitimate children himself, perhaps indicating that he was not the ugly hunchback portrayed by Shakespeare. Jane's punishment was to walk through the streets of London barefoot, wearing only a white sheet. She was then imprisoned in Newgate. After that, her fortunes revived and she married Sir Thomas Lynom, Commissioner of the Welsh Marches.

After two years on the throne, Richard III paid for his usurpation with his life when he lost the Battle of Bosworth Field to Henry, who reigned as Henry VII. Jane Shore died in poverty in London. Sir Thomas More said that there was a moral to be drawn here. But since Jane had survived the reigns of Edward IV, Edward V, Richard III and 14 years into the reign of Henry VII, one can only wonder at what that moral might be.

The Raving Romanovs

It is not only British royals, however, who misbehave. Indeed, the most famous of all scandalous royals was Catherine the Great, who ruled Russia from 1762 to 1796.

From an early age, the German-born Catherine was a very sensual woman. She would lie in bed at night and masturbate with her pillow between her legs. At 16 she was married to her 17-year-old cousin, Peter, the German-born grandson of Peter the Great and heir to the throne of Russia. However, the marriage bed did not hold all the delights Catherine longed for. Peter was an alcoholic, impotent and feeble-minded. For him, bed was where you played with your toys.

For six years, Catherine contented herself with horse riding and voracious reading. But the Empress Elizabeth, Peter's aunt who was Russia's reigning monarch, wanted her to have children to continue the Romanov line. So, on an out-of-the-way island in the Baltic, Elizabeth arranged for Catherine, who was still a virgin, to be left alone with Sergei Saltykov, a Russian nobleman and accomplished womanizer.

After one night with Saltykov, Catherine could not get enough sex. Two miscarriages occurred in rapid succession. Then she went to term with Paul, who was whisked away by Elizabeth and presented to the Russian people as heir to the throne.

Soon after, Catherine's husband Peter underwent an operation, which corrected a malformation of his penis and left him potent. He began taking a string of mistresses. However, he does not seem to have had sex with his wife, who by this time had had a second child by a young Polish nobleman named Count Stanislas Poniatowski.

'I do not know how it is my wife becomes pregnant,' Peter said.

He soon found out when he caught Count Poniatowski leaving their country home in disguise. He accused the Count of sleeping with his wife. Naturally, Poniatowski denied it. Peter then had Catherine dragged out of bed. She and Poniatowski were then forced to have supper with Peter and his latest mistress. Afterwards, Poniatowski was sent back to Poland in disgrace.

Catherine replaced him with an officer in the Horse Guards, Count Grigori Orlov, who soon got her pregnant. She managed to conceal her belly under the huge hooped dresses then in fashion. When she felt the child coming, one of her servants set his own house on fire to distract Peter, who never could resist a good fire. She had three children with Orlov. But they were always farmed out to servants as soon as they were born and only introduced to the royal nursery once no one could really be sure who they belonged to.

Catherine's infidelity drove Peter crazy and, when he came to the throne in 1761, he was determined to divorce her. But Peter was deeply unpopular. He made no effort to conceal his hatred of Russia and his love of all things German. Worse still, he worshipped Frederick II of Prussia with whom Russia was then at war. After just six months on the throne, Peter concluded a peace treaty with Frederick and was planning a disastrous war against Denmark.

Although Catherine had been born in Germany, too, she was much more popular than her husband. Dressed in a lieutenant's uniform, she rode to St Petersburg where Count Orlov was stationed. With the army behind her, she proclaimed herself Empress in Kazan Cathedral. Peter was arrested. He abdicated, but was murdered anyway eight days later by Orlov's brother, Aleksei.

Once on the throne, Catherine refused to marry Orlov, preferring to preserve the Romanov dynasty. He got his own back by seducing every attractive woman who came to court. He became a political liability when he bungled peace negotiations with the Turks. He capped that by seducing Catherine's 13-year-old cousin. Catherine kicked him out of court and he died mad, haunted by the ghost of the murdered Emperor Peter.

Catherine had already met the cavalry officer, Prince Grigori Potemkin. They had fallen instantly in love. This had so infuriated Orlov's brother that he beat Potemkin so hard that he had lost an eye. When Catherine's affair with Orlov ended, she planned to replace him with Potemkin but, after swearing his loyalty, Potemkin retired to a monastery. He refused to return to court until Catherine had sent away all her other favourites.

For two years they had an intense affair. The 35-year-old Potemkin loved to frolic in the royal sauna with the 43-year-old Catherine. However, these activities gave him an enormous appetite. He put on weight which turned the Empress off. However, Potemkin retained his position at court by selecting young men for her pleasure.

Although Potemkin was referred to as 'husband' by Catherine, he hand-picked handsome cavalry officers in their 20s for her. Candidates were first examined by Catherine's personal physician for symptoms of syphilis. Then their virility was tested by one of Catherine's ladies-in-waiting. When Ivan Rimsky-Korsakov, the grandfather of the composer, returned to Countess Bruce for extra tests, she was sacked and a more elderly virility tester was employed.

At least 13 officers passed this exhaustive selection procedure. News spread across Europe, and when Casanova heard of it he set off for Russia. But he was not even considered and contented himself by exchanging 'tokens of the tenderest friendship', swearing 'eternal love' to the beautiful and androgynous Lieutenant Lunin.

Aleksandr Dmitriev-Mamonov had to be excused duty, despite having passed the tests with flying colours. He had made one of the ladies of the court pregnant and had to marry her. This sent Catherine into a sulk, but she still favoured them with an expensive wedding present.

Those who had successfully passed through all the hoops were installed in special apartments below Catherine's, connected to hers by a private staircase. One thousand roubles would be waiting for them there. If a candidate proved satisfactory and a repeat performance was required, the 'emperor of the night' would be promoted to the rank of adjutant-general and given a salary of 12,000 roubles a month, plus expenses. One of her lovers said that they considered themselves 'kept girls'. When she was finished with a lover, he would receive a handsome golden handshake which in one case amounted to an estate with 4,000 serfs. This was a bit heavy on the public purse, but no one complained. Catherine was an autocrat.

Catherine continued this way until she was 60. Then she fell in love with 22-year-old Platon Zubov. This put

Potemkin's nose out of joint as the ambitious Zubov became a rival for power.

The myth has come down that Catherine died when she declared that no man could satisfy her and she tried sex with a horse. The horse, it was said, was lowered on to her by crane. The crane broke and she was crushed to death. There is, however, no evidence to support this scandalous tale. She died at the age of 67, two days after suffering a massive stroke. No equine involvement was suspected.

Catherine the Great was succeeded by her son, Paul, who it seems suffered a mental illness. He was fearful of his mother and, during her reign, built up his own private army. Even after his own coronation in 1796, his paranoia did not disappear. He cut Russia off from the rest of the world, preventing citizens travelling abroad and banning all foreign music and books. Even the wearing of French hats, boots or coats was outlawed.

Failing to kneel before the Tsar's palaces, even if you were on horseback or in a carriage, was an offence punishable by banishment. By the end of his reign, the suspicion of harbouring 'nefarious thoughts' led to a long term in Siberia. Four years after taking the throne, he was murdered by his courtiers, and his son, Alexander, who was one of the conspirators, was installed in his place.

The last of the Romanov Tsars, Nicholas II, was happily married to Queen Victoria's favourite granddaughter, Princess Alix of Hesse. She had already turned down a proposal from the future Edward VII's son, Prince Eddy, heir to the British throne, as she had been madly in love with Nicholas since she first saw him when she was 12. With Victoria's blessing, Alix changed her name to Alexandra when she went to Russia to marry her Tsar.

Their marriage was blissful until they discovered that the Tsarevich, their eldest son Alexsei, was a haemophiliac. In their desperation, they turned to a strolling Siberian priest named Rasputin, who brought scandal to the Romanovs by trading his seemingly magical powers over the Tsarevich's condition for political influence.

Rasputin was a pretty scandalous character from his beginnings in the Siberian village of Pokrovskoye. He was born Grigory Yefimovich Novykh in about 1872, only becoming Rasputin later – the name means 'the debauched one' in Russian. It was not wholly his fault. The local children would bathe naked in the pond and the young girls of the village apparently quickly picked him out for special attention because of his 13-inch penis. A further initiation into the world of sex came at the hands of Irina Danilov Kubasova, the pretty wife of a Russian general. She lured him into her bedroom where she and six of her maids seduced him.

After that, he joined a sect of flagellants named the Khlist, who believed that true mortification of the flesh came through sexual exhaustion. At 20, he married the long-suffering Praskovia Feodorovna who gave him four children. However, he was soon expelled from his village by a respectable priest and he took to the road with his wife and Dunia Bekyeshova, one of Irina Danilov Kubasova's maids who became his life-long mistress. Together they wandered around Russia with Rasputin initiating hordes of other women into the rites of the Khlist in unrestrained orgies. His wife was not fazed by his numerous mistresses.

'He has enough to go around,' she said.

His doctrine of redemption through sexual release attracted numerous respectable guilt-ridden women, allowing many converts to enjoy sex for the first time. His unkempt appearance and peasant manners added to his attraction as a 'holy satyr'. As his biographer, Robert Massie, said : 'Making love to the unwashed peasant with his dirty beard and filthy hands was a new and thrilling sensation.' In fact, many of his lovers dowsed themselves in perfume beforehand as his body odour was so powerful.

By the time he reached St Petersburg, he had a powerful reputation as a mystic, a healer and a clairvoyant. In 1905, he was introduced at court. Soon after, he was called on to tend the Tsarevich. It was found that he could successfully ease the child's condition – perhaps due to hypnosis.

While Rasputin remained a paragon of chastity and humility at court, outside he continued his scandalous ways. Women gathered in his apartment, eager for an invitation to visit his bedroom or the 'holy of holies' as he called it. Usually, he would be found in the dining room, surrounded by female disciples who took turns to sit on his lap while he instructed them on the mysteries of the resurrection. On one occasion, he gave a graphic description of the sex life of horses, then grabbed one of his distinguished guests by the hair and pulled her towards his bedroom, saying 'Come, my lovely mare'.

He would often sing and they would dance wildly, collapsing in a swoon or being taken into the 'holy of holies' for a personal glimpse of paradise. One disciple, an opera singer, was so devoted to him that she would phone him to sing him his favourite songs. Attendance at his gatherings became so fashionable that cuckolded husbands would boast that their wives belonged to Rasputin.

People who tried to convey details of this scandalous behaviour to the Tsar's ears found themselves banished. But in 1911, Nicholas could ignore the rumours no longer when his prime minister drew up a long bill of Rasputin's offences. The Tsar expelled Rasputin from court, but he was soon recalled by the Tsarina, who feared for her son's life.

During World War I, Tsar Nicholas took personal command of his troops, leaving all other government business in the hands of the Tsarina and her personal adviser, Rasputin, who began making disastrous appointments. Rasputin also meddled in military affairs to catastrophic effect. To save Russia from his malign influence, several attempts were made on Rasputin's life.

His enemies were finally successful on 30 December 1916. A gang of conservative noblemen fed him poisoned cake and wine. As he fell into a coma, one of the assassins, Prince Felix Yussupov, a homosexual who had been rebuffed by Rasputin several times, took this opportunity to sexually abuse him. Then he shot him four times. While Rasputin was still alive, a second assassin pulled out a knife and castrated him, throwing his severed penis across the room. It was recovered later by a servant who gave it to a maid. (In 1968, she was still alive, living in Paris, and possessed a polished wooden box in which she kept what looked like 'a blackened, overripe banana, about a foot long'.) Rasputin was then tied up and thrown into the icy Neva river, where he finally drowned.

His assassination redoubled Alexandra's belief in autocracy. She cracked down hard on the Russian people, but within weeks of the death of the mad monk, the Romanovs were swept from power by the Russian Revolution.

Scandinavian Scandals

As well as getting on with it themselves, the British Royal Family have also been good at exporting scandal. A case in point was George III's sister, Princess Caroline Matilda, who was married at the age of 15 to King Christian VII of Denmark. Once ensconced in Copenhagen, she discovered that her husband was debauched and slowly going around the bend. So she took a lover and caused such a scandal that she had to be rescued by the Royal Navy.

It is not surprising that Christian went mad when you consider his upbringing. He was born in 1749. His father, Frederick the Good, was an alcoholic and incoherently drunk throughout most of his reign. Christian's mother, Queen Louisa who was a daughter of Britain's George II, died when he was three. Frederick married again, but his wife, Princess Juliana Maria of Brunswick–Wolfenbuttel, loathed her stepson. This was counter-balanced some-what by Frederick who doted on the child, but only when he was sober enough to recognize him.

A fearsome martinet, Count Reventlow, was appointed as his tutor. He beat the boy unmercifully. Christian's one ambition was to finish his schooling so that he could trav-el around Europe and be as debauched as all the other crown princes. He almost made it, but his father drank himself into an early grave when Christian was just 17.

Ruefully, he took up the reins of state. His first act as King was to appoint Count Reventlow as his Chamberlain. By that time he had become emotionally dependent on his tormentor.

Frederick the Good had already set up the marriage with Princess Caroline Matilda. Christian liked her por-trait well enough, but he was in no hurry to marry. He was keen to sow a few wild oats. But when he started chasing ladies-in-waiting and chambermaids, his courtiers took fright. They were afraid that Christian might go off the rails like his father.

They sent for Princess Caroline Matilda. When Christian saw her in the flesh, he was impressed. She had a pretty face and an inviting figure, and he quickly forgot his objec-tions to marriage.

But even though he had a queen, he was a King and he thought he should spread himself around a bit among his subjects. He and a few close friends began enjoying nights on the tiles in Copenhagen, when not a few pretty young women felt obliged to do their patriotic duty and give their all for king and country.

As well as indulging in wild bouts of womanizing, Christian began to drink heavily. He scandalized Denmark with his relationship with a notorious prostitute who worked under the name 'Milady'. The King would ditch his royal regalia and go out on the town with Milady. During their drunken sprees Christian liked to indulge himself in senseless vandalism and would hurl the grossest insults at anyone who tried to stop him. On more than one occasion he was beaten up. One night he and Milady wrecked a rival brothel; on another, he was pursued by a baying mob to the gates of the palace.

Things got worse when Christian furnished Milady with a mansion and created her Baroness. Something had to be done, so the courtiers forced the King to banish her to Hamburg, where she was kept under guard.

That put an end to one scandal, but those in the inner circles of court feared that another, worse one was about to follow. Christian had learnt Reventlow's lessons too well. Ugly rumours were now in circulation that the King was paying pageboys to beat him; whoever beat him the hardest get the most money. In one bizarre rite, Christian submitted himself to being 'broken on the wheel' with a royal favourite dressed as an executioner standing beside him reading his death warrant.

There was just one thing to be done. The King had to be sent abroad. His ministers though he might sate himself discreetly in the courts of Europe while they got on with the business of government. To keep an eye on Christian, they sent with him a Dr Johann Struensee as his personal physician.

To ensure the maximum discretion – and the maximum fun – Christian travelled under a number of pseudonyms. His first stop was Germany, when he moved on through the Low Countries to Calais, where the royal yacht was waiting to carry him to England.

The moralistic George III did not fully grasp the purpose of the trip. As Christian travelled from Dover to London, George laid on a reception at Canterbury hosted by the

Archbishop. Christian remarked that the last time a Danish King had entered Canterbury he had burnt it to the ground.

In London, Christian adopted the pseuyonym Mr Frederickson and set about bedding as many whores as he could. In the 18th century, London was full of prostitutes and a man could get anything he wanted for a few pence. Mr Frederickson would dangle purses full of bright golden guineas in front of them. There was no way Struensee could restrain him.

The Dowager Princess of Wales, Caroline Matilda's mother, was shocked. So was George III. After a hugely expensive two-month orgy in London, George and Struensee persuaded Christian to leave.

Next stop was Paris, where Christian threw himself into another round of sexual excess. But it was soon clear that the exertion was telling on his health, particularly his mental health.

After six months on the road, Struensee managed to pry him away from the pleasures of Paris. When Christian returned home he seemed a changed man. He held himself with more dignity and bearing and he was kind and considerate to the Queen. His ministers were relieved that the rest cure had worked.

It did not last long. Under the influence of his old friends, he began drinking and womanizing again. But this time it was worse. He refused to attend to any matters of state and it was clear that he was slipping into idiocy.

Struensee saw his chance. He managed to persuade his mistress, Madame de Gabell, to seduce Christian. That way, he thought, he would be able to control the King. Unfortunately, Madame de Gabell was a moral woman. The ethical dilemma that this arrangement put her in was too much for her and she died.

Cursing his luck, Struensee suddenly spotted a better opportunity. He seduced Queen Caroline Matilda.

Together with the Queen Mother, they relieved Christian of the bothersome business of government, leaving him free to give himself up to his pleasures full-time.

All went swimmingly, until Caroline Matilda started appearing in public dressed in men's clothing. Tongues began wagging as to who was wearing the pants in the royal household. But it was Struensee who made the fatal mistake. Unusually for a usurper, he was basically a modern liberal. He instituted much-needed municipal and judicial reform, but foolishly he also established freedom of press. The first thing the papers started printing was stories about the scandal in the palace.

The Dowager Princess of Wales, Caroline Matilda's mother, arrived in Copenhagen and tried to persuade her daughter to flee to England. Caroline Matilda pretended that she did not speak English and refused. The Dowager Princess left empty-handed.

As the scandal grew, Denmark became dangerously politically unstable. The nobility, particularly, objected to Struensee a humble doctor, setting himself up as a backroom monarch. But the Queen Mother knew which side her bread was buttered on. One night in January 1772, while Struensee and Caroline Matilda were out dancing, Juliana Maria went to see Christian. She persuaded him that his wife and Struensee planned to kill him and got the feeble-minded King to sign a warrant for their arrest.

They were seized and Struensee was tortured to death. Caroline Matilda was tried for adultery and found guilty. Her marriage was annulled and she was imprisoned. George III sent a British fleet to rescue her. Fearful of letting the scandal reach the shores of Britain, the already unpopular King George had her taken to Hanover, where she died three years later, at the age of 23.

Christian ruled, in name at least, for another 16 years, first as the puppet of the Queen Mother, Juliana Maria. Then, after 10 years of her less-than-benevolent rule,

Christian's teenage son, Frederick, staged a palace coup and installed himself as Regent.

Not that the Scandinavians were not up to creating royal scandals of their own. In the 17th century, Sweden produced the brilliant and vivacious Queen Christina, who liked to wear men's clothes, refused to marry, gave up the throne and gallivanted around Europe getting into all manner of trouble.

When she was born on 8 December 1626, she was so hairy and cried in such a deep voice that her father King Custavus was told that she was a boy. Gustavus was killed in battle in 1632 when Christina was six. Her mother withdrew to a room hung in black and slept with Gustavus's shroud at her side, under a gold casket containing his heart. This left the young monarch in the hands of five regents and surrounded by male courtiers, who supervised her education. She had no opportunity to develop an interest in feminine pursuits and instead loved to hunt reindeer on horseback in the snow. She rode at such a pace that no one could keep up with her, and she would often stay out in the biting cold for up to 10 hours at a time.

At the age of 18, she took the oath as King of Sweden. There had never been a reigning Queen before. She quickly mastered the art to statesmanship. She also had a great thirst for knowledge. Sleeping only four hours a night, she spent a little time on her toilette and dressed in Hungarian riding outfits of a distinctly masculine cut.

Christina developed a passion for her lady-in-waiting, the beautiful Ebba Sparre, but she married Count Jacob de la Gardie, leaving Christina seething with jealousy. Just when everyone had concluded that she was a lesbian, Christina fell in love with the Count's brother. She heaped honours on him and everyone assumed they were lovers. Eventually, however, she sent him away.

Other suitable suitors were suggested, but Christina fell

out with her government over her refusal to marry.

'Marriage would entail many things to which I cannot become accustomed,' she told them. 'I really cannot say when I will overcome this inhibition.'

To make things worse, she was planning to convert to Catholicism. The French, she had concluded, had much more fun than dour Scandinavian Protestants. To that end, she abdicated in favour of her cousin who became Charles X. The abdication did not just take the form of signing a legal document resigning the position of monarch. There was a bizarre ceremony where she was stripped of her coronation robe and royal insignia. Then she had to lift the crown from her own head.

Christina had already stripped the palace in Stockholm of its furniture, which she had sent to Rome where she intended to settle. She set off via Denmark, dressed as a man and calling herself Count Dohna. In tow was the lovely Ebba Sparre. In Brussels, Christina declared herself a Catholic and threw herself into a round of parties. The scandal sheets happily chronicled her sexual misadventures which grew so outrageous that she was dubbed the 'Queen of Sodom', and the Swedish government threatened to cut off her pension.

In 1655, Christina was welcomed in Rome by Pope Alexander VII as a prize convert. But Christina soon became an embarrassment. She had converted for fun, not piety. She made fun of the Church's holy relics and spoke to her friends in a loud voice during Mass.

Settling in the Palazzo Farnese, she hung the walls with extremely indelicate pictures and had the fig leaves removed from all the statues. She introduced Ebba as her 'bedfellow' and told everyone that her mind was as beautiful as her body.

However, in the evenings, Christina would change out of men's clothing and into more alluring attire to entertain leading churchmen. Cardinal Colonna fell in love with her and the Pope had to send him away from Rome to avoid a public scandal. Christina herself was in love with Cardinal Azzolino, although they managed to be more discreet.

She began dabbling in politics, which quickly made her unpopular, so she quit Rome for France where she received a royal welcome. She stayed at Fontainebleau with her two Italian courtiers, the Marquis Monaldesco, her chief equerry, and Count Santinelli, captain of her guard. The two men loathed each other and vied with each other for the favour of the Queen

Monaldesco had discovered that Santinelli had swindled Christina over a property deal in Rome. To bring this to her attention, he forged a series of letters, which also made reference to her affair with Cardinal Azzolino and her intention of taking the throne of Naples.

However, Christina recognized his handwriting and summoned Monaldesco. She asked him what he thought the punishment for treachery should be. Thinking that she had been convinced by the forgeries and that the forfeit would be paid by Santinelli, he said 'Death'.

She agreed. On 10 November 1657, Monaldesco was summoned to the Galerie de Cerfs in Fontainebleau and asked to read the letters. As he did so, he found the door barred behind him. Santinelli and two guards entered with daggers in their hands. Realizing he had been rumbled, Monaldesco threw himself to his knees and begged Christina for mercy. She merely asked Father Lebel, a prior who had been summoned from the nearby Mathurin Monastery, to prepare Monaldesco for his death. Lebel also begged her to show mercy, as did Santinelli. He said that the case should be taken before the Royal Courts of France. Christina refused and told him to make haste and do his duty, as she strode from the gallery. For the next 15 minutes, she heard Monaldesco's screams as they hacked him to death.

The French were appalled at what they saw as an act of

barbarity. Christina's host, Cardinal Mazarin, advised her to make herself scarce so she fled back to Rome. She was little more popular there and the Pope asked her to live outside the Papal See. As a sweetener, he offered her an annuity and an adviser to oversee her financial affairs – one Cardinal Azzolino.

Meanwhile, a woman named Gyldener was passing herself off as Christina in Sweden. She got away with it for several months. When she was unmasked as a fraud, Christina demanded that she be put to death. Charles X was more merciful and jailed her for a month on a ration of bread and water.

As if Queen Christina had not caused enough royal scandals, she now decided to interfere in European politics. First, she called for the Christian nations to unite to smash Turkey. Then she called on France to help her drive the Spanish out of Sicily, as part of her plan to seize the throne of Naples. Nobody took any notice.

Then Charles X died and Christina thought it was time to return to Sweden. When she reached Hamburg, she received a letter making it plain that she was not welcome in her homeland. She took no notice. In Stockholm, the government had no option but to greet her with due respect and house her in the royal apartments. They even allowed her to use one of the royal estates. But when the locals complained that she was celebrating Mass there, the government had to ask her to leave.

Christina spent the rest of her life wandering aimlessly around Europe, growing fat, unpleasant and eccentric. She put herself up for the vacant throne of Poland but, reviewing her CV, the people of Poland chose the Duke of Lithuania for their monarch instead.

As her health began to fail, she returned to Rome where she died on 19 April 1689, with her faithful Cardinal Azzolino by her side.

Here Comes the Sun

The reputation for debauchery of Louis XIV of France, the Sun King, was despised and envied across the whole of Europe. However, he was not quite as bad as he was made out to be. Instead of exploiting any extramarital opportunity that presented itself, he practised serial adultery, maintaining one favourite at a time whom he replaced when his passion waned.

When he came to the throne in 1661, Louis XIV was married to the Infanta Maria Theresa, the daughter of Philip IV of Spain. Although the marriage was contracted in order to shore up a peace treaty between the two countries, Maria Theresa was deeply in love with her husband, which was a shame. She was short and swarthy and Louis found her dull in the extreme, preferring hunting, gambling and even the business of government to her company.

He began his reign with an affair with his sister-in-law, which was so scandalous that it almost brought down the monarchy. Then he turned to her lady-in-waiting, Louise de la Baume-Leblac, whom he created Duchess de la Valliére. She was the first of four long-term mistresses who bore him 12 illegitimate children in all.

La Valliére produced four. It was only then that the magnetic effect she had had on the King began to flag. He then fell for the beautiful Francoise Arthenais de Mortmart, Marquise de Montespan. The King was used to the routine of dropping around to the house he had bought La Valliére when he wanted sex. Being a creature of habit, he ordered de Montespan to move in with her rival. This was too much for La Valliére, who quit the court and went into a convent.

De Montespan was Louis's mistress for 12 years and produced seven children, whom Louis had legitimized. Like the offspring of Charles II in England, they formed the backbone of the aristocracy. She lost her position in the King's affections when the 18-year-old Duchesse de Fontages came to court with the specific intention of seducing the King.

De Fortages gave birth to a son who died after a month. Then she herself took ill. Poison was suspected. France was in the grip of what was known as the Age of Arsenic at the time. This had begun in 1673, when two priests told the Paris Police Commissioner, Nicholas de la Reynie, that they had heard a number of disturbing confessions from wealthy men and women. A number of them had admitted to murdering their respective husbands and wives. The priests would not break the sanctity of the confessional and name names, but de la Reynie decided to investigate the matter.

He began by trying to track down the suppliers of the 'succession powders' – so-called because they were usually used to ensure the succession of the poisoner. Suspicion fell on a fortune-teller named Marie Bosse. De la Reynie sent an undercover policewoman to consult the clairvoyant on the best way to deal with her troublesome husband. Madame Bosse sold her some arsenic and was arrested, along with her husband, her two sons and another fortune-teller named Vigouorex, who admitted sleeping with all the members of the Bosse family. A huge cache of poison was found in the Bosses' home. Facing torture, La Vigourex and the Bosse family provided a list of their clients. These included a number of prominent members of Louis XIV's court.

Plainly, this was a very delicate matter politically, but de la Reynie explained that although an investigation might embarrass a number of important courtiers, with the epidemic of poisoning that was going on, Louis might find himself the next victim. Louis set up a commission of inquiry.

Officially known as *La Commission de l' Arsenic*, it was known to those who appeared before it as *L' Affaire de la Chambre Ardente*, because de la Reynie, with theatrical flare, conducted the investigation in a room draped in black and lit solely by candlelight. In *La Chambre Ardente*, Marie Bosse and La Vigourex admitted they were part of a devil-worship cult headed by one La Voison – real name Catherine Deshayes.

Madam Deshayes was the wife of a failed haberdasher, who had set up in business making skin-cleansing treatments which, at that time, contained a lot of arsenic. Her experiments had led her to learn about chemistry and she had developed preparations that, she claimed, promoted 'inner cleanliness'.

As a sideline, Madame Deshayes worked as an astrologer. Her clients were rich and aristocratic. To lend weight to her predictions, she had developed a network of informants throughout French society. These were exclusively women and many, including La Vigourex, took pseudonyms.

As an astrologer, La Voison would predict that a woman's husband, say, was going to die suddenly. If the woman seemed pleased at the prospect, La Voison would then supply some poison to hasten the event.

The business was so profitable that La Voison could afford to pay £30,000 for a secluded house in a rundown area of Paris. It was hidden by trees and protected by a high wall. She lived there with her husband, now a successful jeweller, her 21-year-old daughter, Marie-Marguerite Montvoison, and their lodger Nicholas Levassuer – an executioner by trade.

De la Reynie put the house under surveillance, one of his agents, working undercover, overheard one of Deshayes' assistants in a bar drunkenly describing acts of devil worship. The police then picked up two people who had attended meetings at Deshayes's house.

Under interrogation, they said that Deshayes and a 66-year-old priest, L'Abbé Guibourg, regularly conducted Black Masses there. During the service, a naked woman would act as an altar table. She would lie in front of the altar with her legs splayed. The Abbé, wearing an alb with black phaluses embroidered on it, would rest the chalice and wafers on her body. He would intone the Catholic Mass with the words 'infernal lord Satan' substituted for 'God' and 'Christ'. A child would urinate in the chalice and the contents would be sprinkled over the congregation. Then the wafer would be pressed against the breasts and vulva of the woman. As he inserted a wafer into the woman's vagina, the Abbé would chant: 'Lord Satan sayeth in rioting and drunkenness I rise again. You shall fulfil the lusts of the flesh. The works of the flesh are manifest – they are drunkenness, revelling, immodesty, fornication, luxury and witchcraft. My flesh is meat indeed.'

This was the cue for an orgy of indiscriminate sex.

The police raided Deshayes's house. In a pavilion in the garden, they found a room draped in black with an altar in it. The candles on the altar were made from the fat distilled from human flesh.

Deshayes's daughter, Marie-Marguerite, told the police that animals had been sacrificed and their blood drunk. Then, under intense questioning, she admitted that there had been human sacrifices too.

She described how, at one ceremony, the Abbé had said: 'Astaroth, Asmodeus, prince of friendship, I beg you to accept the sacrifice of this child which we now offer you.' Then Guibourg had held the child up by its feet and slit its throat. The blood had spurted into the chalice on the belly of the naked woman. The Abbé had then smeared the blood on his penis and the vagina of the woman, and had sex with her.

One of the children had been Deshayes's own god-daughter, Francoise Filatre. Others had been supplied by the inner circle of devotees or a compliant midwife. Madame Deshayes had had another sideline, as an abortionist, and had often supplied living foetuses ripped from her clients. Victims' entrails were distilled for occult use and the rest of their bodies were burnt in a stove.

It turned out that one of the worshippers was none other than the King's mistress, the Marquise de Montespan. Fearing that she was losing the King's favour to the young Duchesse de Fontages, she had attended three of the 'love masses' to try and win back his favour by acting as the nude altar table.

Catherine Deshayes and the Abbé Guibourg admitted to murdering hundreds of children over a career in Satanism that spanned 13 years. Some 150 courtiers were arrested for poisoning and sentenced to death, slavery in the French galleys or banishment. Madame Deshayes herself was burnt at the stake in 1680. However, the Marquise de Montespan returned, briefly, to favour.

She was eventually replaced – not by a ravishing beauty, but by the middle-aged governess the King had employed to bring up de Montespan's children. Her name was Madame de Maintenon and she had been born in prison. At 17, she had married the elderly poet, Paul Scarron. When he died, she was left penniless and went into a convent before being summoned to court as a governess.

Although she had once been a great beauty, the hardships of life had left her wrinkled and worn. When Queen Maria Theresa died, Louis married de Maintenon morganatically. She was the first and only one of his consorts to have any political influence over him. This proved disastrous.

She urged him to persecute France's Protestants, which led to their mass exodus and also provoked war with

England, Spain, Russia, Holland and most of the rest of Europe.

The Court that Louis XIV established at Versailles was a synonym for scandal. Louis XIII had bought a hunting lodge there in 1624, buying up the entire village in 1632. When Louis XIV came to the throne in 1643 at the age of five, he found himself continually surrounded by intrigue. The solution to prevent this, he discovered in later life, was the magnificent court he built at Versailles, which employed some 22,000 architects, gardeners, craftsmen and labourers. Life there was tightly regulated, from the lever – the ceremony that attended the King getting up in the morning – to the coucher – which attended his going to bed at night. Meals were public ceremonies where courtiers had to remove their hats when speaking to or being spoken to by the King. Officers of the state, lesser royals, army officers and members of the nobility – numbering 15,000 in all – were required to attend court. With so much leisure time on their hands, the cream of society gave itself up to promiscuity and had little time to plot against the King.

Contemporary chronicler, Bussy-Rabutin, remarked : 'Debauch reigned more supremely here than anywhere else in the world. Wine-drinking and unmentionable vice were so fashionable that their evil example perverted the intentions of the virtuous, so they succumbed to the lure of viciousness.'

Even though noblewomen gave themselves freely, a lot of courtiers gave themselves up to homosexuality. This, too, was useful to the King, who could elevate lowly lovers by marrying them off to gay courtiers without running the risk that they might sleep with their husbands. Louise de la Baume-Leblac became the Duchesses de la Valliére, by marrying the notorious homosexual, the Duc de la Valliére. He once tried to seduce a visiting Italian lad named Primi Visconti by observing : 'In Spain, monks do it; in France the nobility do it; in Italy everyone does it.'

Court homosexuals formed themselves into a society, whose leaders were selected according to the size of their sexual organ. Bussy-Rabutin recorded an incident that took place in a brothel where 'they seized hold of a prostitute, tied her wrists and ankles to the bedposts, thrust a firework into the part of her body that decency forbids me to mention, and put a match to it.'

The resulting scandal meant more princes and noblemen had to be banished from court.

Louis XIV was succeeded by his great-grandson, Louis XV, who came to the throne at the age of five. At 15, he married the 23-year-old Princess Marie of Poland. She gave him 10 children in 10 years. Then she called an abrupt halt to their sex life, forcing the 25-year-old King to seek his pleasures elsewhere.

Louis's first scandalous liaison was with the four de Nesle sisters, who came to his bed one after another. Then, when his young mistress, the Duchesse de Chateauroux, died suddenly in 1744, came Jeanne-Antoinette Poisson, the cultivated wife of Charles–Guillaume Le Normant de Étoiles. Madame d'Étoiles moved into rooms under the roof at Versailles and gradually became the King's firm favourite. He created her Marquise de Pompadour, although she is universally known a Madame de Pompadour because she was looked down on by the courtiers as a bourgeoise. Through her natural guile and an ability to make herself agreeable to everyone at court, she began to grow in influence. The King was shy and introverted and had trouble communicating with his courtiers. Madame de Pompadour became his private secretary and moved out of her attic into regal apartments. When she fell out of favour sexually, she maintained her influence by procuring an endless stream of other lovers for him.

She was a patron of the leading artists and architects of the day, and a friend of Voltaire's. She also acted as an agent for the Empress Maria Theresa of Austria. Madame de Pompadour's protégé, the Duc de Choiseul, reversed France's old alliances, realigning France with Austria against the German principalities and England. This led to the Seven Years War, which left France crushed in Europe and Canada in English hands. These defeats were laid at her door. They left her depressed and Madame de Pompadour died in the royal apartments soon after the end of the war in 1764.

Next Louis moved further down the social scale, taking as his mistress the illegitimate daughter of low-class parents – Jeanne Bécu, a hostess in a gambling house. She was the mistress of Jean du Barry, a Gascon nobleman. However, she could not become the King's official *maîtresse en titre* unless she was married to a nobleman. So Jean du Barry generously married her off to his brother Guillaume, the Comte du Barry. The King then moved her into apartments directly above his own in Versailles. The Comtesse du Barry then outstripped even Madame de Pompadour in extravagance. Every day, she bought new jewels and dresses, costing the French treasury the equivalent of £40 million over 5 years.

She also fancied herself as the equal of Madame de Pompadour in political intriguing. Although she allied herself with the faction that brought down the Duc de Choiseul, she succeeded in putting everyone's backs up – including those of Louis's heir and his chief minister. Nevertheless, thanks to Louis's dependence on her, she maintained her place at court. He only sent her away five days before his death as an act of penitence

When Louis XVI came to the throne, he confined du Barry to a nunnery. Despite her humble origins, the Comtesse du Barry aided aristocratic émigrés after the French Revolution, was branded a counter-revolutionary and perished on the guillotine in 1793.

Fall from Grace

Along with the marriage of Charles and Diana, there has been another fairy-tale wedding this century. It was the marriage of the beautiful Hollywood movie star, Grace Kelly, to Prince Rainier of Monaco. In former times, the idea of a reigning monarch marrying an actress would have been a scandal. But in this case, the Hollywood publicity machine had worked overtime to manufacture a virginal image for Grace. It was the antithesis of the truth.

True, Alfred Hitchcock had dubbed Grace Kelly 'The Snow Princess' during the filming of *Dial M for Murder*. But he did so ironically, because of her extraordinary promiscuity on the set. Screenwriter Bryan Mawr recalled a few years later: 'That Grace! She fucked everyone. Why she even fucked little Freddie [Frederick Knott] the writer.'

In the movie business, it was well known that Grace Kelly had slept her way to the top. The famous Hollywood columnist, Hedda Hopper, called her a 'nymphomaniac'. Also, she was not quite the high-society gal that the studios made her out to be either. Her father, self-made millionaire Jack Kelly, was the son of an Irish immigrant and a former bricklayer, who qualified for the Social Register. But he took mistresses from among the wives of Philadelphia's socialites and groomed his daughter to marry a blue-blood. Eager to please daddy, Grace cultivated a refined English accent and came on like a debutante.

She was barely 15 when men started proposing to her. Jack Kelly took it as a mark of esteem that herds of eligible young men would flock to the house. There were so many of them, he could scarcely remember their names.

'You can take her out all you want,' he said. 'But don't think you are going to marry her.'

Only one of them meant anything to her. He was

Harper Davis, the son of a Brick salesman. Her father only discovered that the relationship was serious when Davis graduated from High School in 1944 and enlisted in the Navy. He forced her to break it off,

Years later, when she got engaged to Prince Rainier of Monaco, he asked her if she had ever been in love before. She said, 'Yes, I was in love with Harper Davies. He died.'

When Davis returned from wartime service in 1946, he was struck down by multiple sclerosis. By 1951, he was totally paralysed. Grace would spend hours at his bedside, although he could not move or speak. He died in 1953. When she flew back from Hollywood for his funeral, the studio made great play of the 'Philadelphia socialite' returning for the funeral of her childhood sweetheart.

Grace enrolled in the American Academy of Drama Arts in New York in October 1947. But before she left Philadelphia, she was determined to lose her virginity – but not to her own true love.

'It happened very quickly', she explained later 'I went round to a friend's house to pick her up, and I found that she wasn't there. It was raining outside, and her husband told me she would be gone for the rest of the day. I stayed talking to him and somehow we fell into bed together, without understanding why'.

She did not repeat the experience with the man in question, though she stayed on friendly terms with the couple.

Grace's first sexual encounter was not as accidental as she made it seem. She explained later that she had not wanted to move to New York without knowing what sex was all about, but none of the boys she knew could be trusted to keep a secret. When a friend commiserated saying that it was a pity that her first sexual encounter had not been suffused with love and romance, she replied: 'It wasn't that bad'.

At drama school, she dated the best-looking guy in the

class, Mark Miller. But he had plenty of rivals.

'There were these guys who would call for her,' said Miller. 'I would be thinking that I'm the only love in her life, and some stud would arrive at school. So I'd ask her, "Who's that guy?' and she'd say, "Just some guy I know. He's crazy about me." She would laugh about it and brush it off, like she was just sort of doing the guy a favour. I never gave it too much thought. I was very naïve, I suppose.'

She also had a month-long fling with Hollywood leading man, Alexandre D'Arcy, once hailed as the 'new Valentino'.

'She didn't dress as the sort of girl that would jump into bed with you,' D'Arcy said. But he tried it on anyway. In a taxi, he touched her on the knee. She just jumped into my arms. I could not believe it. She was the very opposite of the homely type of girl she seemed.'

She went back to his apartment on 53rd Street and made love to him without a second thought.

In her second year, one of the drama teachers at the Academy, Don Richardson, took her to his attic apartment on 33rd Street.

'I got the fire going and went out to make some coffee,' he recalled. When he came back, he found she had taken all her clothes off and was waiting for him in bed.

'We had no introduction to this,' he said. 'There was no flirtation. I could not believe it. Here was this fantastically beautiful creature lying next to me…That night was just sheer ecstasy.'

They had to be discreet at the Academy. But somehow, Mark Miller remained in blissful ignorance. Then he only broke it off when he found out she was seeing some stud from Philadelphia.

To make money, Grace would take on assignments modelling lingerie. At lunchtime, she would steal away to Richardson's apartment, and they would make love. Afterwards, she would put her clothes back on and run back to model. She said that these lunchtime sessions were important for her modelling career. They put lights in her eyes. Richardson also marvelled at how she would jump out of bed on Sunday mornings, run off to Mass, run back and jump back into bed with him, naked, with her little gold crucifix around her neck.

Sleeping with Richardson helped Grace at the Academy. He made sure she got good parts in the Academy's productions and coached her. He knew she would never make it on the stage. But when he took a photograph of her he realized that she had what it took to make a movie actress and he took her to the William Morris Agency.

Grace took Richardson home for the weekend to introduce him to her family. But they took against him. He was not a Catholic. He was married, although separated from his wife and currently in the throes of a messy divorce. And he was Jewish. Grace's mother went through his bags and found a packet of condoms. Richardson was thrown out of the house and Grace was lectured on immorality.

She was only allowed to return to the Academy for her graduation. But she seized the opportunity to move in with Richardson. Grace's father tried to buy Richardson off with a Jaguar. Her brother phoned, threatening to break every bone in his body. Richardson refused to be intimidated, but the affair cooled when he discovered Grace was seeing other men.

One of them was the Shah of Iran, who spent a week with her when he was visiting New York. He plied her with gold and jewels. When her mother read about this in the newspapers, she insisted Grace return the jewellery. Grace also received jewellery from Aly Khan.

Richardson recalled her putting on a fashion show for him. She appeared in gown after gown. He could not imagine where she had got them from. Then she appeared, naked, wearing nothing but a gold and emerald bracelet, Richardson had known several girls who had been out with Aly Khan.

'When he first had a date, he would give them a cigarette case with one emerald on it,' he said. 'When he
fucked them, he'd give them the bracelet. I was broken
hearted. I put my clothes on, and said that I was leaving.'

On his way out, he dropped the bracelet in the fish tank.
He left her, naked, fishing around the tank for her bracelet.

She had an affair with Claudius Philippe, banqueting
manager of the Waldorf-Astoria who was on first-name
terms with everyone from Gypsy Rose Lee to the Duke
and Duchess of Windsor. She also set her cap at Manie
Sachs, the head of Columbia records, who was a close
friend of her father.

While touring with the Elitch Gardens stock company in
the summer of 1951, she began an affair with actor Gene
Lyons. Lyons was another divorcee and 10 years older
than her. Then, on 28 August 1951, she was asked to report
to Hollywood to appear in the film that would make her
name, *High Noon*.

Her co-star was Gary Cooper. He was a well-known
womanizer and, although he was nearly 50, he still lived
up to the nickname Clara Bow had given him in the 1920s
– 'Studs'.

The movie began with Gary and Grace in a wedding
scene. All Cooper had to do was say 'I do', take Grace in his
arms and kiss her. The scene was shot over and over again.
Cooper kissed her at least 50 times. Grace made no secret of
the fact that she preferred older men and seduced him.

Grace's affair with her co-star in *High Noon* was the first
of many. Gore Vidal, then a scriptwriter in Hollywood,
said: 'Grace almost always laid her leading man. She was
famous for that in town.'

She also slept with screenwriter Bob Slatzer.

Cooper made a point of not being seen out with Grace.
Nevertheless the affair made the gossip columns and Mrs
Kelly was soon on her way to Hollywood to chaperone her

wayward daughter.

Grace flew back to New York and Gene Lyons, but they were soon parted. She signed a seven-year contract with MGM and headed to Africa to film *Mogambo* with Ava Gardner and Clark Gable. From the moment she landed at Nairobi airport, she began flirting with Gable. He was unimpressed, but once they were out on the set and he found that Grace was the only available white woman for hundreds of miles he succumbed. He was 28 years her senior.

When they arrived in London to shoot the interiors in Boreham Wood, the press asked him about the affair. He denied any involvement.

'I hear you two made Africa hotter than it is,' said Hedda Hopper.

When Mrs Kelly turned up in London, Gable had had enough. He had a guard mounted at the top of the stairs at the Connaught to keep Grace out and he did not return her phone calls. A few weeks later, he was seen doing the town in Paris with model Suzanne Dadolle, with whom he had started an affair before he went to Africa.

Back in New York, Grace consoled herself with Gene Lyons, while seeing Don Richardson on the side. Her affair with Lyons ended when she started an intense affair with leading French heart-throb, Jean-Pierre Aumont, during the shooting of *The Way of the Eagle* for TV. Afterwards, he returned to France and she went back to Hollywood, where she and Gable talked of marriage. Gable considered the age difference insurmountable. In the end, she had to agree.

'His false teeth turn me off,' she told a reporter.

During the filming of *Dial M for Murder*, both Tony Dawson, who played the murderer in the movie, and Frederick Knott, who wrote the original play, fell for her. So did her 49-year-old leading man, Ray Milland.

Milland had been happily married for 30 years.

Although he had had the odd peccadillo, he had steered clear of actresses, which had kept him out of the gossip columns.

His long-suffering wife, Mal, kept her eyes judiciously shut. But she could not turn a blind eye to his affair with Grace, especially when scandal sheet, *Hollywood Confidential*, got hold of the story.

When Milland was spotted getting on a plane with Grace, Milland and his wife separated and Grace moved in with him. However, when Milland's wife agreed to a divorce – their property was in her name – he thought better of it.

Hitchcock was also in love with Grace in his way, and she was happy to gratify his voyeuristic yearnings. She lived a mile down Laurel Canyon from him. He had a powerful telescope and she would purposely leave the curtains open when she got undressed, slowly, at night.

Throughout this period, Grace had also been seeing Bing Crosby. He was married, but his wife of 22 years, Dixie, was an alcoholic and was incapacitated with cancer. Crosby pretty much came and went as he pleased. He lived next door to Alan Ladd, and would use the Ladds' pool house for his trysts with Grace. This upset Ladd as he and his wife were close friends of Dixie's. Ladd suggested they go to a motel, but Crosby was a well-known skinflint. Besides, going to a motel risked a scandal.

Grace was cast in *The Bridges at Toko-Ri* with William Holden, who was just 11 years her senior and her youngest co-star yet. Although he was married with children, Holden was on the rebound from Audrey Hepburn at the time and he and Grace had a fling.

In New York, she met up with Jean-Pierre Aumont again, who introduced her to fashion designer, Oleg Cassini. An accomplished seducer, Cassini set to work. Aumont and Cassini had long been rivals in love, first over Cassini's wife, then over actress Gene Tierney. Cassini bombarded her with flowers, but Grace was heading back to California where she renewed her romantic attachment with Crosby.

Crosby's wife had died and the newspapers were soon proclaiming the affair between the 25-year-old actress and the 50-year-old crooner 'Hollywood's newest romance'. He proposed. She turned him down. But he carried a torch for her for the rest of her life.

Grace invited Cassini out to the Coast. But when he arrived in LA she had little time for him, as she had resumed her affair with Holden. *Confidential* magazine got wind of the affair when reporters spotted his white Cadillac convertible parked outside her apartment one morning. The studio claimed that he was just picking her up for an early call. Holden claimed that the convertible was Mrs Holden's.

'Does anyone think I'm so dumb as to park my wife's car outside another woman's apartment all night?' he told Hedda Hopper.

While Holden's lawyers were demanding a retraction from *Confidential*, Grace's father and brother went to *Confidential*'s office and threatened to beat up the editor. The scandal sheet changed its tack. In the next issue it said: 'Hollywood wives stop biting your nails...this new Hollywood heat wave wasn't grabbing for a guy who already had a ball and chain.' It went on to say that Grace had forsworn married men and implied that she was only bedding single men from now on.

Even though Grace was occupied elsewhere, Cassini did not waste his time in LA. He was seen at Ciro's with Anita Ekberg, Pier Angeli and other beauties. He made sure his adventures made the gossip columns so that, even when Grace was out on location, he could pique her jealousy.

It worked. When she went to France to film *To Catch a Thief* with Cary Grant, she sent him a postcard saying: 'These who love me shall follow me.'

He did and they became lovers. But again, her family

thought he was a poor choice as a husband. Her mother thought there were too many women in his background. Her father dismissed him as a 'wop', although he was actually a Russian Jew by descent. Hollywood looked down on him, too. Hedda Hopper wrote: 'With all the attractive men around town, I do not understand what Grace Kelly sees in Oleg Cassini. It must be his moustache.'

Cassini did not improve the situation by cabling Hopper saying: 'I'll shave off mine if you shave off yours.'

In the face of this opposition, Grace was determined to marry Cassini. But during the filming of *Tribute to a Bad Man*, there were rumours of an affair with her co-star, Spencer Tracy. She was seen out with Bing Crosby and Frank Sinatra, who was a well-known stud and freshly divorced from Ava Gardner. This was all grist to Hedda Hopper's mill. Grace also began a discreet affair with David Niven.

Years later, Prince Rainier asked Niven which of his Hollywood conquests had been best in bed, Niven replied without thinking: 'Grace.' Then, seeing the shocked expression on the Prince's face, he tried to recover the situation by saying unconvincingly: "Er, Gracie...Gracie Fields.'

Sensing the affair was coming to a close, Cassini poured out his heart to Joe Kennedy, the future President's father. Kennedy offered to intercede with Grace for Cassini, then used the opportunity to pursue Grace himself.

At the 1955 Cannes Film Festival, Grace bumped into Jean-Pierre Aumont again and they rekindled their affair. Then she received an invitation to visit Prince Rainier in Monaco. She accepted, but then tried to wheedle out of it when she found she had a hairdresser's appointment that day.

Aumont stepped in, explaining that she could not turn down an invitation from the reigning monarch because she had an appointment at the hairdresser's. At the very least it would be a diplomatic embarrassment for America.

So Grace drove the 50 miles to Monaco. She found that Prince Rainier was a good deal more attractive than she had expected. He showed her around his palace and gardens. It was not love at first sight, but Rainier was very taken with Grace. He was in the market for a princess. As things stood, if he died without producing an heir, the principality of Monaco would be swallowed up by France.

Although charming, the Prince plainly did not make much of an impression on Grace. Two days later, she was photographed kissing and cuddling Aumont in Cannes. One picture showed Grace nibbling Aumont's fingers. *Time* magazine's caption read: 'Grace Kelly, commonly billed as the icy goddess, melted perceptibly in the company of French actor Jean-Pierre Aumont…had Aumont, who came and thawed, actually conquered Grace?'

Cassini's brother Igor, who was a syndicated columnist, claimed that it was all a put-up job, an attempt by Aumont to revive his flagging career. But Aumont told the press: 'I am deeply in love with Grace Kelly' – although he admitted that he did not think that she felt that way about him.

The Kellys were horrified. Grace immediately cabled her family, denying any romance. Her mother, who knew better, cabled back: 'Shall I invite Mr Aumont to visit us in Philadelphia?'

Prince Rainier was upset. Two years before at the Cannes Film Festival, his mistress Gisele Pascal had had a fling with Gary Cooper.

Grace received a curt note from the Prince's spiritual adviser, Father Francis Tucker, thanking her for showing the Prince 'what an American Catholic girl can be and for the very deep impression this has left on him'. And that seemed to be the end of that.

Grace and Aumont left for Paris, pursued by the press. The papers printed rumours that they were going to get married. When the reporters caught up with Aumont, they asked him whether he wanted to marry Grace. He replied: 'Who wouldn't? I adore her.'

To the same question, Grace replied: 'A girl has to be asked first."

Then she launched into a diatribe against the press.

'We live in a terrible world,' she complained. 'A man kisses your hand and it's screamed out from all the headlines. He can't even tell you he loves you without the whole world knowing about it.'

The couple managed to give the press the slip and it was reported that they had eloped. When they were found at Aumont's weekend home in Rueil-Malmaison with his family, the newspapers took this to mean they were already married.

It was not so, but she was keen. When Grace flew back to America alone, she told reporters: 'Differences in our age or nationality present no obstacles in marriage between two people who love each other.'

Once more her family were against her choice of marriage partner. A few days later, she issued a formal statement saying that she and Aumont were 'just good friends.' And she began seeing Cassini again.

Aumont conceded that, with her in Hollywood and him in France, things would not have worked out. Nevertheless, Aumont was one of the few people who got a telegram from Grace, informing him that she was going to get engaged to Prince Rainier before the formal announcement. He married actress Pier Angeli's twin sister, Marisa Pavan, three weeks before Grace's wedding.

By 1956, Prince Rainier had another reason to get married. Three years before, Aristotle Onassis had bought the casino in Monte Carlo, but the economy of the principality was flagging and he was losing money. Gardner Cowles, publisher of *Look* magazine suggested that if Prince Rainier married a movie star it would help lure rich Americans there. Top of Onassis's wish list was Marilyn

Monroe.

'Do you think that the Prince will want to marry you?' Cowles asked her.

'Give me two days alone with him and of course he'll want to marry me.' Marilyn replied.

But the Prince had plans of his own. By chance, friends of the Kellys' had been in Monaco. Unable to get tickets for the Red Cross Gala at the Sporting Club, they had called the palace. Once they mentioned the two magic words 'Grace Kelly', they were invited to the palace. Rainier told them that he was going to America and wanted to see Grace again. Delicate negotiations between Monaco and Philadelphia began. Rainier wanted to see Grace on the set of *The Swan*, which she was filming in North Carolina, but Aumont was with her there.

Instead, the Prince made arrangements to meet her in Philadelphia on Christmas Day. Father Tucker told Grace's father that the Prince wanted to marry his daughter. As always, Jack Kelly was against it.

'I don't want any broken-down prince who's head of a country that nobody ever heard of marrying my daughter.' He scowled. Jack Kelly suspected that Prince Rainier was only after Grace for her money. But when Rainier proposed Grace accepted. There were some advantages to the arrangement.

'I don't want to be married to someone who feels inferior to my success or because I make more money than he does,' she explained. 'The Prince is not going to be "Mr Kelly".'

Oleg Cassini protested: 'You hardly know the man. Are you going to marry someone because he has a title and a few acres of real estate?'

'I will learn to love him,' replied Grace.

Before Grace could marry her Prince, there was a formal marriage contract to be drawn up. Monaco was going through a political and financial crisis at the time and the

Prince demanded a dowry. A figure of £2 million was mentioned. Jack Kelly went through the roof, then paid up. At last, he had one over the Philadelphia blue bloods.

Grace then had to submit to a fertility test. Rainier had taken the precaution of taking his own doctor to America with him. Rainier had had to reject his previous love, the model Gisele Pascal, because she had failed the fertility test. When he had finally given her up, he told Father Tucker: 'Father, if you ever hear that my subjects think I do not love them, tell them what I have done today.'

Later, Gisele married and gave birth to a child, Rainier was devastated. The fertility tests had been falsified as part of a plot by Father Tucker who did not consider Gisele a suitable candidate for the role of princess.

Grace was terrified that the examination would reveal she was not a virgin. Far away from Hollywood gossip, Prince Rainier had apparently been taken in by Grace's chaste screen image and actually believed she was a virgin! Grace took the simple precaution of explaining to the Prince's doctors that her hymen had been broken when she was playing hockey in high school.

Scandal dogged the match from the beginning. At their first public appearance together at a charity gala at the Waldorf-Astoria in New York, a woman rushed up to Rainier and kissed him on the cheek. Grace caused a stir by ordering the Prince to wipe the woman's lipstick off his cheek. Who was that woman? Grace demanded to know. The Prince said he had no idea. The next day, the woman identified herself to the papers as Ecuadorian socialite, Graciela Levi-Castillo.

'He knows who I am,' she said.

Grace had one more movie to make. It was *High Society*, co-starring Bing Crosby and Frank Sinatra. Fearing the worst, Rainier rented a villa in Los Angeles and appeared on the set every day. He appeared puzzled by the private jokes that passed between his fiancée and her two male co-stars.

Although Jack Kelly was pleased that his daughter was marrying into royalty, it was generally considered that Grace was marrying beneath her station. The *Chicago Tribune* wrote: 'She is too well bred to marry the silent partner in a gambling parlour.'

Much of Hollywood confused Monaco with Morocco and wondered how Grace would fare among camels and sand dunes. When he discovered that Monaco was actually a tiny Mediterranean principality, the head of MGM complained that it was no bigger than the studio's back lot.

The myth of Grace's virginity was shattered by her mother, of all people. Overjoyed at the prospect of her daughter's royal marriage, Mrs Kelly talked to reporters and spilled the beans on her daughter's former love affairs. Her revelations ran as a 10-part series in newspapers across America, headlined 'My Daughter Grace Kelly – Her Life and Romances.'

To escape the scandal, Prince Rainier headed for home. But all was not lost. Although it was too late to do anything about the stories running in the American papers, the studios managed to get their hands on the articles and edit them before they went out in Europe. So as far as the citizens of Monaco were concerned, Grace Kelly was still virgo intacta.

Grace still had four years to run on her contract. She wanted to make *Designing Woman* with Jimmy Stewart, but the Prince put his foot down. Realizing that they could hardly sue a princess for breach of contract, MGM swapped her appearance in *Designing Woman* for exclusive rights to film the royal wedding.

Grace made the rounds of Hollywood farewell parties, 'chaperoned' by Frank Sinatra. Then, with a party of 65 guests, she sailed for Monaco on board the *Constitution*. They were met in the Bay of Hercules by the royal yacht. Artistotle Onassis arranged for a plane to drop red and white carnations in the harbour when they docked in Monte Carlo.

Then the problems started. The Kellys and Rainier's family, the Grimaldis, did not get on. Jack Kelly could not find the bathroom in the palace. Since the servants spoke no English, he could not ask them where it was. So he took a limousine to a nearby hotel to take a leak.

At the civil wedding, Grace married her Prince in a religious ceremony at St Nicholas's Cathedral in Monte Carlo.

'Bride is film star, groom is non-pro,' *Variety* reported.

Of her myriad former lovers, only one – David Niven – turned up. Frank Sinatra had been invited, but turned down the invitation when he discovered that Ava Gardner would be there. Press speculation about a possible reconciliation between them would have overshadowed the wedding, he said. Cary Grant also cried off. He was filming *The Pride and the Passion* in Spain.

After the reception, the couple sailed off together on the royal yacht. Grace was not a good sailor and started throwing up as soon as they got out of port. A few days later she fell pregnant.

She spent her confinement alone in the palace. Five months after she gave birth to a girl, she was pregnant again. Despite this, the marriage was soon on the rocks and she would spend long hours on transatlantic calls, pouring out her heart to her friends.

When Grace was away visiting her dying father, Rainier was seen out and about with one of her ladies-in-waiting. On her return, Grace confronted the Prince. He denied everything, but the lady-in-waiting was fired anyway.

To get her own back, Grace invited Cary Grant to stay. Pictures of them kissing at the airport appeared in the papers. Rainier promptly banned screenings of *To Catch a Thief*, which shows them in steamy love scenes together. In fact, they had not had an affair at the time. Grant was one of her co-stars whom Grace had overlooked. That was

135

because Cassini was fresh on the scene at the time. But in the 1970s, after he had separated from his third wife Dyan Cannon, they began an affair. It lasted, on and off, for seven years.

By the early 1970s, like many royal couples, Prince Rainier and Princess Grace had stopped sharing the same bedroom. Soon they went one step further. They stopped sharing the same country. Prince Rainier made a life for himself in Monaco. Princess Grace lived, largely, in Paris. In 1979, there were rumours that she was having an affair with Hungarian documentary film-maker, Robert Dornhelm, whom she saw a great deal of in France. He denied any romantic involvement, but he told the press that he thought having affairs would do her good.

Dornhelm knew that Grace was seeing a number of younger men, whom her friends called her 'toy boys'. One of them was Per Mattson, a 33-year-old Swedish actor who was considered for a part in a film about Raoul Wallenberg that Grace was planning with Dornhelm. They had met at a formal dinner in New York in 1982. He had been whisked up to her hotel room and had stayed there until five o'clock in the morning.

'Grace was used by some of these men,' said her old friend, actress Rita Gamm. 'For them it was not so serious, but for her it was. They did not suffer as desperately and silently as she did.'

New York restaurateur and former model, Jim McMullen, spent a week in Monaco with her. They were also seen together at New York disco, Studio 54. She picked up executive head hunter, Jeffrey Fitzgerald, on Concorde.

'I thought he would hate my lumps and bumps,' she told a friend, 'but he doesn't mind one bit.'

As the years drew on, Grace drank too much, ate too much and put on weight. Meanwhile, the torch of sexual misadventure was passed to a new generation. Both her daughters, Caroline and Stephanie, became notorious. Stephanie threatened to run off with her boyfriend, racing driver Paul Belmondo, son of the French movie star Jean-Paul Belmondo. In a moment of turmoil, Princess Grace confessed to biographer Gwen Robyns: 'How can I bring up my daughters not to have affairs when I am having affairs with married men all the time.'

On 13 September 1982, Princess Grace crashed on a hairpin bend on the Moyenne Corniche and was killed. Although the crash had taken place on French soil, Prince Rainier invoked diplomatic protocols and hampered the police investigation. This promoted all kinds of theories into why she had crashed. A lorry driver said that he had seen the car being driven erratically and that the brake lights had never shown once as the car plunged over the mountainside.

The Mafia was active in the area at the time and it is said that they cut the brake lines. Others claimed that Stephanie, who escaped unscathed from the wreckage was actually driving. But the most likely theory was that Princess Grace had had a minor stroke while at the wheel and had lost control of the car.

At the time of Princess Grace's death, her eldest daughter Princess Caroline, a ravishing young divorcee, was the toast of the European tabloids. In 1983, she was married for a second time to Stephano Casiraghi, the son of an Italian industrialist. He died tragically in a speedboat accident in 1990 leaving her with three small children. As Prince Albert shows no sign of getting married and settling down, Caroline has changed her children's names from Casiraghi to Casiraghi-Grimaldi, with the aim of putting her son on the throne.

Princess Stephanie maintained the role of Monaco's enfant terrible as a wannabe movie star, rock star and fashion designer. She is noted for being the first princess of the house of Grimaldi to give birth out of wedlock.

Fifteen years after the death of Princess Grace she hit the

headlines again with an even more bizarre scandal. In December 1997, *The Sunday Times* revealed that, before her death, Princess Grace had become a member of the Solar Temple. According to the newspaper article, her initiation into the cult involved nude massage and ritual sex.

In October 1994, 23 of Solar Temple's followers were found dead in a farmhouse in the village of Cheiry in Switzerland. Another four were found dead in the cult's headquarters in Canada. Now, if Princess Grace had survived to participate in this ritual murder and mass suicide, that really would have been the biggest royal scandal of all time.

Hollywood
Scandals

Double Speed for Wally

Wallace Reid was the first, but by no means the last Hollywood big name to die a drug addict. It was medical negligence rather than hedonism which led to the death of one of Paramount's most bankable stars of the early 1920s. Nevertheless, the newspapers had a field day, cramming their inside pages with imaginative reconstruction of the padded cell in a mental home in which a half-crazed Reid gibbered his life away. The irony of his death was that the charming and athletic Reid had specialized in playing breezy all-American types. No one typified the clean-cut collar-ad go-getter better than Wally Reid.

Success trapped Reid on a treadmill of cheaply produced starring vehicles, which studio boss Jesse Lasky referred to as the 'frozen custard machine'. This hectic pace helped to kill him. It was while filming *The Valley of the Giants* (1919) on location in the High Sierra that Reid was given doses of morphine to relieve the pain of a back injury sustained in a train crash. The treatment continued in hospital, and when Reid emerged he had become addicted. For a while Wally managed to keep up appearances, but by the time he was cast as a boxer in *The World's Champ* (1922) his strength was fast ebbing away and he could hardly stand. For Paramount, Reid had quite literally become a wasting asset, and there were millions of dollars riding on his career. Fearing the worst, the studio insisted that a doctor accompany Reid night and day for two weeks, but the hapless medic succumbed to the actor's effortless charm and reported that all was well.

But the truth could no longer be hidden. Reid's was one of 117 names to appear on the privately circulated 'Doom Book', complied with the approval of Will Hays, president of the Motion Picture and Distributors Association, the man appointed to clean up Hollywood in the wake of the

Arbuckle scandal. 'The Doom Book's' content were leaked to the press, and the tabloid *GraphiC* splashed a story about 'Hollywood Hop Heads', which pointed the finger at a 'certain male star at Paramount'.

The studio finally went public with the shocking announcement that 'Good Time' Wally was a drug addict, battling his affliction in a private clinic. The sanctimonious Hays appealed to the public not to censure or shun Reid, but to regard him as a 'diseased person'.

The horribly debilitated star died in the arms of his actress wife Florence on 18 January 1923. Billed as 'Mrs Wallace Reid', she later that year supervised and played in *Human Wreckage*, a film based on her husband's experiences as an addict. One of Wally's big hits had been *Double Speed* (1919), a title which would subsequently take on a macabre double meaning.

The Girl Who Was Too Beautiful

A star who slipped through the 'Doom Book' net, and thus escaped the attentions of the foot-in-the-studio-door journalists, was Barbara LaMarr, an exquisite Southern Belle who was one of Louis B. Mayer's favourite leading ladies. The fan magazines dubbed her 'The Girl Who is Too Beautiful'. But she was not too virtuous. Life in the fast lane brought LaMarr six husbands, a battalion of lovers and death from an overdose of heroin at the age of 26.

The studio blamed it all on a strenuous diet. Like the heroine in one of her films, *The White Moth* (1924), LaMarr had fluttered too close to the flames. She was soon forgotten, but achieved a kind of life after death in the 1930s when Louis B. Mayer, casting around for a name for his new Austrian star Hedwig Kiesler, remembered 'The Girl Who is Too Beautiful' and gave us all Hedy Lamarr.

Tough Luck Tootsies

Some stars lived to tell the tale of their addiction. Juanita Hansen, billed as 'The Original Mack Sennett Girl', became hooked while working on the Keystone lot. Soon she was paying $75 an ounce for her cocaine supply. She found her way into the 'Doom Book' when it was discovered that she had been seeking medical treatment for her addiction. End of career. But Juanita was a survivor and made her comeback as the founder of the Juanita Hansen Foundation, waging a war on narcotics addiction just as doctors 'now crusade against syphillis,' as she told the world's press.

There was no comeback for Alma Rubens, wife of Latin Lover Ricardo Cortez and star of *The Firefly of Tough Luck* (1917) and *The Price She Paid* (1924). The price Alma paid was public exposure when, in January 1929, astonished onlookers watched as she ran crazily down Hollywood Boulevard pursued by two men and shrieking that she had been kidnapped. Cornered in a gas station she flashed a knife at her 'kidnappers' who in reality were her doctor and a male nurse attempting to commit her to a private nursing home.

A hopeless heroin addict, Alma was locked in a vicious downward spiral which led to committal in a psychiatric ward of the Los Angeles General Hospital. She emerged to make a comeback bid on the stage in New York. But old habits die hard. In January 1931 Alma was arrested in San Diego's US Grant Hotel. Stitched into her dresses were 40 cubes of morphine. She was led away screaming that she had been framed.

In her last interview she told the *Los Angeles Examiner*: 'As long as my money held out I could get drugs. I was afraid to tell my mother, my best friends. My only desire has been to get drugs and take them in secrecy. If only I could get on my knees before the police or before a judge and beg them to make stiffer laws so that men will refuse to take any dirty dollars from the murderers who sell this poison and who escape punishment when caught by buying their way out.'

Cary Takes a Trip

In the 1950s the major studios attempted to woo back their disappearing audiences with films exploring themes which had previously been considered risqué or taboo. High on the list were movies dealing with drug addiction, among them *The Man With the Golden Arm* (1956), *Monkey on My Back* (1957) and *A Hatful of Rain* (1957). Drug-taking in the plush groves of Beverly Hills took an upward swing in the following decade. Even suave Cary Grant experimented with LSD, revealing a Jekyll and Hyde personality beneath the smooth exterior. The Jekyll character was the one on the screen, while Mr Hyde emerged off the set when the star of *Notorious* (1946) and *To Catch a Thief* (1955) was 'tripping'.

Notable drug users of the time were Dennis Hopper, Jack Nicholson and Peter Fonda, the stars of *Easy Rider* (1969), who took the psychedelic scenic route when making the decade's definitive 'road movie'. As the Swinging Sixties slid into the Sour Seventies, cocaine made a comeback even bigger than Gloria Swanson's in *Sunset Boulevard* (1950). The effects were noticeable on the screen.

In 1978 Jack Nicholson, a heavy cocaine user, directed and starred in *Goin' South*, a rambling comedy Western. Much cocaine was snorted during filming. When *Goin' South* was released, *Time* magazine's film reviewer referred to Nicholson's 'somewhat stoned eyes'. The *Los Angeles Tribune*'s Charles Champlin observed : 'Somewhat confusingly, Jack Nicholson plays the whole role like the before half of a Dristan commercial, with nasal passages blocked. Why, I don't know, and don't care to ask.' Message received and understood.

Fat Man Overboard

Making his movie debut in *Goin' South*, as a crazed Mexican deputy sheriff, was John Belushi. At the beginning of his film career, Belushi was already a doomed man, with a drug habit which gave the Hollywood of the 1980s a cautionary tale to rival all those of the Roaring Twenties rolled together.

An anarchic meatball of a man, Belushi had shot to fame in the TV comedy show 'Saturday Night Live'. The movies beckoned, and after *Goin' South* Belushi had a huge a hit as Bluto the animalistic campus slob in John Landis' *National Lampoon's Animal House* (1978). In real life Belushi was Bluto writ large: glutton, casual trasher of houses and apartments, and consumer of a fearsome amount of cocaine mixed with Quaaludes to take the edge off the cocaine high. Belushi took the drugs to fuel his fragile, complex talent, but they dulled his genius and hurried him along to the final fade-out.

After the smash-hit success of *Animal House*, Belushi was like an express train, careering towards the buffers at the end of the line. He thought he could snort the world up his nose and still keep up the pace. But by the time he was filming *The Blues Brothers* (1980) he was a physical wreck, holed up in his caravan on location in a stupor, pools of urine on the floor mingling with the brandy from an upended Courvoisier bottle, a mound of cocaine on the table at his side. Director John Landis flushed the drugs down the toilet; off the set, hired 'enforcers' tried to keep one step ahead of Belushi in his ceaseless quest for stimulation. It was a hopeless task. Everyone he knew took

145

drugs. On the set of *The Blues Brothers* his distraught wife Judy noted at least 25 regular users.

A Universal Studios doctor who examined Belushi during the filming of *The Blues Brothers* told the film's producer Robert K. Weiss that he had to get Belushi off drugs, adding as an afterthought that the studio might as well get as many films out of the stricken star as it could, because he had only two or three years left at the most. Shades of Wally Reid!

And ironically it was with Reid's studio, Paramount, that Belushi finally wobbled out of control. The ebullient, improvising comedian of 'Saturday Night Live' had become a balding swag-bellied hulk, unable to sleep, think or piece together the shards of a shattered life.

In the happier days Belushi and his partner Dan Aykroyd had given riotous campus 'lectures' to earn quick dollars. At the beginning Aykroyd would always appear to announce that John couldn't begin until he had had his 'injection'. But the joke came true, with a vengeance. By now Belushi was mainlining heroin. Losing his moorings completely, he sank into the sleazy nether world of small-time drug pushers on Sunset Boulevard, one of whom, Cathy Smith, gave him his last injection hours before he died.

At the time Belushi was studying two new film projects. *The Joy of Sex* and *The Noble Rot*. There was precious little joy left in his life, and drugs had long since killed his sex drive. Perhaps *The Noble Rot*, a film about the wine business, was more appropriate, for Belushi had been rooting away before his friends' eyes for months. He died alone on 5 March 1982 in the trash-plastered squalor of Bungalow No. 3 in Los Angeles's Chateau Marmont Hotel. That summer Belushi's actor friend Robin Williams found a sign by Belushi's grave in Martha's Vineyard. It read, 'He could have given us a lot more laughs, but noooooo'.

Fatty Takes a Flyer

At the height of his fame no-one considered Roscoe 'Fatty' Arbuckle a sex symbol. The roly-poly comic was simply one of the most popular and highly paid in the business. In 1917 he had signed with Joseph Schenck at $5,000 a week plus 25 per cent of the profit and complete artistic control over his films. Among those who were given their start in the movies by Arbuckle was Buster Keaton. In 1921 Fatty moved to Paramount to make full-length comedy features on a three-year, $3 million contract. The former plumber's assistant was now a multi-millionaire with a lifestyle to match, complete with a custom-made Pierce-Arrow the size of a tank fitted with a capacious cocktail cabinet. Fatty was on top of the world.

Then disaster struck. In the early 1920s Hollywood was still a horse and buggy town, slumbering around its dusty orange groves. For rest and relaxation of the more sophisticated kind, the movie colony motored north to San Francisco. On 3 September 1921 Arbuckle decided to celebrate his Paramount deal with a party in San Francisco's luxurious Hotel St Francis, where he booked three adjoining suites.

Forty-eight hours later, on Labor Day, the party was still in full swing. Among the revellers was a small-time former model and actress, Virginia Rappe, who had a reputation of shedding her clothes at the slightest opportunity and was notorious as the girl who had given crabs to half the men on the Keystone lot. Virginia had caught Arbuckle's roving eye when she won a 'Best Dressed Girl in Pictures' award. At about three in the afternoon the 330lbs (150kg) comic, his pyjamas flapping around him, locked himself into a bedroom with Rappe. His parting words were, 'This is a chance I've waited for for a long time.'

147

Some time later the party was brought to a halt by Rappe's shrill screams. Fatty stumbled from the bedroom, grinning vacuously. Rappe, thrashing around in pain, her clothes torn to ribbons, was carried out groaning, 'He hurt me, Roscoe hurt me.' Five days later she died in the Pine Street Hospital. A post-mortem revealed that a ruptured bladder had led to the peritonitis which killed her.

A botched attempt at a cover-up failed, and the flood-gates were opened. There were allegations of rape and a theatrically staged arrest of Arbuckle on a murder charge engineered by a politically ambitious District Attorney. Rumours spread that Arbuckle had violated Rappe with a champagne bottle. In Montana outraged cowpokes shot up a cinema showing an Arbuckle film. Three sensational manslaughter trials followed, submerging Fatty in a rising tide of innuendo.

No-one emerged with any credit. Rappe was revealed as a good-time girl, pregnant and suffering from venereal disease. Throughout the proceedings Arbuckle showed no sign of remorse. The first two juries failed to reach a verdict, but in March 1922 the third acquitted Arbuckle, putting it on record that: 'We felt that a great injustice had been done to him . . . Roscoe Arbuckle is entirely innocent and free from blame.'

But you only had to look at Arbuckle to realize that, in many ways, he was far from innocent. Although he went free, prurient minds dwelt on images of the helpless young beauty at the mercy of the slavering beast. A writer for the *Hearst* newspaper chain, which had hounded Arbuckle throughout the trials, offered a sickening valedictory for Rappe: 'Little Virginia Rappe, "The Best Dressed Girl in the Movies", whose up-to-the-minute clothes have been the admiration and envy of thousands, today wears the oldest garment in the world. It is a shroud.'

The trials finished Arbuckle. In a sense, however, he was the victim of circumstances beyond those of Virginia

Rappe's death. During the trial it was revealed that four years earlier executives had been involved in another scandalous party which had been hushed up with some generous bribes. The studio bosses's own hypocrisy had been exposed, and this was unforgiveable. Arbuckle was tossed to the wolves.

After his acquittal Fatty sold his house and fleet of luxury cars to pay the lawyers' fees. Paramount withdrew his films from circulation and consigned two others recently completed to the vaults. It cost them a million dollars. According to Hollywood legend, Arbuckle's old friend Buster Keaton bankrolled the hapless comic and suggested that he direct, under the ironic pseudonym of Will B. Goode. As William B. Goode, Arbuckle's directing credits included a Marion Davies feature, *The Red Mill* (1927) and Eddie Cantor's *Special Delivery* (1927).

Seeking a comeback, he embarked on a disastrous vaudeville tour of Europe and was cruelly booed in Paris. Buster Keaton, who saw him at the time, realized that Fatty just wasn't funny any more. Warners threw him a lifeline, and he ended his days directing two-reelers. He died, broke and forgotten in New York in 1933.

In the wake of Fatty's fall from grace, Will Hays, President Harding's Postmaster General, was appointed as a kind of moral overseer of Hollywood Studios and began to insert 'morality clauses' into their contracts. When Dorothy Cummings signed to play the Virgin Mary in Cecil B. DeMile's *King of Kings* (1927), her contract stipulated that for seven years she was to live life in such a way as to 'prevent any degrading or besmirching' of the role she was about to portray on the screen. When she sued for divorce shortly afterwards, the 'morality clause' was held to be an infringement of personal liberty.

Errol's Wicked, Wicked Ways

A wayward star who took a more serious view of her own shortcomings was Lupe Velez. In the early 1940s Lupe was the quintessential Mexican leading lady. On the screen her hyperactive rhumba cavortings, fractured English, flared nostrils and outrageous mugging made Carmen Miranda look like Little Orphan Annie. Off the screen, her life had been devoted to stimulating, if imprudent diversion, including a steamy romance with Gary Cooper and a marriage to Johnny Weissmuller which quickly turned into a non-stop public brawl.

For a time Lupe was a neighbour of Errol Flynn, a combustible combination which quickly ignited. Errol invited himself into Lupe's bedroom. Stripped and ready for action, he lay down on her extravagantly large bed. Silence descended but not the red hot Mexican tamale. After an interminable wait, Flynn levered himself up to see the penitent Velez on her knees and praying hard underneath a huge crucifix in the corner. At the end of her devotions she crossed herself three times before going down on Flynn.

In the late 1930s Flynn inherited the mantle of Barrymore. On the screen he was the most disarmingly dashing of all Robin Hoods, a lithe swashbuckler with a magnificently muscled body and a carefree smile. Off the set he was a man struggling to survive, an irritable drunk with brittle bones and haemorrhoids. However, he had a reputation as a philanderer to maintain, and set about the task with all the joyless determination of a Casanova.

Whenever his yacht *Sirocco* dropped anchor, boarding parties of local good-time girls would appear more quickly than the time it took Flynn to splice his mainbrace. Errol christened his crew 'Flynn's Flying Fuckers', awarding them a badge of honour – a metal image of an erect penis and testicles – to sport on their lapels. He kept a record of their daily and nightly conquests, marking the points on a scoreboard. Sex had been reduced to little more than physical jerks, performed by same.

Flynn's freebooting ways caught up with him in 1943 when he found himself in the dock on a charge of statutory rape. The suspicion remains that the whole affair was part of a shakedown of the studios by a number of highly placed bent cops. If it was, it backfired badly.

The 'victims' were two Hollywood groupies, Betty Hansen and Peggy Satterlee. Betty, whom the cops had initially picked up on a vagrancy charge, claimed that Flynn had had his way with her at a 'swim-and-sex' party; Peggy's story was that she had danced the hornpipe with Flynn on the *Sirocco* – in front of every porthole.

It soon became clear that the girls were, to say the least, no better than they ought to have been, and far from unwilling sexual companions. Under cross-examination by Flynn's lawyer, Jerry Geisler, Hansen admitted that she 'didn't have no objections' when it came to being balled by Robin Hood, and vouchsafed the information that the star made love with his socks on. Hollywood wags had a field day, pointing out that Flynn's last film had been *They Died With Their Boots On*.

The all-woman jury had no hesitation in acquitting Flynn, whose career suffered not a jot from the hilarious court-room revelations. 'In Like Flynn' became the catchphrase of the day, and in *Northern Pursuit* (1943), his next film, Flynn was able to joke about the whole sleazy affair. The best moment in the movie comes when Flynn assures his bride Julie Bishop that she is the only woman who ever meant anything to him, then turns to the camera and roguishly asks the audience. 'What am I saying?'

Booze, drugs and the haemorrhoids took their toll on Flynn. By the early 1950s he was a puffy shadow of his former self, but still grimly fulfilling his sexual quota, a haggard Stakhanovite toiling away at the coal-face of the libido. Drugs began to play an increasingly baleful part in Flynn's life. In 1953, while filming in Rome, Flynn contracted hepatitis from a dirty needle. In hospital he kept his pecker up with the aid of twice-daily visits from a couple of streetwalkers who administered oral sex. Champagne strictly forbidden in Flynn's supposedly enfeebled condition, was concealed in the flower vase. The flowers died, and Flynn, now himself one of the living dead, was hurrying to keep them company.

Bottled-nosed, bleary and wasted, Flynn died of a heart attack in Vancouver in 1959. He was 50 years old, but the coroner who examined the corpse said that it seemed more like an old man. His last girlfriend, the 16-year-old Beverly Aadland, survived their affair with her virginity intact.

This was the public Flynn, but there was a private and equally sad man who made regular trips to Mexico to satisfy his craving for pubescent girls and teenage boys. Flynn's homosexuality reflected his own confused notion of identity and found bizarre expression in an on-off affair with another mixed-up star, Tyrone Power.

It began in Acapulco in 1946 and was conducted in obscure motels and at the Hollywood home of Edmund Goulding, who had directed Flynn in *The Dawn Patrol* (1938). The strain of this secret life produced some curious side-effects, notably Flynn's habit of exhibiting himself, fully erect, to his strictly macho buddies. They might have found the performance less amusing had they known that one of Flynn's lovers had been the baby-faced 18-year-old Truman Capote, with whom Flynn had slept in New York in 1943. Years later Marilyn Monroe asked Capote if he had enjoyed the experience. Capote replied, 'If it hadn't been Flynn, I wouldn't have remembered it.'

Death of a Director

On the morning of 2 February a team of Los Angeles Police Department officers arrived at a bungalow court apartment on Alvarado Street in LA's Westlake district, then a smart residential area, lapped in the expensive calm which whispers success and money.

They had been called out to investigate a case of natural death, but the scene which greeted them as they entered Bungalow B was anything but calm. The place was a hive of bizarre activity. Two top executives from Famous Players Lasky, a subsidiary of Paramount, were burning papers in the living room fireplace. The instantly recognizable figure of Mabel Normand, the only comedienne of the silent era to enjoy the popularity of a Chaplin or a Lloyd, was feverishly rummaging through the apartment's drawers. An even odder touch was added by the presence in the kitchen of Henry Peavey, a black servant, who was washing dishes, while in and out rushed a succession of unidentified individuals.

One individual who was taking no part in these proceedings was the man who had lived and died in Bungalow B. On the floor lay William Desmond Taylor, one of Paramount's top directors. His face was composed, his clothes carefully arranged; an overturned chair had tipped across his legs. For all the world it looked as if he had settled down for 40 winks. Beside him lay a monogrammed handkerchief, which was picked up by one of the investigators and placed on a cluttered bureau.

Initially there was complete confusion about the cause of Taylor's death. The police were told that a man claiming to be a doctor had walked in off the street, examined the body, informed the film folk that Taylor had died of a stomach haemorrhage and left. He was never identified.

Normand, the studio executives and Peavey confirmed

153

that Taylor had suffered from stomach problems. On the more tricky question of what precisely they were all doing in Bungalow B, milling round Taylor's corpse, the Paramount men and Normand stated that they were retrieving personal letters and telegrams. Normand added that in case it was 'to prevent terms of affection being misconstrued'. Later she admitted that she had visited Taylor the night before.

There was even bigger surprise in store for the puzzled policemen. After clearing the bungalow of its uninvited guests, they turned to the body. As it was lifted on to a stretcher they saw a dark pool of blood on the floor. In Taylor's back there was a small, neat entry wound made by a bullet. Subsequent examination identified the weapon as a Smith and Wesson breaktop .38. The 50-year-old director had not succumbed to stomach cramps; he had been murdered.

The neighbours were questioned. One of them, Faith Cole MacLean, claimed that on the night of 1 February, at about 7.45, she had heard what sounded like a shot inside Bungalow B. Looking out her window, she had seen a stranger wearing a cap and muffler leaving by the bungalow's front door. Later, under questioning, she said that she was no longer sure if the person she had seen was a man or a woman dressed as a man.

The newspapers revealed further astonishing details connected with the Taylor slaying. Searching through Taylor's study, a detective had taken a volume from the shelves – *White Stains*, an erotic work by the necromancer and pornographer Aleister Crowley. When he rifled through its pages, a piece of pale pink notepaper, monogrammed MMM, fell to the floor. Beneath a picture of a butterfly were written the following words: 'Dearest – I love You – Love You – XXXXXXXXX – Yours Always! Mary.'

MMM were the initials of 22-year-old Mary Miles Minter,

Paramount's million-dollar replacement for Mary Pickford and the star of a string of films directed by Taylor.

The police also discovered a cache of pornographic photographs showing Taylor indulging in a variety of sexual acts with a number of leading ladies. In a closet they found a pink nightgown also bearing the monogram MMM. Other closets contained racks of female lingerie, trophies it seemed of the sex life of a superstud.

Who Killed Cock Robin?

The list of suspects eventually swelled to over 300, but the hard core were easily identified. There was Henry Peavey, Taylor's camp valet, who had discovered the body on the morning of the 2nd, and who not long before had been arrested and charged with soliciting young boys in a nearby public park.

Then there was the shadowy figure of Edward F. Sands, who had been hired by Taylor as his secretary. On 12 July 1921, while Taylor was abroad, Sands had absconded with the director's sports car and $4,200 in petty cash. The car had been found but Sands and the money had disappeared. A rumour circulated that Sands was in fact Taylor's younger brother, one Dennis Deane Tanner.

Finally there was Mary Miles Minter, self-confessedly infatuated with Taylor, and her monstrous mother Charlotte Shelby, a former actress and archetypal 'movie mother', grasping, money-grabbing, insanely jealous of her daughter's success and yet determined to hang on to her meal ticket, no matter what the cost.

The investigations rapidly revealed that Taylor himself was a man of mystery. The elegant director, with his impeccable English upper-class accent, had been born William Deane Tanner in humble circumstances in Ireland. He had carved out a successful career in New York as an actor and then an antiques dealer before disappearing in 1908, leaving behind a wife and daughter. He resurfaced in Hollywood in 1913, quickly found work as an actor and then turned to directing. He was soon at the top of his profession, handling the tragic Wallace Reid, Mary Pickford and her successor at Paramount, Mary Miles Minter.

There were as many theories about the motive for murder as there were suspects. Taylor was reputedly involved in the peddling of narcotics; in another version he had fallen foul of a bootlegger (one of the items thoughtfully removed by the studio before the arrival of the police had been a large quantity of bootleg liquor); yet another theory revolved around a score settled by an enemy Taylor had made while serving in the British Army in 1918.

Inevitably the press shone the spotlight on Minter and her gorgon of a mother. It was well-known in movie circles that Charlotte Shelby was the owner of a Smith and Wesson .38, and that on several occasions she had waved it in the faces of those whom she suspected of harbouring lustful designs on her daughter. In fact she was already too late. Several years earlier one of a Taylor's cronies, the director James Kirkwood went through a 'mock marriage' ceremony with the naïve 15-year-old Minter and then got her pregnant. Charlotte had procured an abortion.

Charlotte's alibi was that the entire family had been at home on the fateful night, reading through a script. This was confirmed by Carl Stockdale, an unemployed actor who had partnered Minter in one of her early pictures. Minter claimed that she had not seen Taylor for weeks. Nevertheless, a mass of circumstantial evidence pointed towards Shelby and Minter. But during the 12 months which followed the murder, Minter was questioned by the police only once and her pistol-packin' Momma not questioned at all. This was extremely curious as forensic examination of the jacket worn by Taylor on the night he was murdered revealed three blonde hairs which were positively identified as coming from the head of one Mary Miles Minter. Five years later the case was reopened, and once again mother and daughter found themselves the major suspects named by the press. They were exonerated from blame and declared innocent without trial.

Tragedy stalked in the wake of the Taylor killing. Henry Peavey died in a ghetto flophouse in 1937, claiming on his deathbed that a famous actress and her mother were the killers of his master. The body of the mysterious Sands was found six weeks after Taylor's death, floating down the Connecticut River, a self-inflicted bullet wound in his head. It seems that he was not Taylor's brother.

Mabel Normand, whose career was already on the skids at the time of the murder, was involved in a second scandal in 1923, when her chauffeur shot and wounded an alcoholic oil millionaire with her pistol. Then she was cited as a co-respondent in a divorce case. Her career petered out after a few sad two-reelers. In 1926 she married Lew Cody, who had been her leading man in *Mickey* (1918), one of her biggest hits. It was a doubly dismal affair – both of them were dead within a few years, Normand of drug addiction and tuberculosis and Cody of a heart ailment.

Minter's career had also been on the skids at the time of the murder, her confidence wrecked by the demands of her domineering mother. After six more pictures, Paramount bought out her contract for $350,000. She began to eat to console herself, and the charmingly innocent heroine of the early 1920s swelled into a vapid blonde barrage balloon of a woman, locked into endless litigation with her mother over the dwindling spoils of her brief time in the sun.

The Taylor case was never closed, but there the matter might have rested, gathering dust as memories of the scandal became ever dimmer and those who were involved in it disappeared or died. Then fate intervened, over 60 years after Taylor had been shot in the back by a person or persons unknown.

King Vidor, who died in 1982, was one of Hollywood's greatest film-makers, the director of such silent classics as *The Big Parade* (1925) and extravagant epics like *Northwest Passage* (1939), *Duel in the Sun* (1948), *War and Peace* (1956) and *Solomon and Sheba* (1959).

In the 1960s Vidor was pushed aside by the brash new Young Turks of Hollywood. *Solomon and Sheba* was his last feature film. Thereafter his declining years were marked by a series of unrealized projects. And it was one of these which solved the Taylor mystery.

After Vidor's death, his official biographer, Sidney Kirkpatrick, began to sift through the mountain of material which the director had left behind. One day Kirkpatrick stumbled on a locked strong box hidden behind the boiler on Vidor's deserted ranch. Inside there was a mass of scribbled notes, memos, diary entries, transcripts of interviews and private letters. They all related to the killing of William Desmond Taylor. Kirkpatrick pieced this jigsaw together to produce a fascinating book, *A Cast Of Killers*, which laid to rest the mysteries surrounding the director's death.

Sidelined by the film industry, Vidor had retreated into the past to assemble his last great project. As a young director in Hollywood, he had known many of the major characters in the drama. In 1967 he began his own investigations into the killing. They rapidly became an obsession, and in the process Vidor uncovered incontrovertible evidence of not one but two astonishing cover-ups.

William Desmond Taylor was not the ladies' man he appeared to be when the police opened his lingerie-crammed closets. He was a homosexual with a preference for young boys, who were procured for him by Henry Peavey. Peavey had almost certainly been arrested for soliciting while on a mission for his master.

Taylor entertained his young friends in a room near his home, ostensibly rented for Peavey to sleep in when he had to work late in Bungalow B. The studio, already enmired in the Arbuckle scandal, was well aware of Taylor's habits and moved quickly to limit the damage. The lingerie, the 'pornographic photographs' revealed in the press (but never subsequently seen), and Mary Miles Minter's nightgown were planted by the studio executives who arrived at his home before the police. Thus they secured his status as a legendary ladies' man.

In his investigations Vidor found many discrepancies between the newspaper reports of the events surrounding the murder and its aftermath, and the records in the police files he was allowed to examine. So much of the evidence referred to in the newspapers seemed to have disappeared, or to have never existed at all. The reason for this was simple – it had been destroyed.

At the centre of this tangled web was the Black Widow spider figure of Charlotte Shelby. There can now be little doubt that she was the killer. Like her hapless daughter, she was infatuated with Taylor, a passion which had not been reciprocated by the courtly closet queen.

On the night of 1 February 1922 the pathetic Mary Miles Minter had broken free from the clutches of her mother and rushed off to see Taylor. She must have arrived shortly before Mabel Normand dropped by, and was probably hidden upstairs by Taylor. Meanwhile the demented Charlotte was searching for her baby. She was watching Taylor's house when the doomed director escorted Normand to her car, giving her the chance to slip into Bungalow B. Here she was confronted with Mary Miles Minter emerging from her hiding place. Taylor's fate was sealed, and he was gunned down in front of the terrified Minter's eyes. With all these comings and goings in the critical 15 minutes between 7.30 and 7.45 p.m., it was hardly surprising that neighbour, Faith Cole MacLean, was unsure about the sex of the 'man' leaving the bungalow after the fatal shot.

As we have already seen, Charlotte was not interviewed once by the police in the 12 months following the murder, and in the subsequent investigations conducted by DA Thomas Lee Woolvine, she and her daughter were exonerated. For this she paid a heavy price. Vidor uncovered evidence that in the years following the murder she was making monthly payments of $200 to Carl Stockdale, the man who had proved her alibi. But Stockdale was just a bit player in the drama. Charlotte also had to buy the silence of three successive DA's, Woolvine, Asa Keyes and Burto Fitts. This cost her plenty, and provides the constant undertow in all the civil suits she fought for control of Mary's fortune. Charlotte needed the money to stuff into the pockets of three corrupt public servants.

Finally, 15 years after Taylor's death, the truth was blurted out in court by Mary's sister Margaret, whose marriage to Hugh Fillmore (the grandson of the US President Fillmore) had precipitated another interminable legal wrangle. In open court Margaret claimed that she had provided false testimony during the murder investigation and had further protected her mother from indictment by aiding her in secret conferences with DA Woolvine.

Between them Woolvine, Keyes and Fitts disposed of all the compromising evidence. At one point Leroy Sanderson, one of the LAPD's best detectives, was on the point of discovering the murder weapon. He had a hot tip that Charlotte Shelby's mother had been despatched to the family home in Louisiana with the Smith and Wesson and had thrown it into a bayou. Some neighbours had marked the spot. Sanderson was immediately taken off the case by Fitts. The monogrammed nightgown, Mary Miles Minter's hairs, the shells from the gun, the letters which Mabel Normand feared might be 'misconstrued', the stubs of the cheques made out to Stockdale – they all vanished.

Seemingly safe from indictment, Charlotte and her daughter slid into obscurity. Charlotte was supposed to have died on 13 March 1957 at her daughter's home in Santa Monica. The death certificate did not show the cause of death, and acquaintances continued to report sighting of Shelby, the latest in June 1960. One of Vidor's informants, the Oscar-winning art director George Hopkins, who had been present in Bungalow B on the morning of 2 February and who confirmed Taylor's homosexuality, described Charlotte as a 'vampire bat', sucking her helpless daughter dry. Was she something more, a real-life vampire, one of the undead? In 1967 Mary Miles Minter was still alive, living in seclusion in Santa Monica. She was to be the last person interviewed by Vidor in his morbid quest.

Whatever Happened to Charlotte Shelby?

Vidor's encounter with the forgotten star was like a scene from *Sunset Boulevard*. His first glimpse of Minter as he stood at her front door, was a blurred face peering down at him from behind a grimy upstairs window. Vidor did not recognize the grotesquely obese figure who greeted him at the door. There were no tumbling blonde curls, only a greasy mass of grey wisps clinging to Mary's skull.

Inside the house the outside world was excluded by thick black curtains. In the stifling living room the dust of ages had settled on banks of bric-a-brac from Minter's days of glory – playbills, lobby cards, yellowing movie magazines. As she twittered away abstractedly, thoughts of Gloria Swanson's mad old movie queen Norma Desmond began to drift through Vidor's mind.

Confronted with Vidor's preliminary questions, Minter responded by reading him some of her 'poetry'. Vidor gently pressed her, but she grew increasingly agitated, racked with sobs at every mention of her mother. Pathetically she recalled her woodland 'mock marriage' to Kirkland. Vidor could stand no more, appalled by the sight of this husk of a woman stumbling around the airless room. As he stood up, he looked down at the sheets of 'poetry' which Minter had read to him. There was the now familiar butterfly motif on the notepaper. On the top sheet, in a fine copperplate hand, was written, 'Twisted by Knaves, by Charlotte Shelby'.

A sudden chill gripped the elderly director. Was Charlotte Shelby still alive, as some had claimed, lurking upstairs, still holding Mary's life in her claws? Even more horrible to contemplate, could the woman claiming to be Mary Miles Minter really be Charlotte Shelby? The scenario originally envisaged by Vidor had now assumed the flavour of Grand Guignol, stranded in a nightmare limbo between *Psycho* and *What Ever Happened to Baby Jane?* Vidor had not the stomach to climb the dusty stairs in search of what might have been the most terrible revelation of all. He left. Mary's parting words were, 'My mother killed everything I ever loved.'

Vidor never wrote his screenplay. Mary Miles Minter outlived him by two years, dying on 5 August 1984. To the end she was embroiled in legal actions revolving around the Taylor killing. In her later years she was robbed on at least three separate occasions. After one such robbery, in 1981, she was gagged, beaten and left for dead on her kitchen floor. As the journalist Adela Rogers St Johns observed, the initials MMM ultimately stood for 'Millions, Murder .... And Misery'.

Stalk and Slash

Repulsion (1965), filmed in London by the young Polish director Roman Polanski, is a morbid inside-out version of *Psycho* (1960), charting with chilling technical virtuosity the descent into madness of a young Belgian girl (Catherine Deneuve) living in South Kensington. Her horror of sexuality drives her to batter her boyfriend to death and then slash her lecherous landlord to ribbons with a razor. We follow the journey into madness through her eyes, from the minutely observed obsession with cracks in the pavement, and the distorted view of domestic objects, to the terrifying hallucinations – hands thrusting through the walls of her apartment – which crowd in on Deneuve. A lingering image of *Repulsion* is that of a foetus-like skinned rabbit rotting away on the apartment's kitchen table.

One scene filmed by Polanski did not appear in the final version of *Repulsion*. Deneuve was to have claimed a third victim, a woman drowned in the bathtub containing the corpse of her boyfriend, seeping blood into the water. When the time came to shoot the scene, the actress Polanski had cast for the part could not be persuaded to put her head underwater. So Polanski grabbed a mackintosh and a blonde wig and played the part himself.

The story reveals much of Polanski's morbid nature, and the eerily comic side to his obsessive handling of violence and the sinister games people play with each other. In his films the violence is violence observed. Through his work runs a strong streak of voyeurism.

Polanski himself is the survivor of horror such as few people encounter in the war both his parents were sent to concentration camps. His mother died at Auschwitz.

By the winter of 1968 Polanski was an internationally famous film-maker, the director of *Rosemary's Baby*, a huge box-office success and the harbinger of the horror boom of the 1970s. In January 1968 he flew to London to marry the actress Sharon Tate, who had starred alongside Polanski in his elegant horror spoof, *Dance of the Vampires* (1967). The wedding reception was held at the Playboy Club, and the guest list reads like a roll call of the Swinging Sixties: Peter Sellers, Laurence Harvey, Rudolf Nureyev, Warren Beatty, Vidal Sassoon, Prince and Princess Radziwill, Kenneth Tynan, David Bailey, Brian Jones and Keith Richards. The blonde, petite Tate, who often referred to herself as 'sexy little me', told reporters that the reception was a very 'mod affair'.

Back in Los Angeles, the couple slipped easily into the laid-back, drug-laced lifestyle of the late 1960s. California was still basking in the bogus glow of hippy culture and 1967's 'summer of love'. But now there was a whiff of violence in the air. The Technicolor Dream was soon to end in disillusion and death.

In February 1969 Polanski and Tate moved into a large house in Cielo Drive, Benedict Canyon. Its previous occupant had been Terry Melcher, Doris Day's son. Shortly afterwards Polanski returned to London to work on a screenplay.

One-day in March a hippy turned up at Tate's door asking for Terry Melcher. Theatrical agent Rudi Altobeli, the owner of the house, happened to be visiting. He recognized the short, slightly built hippy and sent him away. The man was Charles Manson.

End Game in Benedict Canyon

On the night of 8 August 1969 the eight-months pregnant Sharon Tate had several guests at the house in Cielo Drive. There was Wojtek Frykowski, an old friend of Polanski from his student days in Lodz. To all intents and purposes, Frykowski was unemployed, living off his friendship with Polanski and using drugs heavily. That night he was on the ninth successive day of a mescalin trip. Accompanying Frykowski was Abigail Folger, a wealthy 27-year-old coffee heiress. Finally there was the 26-year-old Jay Sebring, a fashionable hairdresser, to whom Sharon Tate had once been engaged.

They went out to dinner at the El Coyote restaurant. When they returned, Folger went to bed alone; Frykowski stretched out on the living room sofa, wrapping himself up in a Stars and Strips flag; Sebring accompanied Sharon to her bedroom.

Outside Los Angeles, in the flyblown Spahn Movie Ranch, a ramshackle abandoned film set, another coyote was at work. Charles Manson, ex-jail bird and monstrous patriarch of the 'Family' who lived at the Ranch, had long harboured a grudge against Terry Melcher. He knew that Melcher was no longer living in the house on Cielo Drive, but ordered four members of the 'Family' to kill 'whoever was there'.

Into the night, along the freeways and down the backroads leading to Benedict Canyon drove 23-year-old Charles 'Tex' Watson, 21-year-old Susan Atkins, 21-year-old Patricia Krenwinkel and 20-year-old Linda Kasabian. They were armed with knives and a gun.

Arriving at the house in Cielo Drive, they cut the telephone wires and climbed over the wall into the grounds. Immediately they were dazzled by the oncoming headlights of a car. The car was driven by 18-year-old Steve Parent, a friend of the houseboy William Garretson, who lived in a cottage in the grounds. Parent's car was stopped and its driver shot four times. He was left slumped over the wheel as Manson's four assassins moved in on the house and its sleeping occupants.

Frykowski emerged fuzzily from sleep to find the intruders standing over him. Blearily he asked what was going on. Watson replied, 'I am the Devil. I'm here on the Devil's business.'

Even though he never fully threw off the drug-induced torpor in which he had fallen asleep, the burly Frykowski put up a desperate struggle before the killer got hold of him. Then the others were brought into the living room. Sharon Tate was wearing a bikini-style nightdress. Sebring struggled free and was immediately shot by Watson, who then announced, 'You're all going to die.'

Susan Atkins stabbed Frykowski six times as he fought frantically to break free. Watson followed him as he made a last desperate lunge to get outside, smashing him over the head with the butt of his gun. Then he turned back to Folger and Tate. Folger tried to buy her life with offers of money and credit cards. Tate begged her captors, 'All I want to do is have my baby.' Atkins told her, 'Woman, I have no mercy for you.' Folger managed to stumble through the back door, only to be overhauled and killed by Watson. 'Tex' then returned to complete his horrifying mission, stabbing Tate to death.

A white nylon rope was then knotted around the dead woman's neck and passed across a ceiling beam. At the other end it was tied round the hooded head of Sebring. The whole business had taken about 25 minutes. William Garretson slumbered on undisturbed in the caretaker's cottage. As a final touch, Susan Atkins smeared the word 'pig' in blood on the front door of the house.

The bodies were discovered by the maid the following morning. Doctors rushed to the scene tried unsuccessfully to save Sharon Tate's baby. Sharon was buried on 13 August; alongside her was her 'perfectly' formed son. She was wearing a Puccini mini-dress. The 'mini', one of the fashion symbols of the Sixties, was a sadly ironic touch. For the murders in Cielo Drive had brought the curtain rattling down on the era of Peace and Love. Referring to the instant panic among Hollywood's drug-users, Richard

Sylbert, the art director on *Rosemary's Baby*, told a friend, 'You can hear the toilets flushing all over Beverly Hills.' For Sulbert, 'that marked the end of the fun and games of the Sixties ... It was the end of the joke.'

The Devil's Business

Charles Manson, the evil genius behind the blood-drenched carnage in the house in Cielo Drive, did not stay at large for long. In December 1969, Susan Atkins was imprisoned for another offence and confessed to a cell-mate. Not only was Manson responsible for the Tate killings but also for two murders, only 24 hours later, in which wealthy store-owner Leno Labiance and his wife Rosemary were slashed to death and the words 'Death to Pigs' scrawled in blood on their living room wall.

There is an eerie similarity between Manson and Carol Ledoux, the anti-heroine played by Catherine Deneuve in Polanski's 1965 movie, *Repulsion*. Mason, the social out-cast, and the serenely beautiful Ledoux, whose outer calm conceals inner chaos, have both been so 'imposed upon' – by others and by society – that they can only reassert them-selves through murder. It is almost as if Manson was the ghastly physical embodiment of the dark inner processes of Polanski's mind, summoned up like the Devil in *Rosemary's Baby*.

The director's immediate reaction to his wife's death was to seek to 'control' it in the only way he knew how, by pos-ing for *Life* magazine in a staged photograph on the blood-splashed front porch, the door ajar, hinting at the hell with-in.

Echoes of the killings reverberated through Polanski's subsequent career. In 1971, while filming *Macbeth*, he came to the slaughter of Lady MacDuff and her children. As ever the perfectionist, Polanski himself applied 'red paint' to the face of a small girl playing one of the children. 'What's your name?' he asked as he went about his work. 'Sharon' was the answer. Perhaps the only way in which Roman Polanski can exorcise the murder of his wife and child is to make a film about it.

Thank Heaven for Little Girls

Polanski continued to live on the edge. He had long been notorious for his penchant for young girls – a passion which had been shared by Charlie Chaplin – and in 1977 he accepted an assignment from the French magazine *Vogue Hommes* to shoot a glossy photo spread of young girls of the world.

Polanski's subsequent champagne-splashed photo-session in Jack Nicholson's jacuzzi with a 13-year-old, knowing beyond her years, led to a six-count indictment by a Grand Jury, each count a felony:

Count 1: Furnishing a controlled substance to a minor;
Count 2: Committing a 'lewd and lascivious' act on a child, a 13-year-old girl;
Count 3: Unlawful sexual intercourse;
Count 4: 'Rape by use of drugs', including Quaalude and alcohol;
Count 5: 'Perversion', copulating in the mouth with the sexual organ of the child;
Count 6: Sodomy

If convicted on all six, Polanski faced up to 50 years in prison. Out for the count.

In another of the grisly ironies which stalk through Polanski's life, the date for the trail was originally fixed for 9 August 1977, the eighth anniversary of Sharon Tate's murder. However, in a plea-bargaining arrangement, reached at the beginning of August, Polanski pleaded guilty to the least serious charge, that of 'unlawful sexual intercourse'. Convinced that the child would be stigmatized by the publicity surrounding the case, her father had concluded that the guilty plea by Polanski was sufficient act of contrition.

There were other factors at play. The child's lawyer was worried about her rapid physical development since the incident. Maturing fast, she had developed breasts and would tower over the diminutive Polanski in court. Juries are instructed to put such things out of their minds, but the lawyer knew that it would make his job more difficult. For his part, Polanski's lawyer made an offer that his client would found and fund a theatre arts school for disadvantaged children, where he would also teach. This prompted a member of the prosecution team to observe, 'That would be nifty place for a child molester!'

Polanski had little difficult in charming his probation officer into writing a favourable report on him, but had no success with crusty Judge Laurance J. Rittenband, who eventually ruled: 'Although the prosecutrix was not an inexperienced girl, this of course is not a licence to the defendant, man of the world, in his forties, to engage in an act of unlawful sexual intercourse with her. The law was designed for the protection of females under the age of eighteen years, and it is no defence to such a charge that the female might not have resisted the act.'

Polanski was sentenced to 90 days of diagnostic testing at the State Facility at Chino. A 90-day stay was granted to enable him to continue working on *Hurricane*, a Dino de Laurentiis production.

The director arrived at Chino on 16 December, and spent 42 days there, among inmates he later described as 'the scum of society'. In the meantime he had been dropped from *Hurricane*.

He emerged from prison on 27 January. Final sentencing

was set for 1 February. Hopes that the time at Chino had settled Polanski's debt to society were dashed in the preparations for the final hearing. There is little doubt that the very sight of the film-maker was like red rag to the bull-like Rittenband, who had been enraged by Polanski's open flaunting of his relationship with the 16-year-old Nastassia Kinski throughout the whole saga. In chambers on 30 January he informed Polanski's lawyer that he intended to send the director back to jail for another 48 days, and this only if he agreed voluntarily to deportation after release. Otherwise he would stay in jail.

On 31 January Polanski drove to Los Angeles airport and took the last remaining seat on a British Airways flight to London. In the ensuing uproar Judge Rittenband over-reached himself, telling reporters that because of his crime of 'moral turpitude', Polanski did not belong in America. Protesting that he was in no way biased or prejudiced against Polanski, Rittenband agreed to the reassignment of the case to another judge. No judge was nominated and the case was removed from the court calendar. No sentencing can take place until Polanski's return, something which he has shown no desire to do. In the good old days the final reel always delivered the goods. The bad men bit the dust; the scheming vamp got her come-uppance; the boy got the girl and together they rode off into the rays of a golden sunset. Hollywood liked happy endings, although it was easier to arrange them on the screen than in the frequently disordered lives of its stars. For many of them there was no heart-warming fade-out. 'Exit Screaming' might just as well have been stamped on the last page of their scripts.

In Tinseltown, clawing one's way to the top was merely the preliminary to the gruelling task of staying there. As she grew older, Joan Crawford's savage slash of a mouth and glaring basilisk eyes bore testimony to the strain of clinging to the top of the greasy pole. But few were gripped by a success drive as manic as that which scourged 'Mommie Dearest'. When profiles sagged or hardened into a mask of middle age, when breasts and bottoms dropped, hair fell out in handfuls and memories fogged then the Dorian Gray world of the movie star fell apart.

End of the Rainbow

For others, death was perhaps the wisest of career decisions. Peritonitis carried away Rudolph Valentino, and a Porsche did for James Dean, freezing them for ever in the iconic attitudes of the Great Lover and the Rebel Without a Cause. No middle-aged decline threatens their legends.

Some, however, have staggered to the end of the rainbow to discover not a crock of gold but a crock of shit. Alcohol was John Barrymore's downfall. His dependency was such that in the late 1920s, when he was desperately trying to dry out, he was reduced to gulping the perfume from the bottles on Dolores Costello's dressing table. Few stars have fallen so completely and from such a great height. In 1925 he was at his peak: a triumphant Hamlet on the London stage and, at 43, about to become a romantic swashbuckler to rival Douglas Fairbanks. Ten years later he was in the grip of alcoholism, his memory deserting him and the celebrated matinée idol looks which had earned him the nickname of 'The Great Profile' grown puffy and blurred.

In 1927 Barrymore moved to United Artists at a fee of $150,000 a film. As fast as the money came in he spent it. His rambling estate, 'Bella Vista', consisted of no fewer than 16 separate buildings containing 45 rooms. A dozen servants tended the two swimming pools, trout pond, bowling green, skeet-shooting range and aviary, whose exotic inhabitants included Barrymore's pet vulture

Maloney.

Hard-drinking guests – of whom there was no shortage – could drown their sorrows in a replica English pub or a genuine frontier saloon shipped all the way from Alaska.

Barrymore transferred effortlessly to sound and stayed at the top for another five years. In 1932 five films netted him $375,000 and in MGM's *Grand Hotel*, opposite Greta Garbo, he gave one of the finest performances of his life. But drink was steadily taking its toll. He had developed a paunch and a dewlap under his chin; his glazed eyes were sinking into nests of wrinkles and his voice was becoming increasingly slurred.

In *Dinner at Eight* (1933) he came close to playing himself, a fading matinée idol. In the same year, drink finally exacted a terrible price. During the shooting of a scene for *Counsellor-at-Law* his memory deserted him; after 56 takes he still could not get it right. Next day he played it perfectly, but the writing was on the wall. There was a final brilliant flaring in Howard Hawks's *Twentieth Century* (1934). As Oscar Jaffe, egomaniac producer and ham supreme, Barrymore both celebrated and savaged the notion of 'great acting' in a relentless upstaging contest with Carole Lombard. Then alcohol took over completely.

By the end of the decade Barrymore had been relegated to supporting roles and leads in B-movies, his unfocused eyes gazing beyond the huge prompt cards held up for him to the ruins of his career. Occasionally he rallied. He gave a charming performance in *Midnight* (1939), although his co-star and former lover Mary Astor later recalled that throughout production he had little or no idea what the film was about.

It was a last flicker of the old genius before a sardonic descent into self-parody in a grisly touring play, *My Dear Children*, co-starring his fourth wife, Elaine Barry. Audiences flocked to see Barrymore fluff his lines and fall over the furniture. *My Dear Children* was a production as horrendously inept as Peter O'Toole's *Macbeth* and, with grim irony, as financially successful.

Director Otto Preminger was involved in the production of *My Dear Children*, and in his autobiography he left a vivid picture of the wayward Barrymore in his declining years. Word reached New York from the Mid-West that Barrymore was wobbling out of control. Preminger flew out: 'When we arrived at our destination, Barrymore was waiting for us at the airport, accompanied by the male nurse we had hired to keep him from drinking. Each of them had a bottle sticking out of his coat pocket.'

Preminger was horrified by Barrymore's physical condition. In Chicago he had decided to take up lodgings in a whorehouse, emerging unshaven and hung-over for work. On stage he spent the entire play slumped on a bench centre stage, the action flowing around him, seemingly oblivious to his and the other actors' lines. When the curtain went down for the intermission, Barrymore was too exhausted to be moved. For Preminger, the performance 'went on forever'. On a subsequent night Barrymore's excesses meant that the final curtain did not fall until one in the morning. The audience didn't care. They had come to see Barrymore playing a drunken clown and he was obliging them.

When Preminger taxed Barrymore with his 'abominable' behaviour, the Great Profile replied, 'Well, come tomorrow.' The next night Barrymore was impeccable and word perfect. In his dressing room Preminger asked him, 'Jack, why can't you do this every night?' Grinning broadly, Barrymore replied, 'B-O-R-E-D, my dear boy, bored.'

20th Century-Fox refashioned *My Dear Children* into *The Great Profile* (1940), casting Barrymore as a broken-down old ham actor. His last film was the wretched *Playmates* (1941), co-starring with another doomed Hollywood has-been, Lupe Velez. When the time came for a scene in which Barrymore was to recite Hamlet's soliloquy, the theatre's once-great Prince of Denmark couldn't remember his lines. Turning away from the crew, he mumbled, 'It's been a long time.'

To keep the bailiffs at bay, Barrymore played stooge to guests like Groucho Marx on Rudy Vallee's radio show. One night Mary Astor spotted him alone in the corridor of the radio studio, sagging against a wall like someone 'who just couldn't walk another step'.

Barrymore died penniless in 1942. Sad as it was, his disintegration had been mitigated by a talent for self-mockery which was evident even after his death. There is a famous story, told by Errol Flynn and David Niven – and later fictionally recreated in the film *SOB* (1981) – that when Barrymore died his old drinking companion Flynn went out on a binge to drown his grief. Returning home considerably the worse for wear, he found Barrymore sitting in his customary chair with a fully charged glass in his hand. On closer inspection the thunderstruck Flynn discovered that his old partner in crime had not, in fact, risen from the grave. Barrymore's corpse was on loan from a bribed undertaker.

The story has a sad coda. Twenty-six years later Flynn, by then himself one of the living dead, was hired to play Barrymore in *Too Much Too Soon* (1958). He's just about the only good thing in the film. When Flynn died a year later, there was no one around to play high jinks with his decomposing corpse. Errol had passed way beyond a joke.

The Bottom of the Bottle

One of the saddest tales in Hollywood is that of James Murray, picked by director King Vidor from a gaggle of extras to play the lead in *The Crowd* (1928), the last great silent movie made by MGM. Vidor's instinct had been correct; Murray was a gifted natural actor and gave a moving performance as the anonymous young husband and father struggling to support his family in the Big City. Murray was then cast opposite the rising young Joan Crawford in *Rose-Marie*, a project which was abandoned by the studio, as was Murray when heavy drinking made him unmanageable.

Within a few years he was back at the bottom of the heap, just another face in the crowd. In 1933 Vidor was accosted on Vine Street by an unshaven bum begging the price of a meal. It was an almost unrecognizable Murray. Vidor gave him $10 and took him to the Brown Derby, where Murray made straight for the bar. Impulsively, Vidor offered Murray the lead in his new film *Our Daily Bread*. There was one condition – he had to stay off the sauce. Knowing full well that he was too far gone, Murray rebuffed him and left. Vidor never saw him again.

Hollywood would doubtless have rewritten this scenario as a tearjerker, with the alcoholic Murray, redeemed by the love of a good director, stepping up to receive an Oscar, his white-haired old Mom dabbing her shining eyes in the front row of the audience. Life had drafted a different script. Three years later Murray's emaciated corpse was found floating in the Hudson River.

The incomparable W.C. Fields was quite happy to drink himself to death. Martini was his consuming passion, until it consumed him, and by 1935 he was on two quarts a day. It was said that when Fields travelled he needed three trunks – one for clothes and two for liquor. Wherever he went, whatever he did, there was always a drink in his hand. At home, if the Martini shaker ran dry, he would summon replenishments by blowing on a hunting horn.

Finally, he was persuaded to give up drinking for most of 1937, which proved just how ill he was. While he was in hospital, Carole Lombard presented him with a pig and a bicycle, a reference to a long, rambling and rude joke he had once told her. Perking up, Fields cycled down the clinic's corridors, the pig trotting behind.

The last, and wildest, of his comedies was *Never Give a Sucker an Even Break* (1941). At one point he suggested that the billing be changed to Fields: Sucker. The plot, his calculatedly incoherent farewell to the insanities of Hollywood, concerns the adventures which befall Fields after he drops a bottle of whisky from an aircraft and dives after it.

His alcoholism was now completely out of control and complicated by polyneuritis. There were no more feature films, although Fields managed three cameo appearances in low-budget musicals, looking like a man pickled in gin. He died on Christmas Day 1946, with his sense of timing unimpaired – he had always professed to loathe the Yuletide season.

Buster Keaton, in the 1930s one of Hollywood's great drunk, was more durable. Ironically, the onset of Buster's alcoholism coincided with the period of his greatest creativity, the years between 1923 and 1928, during which he made *Our Hospitality*, *The Navigator*, *The General*, *The Cameraman* and *Spite Marriage*, among the greatest works of the silent cinema.

Fascinated by machinery, Buster always revelled in mechanical props, but when he was persuaded to join MGM in 1928, and relinquish his independence, he was confronted with a machine he could not control, a huge studio. After *Spite Marriage* there was a rapid falling away, accelerated by Buster's drinking, his own 'spite marriage' to the dull and snobbish Natalie Talmadge, and MGM's indifference to his genius.

At his peak Buster had been one of the most graceful of all silent stars, with a profile like a Cocteau cartoon. Four years later drink and disappointment had ravaged those beautiful features, making him old, old old. Even now, however, there was a certain black humour about the effects of the drinking. On a hunting trip with his actor friend William Collier in 1931, Keaton was accompanied by a nubile young Paramount starlet. On the first evening, after a wild ride in a Buster's sand yacht, the two men stayed up drinking. Keaton never got to bed, and was still sitting up with a drink in his hand when Collier roused him just before dawn to go out shooting.

Crouched in the windswept hide, Keaton suddenly groaned, 'I've got to stand up! Listen – my legs – I've no circulation!' Then he yelled, 'It's killing me, help me!' As the two men staggered to their feet, the dim glow of Collier's flashlight fell on Buster's boots. They seemed unnaturally tight. Indeed, they were. At some point in the drunken day before, Keaton had put on his girlfriend's boots, but was so anaesthetized by liquor that he had remained oblivious to the mounting pain until it had become unendurable. In the end he had to be cut out of the boots with a knife.

At the beginning of 1933, while filming the ironically titled *What No Beer?* with Jimmy Durante, Buster disappeared from the MGM lot. He had flown to Mexico with a good-looking nurse, Mae Scribbens, who specialized in the care of advanced alcoholics. She took good care of Buster. One morning in Mexico City, after a heavy night of drinking, he woke up to find her in bed with him. She and Buster were married in Ensenada, California, on 8 January – at a time when Buster was in the middle of a complete alcoholic blackout lasting several days. To the end of his life he could never remember a thing about the marriage.

Keaton was dropped by MGM shortly afterwards. He was cast out into the wilderness. The resourceful Mae kept their affairs afloat with some discreet prostitution. In an afternoon at the Biltmore Hotel she could make up to $100 with a series of calls on 'some of my good men friends'.

Somehow Buster survived. There were a couple of films in Europe, a string of comedy two-reelers, work as a gagman for the Marx Brothers, who treated him abominably, and bit parts in B-movies, notably an enchanting cameo in Reginald LeBorg's *San Diego, I Love You* (1944); and a third, happy, marriage which lasted till his death in 1966.

After the Second World War the French rediscovered him, and he appeared in *Sunset Boulevard* (1950) – as one of the bridge-playing Hollywood 'waxworkers' in Norma Desmond's mansion – and with Chaplin in *Limelight* (1952). He never wholly gave up drinking; to the end he would ask doctors, after a physical examination, if he could drink again. Some must have said yes, for he often did. His genius was finally recognized at the 1965 Venice Film Festival. Behind the cheers there remained a terrible sense of waste. When the cheering died away, Keaton observed, 'Sure it's great, but it's all 30 years too late.'

Bangs and Whimpers

Not content with being the most colourful cowboy star of them all, Tom Mix embellished his extravagant screen image with a largely fictitious account of his adventurous early life: Rough Rider, US Marshal, freedom fighter in the Boer War and in the Mexican Civil War of 1910. The legend was so persuasive that many reference books still record these wholly imaginary exploits as fact. In truth, Mix's army days ended in desertion, and his cowboy days were marked by an arrest for horse stealing.

King of the cowboy corral in the mid-1920s, Mix rode through an amiable fantasy of the West, sporting an increasingly outrageous wardrobe: huge white sombreros, embroidered shirts, skin-tight white pants studded with diamonds, and pearl-handled Colt .45s transformed him into a veritable Beau Brummel of the range. At the height of his popularity he was earning $20,000 a week and the profits of his films were keeping the Fox studio afloat. At the end of the mile-long drive to his palatial home, a big neon sign flashed his famous initials into the night.

By the early 1930s the lights had gone out and Mix had been reduced to touring with circuses. His last film was a tawdry Mascot serial, *The Miracle Rider* (1935).

Five years later, Mix died in a spectacular auto crash which might have come from one of his best films. His body was pulled from the wreckage unmarked and impeccably dressed, his pockets stuffed with cash and cheques. In the pile-up a metal suitcase had struck him on the back of the neck, killing him instantly. The last of the legends surrounding Mix's flamboyant life filled the case with a hoard of gold $20 pieces.

In 1931 the great German director F.W. Murnau rode to death in different fashion. When his car skidded off the road it was being driven by his 14-year-old Filipino manservant, to whom, it was rumoured, the homosexual director was paying some rather intimate and distracting attention. Only 11 mourners attended Murnau's funeral, among them Greta Garbo, who commissioned a death mask of the master director which she kept on her desk.

Here Come the Lizards

In 1967 Jayne Mansfield and her boyfriend-cum-manager Sam Brody were driving to a TV engagement near New Orleans. Their sports car slammed into a truck. The fading star and her lover were decapitated. In the crash, the mutilated body of Jayne's pet chihuahua was squirted out on to the tarmac.

The sheer horror of her end obscured the nightmarish last year of Mansfield's career. In the mid-1950s Hollywood wheeled out a new gimmick to win back the audiences lost to television – big boobs. In a class of her own was Jayne Mansfield, with eye-boggling measurements of 40-19-36.

She hit the big-time in 1956 when 20th Century-Fox, embroiled in a feud with the recalcitrant Marilyn Monroe, signed Jayne to a seven-year contract.

Director Frank Tashlin packaged her principal attributes in a raucous comedy, *The Girl Can't Help It*. Tashlin had started his career in 1928 as animator with Max Fleischer, and in Mansfield's absurd curves he found the closest human approximation to a 'cartoon woman', around whose anatomy he sprayed machine-gun bursts of mocking sight gags. The most celebrated was when Jayne appeared clutching a milk bottle in front of each pendulous breast, bringing a new dimension to the concept of 'Sign and Meaning in the Cinema'. Tashlin believed that 'there's big-breasted women – like walking leaning towers'.

In the end, Jayne seems more pathetic than risible, let alone sexy. The thought of her completely unclothed is enough to make the strongest stomach churn. Remarkably, in *The Girl Can't Help It* she retains a touchingly sympathetic quality, telling Tom Ewell that she just wants to be a housewife and mother, and pretending that she can't sing in order to prevent her gangster boyfriend Marty 'Fats' Murdoch (Edmond O'Brien) from launching her on a showbiz career.

It was Jayne's 'showbiz career' which did her in. Inevitably, the shelf life of her oversized mammaries was limited. Even the most vigorously inflated balloons soon start to grow slack and wrinkled. By the early 1960s she was still making headlines, but her film appearances were now restricted to sleazy exploiters like *The Fat Spy* (1966), playing the daughter of another zonked-out Hollywood veteran, Brian Donlevy; and *L'Amore Primitivo* (1964), in which the flimsy plot required her to perform an extremely primitive strip for a bug-eyed anthropologist and a couple of astonished hotel porters. There were a rumours of a porno film and a list of weird unreleased movies, including *Dog Eat Dog* (1965), *Mondo Hollywood* (1967) and *The Wild, Wild World of Jayne Mansfield* (1967).

By then Jayne's world had progressed from the Wild to the Wooly and Way Beyond. When she sang 'Fly Me to the Moon' in her nightclub act, it was clear that she was zooming out of control through the outer limits of dabbling in Black Magic, sinking two bottles of Bourbon a day and gobbling fistfuls of diet pills to stay awake. Increasingly mountainous, she waddled around in a tiny miniskirt, her arms and thighs blotched with the livid bruises sustained in her frequent brawls with the loathsome Brody. Behind them the happy couple left a trail of bottle-strewn hotel suites caked in the excrement of Jayne's yapping pet dogs.

In one sense at least, her wild behaviour was an expression of disgust, both at what she had become and the predatory and brutal men who had exploited her and brought her to this pass. One night, during her nightclub act, she perched on the knees of an elderly man, yanked out a gigantic, flaccid breast and rammed the nipple into his gasping mouth.

In hospital just before her death, Jayne and Sam went bananas. Dropping LSD, gulping booze and guzzling uppers, they went on a rampage. Within a week the hospital administrator had died of a heart attack.

Mansfield's press secretary Raymond Strait has left a ghastly picture of the hellish pit into which she had sunk in her final days. Visiting Jayne and Sam at home, Strait had gone into the kitchen to mix himself a drink. Suddenly he heard a blood-curdling scream. Rushing back to Brody's leather-lined den, he was confronted by the sight of Jayne climbing the bookshelves, 'her throat filled with such screeching noises that she sounded more animal than human'. Over and over again she moaned, 'The lizards. The lizards! The fucking lizards! Look at them! Oh, my God, look at them!'

Clinging to the shelves with one hand, she jabbed a finger towards the desk. Then Strait saw Brody, crouched in the corner, his eyes set and glassy, masturbating frantical-ly: 'His tongue kept flicking his lips as he hammered him-self toward some incredible satisfaction.' All the while he crooned, 'Do it, baby, do it. Beautiful. Eat the little pussy. Little lizards eat the pussy!'

Strait reeled into the night. He never saw Mansfield again. If ever there was case of Dog Eat Dog in Mondo Hollywood it was that of Jayne Mansfield. The girl just couldn't help it.

Where There's a Pill There's a Way

On the screen Alan Ladd was cool and unsmiling, moving from a stone-faced calm to violent action like a hawser that suddenly snaps under pressure. Off the set, the pressure of being Alan Ladd – enduring the tired old jokes about his lack of height and limited range – finally shattered his brit-tle self-confidence. He once told a friend, 'I'm the most insecure guy in Hollywood.'

Disillusioned, he made a botched attempted to shoot himself in 1962. He was found at his ranch with gunshot wounds which were said to be accidental. Ladd was no stranger to suicide – in 1937 he had watched in horror as his mother, a hopeless alcoholic, died in convulsions after eating rat poison.

He tried again, in 1964, dosing himself with sedatives on top of alcohol. He didn't wake up. Ironically, his last, posthumous appearance was in *The Carpetbaggers* (1964), a rip-roaring tale of sex and skulduggery in Old Hollywood.

Sleeping pills, which had failed to waft Lupita Velez gracefully to the other side, were the chosen method of death for Charles Boyer, Gail Russell, Dorothy Dandridge, Carole Landis (distraught at being dumped by boyfriend Rex Harrison), Judy Garland (found crouched on the lava-tory like a shrunken old crone), and most famously of all,

Marilyn Monroe.

Marilyn had always been one of the most 'difficult' of stars, frequently unable to remember her lines, demanding take after take of the simplest scenes and almost always late on the set. During the shooting of her last film, John Huston's *The Misfits* (1961), co-starring Clark Gable and Montgomery Clift, she was a constant problem, and her regular fits of depression led to an overdose of sleeping pills.

Relations with her husband, the playwright Arthur Miller, had reached breaking point, and they were divorced only a week before the film's première. A terrible melancholy surrounds the movie: a few weeks after filming was completed, Clark Gable died of a heart attack caused by the strain of the location shooting; and Montgomery Clift died six years later, also from a heart attack, caused by heavy drinking.

Marilyn was not long for this world. Crack-up lay just around the corner. She began a new film, the ominously titled *Something's Got to Give*, but after an uninterrupted series of rows she was summarily dismissed. Deserted by her lovers, the last of whom was Robert Kennedy, she slipped her moorings and drifted away. On 5 August 1962 her nude body, an empty bottle of barbiturates beside it, was found by her housekeeper. Surviving fragments of *Something's Got to Give*, particularly a nude bathing scene show that, even in extremis, she had lost none of her elusively luminous beauty that captivated the movie world.

Her story did not end there. Marilyn's death remains an enigma. The question of foul play has often been raised, but never conclusively proved. It was revealed that a secret diary had mysteriously vanished from her bedroom; allegedly, it contained information about her relations with the Kennedy brothers. A private eye claimed that she had been murdered by the CIA to prevent her from revealing a harebrained plot to assasinate the Cuban leader Fidel Castro. Others have suggested that she knew too much about the Mob's designs on the Kennedy brothers, which ultimately led to the assassination of President John F. Kennedy.

The endless flood of speculation and theory washes over her body, sprawled sadly in death. They won't stop pawing over Marilyn in death, just as they pawed over her in life. But the essential Marilyn remains with us on celluloid. Cameramen may often have cursed her, but the camera loved her till the end.

'The Joker is Wild'

With the presence of the Mafia, Hollywood set about cleaning up its films about the Chicago Mob from which it now strained (on screen) to keep a puritanical distance. Good old Frank Sinatra, about whom more scurrilous speculation regarding Mafia links has been made than any other entertainer, played the part of Joe E. Lewis in *The Joker is Wild* (1975). Predictably Hollywood reduced the hoods in the film to the level of cartoon wise-guys. In reality, Lewis was a singer-comedian whose throat had been slashed for his unfortunate refusal to tread the boards of a Mafia nightclub. 'Machine Gun' Jack McGurn was the nasty with the knife on whom history was to pile the telling evidence that he masterminded the St Valentine's Day Massacre. In the film the studio conversion kit turns the hit-man into a yapping wisecracker who would be a more suitable match for Bugs Bunny.

McGurn's loyal tribe, who were left intact when 'Machine Gun' was blown off the streets in 1936, were the most influential monsters in the State when Sinatra made the movie. Chief Mafioso was Sam Giancana, once a gunslinger for Al Capone, who took over the Chicago outfit in 1959. A tough-nosed operator, he was quick to boost the Mob's already massive income form Hollywood and Las

Vegas. With his celebrity chums, and especially his long-term shenanigans with singer Phyllis McGuire, it comes as no surprise at all that his daughter, Antoinette, craved a life in the spotlight. Dad immediately fixed a top-level meeting for her at MGM.

She had been quite open about her father's grip on the studios: 'If Sam wanted to send his little girl to Hollywood, or if he just wanted a friend to play a movie role, or if he just wanted to see the studio sights and meet some stars, he got what he wanted, and he got it with red carpet treatment.'

Hollywood has yet to make a movie about its own seedy partnership with the Mafia. Applauded at the time for its unzipping of hoodlum rule on the Brooklyn shore in *On The Waterfront* (1954), it would never have had the gall to turn Brando into Bioff and so detail the gift-wrapped package which it had already been delivering to the Mafia for years.

The almost invisible line between the Mob and the moguls is further blurred when one considers the links between actors and hoods. Jean Harlow had a long-term relationship with Longie Zwillman, the new Jersey prohibition king, while George Raft spent all his time as a boy on the streets of New York with all kinds of toughies, some of whom later took centre-stage as star gangsters. On of Raft's boyhood buddies was Bugsy Siegel, the bootlegger and chief hit-man for Murder Inc., who improved his career credit when he turned acres of sand into Las Vegas and so thoughtfully created a limitless new cash flow for the 'Families'.

As Raft's star faded from sight, he was happy to accept work which was sought out for him by both Siegel and Mayer Lansky, the financial whizz of the entire syndicate.

Even today the links persist. James Caan, who in *The Godfather* played the hot-headed Sonny whose life is ended by rival bullets at a New Jersey toll booth, seemed to step straight off the set when he appeared in court to defend an 'old friend', Andrew Russo. Recently released from a five-year jail term for bribery and tax evasion, he was now taking the stand for bribery and extortion. Considered by the FBI to be a high-flying member of the Colombo family (one of New York's top five), he was extolled by Caan who came out with the classic cliché: 'I don't know if there is a Mafia.' The prosecutor, Rudolph Giuliani, was amazed that Caan could even speak because, as he said, 'I thought he was killed at the toll booth.'

Caan seemed also to be intimately acquainted with Mafia protocol. Loyally providing verbal support for Russo's chum, Carmine 'The Shake' Persico (the Colombo family boss), he kissed Persico, Brando-style, on the cheek.

Caan and Russo seem to have become friends during the shooting of *The Godfather*. At that time Joe Colombo was still running his own family. As a ruse to lessen the pressure from the FBI flatfoots, he founded the Italian American Civil Rights League which began to claim that 'Mafia' was term of racial abuse which the FBI, not to mention the Italian-haters amongst the WASP establishment, was guilty of spreading willy-nilly. This led to a veto on the terms 'Mafia' and 'Cosa Nostra' in not only all FBI public statements but also in *The Godfather* itself.

The Peraino offshoot of the Colombo clan was not content with just shaping films but wanted to actually make them. Louis 'Butcher' Peraino and former Brooklyn barber, Gerald Damiano, were the puppeteers behind *Deep Throat* (1972) and its star Linda Lovelace. After dropping $22,000 into the pot, the final reward for the Colombos was around $100m. Peraino and his brother Joseph soon sank their teeth into Hollywood with tasteful excursion which included *The Devil in Miss Jones* (1973), Andy Warhol's *Frankenstein* (1974), *Return of the Dragon* (1973) (starring Bruce Lee) and the enormous cash-creator, *Texas Chainsaw Massacre* (1975). One producer even told the *Los Angeles*

Times that, when you dealt with the brothers, you never knew whether you were negotiating for your picture or your life.

Francis Ford Coppola, director of *The Godfather*, was again blessed with Mafia involvement in *The Cotton Club* (1984). The money-men who funded the picture were Ed and Fred Doumani, who still own the El Morocco casino in Las Vegas, a joint which had hosted visits-plenty from FBI investigators who have the nasty guff of gangland connections in their nostrils.

When the film's budget disappeared off the graph, soaring from $20 million to $47 million, the brothers sent a 'good friend' to teach Coppola basic book-keeping. Joey Cusumano arrived as the producer and, unsurprisingly, the high-spending director finished filming before the deadline. Still, Cusumano, who was followed for six months by two FBI cars for 24 hours a day, couldn't return the $27 million which had left a gasping hole the Doumanis' pocket.

The Doumanis, of course, kept their distance from the film set by staying in Las Vegas. They epitomize the new era of sleek mobsters who do not run around like Bioff emptying gun barrels at those who transgress. Instead they employ smooth-talking puppets as respectable fronts for their operations. Even today, if you want to make a trouble-free movie, you have to be able to negotiate the complex path which eventually leads back to the Mob. Willie Bioff would approve.

Here Comes Hedda

By the early 1940s, Louella had a rival, Hedda Hopper, charitably described by Ray Milland as 'an unmitigated bitch . . . venomous, vicious, a pathological liar and quite stupid'.

Hedda was nudging 50 before she hit the big time. In the mid-1930s she was just another general-purpose actress whose career was going nowhere. Ironically, Louella had been one of her early boosters in the silent days, dubbing her the 'Queen of the Quickies'. Now she was living on her wits and her friendship with MGM screenwriter Frances Marion and Louella's old chum Marion Davies. It was Davies who gave Hedda her start in journalism in 1935, writing a weekly fashion column in *The Washington Post*.

Initially Louella continued to root for Hedda, but in 1939 they had become deadly rivals. 'Hedda Hopper's Hollywood', syndicated by Esquire Features, was appearing in the *Los Angeles Times*, the *New York Daily News*, and *The Chicago Tribune*. For the first time Louella had a serious competitor, a development which was welcomed by the studios. The gloves came off and a battle was joined which lasted for 20 years. Frequently the stars were caught in the crossfire. If one of them favoured Louella with a juicy morsel, he would quickly find himself the object of one of Hedda's vendettas. And vice versa.

Louella always affected a flutteringly vague manner which, until her later failing years, concealed a mind like a bear trap. Hedda adopted a brasher approach. She revelled in pointing dramatically at her home on Tropical Drive in Beverly Hills and chortling, 'That's the home fear built!'

Like Louella, Hedda had only the haziest grasp of what real journalism was about. Sometimes this could be almost endearing. Ringing the *Los Angeles Times* with a scoop, she shrieked down the line, 'Stop the presses – whatever that means!'

She started as she meant to go on. In her very first column she reported that Greta Garbo, who was soon to marry Leopold Stokowski, had undergone inspection by the famous conductor's patrician Philadelphia parents. Not only did the romance prove to be non-existent, but so did the Philadelphia relatives. This rivalled the immortal story filed by Louella that Sigmund Freud was going to be hired by Warners to act as the technical adviser on the Bette Davis weepie, *Now Voyager* (1942). Presumably Jack Warner had paranormal powers, as Siggy was busy being dead at the time.

All too rarely did Hedda's carelessness with these awkward little facts catch up with her. When she refused to stop running a story that Joseph Cotton was having an extramarital affair with Deanna Durbin, Cotton took his revenge. Espying the statuesque Hopper at a party, he promptly planted a hefty kick in the middle of her fat backside. On another occasion Ann Sheridan, taxed beyond endurance, dumped a plate of mashed potato in her lap.

Hedda never forgot or forgave the slights and petty humiliations she had endured in her days as a humble supporting actress! Years before, she had been snubbed on the set by Joan Bennett. When Bennett's husband, producer Walter Wanger, shot her lover, the agent Jennings Lang, in the groin, Hedda had a field day, wallowing in righteous indignation.

Joan Bennett responded by sending Hedda a unique Valentine – a skunk – with the accompanying note:

> Here's a little valentine
> That very plainly tells
> The reason it reminded me so
> Much of you–
> It smells!

However, the majority of stars were happy to lick her boots, as is evidenced by this fawning telegram signed by Gary Cooper, William (Hopalong Cassidy) Boyd, John Wayne, Harry Carey and Roy Rogers:

HEDDA YOU OLD HOPTOAD FIRST YOU WENT TO TEXAS. NOW YOU'RE IN ARIZONA THAT'S COW

COUNTRY AND THAT MEANS COWBOYS. AND COW-
BOYS MEANS LOTS OF FUN FOR ALL AMERICA. SO
HAVE A GOOD TIME. BUT FOR GOSH SAKES DON'T
FORGET TO COME BACK TO US. REGARDS AND SUC-
CESS FROM THE 'ARIZONA GANG'.

Presumably the reference to 'cow country' was merely a
Freudian slip.

According to one story, Merle Oberon, reeling from
Hedda's attacks, took her out to lunch at the Vine Street
Derby. When Merle asked what had caused this tidal wave
of bile, Hedda replied exultantly, 'Nothing, dear. It's bitchery. Sheer bitchery.'

Hedda reserved her most pungent bitchery for Louella.
On one famous occasion they both attended a show staged
at Hollywood's Moulin Rouge for opera star Helen
Traubel. In the finale a small flock of doves was released.
They were supposed to settle tastefully on the girls of the
chorus line but, distracted by the lights and music, they
flew about the auditorium in confusion. As the feathers
began to drift down on to the audience, Hedda leapt to her
feet, hissing, 'Let's get out of here! Those birds are going to
shit! And when they do, I hope they hit Louella's bald
spot!,

The shit certainly hit the fan when, in her autobiography,
The Whole Truth and Nothing But, Hedda claimed that she
had tried to dissuade Elizabeth Taylor from marrying
Michael Wilding because he had had a homosexual relationship with Stewart Granger. Straight back zinged a
libel suit for $3,000,000. The book was closed with a sub-
stantial out-of-court settlement and a full apology from
Hedda.

In a world in which everyone was either on the way up
or on the way down, this pair of carrion crows clung to
their perches for nearly 20 years. In part their success lay
in their crude but instinctive feel for public opinion.

Hedda and Louella were never ones to swim against the tide. They were seldom, if ever, the first to break the real Hollywood tragedies, like Frances Farmer's mental collapse. In cases like these, they were content to trot along in the rear, happy to put the stiletto heel into a woman who was already down.

Ultimately, they were the studios' creatures, and in their coy references to sex (for which read 'dating') or heavy drinking (for which read remarks alike, 'Aren't all those late-night revels taking their toll on Constance Bennett's beauty?') they acted as apologists for the erratic antics of the stars. For all their power, they never pushed their luck too far.

As Louella frequently observed in, her column, 'Tempus sure does fugit!'. It made them old and confused struggling to survive in a world which had left them, and the studio system on which they fed, far behind. David Niven once remarked that Hedda and Louella had skins as tough as a brontosaurus. Now they were brontosauri, near-extinct dinosaurs, grazing fretfully on increasingly meagre pastures.

As she became increasingly doddery, Louella relied almost exclusively on studio hand-outs to fill her column. She would drift through film-land parties, stuffing them abstractedly into an enormous handbag. At one party she was approached by a young gatecrasher proffering a hand-out on which several stars had already signed their autographs. Not realizing that she, too, was being asked to sign, she shot out her claw and crammed the crumpled paper into her bag. Later, in her office, an assistant found her gazing tearfully at it and wailing, 'What are they trying to tell me?' The message, Louella, was : 'You're all washed up!'

Hedda finally succumbed to the double pneumonia in 1966. Louella outlasted her rival by six years, ending her days in a nursing home where she sat mute before the

191

television, bathed in the ghostly glow of the stars she had alternately fawned upon and terrorized.

Strictly Confidential

In the 1950s there was one magazine which was happy to 'boldly go' where no one feared to tread – *Confidential*, the sleaze sheet owned by Robert Harrison.

Confidential appeared in 1952, at a time when the power of the major studios was on the wane, in their heyday, the heads of studios were the first to be called if a star wandered on to the wrong side of the law. MGM's Louis B. Mayer arrived at the scene of the suicide of Jean Harlow's husband, Paul Bern, a full two hours before the boys in blue. Significantly, it was Mayer who handed over the suicide note allegedly written by Bern, and who ensured that the tricky questions raised by the coroner's inquest were suppressed. He was protecting his investment. But times were changing, many of the stars were now freelancers who could no longer rely on the old-time studio empires, with their almost limitless resources, to protect them.

Into this squalid arena oozed slimeball Harrison, a former porn-merchant who had cut his journalistic teeth on a legendary scandal sheet, the *Daily Graphic*. Harrison based his editorial approach on the bullying tactic adopted by the House Un-American Activities Committee (HUAC) investigators in the Communist witch-hunts of the late 1940s and early 1950s. Innuendo and guilt by association were the order of the day. Truth was usually tossed out of the window.

Confidential's motto was: 'Tells the Facts and Names the Names'. Its style was mixture of *Police Gazette* and Mickey Spillane on speed. Its formula was simple: an unflattering candid shot of a star and then a story alleging homosexuality, misogyny, drunkenness or vicious domestic strife.

And those were the flattering profiles! How about some samples? LIZABETH SCOTT IN THE CALL GIRL'S CALL BOOK

Just a roving check ma'am and out popped . . . The vice cops expected to find a few big name customers when they grabbed the date book of a trio of Hollywood Jezebels, but even their cast-iron nerves got a jolt when they got to the S's! In recent years Scotty's almost nonexistent career has allowed her to roam farther afield. In one jaunt to Europe she headed straight for Paris and the left bank where she took up with Frede the city's most notorious lesbian queen and operator of a nightclub devoted exclusively to entertaining deviates just like herself!

Or:

KIM NOVAK AND SAMMY DAVIS JR

Who broke up their romance?
Exclusive! Boy meets girl, boy gets girl ... It's a Hollywood movie plot no more. Here's how Hollywood broke Sammy's spirit on the rocks. It's the tragic love story of the century. In Romeo and Juliet the lovers could only be reunited in death ... when their parents wouldn't let them marry. In real life a king gives up his throne for the woman be loves and gives up a $5 million bank account. In this case SAMMY DAVIS JR WOULDN'T GIVE UP THE NEGRO RACE! *Kim Novak wouldn't give up the white race! Of course, there was the fact that his skin was black and her skin was white, but in Hollywood there's no such thing as a color line.*

Harry Cohn, the volatile head of Columbia, took Sammy aside and said, 'Do you realize this girl is worth $20 million to me? Have a fling for a few months, but don't get married.' A dramatic decision had to be made ... Sammy made it. He married a colored girl. Maybe his marriage had something to do with the visit Sammy received from two of Cohn's thugs, who said to Sammy, 'YOU HAVE ONE EYE NOW. WANT TO TRY FOR NONE? WELL THAT'S THE WAY FOR FUTURE

LOOKS IF YOU DON'T MARRY A COLORED GIRL WITHIN THREE DAYS OR ELSE!' *A few months later Cohn himself was dead. Rumors going around Columbia said that [Kim and Sammy's] romance had killed Harry.*

Harrison's informants were a motley crew of high-class hookers, out-of-work actors and washed-up journalists. Sometimes Hollywood's elite informed on each other. The Harry Cohn story was supplied by producer Mike Todd, a man only marginally less of demented egomaniac than the beast of the Columbia lot. Stories were also fed to *Confidential* by two gossip-columnists, the odious Walter Winchell and his rival Lee Mortimer. Winchell even plugged the magazine on television.

Infra-red, ultra-rapid film and high-powered telephone lenses were some of the paparazzi techniques used by *Confidential* to pry into the private lives of the stars. In this way it required intimate pictures of a domestic slugfest between British actor Anthony Steel and his busy wife Anita Ekberg.

It was with this kind of 'research' that Harrison black-mailed the stars. Many paid up to avoid being splashed across the pages of *Confidential* in exposes like : *Dan Dailey in Drag; PSSST! Vic Mature: That Cute Trick You dated? 'She' was a 'HE'; Errol Flynn and His Two-Way Mirrors; The Best Pumper in Hollywood? M-M-M-Marilyn M-M-M-Monroe; and an old chestnut, Rory Calhoun – But for the Grace of God Still a Convict!*

Eventually the worms began to turn. The day after *Confidential* had featured a compromising item about Grace Kelly, her father burst into Harrison's New York office, smashed up his desk and poked the fearless publisher on the jaw. Early in 1957 Dorothy Dandridge, the black star of *Carmen Jones* (1954), filed a $2 million suit against *Confidential* after it had printed a feature on her allegedly naked cavorting in the woods with a bunch of fun-loving 'naturists'.

The floodgates were opened, and the stars began to line up to take legal potshots at their tormentor. Immediately alarm bells began ringing in the studio. If the stars were to take the stand, heaven knows what embarrassing revelations some smart-ass attorney might coax out of them. Once again it was cover-up time. When they failed to persuade California's Attorney-General to kill the actions against *Confidential* (by the subtle method of threatening to withdraw the industry's financial support for the Republican Party) the studio ensured that all the stars were as far away as possible, 'on holiday', when the proceedings began.

There were only two exceptions: Dandridge, who withdrew her complaint after a considerable out-of-court settlement; and fiery red-headed, green-eyed Irish-born star Maureen O'Hara, who was holding out for damages of $5,000,000.

Confidential had run a story in which it alleged that O'Hara played a game of 'Chinese Chest' in the loge section of Grauman's Chinese Theater with a South American gigolo. *Confidential* told its readers: 'The couple saw a couple who heated up the balcony as if it was July. Maureen, blouse unbuttoned and her hair in disarray, had assumed, in order to watch the movie, the oddest posture ever to be beheld in the entire history of motion pictures. She was stretched out on three seats, the lucky South American occupying the middle chair, while a picture denouncing juvenile delinquency was shown on the screen.'

The judge, obviously a man with a sense of humour, decided to re-enact the sordid scene in situ. The manager of Grauman's played Maureen's lucky Latin lover, and a reporter stood in for the tawny-haired star, raising her legs in the air for the edification of the jury. The seats were then minutely examined.

After these surreal solemnities, real-life took over. On 16 August one of *Confidential*'s editors, Polly Gould, committed suicide. She had been due to take the stand the following day. Her death was not unconnected with the fact that she had been playing both ends against the middle – acting a stoolie for the DA and keeping Harrison informed of impending legal moves against him.

On the 17th O'Hara made her first appearance in court, brandishing a passport which seemed to prove that she had been in Spain at the time of the back-seat canoodling. But the witnesses would not be budged. Maureen's sister, an Irish nun, took the stand to vouch for the star's spotless character. There was even a lie detector test which proved inconclusive.

Eventually *Confidential* was ordered to pay $5,000 damages. Cheap at the price, perhaps, but only the first of a series of much more expensive settlements with a dozen stars. Liberace, for example, took the magazine for $40,000.

Shortly afterwards, Harrison's editor-in-chief, the rabid Red-baiting Howard Rushmore, shot and killed his wife while riding in a cab in New York's Upper East Side and then turned the gun on himself. Harrison sold *Confidential* and launched a new scandal sheet, *Inside News*. But his days were numbered. There was now pap aplenty for the public pouring from their television screens. And the stars were revealing all in 'fuck and tell' autobiographies like Errol Flynn's *My Wicked, Wicked Ways*, which was published in 1957. *Confidential*'s reign of terror was over.

However, its spirit lives on. Doesn't *Confidential*'s parade of outrageous fabrications, its prurience, homophobia and total absence of any journalistic standards have a depressingly familiar ring? Yes, *Confidential* is alive and well, flourishing in the boob-splattered pages of Britain's tabloid press.

Lights. . .Camera. . .ACTION !

On many a set a boxing referee might have been more useful than a director. Rivalries between a studio's top stars were the very stuff of Hollywood gossip, spoon-fed to the public by Hedda and Louella and not infrequently engineered by the studios themselves. In the early 1920s Paramount fermented a feud between their exotic foreign import Pola Negri and homegrown star Gloria Swanson. It was as phoney as Negri's name (she was born Barbara Appolionia Chalupiec), but it helped sell movies.

However, no one needed to stoke up the fires of an artificial quarrel when Bette Davis and Miriam Hopkins squared up to each other while making *Old Acquaintance* in 1943. Sparks also flew during the stormy filming of *The Women* in 1939. When Joan Crawford grabbed the role of the hardboiled vixen Crystal, she continued to play the part off the set, bitching about her hated co-star Norma Shearer and being bawled out by director George Cukor.

Joan could drive anyone to distraction, but it never took much to excite the peppery Hungarian director Michael Curtiz. While directing *Mildred Pierce* (1945), he grew so frustrated with Crawford's tantrums that he tore the shoulder pads off her dress.

Curtiz was a hard-driving bully who was equally careless of the lives of the extras in the flood scene in *Noah's Ark* (1928) and the lives of the horses in *The Charge of the Light Brigade* (1936). He was famous for his mangled English, and colloquialisms every bit as extravagant as those uttered by Sam Goldwyn. While filming *The Charge of the Light Brigade*, Curtiz spotted David Niven at the side of the set, sharing a laugh with Errol Flynn about something he had just roared over his megaphone. Turning the loud-hailer towards the grinning actors, Curtiz bellowed, 'You think I know fucking nothing! Well let me tell you I know fuck all!'

'Difficult' stars are not unknown in these enlightened times, not the least of them the overbearing Barbra Streisand. As an ex-roommate once observed, 'Barbra has settled for more.' Inevitably this means that others get less of everything, particularly co-operation. After she had stomped furiously off the set of *Hello Dolly!* for the umpteenth time, exasperated co-star Walter Matthau yelled after her, 'Just remember, Betty Hutton once thought she was indispensable!' and was greeted with a round of applause from the assembled technicians. After another violent altercation he delivered himself of the understandable if hyperbolic opinion: 'I have more talent in one of my farts than you do in the whole of your body!' After the filming was over, he reflected, 'I have no disagreement with Barbra Streisand, I was merely exasperated by her tendency towards megalomania.'

Fun and Games with Roman

Directors frequently suffer at the hands of temperamental stars and producers. After the troubled filming of *Macbeth* in 1971, director Roman Polanski sent producer Victor Lownes a solid gold prick as a mark of his esteem.

Revenge can sometimes be exacted on the set. On *Cul-de-Sac* (1968) relations between Polanski and gravel-voiced character actor Lionel Stander were somewhat strained. One day over lunch Polanski asked Stander if he could drink a bottle of milk in one go. 'Sure!' replied Stander, grabbing the nearest bottle and gulping it down without a pause. When he had finished, Polanski looked up from consulting his watch and said, 'Fantastic! Eleven seconds. Can you do that when we shoot?' 'Sure!' replied Stander. It took 16 takes – 16 pints of milk – before Polanski was satisfied. In another scene Polanski forced Stander to eat 22 raw eggs.

Filming with Polanski is never less than lively. On Chinatown (1974) the excitable little director found Jack Nicholson watching baseball on a portable television when he was urgently needed on set. Seizing an iron bar he began to smash up the television while Nicholson, incandescent with rage, tore off all his clothes in front of the crew. Shooting had to be abandoned as by now both men were too hysterical to resume work. On the same film, Polanski was constantly at odds with Faye Dunaway over the interpretation of the femme fatale she was playing. To annoy her between takes, he recited Rimbaud to her in French.

Sometimes the boot is on the other foot. James Cagney once flattened a director who persisted in making him repeat a single line. He then phoned Jack Warner and told him, 'You can come and pick up your boy – I just laid him out.'

Lee Marvin, berated by Joshua Logan for his drunken antics on *Paint Your Wagon* (1969), responded by urinating all over the director's boots.

The Face on the Cutting Room Floor

The ultimate sanction is consignment to the cutting room floor. When Buster Keaton threatened to upstage Charles Chaplin in the scene they shared in *Chaplin's Limelight* (1952), the Great Stoneface's best moments were slashed from the film.

John Ireland never became a top-line star, although he had his chances, notably in Howard Hawks's *Red River* (1948), which might have given him a big break had not his role been drastically cut during production. The film's screenwriter Chase Borden claimed that Hawks reached for the guillotine to punish Ireland for rustling the film's leading lady, Joanne Dru, from his own corral. As Hawks was married at the time, revenge had to be clandestine.

The beans were spilled when Chase lunched with Hawks and the film star John Wayne. While Hawks was in the men's room, Wayne told the writer that Ireland's character was going to be dropped from the film because 'he's fooling around with Howard's girl'. Chase protested, 'What the hell's that got to do with making a picture! I don't care if he's fooling around with the Virgin Mary, you've got a picture to make and the guy's good!' Wayne replied, 'He's out and that's it.'

Hawks stonewalled when challenged about the vendetta, claiming that he was sick of Ireland's late-night drinking and pot-smoking sessions, which left him more than a little fuzzy when it came to an early-morning call. Nevertheless, Ireland disappears over the horizon for long sections of *Red River*. When he finally reappears, it is for the sole purpose of being casually gunned down by John Wayne. Hawks's pettiness availed him nothing, as Dru and Ireland were married shortly after completing the film.

Upstage, Downstage

The heavyweight German star Emil Jannings resorted to more brutal methods with Marlene Dietrich when filming Josef von Sternberg's *The Blue Angel* (1930), the movie which made Marlene a star.

In the late 1920s Jannings had hovered portentously over Hollywood like a giant Zeppelin, the legend 'Great Actor' emblazoned in Gothic script on its sides. But the talkies had revealed Jannings's thick German accent and he was packed back to the Fatherland by Paramount clutching the Academy Award he had won in 1928 for his performance as the broken Tsarist general in *The Last Command*.

In *The Blue Angel*, Jannings played the stuffy schoolmaster bewitched then broken and humiliated by Marlene's incomparable nightclub slut Lola-Lola. Halfway through shooting Jannings realized that the film was being effortlessly stolen from him by a woman who didn't seem to be acting at all. Therein, of course, lies the mystery of cinema. Hysterical with rage, the 'Great Actor' burst into von Sternberg's office, moaning, holding his head and railing against that 'nincompoop idiot fool I'm working with!' Somewhat less than tactfully it was pointed out that it was he, the great Emil Jannings, who had requested Dietrich in the first place. He decided quite literally to take matters into his own hands.

In the scene in which he was to attack Lola-Lola, he seized Dietrich and flung her on a couch, his stubby fingers in a vice-like grip around her neck. Marlene fought to break free, but Jannings was not about to let go. Suddenly von Sternberg realized that this was for real. Jannings had flipped and was really trying to throttle his co-star. He rushed onto the set and dragged off the hulking actor, who was promptly struck in the face by Hans Albers. Jannings dissolved into tears and stumbled from the set. Marlene, whose genuine terror plain to see in the finished film, was rushed to her dressing room and revived. She bore the bruises on her neck for several weeks, and Jannings narrowly escaped an attempted murder rap.

Joan Crawford took stern measures against Mercedes McCambridge while making Nicholas Ray's baroque Western *Johnny Guitar* (1954).

Mercedes's bravura acting style was clearly stealing Joan's thunder as well as winning spontaneous applause from the crew. Joan went on the warpath, and to avoid battle royal on the set Nicholas Ray was obliged to shoot McCambridge's scenes at the crack of dawn. Spying on an early-morning shoot, Joan's paranoia was confirmed. The bitch was upstaging her! Medusa eyes ablaze, she stalked off to her rival's dressing room and proceeded to shred all her costumes to ribbons. Not content with this, Joan spent the next two years trying to make sure that Mercedes never worked in Hollywood again.

Two of the greatest upstagers of all time, Mae West and W. C. Fields, were paired for the first and last time in *My Little Chickadee* (1940), the comedy equivalent of *King Kong* v. *Godzilla*. Throughout production the stars sniped away at each other. Of the bibulous Fields, Mae observed: 'There is no one quite like Bill. And it would be snide of me to add, "Thank God". A great performer. My only doubts about him come in bottles." Precisely, Mae. Fields won the bout on a technical knockout, slyly filching Mae's most famous line and asking her to 'come up and see me some time ... in Philadelphia!'

Fields's magnificently bleary eye focused with unfailing accuracy on the absurdities and pettiness of life. Drink-sodden, florid of speech and nose, a relentless misogynist and child hater, he reserved a special place in his demonology for women and children. He had a special way of dealing with his tiny antagonist Baby LeRoy, the child star with whom he first locked horns in *Tillie and Gus* (1933). When asked about his small co-star, the curmud-geonly Fields replied, 'Fella named LeRoy, claims he's a baby.' On one famous occasion he spiked LeRoy's orange juice with gin. When the liquor began to take effect and Baby was carried away, Fields strutted round the set, tri-umphantly proclaiming, 'The kid's no trouper!'

Marlene Dietrich was the focus of an equally infantile feud between her co-stars Edward G. Robinson and George Raft when they were making *Manpower* (1941). Both men had the hots for Dietrich, although the enigmatic Marlene was not going to lay. She preferred lanky all-American types like John Wayne and Jimmy Stewart. The needle between Raft and Robinson was increased by the latter's niggling advice to Raft on the best way to deliver his lines and handle business. The tension finally exploded into a punch-up on the set which was captured by a *Life* photographer.

Raft was ever-ready with a swift right. Two years later, on *Background to Danger*, he filmed a scene in which he was tied to a chair by heavies Peter Lorre and Sydney Greenstreet. Lorre enjoyed himself hugely, laughing sadistically and blowing cigarette smoke into Raft's eyes. As soon as he was untied, Raft made straight for Lorre's dressing room and decked the diminutive character star.

Edward G. Robinson picked on someone his own size when he was filming *Barbary Coast* (1935) with Miriam Hopkins. He considered Hopkins 'Puerile, silly and snobbish', an opinion confirmed by her insistence on wearing a series of elaborate costumes which made Robinson look even more dwarf-like than usual. To add insult to injury, she demanded a box for him to stand on during their scenes together. When the script called for Edward G to slap Hopkins on the cheek, he floored her with a right uppercut to the jaw.

Ever the 'serious actress', Bette Davis wanted Laurence Olivier as her co-star in *The Private Lives of Elizabeth and Essex* (1939). Instead she got Errol Flynn. Not in the same league, my dear, and, to boot on a higher salary than the smouldering Davis. Bette relieved her disappointment on the set by delivering a 'stage slap' to Flynn of such force that the brittle he-man was knocked cold.

Try as they might, some stars just never hit it off. Laurence Olivier was determined that Vivian Leigh should appear opposite him in *Rebecca* (1940). Producer David O. Selznick wouldn't play ball. After Scarlett O'Hara, the mousey little heroine of *Rebecca* was just too big a character change. Moreover, Selznick felt that the public, might react unfavourably to real-life lovers. Olivier and Leigh smooching on screen, particularly as they were both married to other people at the time. So Larry got Joan Fontaine, who had to endure the stream of obscenities he whispered into her ear during their screen clinches. Sadistic director Alfred Hitchcock played along with it all, as Fontaine's obvious distress conveyed precisely the vulnerability for which he was searching.

The sweet nothings Spencer Tracy whispered into the ear of starch Irene Dunne while they were filming *A Guy Named Joe* (1943) were of an equally explicit nature. Grumpy, hard-drinking Spence was strongly attracted to *noli me tangere* types like Dunne and, most famously, Katharine Hepburn. When the script called for canoodling, Tracy gave Dunne a graphically detailed description of what he really wanted to do with her. Studio boss Louis B Mayer had to be called in to read the riot act to his horny leading man.

Vivien Leigh had a different close-up problem with Clark Gable while making *Gone With The Wind* (1939). Her love scenes with the 'King' were made almost unendurable by the blasts of fetid breath caused by his less than satisfactory dentures. Twenty-five years later, while making *Ship of Fools*, Leigh had an equally distressing close encounter of the vaporous kind with Lee Marvin when she was stiffed by his alcohol-scented attentions.

Diplomatic Fred Astaire always refused to be drawn on which of his leading ladies was his favourite dancing partner, although it was well known that there was little love lost between him and Ginger Rogers. In the 1970s he politely declined an invitation to a reunion with Ginger at a Lincoln Center tribute, leaving his erstwhile co-star to kiss a top hat for the benefit of the press. As Fred once admitted to the actress Dana Wynter, 'Ginger was so heavy!'

Are you Now or
Have You Ever Been. . . ?

It did not take long for the tentacles of rabid Red-baiting politics to spread through Hollywood. In 1945 there had been a series of labour disputes at the major studios, which in October climaxed in a riot outside the Warner studios at Burbank. A year later trouble flared again, with skirmishing between police and pickets breaking out at Warners and MGM.

In 1947 the House Un-American Activities Committee (HUAC) moved in on Hollywood, convinced that the labour unrest had been Communist-inspired. HUAC had been formed in 1937 and in 1940 was conducting investigations into Hollywood under the chairmanship of Texas Democrat Martin Dies, a man so right-wing that the practically disappeared off the political Richter scale. At one point he even suspected Shirley Temple of being a Communist! Defiant anti-intellectualism was the order of the day on HUAC. At one hearing a witness unwisely quoted the Elizabethan poet Christopher Marlowe, where upon he was interrupted by Joe Starnes, Dies's henchman, who rasped. 'You are quoting from this Marlowe. Is he a Communist?' In the postward years HUAC's principal role was the exploitation of public ignorance and hysteria about 'Communist conspiracy'. Officially, its members had the power only to suggest alterations to any new law. In fact, HUAC had the power to wreck people's lives, using innuendo, hearsay and malice, under the protective umbrella of the right-wing press.

Prominent among HUAC's supporters in the press was columnist Hedda Hopper, who was stomping the country addressing women's clubs, urging them to boycott films which featured 'Communist actors'. Hedda was also

made Vice-President of the Motion Picture Alliance for the
Preservation of American Ideals, among whose leading
lights were director Leo McCarey and actors John Wayne,
Ward Bond, Robert Taylor and Hollywood's self-appointed 'expert' on Communism, Adolphe Menjou.

Adolphe was firmly of the opinion that sneaky Red actors
could infiltrate Communists notions into a film merely by
the inflection they cunningly gave their lines. He predict-
ed that a Communist take-over of the United States was
imminent and declared that he was going to live in Texas
'because the Texans will shoot all Communists on sight'.
Clearly it did not occur to him that the good ol' boys of the
Lone Star State might just as easily gun down dandified little Hollywood actors when they appeared on the horizon.

Menjou's penetrating insights into the Red menace set
the intellectual tone of HUAC hearings, which opened privately in the spring of 1947, its chairman was J. Parnell
Thomas, a corrupt reactionary who was later jailed for
payroll padding. One of the more pernicious members of
the Committee was the anti-Semitic Mississippi
Congressman John Rankin, who announced his dismay on
discovering that Danny Kaye's real name was Daniel
Kaminsky. It would have been laughable if the consequences of HUAC's deliberations had not been so tragic.

HUAC discovered that there was no shortage of 'friendly' witnesses. Ginger Rogers's monstrous mother Lela
proudly told the Committee of her daughter's patriotic
refusal to deliver the line 'Share and share alike – that's
democracy', in *Tender Comrade* (1943), a piece of wartime
moral uplift about women war workers. Sharing things?
Good heavens, we can't have any of that in the land of the
free!

Gary Cooper stepped forward to provide a critique of
Communism straight from *Mr Deeds Goes to Town*: 'From
what I hear of it, I don't like it, because it isn't on the level',
a sentiment which might well have been applied to HUAC

itself. Was Gary worried that someone might remember that in the more innocent days of 1938 he was voted top male star in a poll of the delegates to the American Communist Party's national convention taken by the *Daily Worker*? (That well-known fellow-traveller Claudette Colbert was their favourite leading lady.)

Robert Montgomery told the Committee, 'I gave up my job to fight a totalitarianism called Fascism. I am ready to do it again to fight the totalitarianism called Communism.'

After the 23 'friendly' witnesses came the turn of 19 'unfriendly' witnesses. Of these, eight writers, a producer and a director – who became known as the 'Hollywood Ten' – declined to testify before the Committee and were held in contempt of Congress.

The Hollywood Ten were John Howard Lawson, Dalton Trumbo, Lester Cole, Alvah Bessie, Albert Maltz, Ring Lardner Jr, Samuel Ornitz, Herbert J. Biberman, Edward Dmytryk and Adrian Scott. They were by no means insubstantial figures. Scott and Dmytryk were RKO's top producer-director team, riding high on the success of *Crossfire*, a hard-hitting indictment of anti-Semitism and the studio's most profitable film of 1947. Dalton Trumbo was one of the highest-paid screenwriters in Hollywood, and among his credits were *A Guy Named Joe* (1943), *Thirty Seconds over Tokyo* (1944) and Ginger Rogers's favourite film, *Tender Comrade*. Ring Lardner's credits included *Woman of the Year* (1942), *The Cross of Lorraine* (1943) and *Tomorrow the World* (1944).

Under the leadership of John Howard Lawson the Ten refused to answer the question: 'Are you now, or have you ever been a Communist?' Rather than refuse to testify on the grounds that they might incriminate themselves (according to the Fifth Amendment), they regarded the Committee itself as unconstitutional. Lawson stated, 'I am not on trial here . . . the Committee is on trial before the American people.'

A Committee for the First Amendment, chaired by John Huston, was formed to protest against HUAC's infringement of the constitutional rights of the Hollywood Ten. A planeload of stars, among them Humphrey Bogart, Lauren Bacall, Richard Conte and Danny Kaye, flew to Washington in a blaze of publicity. However, they quickly caved in when pressure was applied by the Truman administration.

According to the writer-director Abraham Polonsky, soon to become another victim of the Red purge: 'General Beadle Smith was sent to Hollywood and he met the important Hollywood owners. A policy was laid down to call these stars and director off – the important ones. Pressure was put on them through their agents and the whole thing melted in about two weeks. It finally came down to a meeting and Humphrey Bogart turned around and looked at a half empty room – the first meetings were held at George Chasen's, and you couldn't get in – it was like an opening night at the opera – everybody wanted to be in on this. Anyway, Humphrey Bogart looked round this room and said: "You don't think I'm going to stand up there all by myself and take a beating – I'm getting out too." And he walked out of the room. Then Huston said, "Well, it's hopeless, fellows,' and left for Europe. The final meeting was held and the only people present were Willie Wyler, the permanent secretary, myself and one other. Wyler said, "Well, I think we can use our time better than this." And it was true.'

The industry did not lift a finger to help the Hollywood Ten. In November 1947, at a meeting in New York, the Association of Motion Picture Producers declared that the Ten had 'impaired their usefulness to the industry', a phrase of which Stalin himself might have been proud, and that they would not be re-employed until they had purged themselves of the contempt and sworn under oath that they were not Communists. The Association went on to pledge that the industry would not 'knowingly employ a Communist or a member of any party or group which advocates the overthrow of the Government of the United States by force or by any illegal or unconstitutional method'. Thus began the dreaded 'blacklist', on which were placed the names of writers, directors and actors who were suspected of the slightest traces of left-wing sympathies.

A surprising opponent of HUAC was Sam Goldwyn, no lover of Communism but a man who felt that the gathering witch-hunt was itself un-American, Goldwyn thought that those in Hollywood making the most noise about the Communist threat – men like Louis B. Mayer and Jack Warner – were blustering hypocrites. They had been happy to sanction films like *Song of Russia* and *Mission to Moscow* during the War and could not disown them. Goldwyn intervened to prevent a close friend, the screenwriter Robert Sherwood, from being hauled before the Committee to explain certain 'suspect scenes' in, of all films, the Oscar-laden hit *The Best Years of Our Lives* (1946).

Sherwood was luckier than the Hollywood Ten, who underwent a prolonged legal agony. The proceedings against them dragged on for over two years before any of them served time in prison. Then, in 1949, Red mania exploded on the front pages in even more virulent form, with the conviction of the former State Department official Alger Hiss on a charge of espionage – the first major political triumph of a young Republican Congressman, Richard Milhouse Nixon.

Politicians in both the Republican and Democrat Parties were now convinced that the very fabric of government was infested with Communist infiltrators. Perhaps the entire State Department was a nest of spies: could Franklin Delano Roosevelt have been a crypto-Commie? And what about Harry Truman? In these feverish times anything seemed possible to those blinkered by bigotry. Fuel was added to the flames when the Korean War broke out in June 1950.

HUAC remained the focus of the witch-hunt, but numerous self-appointed committees now sprang up like mushrooms, combing libraries and bookstores for Red propaganda. Reactionary sheets like *Red Channels* and the pamphlets issued by the Catholic Information Society fingered celebrities who had supported liberal causes and Communist 'front' organizations. Their model was *The Red Network*, published in the early 1930s by a fanatical night-winger. Elizabeth Dilling, who believed that the YMCA was a Communist 'front' and that Eleanor Roosevelt was a 'dangerous pacifist'.

And then there was Joseph McCarthy, an obscure junior Senator from Wisconsin, who on 9 February 1950 delivered a speech to the Women's Republican Club in Wheeling, West Virginia, in which he claimed to be in possession of a list of 205 employees of the State Department who were known to the Secretary of State Dean Acheson to be card-carrying Communists. In Wheeling itself, where McCarthy's campaign began, public-spirited citizens made a shattering discovery. Inside packets of a certain brand of ideologically sound US bubble gum were give-away cards informing unwary schoolchildren that the USSR, with its population of 211 million, had its capital in Moscow and was 'the largest country in the world.' The very foundations of democracy were trembling. The bubble-gum cards were seized and burnt.

After the bonfire a Mrs Thomas J. White, who sat on the Indiana State Textbook Commission, declared: 'There is a Communist directive now to stress the story of Robin Hood... because he robbed the rich and gave it to the poor. That's the Communist line. It's just a smearing of law and order.' McCarthy's bullying 'inquiries' lasted until April 1954, when the American people finally grew weary of him. It would be cheering to think that an overwhelming revulsion swept him away, but the truth is that McCarthy was one of the first great casualties of over-exposure on television. People simply grew bored with him.

Art for Art's Sake, Money for Christ's Sake

The most recent Hollywood furore stemmed from Martin Scorsese's *The Last Temptation of Christ*. Even while shooting was still in full swing, stories leaked out about the film's alleged debunking of Christ and glimpses of his sex life. The film, which twins Willem Defoe as Jesus and Barbara Hershey as Mary Magdalene, also portrays a 'wimpish' Christ in the eyes of the fundamentalists. Their consequent actions served to underline both their single-minded vigour as well as their financial clout.

First they offered to reimburse Universal for their $10 million plus expenditure on the film, so they could collect all the copies which they would then ceremoniously burn. Universal hit back via a series of newspaper advertisements:

> While we understand the deep feelings which have prompted this offer, we believe that to accept it would threaten the fundamental freedoms of religion and expression promised to all Americans under our Constitution.
> In the United States no one sect or coalition has the power to set boundaries around each person's freedom to explore religious or philosophical questions whether through speech, books, or film.
> These freedoms protect us all. They are precious. They are not for sale.

The reply from the aggrieved was as solid as ever. They felt the plans by MCA chairman Lew Wasserman and president Sid Sheinberg to proceed with the film's release

211

would fan the flames of anti-Semitism'. In other words the real sub-text was simply that two Jews (Wasserman and Sheinberg) had no business touching a picture which questioned the nature of Jesus Christ.

Aside from protests outside the Burbank offices of MCA, there were also anti-Jewish demonstrations outside the home of Wasserman himself. The Christians flew an airplane over his roof with a banner which proclaimed, 'Wasserman fans Jew hatred with Temptation'. Next they delivered an effigy of a blood-splattered Christ being ground into the earth by a businessman.

Jack Valenti, President of the Motion Picture Association of America, lent his muscle to the fight by helping Universal: 'No one,' he said, 'no matter how passionate their opposition, can or should prevent the entry of a point of view, whether it is creative, political or philosophical.'

On his side were a group of mainstream churchmen, none of whom, having been shown an unfinished version of the film by Scorsese, believed that it ought to be banned.

Scorsese, himself a deeply spiritual man who once trained for the priesthood, is the last director to make a two-cents version of the Christ story. You only have to examine his previous output to witness his obsession with the conflict between body and soul, material and spiritual. This did not deter the protesters who deemed it unnecessary to view a single frame of film.

Scorsese was clearly disturbed by the strength of the protests. He sincerely claimed that the film had been made 'with deep religious feeling. I believe it is a film about suffering and the struggle to find God. It was made with conviction and love, and so I believe it is an affirmation of faith, not a denial.'

'Further,' he went on, 'I feel strongly that people everywhere will be able to identify with the human side of Jesus as well as his divine side. I urge everyone to withhold judgement until we are able to screen the completed film.'

The Last Temptation of Christ was eventually released in the States in late September 1988 and in Britain shortly afterwards. Thankfully a planet away from the biblical epics in which actors talked to the sky, it is a personal look at the self-doubts which may well have gripped Jesus-the-man when asked to be Jesus-the-son-of-God. The censorious Christian zealots were eventually trampled underfoot and the producers cleaned up. Useful publicity full marks; outraged protesters zero.

A Sale of Two Titties

In 1943, the censors found something solid to cling to in the shape of Jane Russell's chest which had a lead part in Howard Hughes' *The Outlaw*. Afraid that Jane's best friends might cause grown-ups to go home and have sex, they enjoyed themselves thoroughly in the midst of controversy and litigation. Director Hughes found it tough to keep his camera from peeking down Jane's dress, and, when the drooling public was generously allowed in to see the film six years later, they found a lukewarm western featuring Russell's red-hot cleavage.

Filth Dressed as Art?

Censors the world over had fun with *Last Tango in Paris*. A record opening in Paris was followed by the film's confiscation in Italy, after which a court in Bologna refused to believe that it took 'persistent delight in arousing base, libidinous instincts.' United Artists, meanwhile, sneaked it into small theatres in New York, Los Angeles, Boston, Washington, Philadelphia and Toronto.

The whole episode was confused by some critics who regarded the sweaty writhings of Marlon Brando and

Maria Schneider as a movie milestone and others who regarded it as filth dressed as art. Bernardo Bertolucci, the director, pretentious as ever, played to the gallery of jabbering TV celebrities who had now joined in the spectacle, by exclaiming: 'Pornography is not in the hands of the child who discovers his sexuality by masturbating, but in the hands of the adult who slaps him.' Quite.

For once one almost felt sorry for the censors as they slithered in the mud, desperately trying to shape public taste. Emerging in this case as perplexed humans, they are more often regarded as well-dressed bores who live in a cupboard.

Absence of Malice?

It was after the 1982 Academy Awards that an aggrieved film fan felt moved enough to place an ad in the pages of *Daily Variety*. It read: To the members of the Academy: I would sincerely like you to see *The Verdict* once more and tell me what Paul Newman has to do to win an Academy Award.

Supervisor Ed Jones
Ventura County

Newman had yet again been cheated of his due. Critically acclaimed for his role as a boozy, self-doubting lawyer, the five-times nominee was hungering for the top prize. Throughout the year staff at 20th Century-Fox had referred to *The Verdict* as Paul Newman's Academy Award movie. Newman's own view, declared to *Time* magazine, was that, 'It was such a relief to let it all hang out in the movie – blemishes and all.'

Needless to say, when the critics once again spoke sense, the Oscar decision-makers recoiled. In the *New York Times* Janet Maeslin wrote: 'A solidly old-fashioned courtroom drama such as *The Verdict* could have gotten by with a serious measured performance from its leading man or it could have worked well with a dazzling movie-star turn. The fact that Paul Newman delivers both makes a clever, suspenseful, enthralling movie even better.'

Still, the Oscar flame had already scorched Newman back in 1964 when the Awards were trotted out for the past year's work, which included *Hud*. Back then the *New Yorker* was bold enough to print: 'The Academy may as well give him an Oscar right now and get it over with.'

The picture was so powerful that critics felt it could do no wrong. *Daily Variety* led the pack at an early stage: 'A picture comes along and grabs you by the throat. You sit there, spellbound. You say, "This is the way it really is." You don't merely see the picture, you live it. And when it's over, you've changed. You see life in a new way. *Hud* is such a motion picture.'

The *New York Times* expertly tapped the core of the movie: 'A drama of moral corruption – of the debilitating disease of avaricious self-seeking – that is creeping across the land and infecting the minds of young people in this complex, materialistic age.'

Bosley Crowther loved *Hud* because it seemed to him, 'a profound contemplation of the human condition'. One suspects, however, that what the mass audience most enjoyed was watching the swaggering Newman, all curling lip and arrogant stare, eat people up as an amoral Texan who, by fooling around with countless girls, causes a squeaky clean community to break out in a collective rash. *Life* neatly summed up Newman's appeal: 'Hud is the sort of non-hero who has become Paul Newman's special province.'

The whole picture scored with glowing reviews for other performers as well. Melvyn Douglas (the pure-at-heart patriarch), Brandon de Wilde (the naïve nephew) and Patricia Neal (the housekeeper Newman tries to rape) were all allowed to bask in the critical spotlight. De Wilde, in fact, was finally the only lead from *Hud* who was not nominated for an Oscar.

And yet, despite a set of great performances, it was Newman who swamped the picture. Director Martin Ritt was able to tap Newman's cool stare and brooding presence and employ it to not only define the behaviour of the other characters but to dominate the entire film. When his name was called up during the readout from the podium, he received an especially warm round of applause, but no Oscar (Newman finally received an Oscar in 1986 for *Color of Money*).

The Politics of Envy

Fortunately, Steven Spielberg has a beard to help bury his anxiety. It is quite outrageous that he is regularly cold-shouldered by Tinseltown's venerable rulers who presumably deeply resent the success which was his from the word go. He had barely left film school when, at 25, he directed *Duel* in 1971 for CBS and proved himself an edge-of-the-seat talent. Despite his untainted track record (apart from the bitsy *1941* which almost blew the bank for two studios), he has always been kept at arm's length by those who turn a deeper shade of green at the thought of his achievements.

That he has almost single-handedly brought back millions to the cinema the world over and also makes terrific movies is clearly not a prerequisite for Oscar success. Much better to dish out the golden trophy to some third-rate slodge whose director is not a threat. To boot, Spielberg is also a decent chap which is bound to boost the hatred factor against him. Now that his long-time lover and current wife Amy Irvine is about to prise his squillions from him via the divorce courts, he might just be brought more into the Hollywood fold. If, in court, he is seen to

have been fooling around, or, alternatively, to be a beard-
ed devil, he will surely be acclaimed as 'one of the boys'
and so go on to reach Oscars-a-plenty.

For now, though, he is isolated by success. How could
he have felt, when, sitting there watching a procession of
colleagues go forward to claim their statuettes, he was
completely ignored at the 1977 Academy Awards? *Close
Encounters of the Third Kind* had shown itself to be a creative and commercial smash and shot Spielberg into the
superleague.

Even during shooting there were rumours that *Encounters*
was something special. The *New York Times* printed that
the feature 'has been cloaked in almost as much secrecy as
the Manhattan [atomic bomb] Project.' *Time* magazine had
its foot firmly jammed in the studio door and could only
come up with: 'Cast and crew have been forbidden to discuss the movie's contents in interviews – security guards
have watched over its sets round the clock, at one point
assiduously ejecting Spielberg when he showed up without his ID badge.'

Richard Dreyfuss, who played lead in the movie, ignored
the press for some time until he finally blustered: 'If I told
you anything Steve would kill me. All I can say is that in
Jaws, the shark was the star of the film; in this film, the film
is the star of the film. 'Spielberg himself admitted to
American Film: 'I didn't clamp the lid down because of
egocentric reasons...I wanted to surprise. And the only
way in the world you're going to do that is by keeping
quiet about what's in it.'

Columbia's top brass leaked sweat when a journalist
from *New York* magazine used bribery to glean a ticket for
the film's first preview (a semi-secret low-key screening) in
Dallas, and later wrote: 'I can understand all the appre-
hension. In my humble opinion, the picture will be a
colossal flop.' The studio's cage was rattled even further
when share prices dropped at once, but it gritted its teeth

anyway and flew in critics from every corner of the States to meet Spielberg and his cast. They appeared sincere when they gushed: 'I want to thank you, Steven, for giving us this film' (producer Michael Phillips); and, 'I think of it as a religious film' (actress Melinda Dillon).

These US critics, and most others the world over, were next to make the intruder from New York a complete fool. The reviews were quite sensational, and 'masterpiece', 'creative heights' and 'Spielberg is King' littered newspaper columns around the world. Rona Barrett, normally of the 'please-me-or-forget-it' school of sensitivity, was soon frothing at both ends: 'An incredible experience,' she wrote, 'Steven Spielberg proves himself to be a consummate movie-maker and an artist of rare insight.'

Encounters simultaneously hit the cover of Newsweek in which Jack Kroll scribbled: '*Close Encounters* is the friendliest, warmest science-fiction epic you've ever seen. It brings the heavens down to earth.' Roy Bradbury in the *Los Angeles Times* let his enthusiasm rip: '*Close Encounters* is, in all probability, the most important film of our time.'

There was only the odd sourpuss. One of them was Rex Reed who grumbled about 'a wasteful depressing failure....Living in New York, I'm surrounded by enough intergalactic freaks already.' Clearly movie fans did not agree with old Rex. Queueing from day one, they have succeeded in making the film one of Columbia's most lucrative films ever.

With the run-up to the Oscars the fangs were out to give Spielberg a nasty bite. When it was announced that he had not even been nominated in the 'Best Picture' category, it was generally perceived that Steven was not the most popular kid on the block, even if he was the most talented. By being refused that nomination, he ended up in the tacky company of *Saturday Night Fever* which, although it had entertained millions, was hardly a creative first like Encounters.

The *Christian Science Monitor* quite rightly fumed: 'What happened to *Close Encounters of the Third Kind*? Its blood brother, *Star Wars*, is lots of fun, but the picture that represents a whole year should have more heft – which is exactly what *Close Encounters* has to offer.'

Spielberg knew he would be boxing with his chum George Lucas, who had made *Star Wars*, in the 'Best Director' category, but Spielberg was clearly the better choice, since he laced his special effects with deep human experience and credible acting. As it was, *Close Encounters* was embarrassingly absent from the most prestigious categories but did manage to score a first for 'Best Cinematography', and secured a begrudging additional prize for sound effects editing.

By 1982 it seemed as if *ET* might finally fly the flag for Spielberg at that year's Academy Awards. With great reviews, it also broke all existing box-office records from day one and did in fact manage to collect nine nominations. Rex Reed got it right this time when he wrote back from the Cannes Film Festival, trumpeting that Spielberg 'showed the Godards and the Antonionis and the Fassbinders who had bored everyone into a state of catatonia for the previous two weeks how real movies are made.' Sheila Benson of the *Los Angeles Times* made even Reed's proclamation seem shy by comparison: 'It may be the film of the decade and possibly the double decade.' Even the *New Yorker*'s notorious Pauline Kael enthused that it was 'a dream of a movie – a bliss out'.

'ET phone home' was the year's catch phrase. It adorned bumper stickers, political cartoons and entered conversations all over the world. Neil Diamond was so moved that he recorded 'Turn on Your Heart Light' which tweaked American heartstrings and became a must for weddings and bar mitzvahs. After Spielberg licensed more than 50 entrepreneurs to sell *ET* to the universe, the billions rolled in.

But on Awards night *ET* was soundly trounced by *Gandhi*,

Sir Richard Attenborough's eulogy on a great man. Attenborough is typical of the kind of dull British director who can turn sparkling material into a routine exercise. Hamstrung by its theatrical approach, Gandhi was a linear plod which threw up one damn experience after another. Praised for months in advance because of its respectably serious subject-matter, and with Attenborough blabbing on to countless journalists, it was the ideal film to expose Hollywood's hypocrisy. It so often turns its back on the populist pictures which earn the millions required to keep the whole industry afloat and instead opts for decent-but-dull arthouse fodder so as to tart up its tarnished credibility.

Vincent Canby of the *New York Times* was furious: '*ET* and *Tootsie* are films. *Gandhi* is a laboriously illustrated textbook.' His colleague Janet Maslin agreed: 'Someday, the sweep that brought *Gandhi* eight Awards may be known as one of the great injustices in the annals of Oscardom.'

Spielberg, nice guy that he is, sat on his pride though it must have been difficult. Trying to joke around, he said, 'Look we tried our best. We stuffed the ballot boxes, we just didn't stuff them enough.' To the *Los Angeles Times* he said, 'We were almost precluded from awards because people feel we've already been amply rewarded. . .The tendency is for important films to win over popcorn entertainment. History is more weighty than popcorn.'

Who's Afraid of Richard Burton?

Richard Burton was another to find himself cheated by the suits who run the Academy. Before the 1970 Awards, at which he was up for 'Best Actor' for *Anne of the Thousand Days*, he quipped: 'Oh, I suppose 30 years from now Peter O'Toole and I will still be appearing on talk shows plugging for our first Oscar.' This, the fourth nomination for Peter O'Toole, for *Goodbye Mr. Chips*, was already Burton's fifth.

Elizabeth Taylor, not surprisingly, indicated where her preference for the Award lay: 'We want Richard to win an Oscar,' she exclaimed. 'I've won an Award. Richard never has you know.'

Unlike the 1966 ceremony where Burton and Taylor were nominated for *Who's Afraid of Virginia Woolf* (She won), they decided to attend this time round. Indeed Liz explained to CBS that she regretted that her husband had not won for *Virginia Woolf*, since she considered it 'his greatest performance because the weak character is so unlike him.'

Newspaper stories at the time revolved around Liz's intention to wear the $1.5 million diamond necklace which Burton had given her. Yet even it was upstaged by Taylor as she failed to mask her disappointment when Burton fell at the final hurdle.

Their desolation could not have been helped by John Wayne who scooped first prize for *True Grit*. Backstage, he told a reporter from the *Oklahoma City Oklahoman* the following: 'It's ironic that I got the Oscar for a role that was the easiest of my career. I just hippity-hopped through it.'

Oscar's Origins

Perhaps the greatest Oscar scandal of all concerns the reason for the Academy's existence in the first place.

In 1926 Hollywood was film-factory and Louis B. Mayer, the snarling despot at Metro-Goldwyn-Mayer, was the biggest of the studio barons. Keen to keep power confined to a few hands, preferably his own, he founded the Academy as a means of thwarting the unions which studio craftsmen were queueing up to join.

Things reached a pretty pass when Louis B. instructed the studio art director to build him a brand new house. He spat fire when he learnt that unionized studio labour would be unsuitable since it cost way too much. Enter Louis with big muscles and hefty jackboots.

Over Sunday dinner at his now-finished Santa Monica beach house, he concocted a body which would mediate labour disputes, give a PR gloss to the entire film industry and also be an elite club which would stage yearly banquets. When he snuck in his two lawyers, Edwin Loeb and George W. Cohen (known as ' the father of motion-picture contracts'), Louis's charitable intentions were plain as pie.

To read Hollywood is to be master of the sub-plot. When next you see a glossy, tanned star thanking his mother for having the foresight to give birth to him, just think that the expensive party which gives out the Academy Awards was an attempt to squash the slaves who built Hollywood. Under every smile a scandal.

'Where's the Rest of Me?'

What about the blissful twinning of old gunslinger Ronnie Reagan with Jane Wyman? Hedda and Louella and all Hollywood had them marked as the most together couple in town. Certainly it was not only impossible to imagine them having sex outside of their marriage, or perhaps even within it, but it also seemed unlikely that they ever even had rows about who would put the cat out at night.

So their 1949 divorce shook whatever grip morality still exerted on Tinseltown. Rattled to the back teeth, onlookers soon realized that hard-headed jealousy and biting resentment were the cause. In 1948 Reagan admitted to Hedda Hopper: 'If this comes to a divorce I think I'll name *Johnny Belinda* co-respondent.' This was the 1948 film in which Wyman was such a knockout as a deaf-mute that she scooped up an Oscar at a time when Ronnie, whose acting style consisted of pointing his suit at the camera, was almost disappearing from sight. (It was his ultimate screen triumph as President which would restore his fortunes in later years.) In the months following Wyman's Oscar success, the cute couple was out for dinner one evening. The waiter, with sarcastically raised eyebrows, asked; 'And what will Mr. Wyman have?'

The only 3-D performance which Reagan managed to squeeze from his cardboard character was his role as amputee Drake McHugh in *King's Row*, directed by Sam Wood in 1942. Upon waking up after losing both his legs in an altercation with a train, the future President of the US uttered the immortal words: 'Where's the rest of me?' Savouring it as his best performance, Ronnie modestly screened it to guest after guest at his dinner parties. When the marriage was crumbling into tiny pieces, Jane said to a friend, 'I just couldn't watch that damned *King's Row* anymore.' In the divorce courts she tactfully referred to his new fascination with politics as the main reason.

However, Reagan was not one to give a tarnished image much elbow room. Proving even at this early stage that he had the non-stick quality which kept dirt at a distance, he met his present wife Nancy Davis (born Anne Frances Robbins) and soon swung back onto the track of decency. They first met when gleaming Ron was the liberal president of the Screen Actors' Guild and Nancy was a true-blue who was ridiculously suspected of Commie connections. More daft a link is difficult to imagine. Taking her out to dinner to indicate that they had pointed the finger at the wrong Nancy Davies, Ron got heavily involved with a woman who, in *The Next Voice You Hear*, heard the voice of God on the radio. She married Reagan in 1953.

Nancy certainly seems to have squeezed any namby-pamby liberal tendencies out of her husband. A reasonable Democrat in an earlier life, he now fired off broadsides against homosexuals (as Governor of California, he fired two of his staff for being gay) and indulged in right-wing knee-jerking to such an extent that he was fired as a TV presenter from 'General Electric Theater'.

Ronnie seems to have been a toy in Nancy's hands. Her surgeon stepfather was said to have been 'intolerant of minorities'. To the astonishment of the press hacks at a Chicago fundraiser in 1980, she gushed to her hubby over an amplified phone line that she wished he could be there to 'see all these beautiful white people.'

In Like Clint

Just as solid as Ron and Nancy were Clint and Maggie Eastwood. Despite the queue of lovelies present on any film lot for a hoped-for fling with Dirty Harry, the chin himself was seemingly devoted to Maggie and the two kids. He would go to any lengths to protect them from press snooping.

Sondra Locke, who Clint is eventually married, first popped up to act in *The Outlaw Josey Wales* in 1976, after which she returned to face Clint in *The Gauntlet*. The crew noticed the closeness of the couple and notions of a romance were paraded in print when they turned up for the première of a film called *First Love*. It was generally felt that they were having a close encounter of the first kind.

It was agent William Morris who jammed his foot firmly in his mouth when he said: 'We understand Clint is looking for a script as a basis for another movie in which Miss Sondra Locke will star. He will perhaps both direct and star opposite her in any new film.'

From this point on Sondra was never off the screen. *Every Which Way But Loose* in 1978 led to *Any Which Way You Can* and *Bronco Billy*, both in 1980. For a man who claims to shun the limelight, it was a mite foolish to take Sondra along to a celebrity motor race after which Miss Locke clumsily exclaimed: 'Everybody would love for us to say, "Its all true, we are madly in love." But people will believe whatever they want to believe. Even if it was true – which it isn't – I certainly would not talk about it.'

Maggie must have felt like an island. She had clung to Clint during the TV series 'Rawhide', including the time when it was temporarily cancelled, and backed him in his decision to make *A Fistful of Dollars*, the first of the 'Spaghetti Westerns' in 1964, when others advised against it.

She also had a relaxed attitude towards his celebrity status. Once when sitting outside an Italian café, Clint was asked to pose with a beautiful Oriental model. Soon the picture appeared with the caption: 'Could this love affair end in marriage?' Maggie was good at laughing all this off.

Clint once talked to a journalist about other women: 'I guess Maggie understands these are the hazards of my business, but Maggie is a very smart lady. I respect her and her opinions, although we don't always agree.'

To another he let a small but significant cat out of the bag. 'Maggie doesn't own me. The worst thing is owning people. I don't want to own anybody; shared maybe, but not own lock, stock and barrel.'

He continued: 'To me love for a person is respect for feelings. Love is respecting privacy, accepting faults, but I don't believe it's a one-way street. The sophisticated woman accepts that the chances are a guy's not being 100 percent faithful.'

Exit Clint from his $3 million house, leaving Maggie with Kyle, ten, and Alison, six. After deciding to kick Clint down the garden path for good, she has since emerged to successfully claim his millions.

In topsy-turvy Tinseltown, where suburbanites are really sex fiends, and half-baked actors later come out of hiding to run the world, it comes as no surprise to find that marriage is often shown the door along with honesty, decency, trust and other interfering virtues.

Time of Corruption

In a recent edition of the August *New York Times*, three of its best reporters commented on the far-reaching nature of corruption. Robert Lindsey, Jeff Gerth and Aljean Harmetz wrote of 'a pattern of questionable financial practices throughout the motion picture industry. According to Columbia and law enforcement sources, the film business is permeated by financial irregularities that extend from the executive suite to the movie backlot to the local theater box office...'

It was Richard Brooks, the Academy Award-winning writer and director who said ten years ago: 'Nobody can skim as well as Las Vegas because they invented it. But Hollywood is second. It's a time of corruption.'

Brooks's utterances came in the aftermath of the greatest Hollywood financial scandal in years, that of David Begelman and the forged cheques in 1978. This had such an unsettling effect throughout the entire industry that it has seen executives clinging to their cashmere coats with guilt and actors looking at them sideways even more than before.

The long and complex saga which was to unseat Begelman (then president of Columbia) began with an everyday meeting between actor Cliff Robertson (best known for his 1976 lead role in *Obsession*) and his secretary Evelyn Christel who arrived at the Robertson residence on 25 February 1977 to leaf through the day's correspondence.

Robertson, whose strict presbyterian upbringing made him a stickler for right and wrong, was already scoffed at in Hollywood because he led a satisfying family life and didn't need the industry. In amongst the usual correspondence was a tax statement which claimed that Robertson had received a cheque the previous year for $10,000 and would he be so kind as to cough up the tax on it. Seeing that Cliff had done no work for Columbia during this period, it struck him as just slightly odd.

As gestures of good will from the studios, actors and directors are often paid lump sums on an ad hoc basis so that loyalty and cordial relations can be maintained. It is not unusual, for example, for a director to be given a spanking new limousine at the end of a shoot.

After persistent enquiries by Robertson and his secretary, Columbia claimed the $10,000 had been paid to assist Robertson on the promotional tour for *Obsession*. Clearly more than Robertson would be likely to spend in those circumstances, such a fistful comes fittingly into the 'goodwill' category. Yet Robertson had never received such a cheque so he wasn't too keen to pay tax on it.

After negotiating the complex web that is now Hollywood. Robertson eventually discovered that Begelman had forged a cheque in his name and received $10,000 in American Express travellers' cheques.

After the details of Begelman's crimes were teased out in court, it was revealed that the president of Columbia had pocketed a mere $60,000. A manic greed seemed to be driving the personality of a man who had been earning an easy third of a million dollars per year.

Just when Begelman was being traumatized by current complainants, up popped the spectre of Sid Luft who thought the time was ripe to revive a lawsuit. The ex-husband of Judy Garland, he had filed a suit against Begelman in 1966, accusing him of writing phoney cheques on his wife's account.

Luft's suspicion of Begelman went back as far as 1961 when Garland hired Begelman (then an agent) to manage her affairs. It was two years later when Luft regained control of his wife's career that he and his accountant found discrepancies in the books.

First off were 13 cheques for $36,000 which Begelman had forged in Garland's name and cashed in at different Las Vegas hotels. Next to flee Miss Garland's cosy nestegg was the tidy sum of $50,000 which sped its way from a Garland account in London to a mystery account in New York. Guess whose? Then, by what must surely have been an error of bureaucracy, a further $10,000 was switched from an account, which honest Dave held in trust for Garland, to an account in his own name.

Finally, there was the matter of an expensive Cadillac which Judy should have received for her appearance on the Jack Paar TV show in 1962. Registered in the name of Begelman, it was a luxury to which Garland never even knew she was entitled! The fleecing of Judy assumes a particularly sad twist when it was revealed by two of her children, Liza Minelli and Joseph Luft, that their mother had died a virtual bankrupt.

Despite the gravity of his crimes, Begelman received only three years' probation and a $5,000 fine which is apparently appropriate for a first offender in the realm of grand theft. In sentencing Begelman, Judge Thomas Murphy graphically outlined Begelman's greed through-innocence: 'if you had painted your hand red and let it drip on the floor you couldn't have better called your crime to anyone's attention.'

As well as being ordered into psychiatric care, he was also instructed to produce something of benefit to the community. The result was *Angel Death*, a documentary on the legal dangers of drug abuse. Perhaps a full-blown feature on the fatal attraction of hard cash would have been more suitable. Michael Douglas and *Wall Street* had yet to arrive.

Yet the startling aspect of the Begelman scandal was not simply that a millionaire would go to such grasping lengths to cheat that extra dollar from an ignorant victim but the effect these revelations had in Hollywood.

Columbia, despite being rattled to the back teeth, consoled its shareholders with the solid fact that its then current biggie, *Close Encounters of the Third Kind*, had just topped $50 million at the box office. The super-sell of toys, T-shirts and assorted trivia would be certain to placate them even more.

Fixing the Books

But elsewhere the sordid scandal caused plenty of high-profile reaction. Fraud was now revealed as a natural part of everyday life in Tinseltown: bribes to studio executives from independent producers eager to secure backing, the pocketing of money from production budgets by cash-hungry producers, not to mention the concealment of profits by distributors and the outright lies of cinema owners about the number of tickets sold.

One famous result was the filing of a suit against Allied Artists by Sean Connery and Michael Caine, who insisted loudly that the profits they were due from *The Man Who Would Be King* (1978) had never arrived in the post. After filing in a New York court, Connery explained: 'I've never stolen from anybody in my life. To work in good faith and be cheated is wrong; I'm tired of being robbed.' More courageous than most actors perhaps because he is more secure in his career and star-status, Connery was till then one of the few to have complained in public.

Now actors lined up to vent their wrath on their employers. Many complained that overheads, distribution, equipment hire, and even advertising publicity and phone calls, were being deducted from the cost of the picture before they received their share. Robert Montgomery, a New York lawyer, commented: 'I don't think this is cheating in the criminal sense, but I do think managements take advantage of every possibility available to them.'

Next to mouth off as a result of Begelman's antics were the cinema owners who complained about the shoddy behaviour of the big studios. 20th Century-Fox ended up in court trying to fend off the accusation that they would only release the highly lucrative *Star Wars* to some cinemas provided these venues would allow themselves to be lumbered with *The Other Side of Midnight*, which was then trying to scratch a living. Marvin Goldman, president of the National Association of Theater Owners, summed up national feeling which had exploded as a result of Begelman and his paltry cheques. 'I think if our industry was held up to the light and you shook it a lot of worms would fall out.'

The Film That Sank a Studio

The other major modern financial scandal has to be the mad wastage behind the making of *Heaven's Gate* by Michael Cimino, the man who made *The Deer Hunter*. *Heaven's Gate*, released in 1980, is a film that has become synonymous with massive egos, chronic mismanagement, epic malpractice and spending sums equivalent to the annual turnover of small nations. So great was the disaster that it sank United Artists for good.

A big screen western with a production budget of $7.5 million finally cost $36 million. Decisions about the movie were being made by people who were thousands of miles apart and who were not even in regular contact. Cimino even managed to keep the film from his employers so that they were unable to see a single frame before the disastrous opening night.

One of the many blunders was that Cimino, inexplicably, had never actually signed the budget agreement. Lawyers began to pull out their hair as they tried to give some legal substance to the studio's insistence on keeping costs down. Meanwhile the maverick Cimino, whose obsessive perfectionism was an equal match for his outsize ego, was flagrantly defying orders from Hollywood.

By placing cast and crew on call and on overtime, he hoped to finish the film to meet the Christmas 1979 deadline. Instead the work schedule expanded to fill those extra hours so that, as it was later calculated, a day was lost for each day shot. Normal rates were boosted by double time and triple time on Sundays, while enough film to stretch round the planet and back was causing the Hollywood bosses to bark like mad dogs.

On the set itself there was no frenzy whatsoever as Cimino fed hundreds of thousands of feet of film into his constantly whirring cameras in an all-out attempt at perfection. Everything moved at a pace which, if any slower, would have ground proceedings to a halt. Frantic accountants had by now worked out that production costs had shot into the twilight zone and were running at over $1 million a week.

Executive Derek Kavanagh flew to Montana where the film was being shot. As well as examining the amount of screen-time shot, he also scrutinized camera and production reports and rounded up accounts paid and owing. He concluded that shooting would never be completed by Christmas and remarked too that certain local roads were to close for a time and so the schedule would be stretched even further.

Cimino, he calculated, was running through a massive two hours of film to shoot just over half a script page, which would eventually result in only 2 minutes on the screen. For this freewheeling addiction to his art, he was burning up $200,000 a day.

Before the prologue and epilogue were added to the film, not to mention expensive post-production, the total for shooting came to $27,024,884.29. These add-ons caused the budget to sky-rocket to $44 million (now including promotional costs), a figure which seems to knowingly mock the first budget estimate of $7.5 million.

Cimino's big-headed notion of art at any price is crazy when you realize that a film is not a personal whim which is exercised in a commercial vacuum but a product which has to be made, sold and marketed like any other.

That the film was trashed by critics and ignored by the public highlights even more the foolishness at the heart of its making. Hollow laughter could be heard throughout Hollywood. Artistic holes abound in a movie which shunts credible characters and storylines aside in its mad pursuit of wide-screen effects. Cimino's obsession with detail ensured that characters were two-dimensional and left most audiences stone cold. However, since the film was re-released in a form close to its original length, it has been re-appraised by some critics. But the public still has yet to flock.

Burning Banknotes

The carefree spending on *Heaven's Gate* seemed to hit Hollywood like a nasty disease. *Star Trek* (1979), *The Wiz* (1978), *The Blue Brothers* (1980), *Reds* (1981), *Raise The Titanic* (1980) (which sank Lew Grade) and *1941* (1979) (with which golden boy Stephen Spielberg almost sank two studios) all notched up budgets of between $25-30 million.

Certain expensive failures have also been largely due to a surreal mismatch of man and material. Which studio greysuit could have possibly thought that John Schiesinger, he of *Far From the Madding Crowd* (1967) in screen and *Der Rosenkavalier* at Covent Garden, would be the perfect choice for *Honky Tonk Freeway* (1981) whose cast of loopy characters required a less straight-laced director?

Or who mistakenly thought that Hugh Hudson, director of *Chariots of Fire* (1981), possessed a natural empathy for the American War of Independence and so allowed him to burn banknotes on *Revolution* (1985). Luciano Pavarotti sang perfectly well in *Yes, Giorgio* (1982), but was risible in his attempts to carry on a screen romance, while the unfettered creativity of Roman Polanski was quite wrong for the literal-minded nature of *Pirates* (1986). All these films, which lost fortunes, were part of a new era of the colossal overspend.

This is the sort of bone-headed profligacy and idiotic tunnel vision which hits Hollywood for six. In a brief two week period during summer 1984, the top management of three studios were all shown the door, while within three years of the *Heaven's Gate* free-for-all the same switch had occurred in every major Hollywood production company. It only takes a self-serving director on a set, with an ego larger than the budget available for his entire production, or a smooth-talking executive who fancies a spot of extra cash, to cause thunderbolts throughout an industry which is just learning to walk again. The cigar-chomping chin-jutting mogul is a favourite image of Hollywood which has been diluted to the level of strip cartoon. Stand-up comics both here and in America, as well as our own Goons and Pythons, have relished acting out the universally accepted caricature of the barking studio head who acts on whim and impulse and fires people he doesn't even employ.

Yet those comic creations sprang originally from a close-knit batch of Hollywood bosses whose obsessive spite and malice caused them to break employees or competitors into tiny pieces.

Joseph Patrick Kennedy hid much beneath the schoolboy grin and rogue-Irish charm. Later to bathe in the reflected glory of his gleaming family, it seems almost impossible to believe that he was possessed of a streak so harsh that he could box men into a corner so they could scarcely breath.

Harry the Hustler

An obsession with movie-making certainly kept hell-fire tactics in their place. A telling encounter between a writer and Harry Cohn, who ruled Columbia Pictures, speaks volumes:

'Whaddaya been doing?' Cohn asked the writer, whom he had not seen in some time.

'I've been in retirement writing a book.' Answered the writer.

'Is there a picture in it?' demanded Cohn.

'No, I don't think so.'

'Too bad,' ended Cohn, 'I'd like to have read it.'

The business clout, Jewish wit, dismissive manner and obsession with movies is the substance of a conversation which could have been held between young writer and any one of the maverick studio bosses.

Harry Cohn, the most savage of dictators, was named 'White Fang' by writer Ben Hecht. Jewish by birth and of mixed German-Russian parentage, he seemed keener than the others to squash his roots to the point where he often sounded anti-Semitic. Once at a large party which he was hosting for studio staff, he commented on the mass rush to the buffet table, by spitting out disparagingly, 'Look at those Jews eat.'

As a youngster in New York City, he had shifted around as a pool hustler, song plugger and trolley bus driver. In his driving job he was so adept at creaming the takings that his bosses always told him that they were glad he had the decency to bring the bus back at night.

From the early 1920s to the late 1950s Cohn ran an empire which produced *It Happened One Night* (1934), *All the King's Men* (1949), *From Here to Eternity* (1953) and *The*

Bridge On the River Kwai (1957). Yet his workaholic employees who made these films possible knew the darker meaning of Cohn's maxim: 'He who eats my bread and sings my song.'

Cohn had been trying for a long time to lure a bright, thoughtful and sensitive young chap to Columbia. When the twin weapons of persuasion and charm failed – and Cohn could easily summon up charm at will – dollars and power were offered up instead. When appointed as an executive producer with a hefty bank balance, the young fellow at once set to work on a script with two writers. Cohn himself offered a batch of ideas which were rejected by the creative threesome. The new arrival complained to Cohn that the vote was three to one in their favour. 'You're wrong,' explained Cohn, 'it's one to nothing.'

Cohn fired the two writers immediately and from that day on reserved his meanest remarks for the producer. Over dinner in the corporate dining room he would turn to the young man with the abusive question. 'All right, Jewboy, what do you think?', while on one memorable occasion, as a number of Columbia big-shots were about to shoot off to a preview, he smiled at his victim with the remark – 'Who do you think your wife's fucking tonight?' Shortly after this the put-upon employee fled Cohn and his venom.

At press conferences to announce a new film, Cohn constantly referred to the male and female leads as 'the prick and the cunt' Plenty of written evidence quotes Cohn as remarking 'This time the prick will be played by. . .and the cunt by. . .'

Even his own family was not spared. On one occasion, when Sam Goldwyn and his wife came to dinner, Cohn received a call which caused him to break out in the most vulgar expletives. This coincided with one of his sons coming downstairs to wish his parents goodnight. Goldwyn, himself a hated studio head, butted in: 'Harry, you shouldn't talk like that in front of the boy. It's not right.'

'It's time he learned,' snapped Cohn and continued breathing foul abuse down the phone.

Unsurprisingly, Cohn became a major fan of Benito Mussolini after making a documentary on him so he went to visit the dictator in Italy. He loved the complex web of corridors which led to his office as well as the raised circular desk which lent Il Duce the proper pomposity. On his return to Hollywood, Cohn modelled his own office after it, refusing, like Mussolini, to take Novocaine for pain and kept the despot's photograph on his desk until he became unpopular,

As super-salesmen for the concept of the Free World through screens across the world, the most powerful men in showbusiness were in fact practising a tyranny which so many new immigrants had fled in the old world and which had no place in countless film versions of the American Dream.

'He Bit Me on the Breast'

One story in particular shows his poisonous drive. It centres on the supposed encounter between one Eunice Pringle, a teenage waster who dreamed of neon lights, and Alexander Pantages, an energetic entrepreneur who owned the Hollywood Pantages, the first really impressive art deco cinema. The theatre, in fact, lives on even now as a convenient stop-off for touring Broadway musicals. He also ran a less grandiose cinema in downtown Los Angeles. It was here that Pringle collapsed into noisy hysterics after her supposed rape by Pantages.

A cinema employee was startled to witness the plump Eunice, wrapped in a revealing red dress, running terrified from the caretaker's broom cupboard. With shrieks-aplenty which could easily be heard by the audience above the soundtrack of the movie they were watching, she pointed accusingly at a respectable-looking, well-groomed man who was in his office next to the broom cupboard. It was, of course, Pantages. The panicky Pantages declared himself innocent to a traffic policeman who had by now been called in to investigate.

Pantages was an immigrant from Athens who splendidly exemplified the American Dream. Having sold papers and shone shoes, he vanished to Alaska during the Klondike gold strike and returned with a stash of gold nuggets. He bought his first theatre, a vaudeville venue in Seattle and, with his flair for energetic promotion, kept the public flooding in. Adding films to the bill, he soon built up his collection to 60 theatres which stretched from Canada to Mexico. By 1929 Pantages had amassed a fortune of $30 million.

However, in court his gruff, broken English did not appeal to the jury who by now had been fed constant descriptions of Eunice as 'the sweetest seventeen since Clara Bow' (*Herald-Examiner*), and 'a full-blown beauty' (*Los Angeles Times*).

To bolster the effect she turned up in court wearing a girlish frock of which Mary Pickford would have been proud and the kind of flat shoes which hardly suggest temptation. Claiming that she had gone to the cinema to show Pantages a new act she had developed, she then proceeded to intricately detail the encounter in the broom cupboard.

'He said he wanted me for his sweetheart. I told him I was not interested in sweethearts. I was interested in work, but he continued his advances. He seemed to go crazy. He clapped his hand over my mouth – he bit me on the breast.' Fainting immediately, she came round to find her dress hoisted and Pantages' privates on parade. With her girlish air and home-spun clothing, how could the jury resist Eunice? They could not.

Despite Pantages' protestations that with sex being freely available throughout movieland, he had no need to resort to rape in a broom cupboard, and despite noisy rumours that Eunice's agent was a sharp practitioner who had used her as part of some scam, Pantages was sent down for 59 years.

A timely first which was to leave an indelible mark on the law courts also served to help Pantages. His lawyer, Jerry Geisler, succeeded in gaining permission for the morals of a minor to be held up for inspection in court. Waving his evidence in front of the California Supreme Court, Geisler secured a re-trial for 1931. Declaring that 'the testimony of the prosecutrix was so improbable as to challenge credulity' and watching Geisler and Ehrlich, his associate, enact the supposed rape in court, they concluded that the assault described by Eunice would have been impossible in a broom cupboard.

An old lady who managed the Moonbeam Glen Bungalow Court, where Pringle and her devious agent had lived as man and wife, was wheeled on as an eleventh hour witness. Not particularly willing to help Pantages, she was confronted by extensive Bible readings from Ehrlich who convinced her of her moral duty. She singled out the conniving Eunice as a tenant and so Pantages finally savoured justice.

This is where the beaming Joe Kennedy comes in. Kennedy acquired RKO through his movie company FBO. RKO was quick to devour the Orpheum cinema circuit whose only rival on the West Coast was, surprise, surprise, Pantages. Eunice finally confessed on her deathbed in the manner of gripping Hollywood melodrama that it was mogul Joe, the father of a future president, who had secured Eunice's compliance in the stitch-up so that Pantages would become an immediate nonentity and leave his cinema chain up for grabs. However, thanks to the maverick efforts of Jerry Geisler, who now leapt from backroom lawyer to the grand heights of 'Lawyer to the Stars', Kennedy's scheme never got off the starting block. Although this seedy incident squashed his ambitions as a big-shot movie-man, it did not deter him from quickly entering the equally morally ambiguous arena of national politics.

A neat irony completes the story. With Kennedy shunted aside, Warner Brothers took over the theatre where the incident occurred and later screened all the movies by Errol Flynn. It was the legal breakthrough which Geisler achieved that was of direct help to Flynn when he was maliciously accused of rape by two underage girls.

Hollywood Schmollywood

This sly scheme of Kennedy's seems the last word in civilized behaviour when compared to the rough-shod tactics of the other upstart moguls. Eastern European cities like Warsaw, Kiev and Minsk had propelled towards America a new generation of the ambitious and determined who were street hustlers first and English-speakers last. Mostly Jewish, they were quick to rid themselves of long-winded surnames and assume instead names more palatable to a homogenized community. Mayer, Warner, Zukor and Selznick were the result. Their collective rise from back-street to boardroom was a strong feature in helping to create the all-pervasive idea of the American Dream.

Between them the future dinosaurs were glove salesmen, furriers, pool hustlers and rag-and-bone men before finding a common bond in the world of nickelodeons. (These devices willed the customer to part with a few cents and delivered in return a peepshow, one's fortune or weight.) They firmly joined hands to jump into the untested waters of the movie business. Determined not to catch a cold, and ignoring criticism of the corrupting nature of the film and how it could leave the viewer with a permanently strange squint, they, as immigrants, were quick to divine the appeal of a medium which could crash through class, race and language barriers.

There was also the simple paradox that these Jewish pragmatists were selling Gentile features and customs across the planet. The cute blonde hair and demure manners of Mary Pickford were a perfect match for their intentions. When Jesse Lasky of Paramount was rushed to hospital with a heart attack, he hastily replied 'American' to a simple question about race. The young Jewish official said, 'Now, now. Mr. Lasky. We are Jewish aren't we?'

'Jewish, oh yes, yes, Jewish,' stuttered the surprised Lasky. These moguls, as capable of creative salesmanship as of whimsical cruelty, were paid a twisted compliment by Joseph Stalin who complained that if he could only control the film industry he could control the world.

Warner Brothers was one of the great dynasties. Sam, Albert, Harry and Jack were the four brothers. Sam, by far the most likeable, had pioneered the use of sound in *The Jazz Singer* but unfortunately died the day after it opened on 6 October 1927. It was Albert, in his capacity as Treasurer who spouted fire over the stars' vast pay cheques, while Harry displayed plenty of entrepreneurial flair. He was once described by Jack as having the 'toughness of a brothel madam and the buzzing persistence of a mosquito on a hot night'. Jack was head of production and so became the best known of the famous four. He was the would-be actor who actually sang illustrated songs in his very first Warner cinema.

Rock's Pillow Talk

That same discrepancy between an image dreamed up by Hollywood and a quite different reality is relevant to the life of Rock Hudson.

For more than 30 years Hudson was the leading torch-bearer for all-American masculinity. One of the biggest screen heroes of this century, he sported a 6 ft 4 in (193 cm) frame, clean-cut looks and a healthy natural manner which appealed enormously to millions of women fans.

He placed a seal on his masculinity when, in 1956, he played opposite Elizabeth Taylor in *Giant*, a film which brought him a 'Best Actor' Oscar nomination. He then proceeded to make three pictures with Doris Day in the late 1950s and early 1960s in which he established a new trend of sexy sophistication. Even 20 years later Rock was still able to trot out his masculine charm when he starred opposite Linda Evans in 'Dynasty.'

It was shortly after this that Hudson confessed to a stunned world that he was not only gay but also dying of AIDS. This he did selflessly as a means of dispelling the malice and prejudice which AIDS sufferers have had to endure. In this brave attempt to create a better climate, Rock became a hero all over again, this time to a different audience.

In 1954 Rock proved himself a fully-fledged star when he appeared opposite Jane Wyman in the remake of *Magnificent Obsession*. It was at this time that the scummy tabloid magazine, *Confidential*, called Hudson's bosses to announce with pride that it had in its sweaty paw some damning evidence which proved beyond doubt that Rock was homosexual. With the arbitrary pragmatism so typical of Hollywood, they safeguarded Rock's secret by twisting the arm of the magazine and instead fed a minor gay actor to the lions. The scapegoat was George Nader.

With a career which only really required him to point his biceps at the camera and utter a few semi-intelligent words, Nader flaunted himself more on the covers of Hollywood fan magazines than he acted in films. Yet even his tiny successes in Hollywood were ruthlessly stamped out by the studio barons who now bought silence on Hudson for an exposé on Nader.

Nader made a last bid for the spotlight in the early 1960s with a couple of television series which failed, so instead he headed for West Germany where he became the number one star due to a succession of ersatz James Bond thrillers. But when spy films became passé, Nader brought his earnings back to Hollywood and retired in some degree of comfort.

The Hollywood publicists and gossip-columnists resorted to stop-gap tactics to protect Hudson. In 1955, he eloped with secretary Phyllis Gates and the result was a marriage which lasted three years. This created a smoke-screen around his private life, as did his masculine achievement in *Giant* which was released the following year. For the next 15 years, chatterings about Rock's sexual preferences were dismissed as nothing more than malice or jealousy.

Hudson had, in fact, been fixed with a woman before this. The first girl he was seen flirting with in public, and thus by extension cavorting with in private, was the singer-dancer Vera-Ellen whose face may well be remembered for her role as Rosemary Clooney's sister in *White Christmas* (1954). Encouraged by Henry Willson, his agent-manager, with whom he was drinking at Ciro's nightclub in Hollywood in 1949, to go and talk to her. Rock interrupted her dance and the result was a series of highly public dates.

The Press Photographers' Costume Ball was not far off and Rock and Vera-Ellen stole the show by dressing up as 'Mr and Mrs Oscar', the Academy Award statuettes.

Covered with gold paint, they sported splendid plastic heads, bathing costumes and swords from the props department. They won the first prize. The gossip-writers claimed that Rock had proposed to the young lady but had been flatly rebuffed. And so the effective and reassuring publicity blanket gave the public not the slightest inkling that, not only would Rock never dream of marriage, but that he was also completely gay.

It was gay activist, Armistead Maupin, a columnist on the *San Francisco Chronicle*, who commented on this: 'Rock had learned the lesson well in Hollywood. He played by the rules. These rules say that you keep quiet about being gay and everyone will lie about it for you. The gossip columnists will make up girlfriends for you and everyone in Hollywood will know you're gay except the public.'

It was also to Maupin that Rock confessed he might finally reveal all to the public. 'Rock seemed to take to the idea and said, 'One of these days I'm going to have a lot to tell,'' I thought it would be a good idea because he was actually the same in private life as on the screen: very masculine and natural. You could see the idea would be difficult for some men of his generation – he was never able to bring himself to go public about it.'

As the years passed, and Rock's PR machine was seen as nothing more than a desperate veil, stories about his real-life frolics hit the headlines. In the early 1970s, invitations to a party were sent out by a San Francisco gay couple who were known for their out-to-lunch gatherings. This time the event was to be the wedding reception of Rock Hudson and Jim Nabors. Hudson was able to dismiss such a practical joke with his virile charm but Nabors was kicked into touch by the powerful pen-pushers. Having signed to CBS in 1971 for his own variety show, he now found that it was cruelly cancelled. As in the case of George Nader the star had won out at the expense of the nonentity. Nabors upped and left Hollywood and settled in Hawaii. It was only through the loyalty of friends like Burt Reynolds, who cast Nabors in his films, that he was able to work again.

The sad irony in this case was that Hudson and Nabors were not in fact conducting an affair. Maupin, as usual, proves a credible source on the life of the star: 'Rock used to explain the story at dinner parties. In point of fact he and Nabors were just good friends. But the rumours made it impossible by them to be seen together, which is very sad.'

In the late 1970s and early 1980s one Tom Clark moved in with Rock Hudson. Because Rock had fired Henry Willson at the end of the 1960s, it was a simple convenience to refer to Clark as Rock's 'manager'.

The two had met when Clark was working as a publicist at MGM. He soon became the star's accounts adviser, secretary and friend and took part in plenty of Rock's well loved Hollywood pub crawls.

A confidante of Hudson's explains: 'It came to the point that he was dependent on Tom, because Tom babied him; he made sure Rock had a warm sweater on, he made his plane reservations, his dinner reservations, he made sure that Rock's clothes were out of the dry cleaners, he did everything for him. Rock loved that.'

Rock displayed a giant appetite for sex during his last 20 years in Hollywood. Famous and notorious men, not to mention would-be actors were able to share Rock's affections. One well known agent has said: 'Rock Hudson helped several people get started in show business.'

One in particular was a football player who lived with him in the early 1980s. Introduced by Rock to all the right people, he landed a plum role in a national television series after which he cut Hudson dead and pretended never even to have met him, lest his own macho image be dented. He has since gone on to be the star of several national series.

It was this generosity which Rock possessed right to the end, when (and it must have been tough for him) he confessed his homosexuality for the benefit of others. By this time he had recorded 'Dynasty' on whose set he had arrived with sunken eyes and cheeks, as well as bony wrists and ankles. Desperate publicity claims about dieting and intentional weight-loss ('he loves the idea of being slender again') would not wash this time. But the old macho maverick died fittingly with the same respect he had enjoyed at the height of his career due to this last gesture of magnanimity.

At least Rock never suffered in the manner of other Hollywood homosexuals, many of whom were discarded by the studios. William Taten Tiden III, better known as Big Bill Tiden or 'Stumpfinger', was a star tennis player who soon became a silent movie actor. He had a predilection for young boys which finally nailed his career and shattered him personally. Once caught fondling a young boy in a car, he was later found waiting outside the school gates for another and finally used up all his money in the law courts. Abandoned by his high-flying friends, he died of a heart attack.

The likeable William Haines, a popular MGM star of the 1920s, went the same way. A comic queen who camped it up on set and would often greet male cast and crew with an affectionate pat on the bottom, he was finally caught with a sailor in a seedy downtown YMCA. His film career ended forthwith, although he went onto have a highly successful career as interior designer to the stars.

Hollywood homosexuals were always open to crude decisions by the dictators-on-high who would drop them at a snap if their leanings showed any sign of becoming public knowledge. In the context of cinema, what these actors really symbolize is the yawning gap between fantasy and reality. What the public believes is exactly what Hollywood wants it to.

Political Scandals

Zippergate

The story of President Clinton and his peccadilloes was the political scandal of the 20th century. Although President Nixon would have been impeached if he had not resigned following the Watergate scandal, Bill Clinton continued to tough it out – even after finding himself the first president to be impeached since Andrew Johnson, who was tried by the Senate in 1868.

Interestingly, like Clinton, Johnson was accused of adultery. But the substantive charge that brought him to an unprecedented two-month trial was violation of the Tenure of Office Act, which was designed to stop the President sacking Northern carpetbaggers who had seized Federal posts in the South under the authority of Congress after the Civil War. Johnson, a Southerner, sought reconciliation between the states and refused to accept the act. He caused a scandal by defying Congress and sacking the Secretary of War, Edwin Stanton.

When Stanton refused to stand down, Congress rallied around him and Johnson found himself the first president to be impeached. Although Johnson was a Republican, it was the Republicans who were out to get him. Abraham Lincoln had been a Republican and the Republicans on Capitol Hill were vehemently opposed to Johnson's kidglove treatment of the defeated Confederacy.

The newspapers vilified Johnson as 'the Great Criminal' and accused him of everything up to, and including, being one of the conspirators in the plot to assassinate Lincoln – and, of course, adultery. Illinois senators were warned that if they voted for acquittal, they would be hanged when they returned home. And the mistress of Kansas Senator Robert Ream was told that if she had any influence on him, she had better use it to get him to vote to convict.

Johnson acted with great decorum throughout the Senate

trial. He held himself above the fray, refusing to dignify the proceedings with his presence. The final vote was 35 to 19, just one vote short of the two-thirds majority required by the Constitution.

However, 1868 was an election year and Johnson lost any chance of a second term in the White House. He returned to his home state of Tennessee where he stood for election to Congress in 1870. He lost. He lost again in 1872, but was returned to the Senate in 1874, where he was warmly greeted by a number of senators who had voted for his conviction six years before.

Bill Clinton's impeachment also began with something more substantive than adultery. The investigation began with the appointment of a Special Prosecutor to look into a land deal, known as Whitewater. In August 1979, while Clinton was an Arkansas state attorney and campaigning for his first term as governor, Bill and Hillary Clinton bought 230 acres of river front land in the Ozark Mountains of northern Arkansas, which seemed prime for development. They paid no money. The deposit was provided by the couple's friends, Jim and Susan McDougal.

The land was never developed and the Clintons made no money out of the deal. However, some time later the McDougals' mortgage company ran into difficulties and the McDougals ended up in jail. It was discovered that the land had originally been sold at a very favourable price by a major logging company, which seemed to get an easy ride from Bill Clinton, who was in the governor's mansion. There were also allegations that Whitewater accounts were used to funnel money to Clinton's campaign funds.

Hillary Clinton's extraordinary success at commodities trading also came under investigation. Her activities at the Arkansas law firm of Rose Law, where she had worked on some of the McDougals' other dealings, came under scrutiny when her colleague there, Vince Foster, who had gone on to become a White House attorney, was found shot in the head in a park in Washington. The coroner's verdict was suicide, but many suspected that there was more to it. One persistent rumour was that Vince Foster and Hillary Clinton had been having an affair.

Hillary was also accused of illegally firing seven members of staff working in the White House travel office, replacing them with cronies from Arkansas. And the White House was accused of making illegal use of FBI files.

However, these cases were extraordinarily arcane and convoluted. They failed to catch the public's imagination and the investigation was getting nowhere until the Special Prosecutor got lucky. A young woman named Paula Jones sued Bill Clinton for sexual harassment. She alleged that while he was Governor of Arkansas, a state trooper had told her that the Governor wanted to see her and had taken her up to Clinton's hotel room. There, she said, Clinton had pulled out his penis and asked her to kiss it. She had declined. However, when the magazine *American Spectator* said that she had slept with Clinton, she brought a suit against him for 'severe emotional distress' in an effort, she claimed, to clear her name. Paula Jones had been a state employee at the time, so Clinton was her boss. If he had made any unwanted overture – particularly such a gross one – she had an open-and-shut case. But Clinton denied that any such incident had ever taken place.

The Special Prosecutor asked the Attorney General to extend his remit to investigate the Paula Jones case, on the grounds that he might be able to prove a pattern of lying that would be pertinent to the Whitewater affair. That Special Prosecutor was Ken Starr and he had been involved in the preparation of Paula Jones's suit.

It was no secret that Clinton was a womanizer. Born in Hope, Arkansas, in 1946, he had wanted to be a politician in the Kennedy mould, especially after meeting his hero in the White House when he was 13. While a Rhodes scholar at Oxford, he was such a fearless stud that he had propositioned arch-feminist Germaine Greer.

At Yale Law School, he met Hillary Rodham. who shared his political ambitions. She went with him to Arkansas as his campaign manager in the 1974 congressional race. He lost.

While Hillary was running his campaign, Bill was having an affair with one of his other campaign workers. Nevertheless, Bill and Hillary were married in 1975 and she stood by him throughout six terms as Governor of Arkansas, although his extramarital affairs during that period are now the stuff of legend.

When Clinton decided to run for the presidency in 1992, his good looks and Kennedyesque charisma soon put him ahead of the field. And the rumours of his marital infidelity did him no harm. During the New Hampshire primary in February 1992, supermarket check-out scandal sheet *The Star* ran the banner headline, 'DEMS FRONT-RUNNER BILL CLINTON CHEATED WITH MISS AMERICA.'

It then went on to name five women whom Clinton was alleged to have slept with, including former Miss America and *Playboy* centrefold, Elizabeth Ward Gracen. Bill denied everything and the major newspapers dismissed the allegations as the 'unverified reports of supermarket tabloids'.

The Star hit back with 'MY 12-YEAR AFFAIR WITH BILL CLINTON'. This time it wheeled out former Little Rock night-club singer Gennifer Flowers. She was, in newspaper terms, the 'smoking bimbo'.

In an interview, she said: 'We made love everywhere, on the floor, in bed, in the kitchen, on the cabinet, the sink... I called his testicles "the boys" and he called my breasts "the girls".'

She also said that he once tried to have sex with her in the men's room in the governor's mansion while Hillary was entertaining on the lawn outside. He even used his jogging as cover – he jogged over to her apartment, made love to her and jogged home. That way, his being sweaty did not arouse Hillary's suspicions.

'I admired his stamina,' Flowers said, 'being able to make love with such enthusiasm after running. I used to tease him about running back much slower.'

Naturally the media loved such tales. In a press conference in 1992, one reporter brought the house down by asking Flowers: 'Did the Governor use a condom?'

Such salacious details were much more interesting to the general public than the political issues at stake in the election, and after a few queasy moments Clinton bounced back in the polls.

Soon his campaign team managed to turn his womanizing into an advantage. With consummate skill, they called CBS and demanded the right to reply to Flowers' accusations on the network's prestigious *60 Minutes* programme. Their timing was perfect. Clinton got on the show directly after the Superbowl, guaranteeing a massive audience of slightly inebriated males. With Hillary beside him, Clinton admitted that there had been problems in their marriage. When asked whether that meant that he had committed adultery, Hillary answered coolly: 'People who have been married a long time know what it means.'

It was a riveting performance. In one fell swoop, the two of them blew every other candidate out of the water. Hillary made only one slight slip when she said that she was not there just to 'stand by my man like Tammy Wynette'. She later apologized to Tammy when the spin doctors realized they were in danger of losing the Country and Western vote.

Later, Clinton admitted to having smoked marijuana but 'he did not inhale'. Besides, he had done it while he was a student in England, so he had broken no American law. Not even his admission that he had dodged the draft during the Vietnam War prevented him from winning the 1992 presidential election. Committing adultery, smoking dope and dodging the draft actually endeared him to the baby boomers who now made up the bulk of the voters. However, these things alienated him from the old-fashioned religious right. This sector hated him with a passion and would do anything to bring him down.

Once Clinton was in the White House, the state troopers from Arkansas who had guarded him when he was governor, revealed that Clinton had had hundreds of women.

'There was hardly an opportunity he would let slip to have sex,' one said. This included being given oral sex by a woman in the back of a limousine in the parking lot of his daughter's school, while he was waiting to pick up his daughter, Chelsea.

Alleged lovers included the wife of a prominent judge, a local newspaper reporter, a former state employee, a sales clerk from the cosmetics counter at a Little Rock department store and a black prostitute named Bobbie Ann Williams. She claimed that Clinton had fathered her mixed-race child in one of their 13 sex sessions.

Sally Perdue, a former Miss Arkansas, claimed to have had an affair with Clinton in 1983, when she was a radio-show host in Little Rock. After the affair was over, she claimed a Democratic Party official had promised her a $40,000 job if she 'behaved like a good girl'. The implication was, she said, that otherwise she might get her legs broken.

Rock'n'roll groupie Connie Hamzy had a brush with Clinton. She told *Penthouse* magazine that a Clinton aide had approached her as she lay sunbathing by a swimming pool in a scanty bikini. She boasted that she had fondled the future president.

Blonde power-company executive Jo Jenkins denied having an affair with Clinton, but his phone record revealed that he telephoned her 11 times in one day. One of the calls, late at night, lasted 94 minutes. According to Gennifer Flowers' book, *Passion and Betrayal*, Clinton liked to indulge in mutual masturbation sessions while talking to his lover over the phone. Flowers said she had to fake it as telephone sex did not turn her on.

All these allegations did Clinton no harm. They merely enhanced his reputation as a stud. There has long been talk inside the Beltway that Bill and Hillary had made a pre-presidential pact long ago. She would stand by him and cover up for his womanizing, if he gave her a big job in government. When they got into the White House, she was put in charge of a revolutionary health-care plan that would give Americans a health service along the lines of Britain's NHS. However, right-wing Republicans characterized the Clinton health-care plan as a Communist plot and the insurance companies stumped up millions to run a series of TV commercials to protect the private system that brought them in a vast fortune each year. The health-care programme was soon in tatters and Hillary was out of a job.

The only real danger to Bill Clinton came from Paula Jones. She now had powerful backers, wealthy right-wing Republicans, and threatened to take him to court. The White House responded to her allegations by trying to trash her. Clinton's spin doctor, James Carville, called her 'trailer park trash'. The Republicans gave her a make-over and she pressed on.

She did not want money, she said. All she wanted was an apology. But for Clinton an apology would mean an admission. That was not a chance he was prepared to take. Jones upped the ante by promising the press certain salacious details that would make her case stand up in court. She could, she said, describe in detail some 'distinguishing characteristics' of Clinton's genitals. The media went wild with speculation about what these 'distinguishing characteristics' might be.

The White House tried to keep the lid on things by claiming that, as President, Clinton could not be taken to court while in office. That was a matter that had to be decided by the Supreme Court and, while waiting for their ruling, Clinton squeezed through the 1996 election. His Republican opponent, Bob Dole, could not make political capital out of Paula Jones's allegations. He could hardly play Mister Clean. He was a twice-married divorcee, who was guilty of a little intramarital shenanigans himself. Besides, he was as old as Father Time and dared not risk playing the sex card against a younger, demonstrably more virile man. Clinton may not have been able to keep it in his pants, but at least he could get it up.

In November 1996, the American people went to the polls and gave an overwhelming endorsement to adultery. The economy was booming and presidential peccadilloes did not hit the voters in the pocket. Besides, when Clinton turned on the charm, the country – like Hillary – would forgive him anything.

It did not work on the Supreme Court though. Even in the Paula Jones case, the justices argued that 'justice delayed is justice denied'. In America, they insisted, no one, not even the President, is above the law. A hearing in the Paula Jones case was set for May 1998.

The President's lawyer came close to stopping the lawsuit with an 11th hour comprise. Slick Willie, it seemed, was about to slide again. But, in hubris, a White House aide told CNN that Paula Jones was pulling out because she knew her case was hopeless.

Paula put her foot back on the gas and, for the first time, spoke of the President's genital peculiarity. When he had dropped his trousers and asked her to kiss his dick back in Little Rock, she said, it was erect – but bent. And she demanded $2 million for 'emotional distress'.

To limit the damage, Bill and Hillary took a romantic holiday for two in the Virgin Islands, of all places, along with half the world's press. The happy, if slightly overweight, couple were pictured dancing on the beach in their swimming costumes. This seemingly spontaneous act of affection was a carefully rehearsed photo opportunity.

Some commentators were taken in by the Caribbean idyll. It was said that Hillary was no longer faking it. She had actually fallen in love with the big lug again. But fate was closing in.

First, President Clinton was called to testify under oath in a six-hour closed-door hearing as part of the discovery phase of the Paula Jones case. Paula sat only feet away. Under tough cross-questioning by Jones's lawyer, Clinton was asked whether he had ever been in 'close proximity' to Paula. Clinton said he could not recall meeting her. He denied dropping his trousers and asking her to 'kiss it'. His attorney added: 'In terms of size, shape, and direction the President is a normal man,' although the attorney did not say how he knew this. The President was then cross-examined generally about his sex life.

Also called to give a deposition was a young woman named Monica Lewinsky. She had been an intern in the White House. She was asked whether she had had sexual relations with the President. This was relevant because, if Clinton had asked her for sex, it would show that he made a practice of importuning employees. Monica stoutly denied any such sexual relations had taken place.

One person who knew that this was not true was 48-year old Linda Tripp. She had been an aide in the Bush White House and had stayed on as one of the transitional team that smoothed the hand-over of power when Clinton entered the Oval Office. Her other claim to fame was that she had served Hillary's law partner, Vince Foster, his last hamburger before he committed suicide – or was ruthlessly gunned down by the Clintons' hired assassins, as right-wing conspiracy theorists were now saying.

A committed Republican, Tripp was no Clinton fan. She had already reported that she had seen another White House staffer, Kathleen Willey, leaving the Oval Office after an interview with Clinton 'flustered, happy and joyful... dishevelled, her face was red, her lipstick was off'. Willey refused to comment publicly and Tripp was denounced as a liar by the President's lawyers. Reluctantly, Willey was forced to make a deposition in the Paula Jones case. She later told all on TV. The President, she said, had placed her hand on his member. She was asked whether the Chief Executive had been aroused. 'Yes,' she said.

Linda Tripp did not like being called a liar and she was determined to get her own back. She already had another card up her sleeve. After she had left the White House, she had gone to work at the Pentagon. There, she befriended a young graduate named Monica Lewinsky, who had also transferred from the White House. In the powder room, Lewinsky revealed that she had pleasured the President in a small room off the Oval Office. This was the same room where a former president, Warren Harding, was caught in flagrante with his young mistress Nan Britton by his wife.

Tripp consulted New York literary agent and long-time Clinton-baiter, Lucienne Goldberg. Goldberg had been a $1,000-a-week Republican spy in the McGovern camp in the 1972 Nixon 'dirty tricks' campaign. She went on to represent Mark Fuhrman, the racist cop caught lying in the O.J. Simpson case.

Goldberg lapped up Tripp's tale, but to make anything of it they would need evidence. Lewinsky had turned to Tripp as a shoulder to cry on and Tripp began taping Lewinsky's phone calls, pumping her for erotic detail. Everything she said directly contradicted what both Clinton and Lewinsky had said in their depositions.

Lewinsky said that her affair with the President had begun not long after she arrived in the White House. She was just 21. The daughter of a wealthy Californian physician, she had been to school in Beverley Hills. The video of her High School prom shows her in clinches with a string of boys. At college in Portland, Oregon, she was considered 'a bit flash' at the raucous barbecues the students held. There were even rumours of an affair with the professor. Monica was apparently a young woman with a taste for older men.

After graduating in 1995, her mother arranged for her to be an unpaid intern, or trainee, in the White House.

'There goes trouble,' said the White House staffer who interviewed her for the job.

She was given a desk that lay between the Oval Office and the President's private apartment. Every time the President walked by, it was plain that he noticed her. She wore low-cut blouses with the top three buttons undone. Under the desk, her short skirts revealed lacy stocking tops. The President even commented on the thong she was wearing that rose above the top of her skirt.

At first, White House wags put his attentions down to innocent flirtation. No one suspected that there was anything going on between them. But tongues started wagging when she turned up one night with a private visit pass. These are rarely issued to staff. She said she was visiting a close personal friend in the Chief of Staff's office, but the person whose name she wrote in the security log had already gone home.

Gifts were exchanged. Monica bought Clinton the tie that he wore when he gave his State of the Union address in 1997. He sent her flowers, and gave her a book of erotic verse and a dress, which she kept, unwashed, as a *memento amori* because, she boasted, it was stained with presidential semen.

Secret Service men were overheard saying that she should not be visiting the President's apartment so often – especially not when Hillary and Chelsea were away. She also appeared on the guest list at Camp David.

When gossip spread throughout the White House, Monica was transferred to a paid job in the Pentagon. There she developed a crush on another older man. But she continued to see the President, arriving late at night in figure-hugging dresses.

She began to get disillusioned, however, when she discovered that she was not the only filly in Bill's stable. She began to record her own phone calls with the President. Some of the conversations were very explicit indeed. There were hot telephone sex sessions. Memorably, the President expressed his desire to 'coat you with my baby gravy' – not an appetizing image, perhaps, but hardly a federal offence.

Tripp went to Kenneth Starr, the Special Prosecutor on the Whitewater scandal. She convinced him that Clinton had lied under oath in his deposition in the Paula Jones case, and that Clinton, via his attorney and close friend Vernon Jordan, had also asked Monica to lie under oath.

Starr got the FBI to wire Tripp's capacious cleavage. She invited Lewinsky for cocktails at the Ritz Carlton in Crystal City and the G-men taped their girl talk. Lewinsky began complaining to Tripp that the President was cheating on her with four other women – three of whom worked in the White House. It seemed he was running a state-sponsored seraglio. She called him 'The Creep,' and `El Sicko' and admitted giving Clinton oral sex, which the FBI gleefully taped.

Monica said she had asked Bill Clinton why he did not settle the Paula Jones case out of court. He apparently replied: 'I can't – because then they would all come out of the woodwork.'

'Were there that many?' Lewinsky had asked.

'Hundreds,' Clinton had replied.

The Federal agents moved in. They seized from Lewinsky's Watergate flat a copy of Walt Whitman's *Leaves of Grass* – which contains the line 'Copulation is no more rank to me than death' – inscribed by the President's own fair hand. They also seized jewellery that Clinton had bought for her while on holiday in Martha's Vineyard with

Hillary. Meanwhile, Starr gave 24-year-old Monica an eight-hour grilling.

The media were fascinated by just who these 'hundreds' of other women could be. Soon the bimbo hunt was in full cry. Forty-eight-year-old Dolly Kyle Browning claimed that she had begun an affair with Clinton in high school that had lasted into his White House days. She claimed to have made love to the President three times in a senator's hotel room. And, while he was governor, they had had sex in the basement of the gubernatorial mansion, frolicked in houses borrowed from friends and made love in a neighbour's back yard.

Then there was leggy Susan McDougal, who went down for 18 months for refusing to testify against Clinton over Whitewater. Her husband, Jim, said that he had intercepted an 'intimate' phone call between his wife and the President, and that she had later admitted the affair. Again she stuck up for the President.

'I'm a small town girl,' she told the press, 'a Southern Baptist, I wouldn't do that.'

Sheila Lawrence was then accused of making love to President Clinton while her millionaire husband turned a blind eye. In return, he was made US ambassador to Switzerland. When he died, Clinton rewarded Sheila's discretion by having her husband's remains interred in Arlington National Cemetery, where John F Kennedy is buried. His remains were later moved when it was discovered that Lawrence had lied about his military service.

Fearing she was being upstaged, Gennifer Flowers went on CNN with more details of her affair with Clinton. She told chat-show host Larry King: 'He's a chance taker and he will make you take chances. He wanted to make love with Hillary nearby.'

Clinton, she said, had made her pregnant and she had had an abortion. Meanwhile, Bill was caught on tape saying Flowers could 'suck a tennis ball through a garden hose'.

Back in Little Rock, Sally Perdue told the nation that Clinton liked nothing than better to cavort around her bedroom dressed in her black nightie. And 33-year-old Bobbie Ann Williams took a lie detector test in an attempt to get child support for her seven-year-old son and Clinton lookalike, Danny. Strapped to the polygraph, she claimed that her first paid encounter with the Governor took place behind a hedge in Little Rock. Later, she said, she had organized three-in-a-bed sessions for him with another prostitute. The polygraph operator was sweating. She was not. The needles remained as steady as her accusations.

Former Miss America and *Playboy* centrefold Elizabeth Ward Gracen, who was by then a prominent TV actress, left the country rather than be subpoenaed in the Paula Jones case. She later admitted to having sex with Clinton when she was 21, but insisted that the sex was consensual.

The spin doctors were maintaining that any sexual contact Clinton had with these women was oral. This was vital. Under the Constitution, a president can only be impeached for 'high crimes and misdemeanours'. Technically, adultery is a misdemeanour in the District of Columbia. However, Clinton and others maintain that oral sex does not constitute adultery because it is not mentioned, or condemned, by the Bible. This was the key to Clinton's defence, because none other than Newt Gingrich, Republican speaker of the House of Representatives at that time and Clinton's bitterest enemy, had used that very argument in his bitterly contended divorce case.

Clinton famously appeared on television, wagging his finger at the press and saying: 'I did not have sex with that woman, Miss Lewinsky.'

But slowly, he confessed to being 'emotionally close' to Monica. Hillary went on the chat shows and said she still loved and trusted her husband – only to be dubbed 'the world's most powerful doormat'. There was a rightwing conspiracy to bring her husband down, she said.

And, in a way, it was true. Special prosecutor Ken Starr was a committed Republican. He had spent $25 million and three years getting nowhere with the Whitewater investigation. But now, at last, he had something.

In the midst of the crisis, Clinton delivered a barnstorming State of the Union address. He held his nerve and things began to turn in his favour. The federal judge in charge of the Paula Jones case quashed her suit. Even if the incident in the hotel room she described had occurred, she had no civil case because she could not prove that she had been materially damaged by Clinton's behaviour. Indeed, after the incident, she had been promoted. And she could not show any emotional damage since she had gone on to get married.

Even so, Starr maintained that if Clinton had lied under oath in his deposition in the case, he was guilty of perjury. If he had put pressure on Monica Lewinsky to lie, then he was guilty of suborning a witness. And, if he had had some gifts he had given Monica Lewinsky removed from her flat – as was now being alleged he was guilty of obstructing the course of justice. As President, Clinton was the chief law officer of the United States, so these were serious – impeachable – offences.

Starr managed to make a deal with Monica Lewinsky. If she testified in graphic detail to the Grand Jury, holding nothing back, he would guarantee her immunity from prosecution. If she did not testify, he would charge her with perjury over her testimony in the Paula Jones case. At her trial, Clinton would be called as a witness, so he would be exposed anyway.

Monica had no choice. She took the deal. She told the Grand Jury that she had both given and received oral sex with the President on numerous occasions. She said that she had entertained him by dancing around naked and performing sexual acts with a cigar. She also said that he had penetrated her, but he had not 'finished off' inside her.

This was enough of a loophole for Clinton to continue to argue that he had not had sex with her. Within the narrowest Biblical definition, a sexual act means one that could result in reproduction. This was a whisper away.

She also handed over the semen-stained dress that she had kept. The semen proved to match a sample of DNA provided by the President.

President Clinton then consented to testify to the Grand Jury. But he would do so, not in person, but by a closed circuit TV from the White House. Again, he stuck to his guns. Although he admitted an 'inappropriate relationship' with Monica Lewinsky, he denied having sex with her under the definition provided in the Paula Jones case. He denied lying under oath and he denied asking anyone else to do so.

He went on television and admitted that he had deceived the country and brought pain to his family, and he asked for forgiveness. The press screamed that if he had only admitted that he had had sex with Monica Lewinsky in the first place, he would have been forgiven and the whole thing could have been forgotten. But that was the one thing he could not do. If he admitted that he had had sex with Monica Lewinsky, he would be admitting that he had committed perjury, both in his deposition in the Paula Jones case and in his testimony to the Grand Jury, and that he had lied to the American people. Besides, he was rising in popularity in the polls.

Although almost every detail of the evidence presented to the Grand Jury had already been leaked, the House of Representatives voted to publish the Starr report both as hard copy and on the internet. Clinton's televised testimony was also released. The Republicans in the House hoped that this would do the maximum damage to the Democrats before the congressional elections in November 1998.

It did the Republicans no good. The tide of gains in the House of Representatives that been flowing with them since Bill Clinton had first entered the White House now ebbed, although they retained a majority. And in the Senate, they failed to gain the two-thirds majority they would need to remove him from office. Despite this, the House of Representatives voted to impeach him anyway.

According to the *National Enquirer*, the impeachment rattled Hillary and she lashed out at Bill. His Secret Service guards had to fend her off. Courtesy of *The Star*, Bobbie Ann Williams had her son's DNA compared with that provided to the Starr Committee by Bill Clinton, and it was found that the President was not the father.

Meanwhile, the Senate duly sat and tried the President, with the Republicans dragging out the proceedings in the forlorn hope that some new and even more scandalous evidence against the President would be unearthed. Meanwhile, Bill Clinton continued to soar in the polls.

The Profumo Scandal

The biggest scandal in British public life took place, ironically, in the Swinging Sixties, when everyone was supposed to be having a lot of sex and having a good time – apart from government ministers that is. When it was discovered that Minister of War, John Profumo, had been sharing a prostitute with the naval attaché at the Russian embassy and had lied to the House of Commons about it, he was forced to resign. But that was not the end of the matter. Soon after, the Prime Minister, who had been fatally damaged by the affair, resigned and the following year the Conservative government was swept from power.

The scandal centred around Christine Keeler who, at the age of 15, quit her home in the Buckinghamshire village of Wraysbury for the bright lights of London. Within months, her self-confidence and good looks had taken her from being a waitress in a Greek restaurant to being a part-time model and a topless dancer in Murray's Cabaret Club in Soho, where she earned £8.50 a week. There, fellow show-girl Mandy Rice-Davis, a perky 17-year-old from Birmingham, introduced her to her friend Stephen Ward.

Ward was a thin and elegant man in his late 40s. He was a talented artist but earned his living as an osteopath. He numbered among his clients several high-ranking members of the establishment. These included Lord Astor, who let him a cottage in the grounds of his Cliveden estate for the peppercorn rent of £1 a year, and Sir Colin Coote, Editor of *The Daily Telegraph*, who associated with the head of MI5, Sir Roger Hollis – whom Peter Wright later named as the fifth man in the Cambridge spy ring.

Ward liked doing favours for people. He also liked drugs and the company of pretty women, including prostitutes. Christine Keeler and Mandy Rice-Davis moved in with him in his London flat in Wimpole Mews and would go with him to Cliveden at weekends for parties in his cottage.

In June 1961, over lunch at The Garrick, Coote introduced Ward to the Soviet naval attaché, Yevgeny Ivanov. MI5 had singled out Ivanov as a man who might easily succumb to the temptations of the West. They thought that a weekend party with some of Ward's attractive young female friends might be just the thing to turn him. The defection of such a high-ranking Russian official would be quite a prize. Specifically, MI5 wanted Ward to 'honeytrap' Ivanov with Keeler.

Ward invited Ivanov down to Cliveden on Sunday 9 July 1951. He took Keeler down there the night before when the Astors were holding a dinner party in the house. Keeler wanted to go swimming and Ward dared her to go in the nude. When she did, he stole her swimming costume.

Lord Astor and John Profumo were out in the gardens for an after dinner stroll when they spotted the beautiful, naked 19-year-old in the swimming pool. Christine realized that they were coming and struck out for the edge of the pool. She emerged nude and grabbed a small towel to cover herself, moments before the two men caught up with her.

The two middle-aged men were fooling around with the near-naked girl when suddenly the floodlights were turned on. The rest of the guests – including Profumo's wife – came out into the garden, too. Christine was introduced. Later, Profumo, managed to give her a guided tour of the bedrooms at Cliveden.

At 46, Profumo was a rising Tory politician. The son of a successful barrister, he was independently wealthy and lived the life of a Tory squire. Educated at Harrow and Oxford, he served on the staff of General Alexander during World War II, rising to the rank of lieutenant-colonel. He was elected to Parliament for Stratford-upon-Avon in 1950 and joined the government in 1952, rising to the position of Secretary for War in 1960. In 1954, he had married the actress Valerie Hobson.

The day after Christine met Profumo, Ivanov turned up at Cliveden. Ward laid on a swimming party as a way of introducing him to Christine. She fancied Ivanov immediately. She told the *News of the World*: 'He was MAN. He was rugged with a hairy chest, strong and agile.'

However, when they decided to have a piggy-back fight in the pool, it was Jack Profumo's shoulders she clambered on to, not Ivanov's. That evening, Christine left with Ivanov, but not before Profumo had asked her for her phone number. Christine was flattered and told him to contact Ward.

Back at Ward's Wimpole Mews flat, Christine and Ivanov demolished a bottle of vodka. Then he kissed her.

'Before I knew what was happening, I was in his arms,' she said. 'We left serious discussion and I yielded to this wonderful huggy bear of a man... He was a wonderful lover.'

Two days later, Profumo, phoned and came round. On his third visit, he began to kiss her and soon, 'I was returning his kisses with everything that I suddenly felt for him,' she said.

Profumo would always call first before he came round for what Keeler called a 'screw of convenience'. They had to be discreet. With Ivanov, she went out on the town, but Profumo could not risk being seen out with her in a pub or restaurant. Occasionally though they went for a drive. As well as having sex at Ward's flat, they had it in Profumo's red mini and a black car he borrowed from the Minister of Labour, John Hare. And once, when his wife was away in Ireland, Profumo took Christine back to their house in Nash Terrace near Regents Park. It was late and the butler and staff were asleep. Profumo took her directly to the bedroom.

Profumo had no idea that he was sharing his mistress with Ivanov. He was deeply attached to her. But she did not share his feelings. For her, sex 'had no more meaning than a handshake or a look across a crowded room,' she said. Meanwhile, Profumo showered her with expensive gifts and money – ostensibly to buy her mother a birthday present.

After a month, MI5 learnt about Profumo's affair with Keeler. Fearing that it compromised their entrapment of Ivanov, Hollis asked the Cabinet Secretary, Sir Norman Brook, to warn Profumo. On 9 August 1961, in panic, John Profumo wrote a note to Christine Keeler:

Darling,
In great haste & because I can get no reply from your phone.
Alas something's blown up tomorrow night & I can't therefore make it. I'm terribly sorry especially as I leave the next day for various trips & then a holiday so won't be able to see you again until some time in September. Blast it.
Please take care of yourself & don't run away.
Love J

I'm writing this cos I know you 're off the day after tomorrow & I want you to know before you go if I still can't reach you by phone.

It was this note that sealed his fate.

Despite the warning, Profumo continued seeing Christine Keeler for another four months. During that time, he took amazing risks. One evening an army officer turned up at the flat looking for Ward.

'I had to introduce him to the War Minister,' said Keeler. 'The colonel couldn't believe it. Jack nearly died.'

Profumo only broke it off in December because Keeler refused to move out of Ward's flat and into a discreet love nest that he was going to buy for her.

MI5 began to lose interest in the plan to honeytrap Ivanov. They were finding Ward increasingly unreliable. Keeler had moved on, too. While scoring marijuana for Ward, she had met West Indian jazz singer, Lucky Cordon, and, through him, another West Indian named Johnny Edgecombe. She had begun sleeping with both of them. This had led to a fight at an all-night club in Soho in October 1962, where Cordon got his face slashed. Keeler moved in with Edgecombe briefly. When things did not work out, she moved back into Ward's flat. One night, Edgecombe came round to try and win her back. It was late and she would not let him in. He pulled a gun and blasted the front door. The police were called and Edgecombe was arrested and charged with attempted murder.

After this incident, Ward asked Keeler to leave the flat. She turned to one of his patients, solicitor Michael Eddowes, for help. She told him that she and Ward had actually been spying for the Russians and that Ward had asked her to find out from Profumo about British plans to arm West Germany with nuclear weapons.

She told the same story to former Labour MP, John Lewis, who had a personal dislike of Ward. He passed the information on to George Wigg, a Labour MP who disliked Profumo after he had bested him in the House. In January 1963, Paul Mann, a journalist, took Keeler to the *Sunday Pictorial*. Keeler showed the *Pictorial* the note that Profumo had written and the paper offered her £1,000 for her story.

However, the newspapers were exceedingly cautious at the time. The previous year, the exposure of the spy John Vassall, an admiralty clerk who had been passing secrets to the Soviets, had led to a Tribunal of Inquiry that had investigated the role of the press in the affair. In the course of it, two journalists had been sent to prison for refusing to name their sources.

The *Pictorial* contacted Ward, who managed to convince the paper that Keeler's story was a pack of lies and publication was dropped. This annoyed Keeler so she went to the police and told them that Ward procured call girls for his rich clients. A few days later, Profumo found himself being questioned by the Attorney General Sir John Hobson, the Solicitor General Peter Rawlinson and the Chief Whip Martin Redmayne. He denied any impropriety with Keeler. Although sceptical, they chose to accept what he was saying.

Prime Minister Harold Macmillan was briefed. A man of the world, he said that if Profumo had had an affair with Keeler he had been foolish, but sleeping with a pretty young woman, even if she was alleged to be prostitute, was hardly a sackable offence. Everyone hoped that that was the end of it. But on 8 March 1963, a small-circulation newsletter called *Westminster Confidential* ran a piece about the story that the *Pictorial* had dropped. It repeated the allegation that both the War Secretary and a Soviet military attaché, one Colonel Ivanov, were the clients of the same call girl.

On 10 March, George Wigg, who by this time had a bulging

dossier on the relationship between Profumo and Keeler, took it to the Labour leader, Harold Wilson. Wilson urged caution, but events now had a momentum of their own.

On 14 March, Johnny Edgecombe came up for trial at the Old Bailey. The key witness, Christine Keeler, was on holiday and it was rumoured that she had been whisked out of the country to keep a lid on the scandal.

The next day, the *Daily Express* ran the headline, 'WAR MINISTER SHOCK'. It claimed that John Profumo had tendered his resignation for 'personal reasons'. Down the page was a picture of Christine Keeler under the headline, 'VANISHED'.

The *Express* later claimed that the juxtaposition of the two stories was purely coincidental. But everyone put two and two together.

On 19 March, during a debate on the Vassall case, George Wigg, under the protection of parliamentary privilege, raised the rumours circulating about the War Minister. He was supported by Barbara Castle and the Labour front-bencher Dick Crossman. The government was flustered. The Home Secretary, Henry Brooke, told the Labour critics that if they wanted to substantiate their accusations, they should use a different forum, one that was not shielded from the laws of libel by the cloak of privilege.

Profumo had one supporter though – backbench Labour MP, Reginald Paget.

'What do these rumours amount to?' Paget asked rhetorically. 'They amount to the fact that a minister is said to be acquainted with an extremely pretty girl. As far as I am concerned, I should have thought that was matter for congratulation rather than an inquiry.'

Profumo was then grilled again by the Chief Whip, the Leader of the House Iain Macleod and Bill Deedes, Minister without Portfolio and future editor of *The Daily Telegraph*. Profumo again insisted that he was innocent. He then made a parliamentary statement. In it he admitted knowing

Christine Keeler, but said he had not seen her since December 1961. He also said that he had met Stephen Ward and Yevgeny Ivanov. He denied that he was in any way responsible for her absence from the trial and stated categorically: 'There was no impropriety whatsoever in my acquaintanceship with Miss Keeler.' He threatened anyone who repeated the allegations outside the House with a writ.

A few days later, the newspapers caught up with Christine Keeler in Madrid. She confirmed what Profumo had said, but George Wigg would not leave it at that. He went on the *Panorama* TV programme and said that Ward and Ivanov were security risks. The next day, Ward met Wigg and tried to convince him that it was not true. He failed. More than ever, Wigg believed that Profumo had lied. He wrote a report of his meeting with Ward and gave it to Harold Wilson, who passed it on to Macmillan.

Although the Vassall case was keeping the British press subdued, there was no such reticence in the foreign papers. Profumo issued writs against *Paris Match* and *Il Tempo Illustrato*, which both said that he had been bonking Christine Keeler.

In an attempt to salvage the situation, the Home Secretary told the Metropolitan Police to try and find something on Ward. This was highly irregular. The police are supposed to investigate crimes and find out who committed them, not investigate people on the off chance they have committed a crime.

It soon became clear to Ward's friends and clients that he was in serious trouble. They deserted him in droves. Mandy Rice-Davis was arrested on trumped-up charges and held in prison until she agreed to testify against Ward.

Ward desperately wrote to everyone he could think of, protesting his innocence. Harold Wilson received a letter. He showed it to the Prime Minister, who agreed to set up a committee of inquiry under Lord Dilhome. Profumo was on holiday at the time. When he returned, he realized that the game was up. He could not face a committee of inquiry and lie again, so he went to see the Chief Whip and Macmillan's Parliamentary Private Secretary, told them that he had lied and resigned.

His letter of resignation and Macmillan's reply were published the next day.

'I misled you, and my colleagues, and the House,' Profumo wrote, but, he explained, 'I did this to protect my wife and family.'

Macmillan's terse reply said: 'I am sure you will understand that in the circumstances I have no alternative but to advise the Queen to accept your resignation.'

The very day this exchange appeared in the papers, 5 June 1963, there was more drama. Christine Keeler's other West Indian boyfriend, Lucky Cordon, came to court on the charge of assaulting her outside a friend's flat. Keeler turned up in court in a Rolls Royce.

From the dock, Cordon accused her of giving him VD. She responded with an outburst from the public gallery. The newspapers lapped it up. Cordon was sent down for three years, which was overturned on appeal.

Ward appeared on TV on 9 June and denied that he had encouraged Christine Keeler to have an affair with John Profumo because he had a friend in the Soviet Embassy. The following day he was arrested and charged with living on immoral earnings.

By this time, newspapers world-wide were running the scandal on the front page. Mandy Rice-Davis told the *Washington Star* about society orgies in London. She mentioned that at one dinner party, a naked man wearing only a mask waited on table. The hunt for the masked man was on. Was it a senior judge, a cabinet minister or a member of the royal family?

Under the headline, 'PRINCE PHILIP AND THE PROFUMO SCANDAL, the *Daily Mirror* vehemently dismissed the 'foul rumour' that Prince Philip was involved. The

Queen's Consort was a member of a gentleman's association called the Thursday Club, which also boasted Stephen Ward among its membership.

Allegations flew thick and fast. Everyone in any position in society was now a target. The Bishop of Southwark, Mervyn Stockwood, appealed for calm.

Politically the question came down to: how had John Profumo managed to lie about his affair for so long? Macmillan, who had taken a lenient attitude to the matter back in January, was now in the firing line. Colleagues began to sense that his tenure of office was drawing to a close. Lord Hailsham quit his title to become a contender for the premiership. He threw his hat into the ring by appearing on television and condemning Profumo for lying. Again, Reginald Paget rallied to Profumo's defence.

'When self-indulgence has reduced a man to the shape of Lord Hailsham,' he said, 'sexual continence involves no more than a sense of the ridiculous'.

Milking the situation for all it was worth, Mandy Rice-Davis told the *Sunday Mirror* that the Soviet military attaché and the War Minister had missed bumping into each other at Ward's flat by a matter of minutes on a number of occasions.

Michael Eddowes issued a press statement, saying that he had warned the Prime Minister of the security risk as early as 29 March. Meanwhile, Christine Keeler sold her 'confessions' to the *News of the World*, which began serializing them.

The Times attacked the Conservative government for its lack of moral leadership. To this, Lord Hailsham responded petulantly: '*The Times* is an anti-Conservative newspaper with an anti-Conservative editor.'

Even the *Washington Post* got in on the act, saying that 'a picture of widespread decadence beneath the glitter of a large segment of stiff-lipped society is emerging.'

Labour went on the offensive. In a debate in the House of Commons on 19 June, Harold Wilson said that the

Profumo scandal had 'shocked the moral conscience of the nation'. Pointing the finger at the Prime Minister, he said that for political reasons he was gambling with national security.

Macmillan could not even count on the support of his own backbenchers. Conservative MP, Nigel Birch, stated the simple facts of the case.

'I must say that [Profumo] never struck me as a man at all like a cloister monk,' he told the House. 'And Miss Keeler is a professional prostitute. There seems to me to be a basic improbability that their relationship was purely platonic. What are whores about?'

Addressing the Prime Minister directly, he said: 'I myself feel that the time will come very soon when my Right Honourable Friend ought to make way for a much younger colleague.'

Macmillan survived the debate but was badly wounded. Four days later, he announced an official inquiry under Lord Denning. It did not save him. Macmillan resigned in the early autumn, shortly before the party conference. He was replaced by Sir Alec Douglas Home, but the Conservative government was tainted by the scandal and was swept from office the following year.

Although Lord Denning was supposed to look into possible breaches of security caused by the Profumo scandal, like Ken Starr, he concentrated on the salacious aspects – so much so that when he cross-questioned witnesses, he often sent the official stenographer out of the room to save her, or perhaps his own, blushes.

When Ward went on trial at the Old Bailey, the world's media were there in force. Again, the salacious details were played up. One newspaper in New Zealand was prosecuted for indecency for merely reporting the case.

The star of the show was undoubtedly Mandy Rice-Davis, whom the judge mistakenly addressed as Marilyn Monroe. When it was put to her that Lord Astor had denied that he had met her at his house parties at Cliveden, she said: 'Well, he would, wouldn't he?' That remark is now in the *Oxford Dictionary of Quotations*.

In his summing up, the judge pointed out that none of Ward's highborn friends had come to testify on his behalf.

'One would have thought from the newspapers that this country has become a sink of iniquity,' he told the jury. 'But you and I know that the even tenor of family life over the overwhelming majority of the population goes quietly and decently on.'

He might as well have been putting the noose around the defendant's neck. The judge was implying that Ward was not just guilty of introducing rich and powerful people to a couple of attractive and available girls, but that he was responsible for the general loosening of moral standards that many people felt was engulfing the country. Ward knew that he was being made a scapegoat.

'This is a political trial,' he told a friend. 'Someone had to be sacrificed and that someone is me.'

On the night of 3 July 1963, Ward took an overdose of sleeping tablets. He left a suicide note saying that, after the judge's summing up, he had given up all hope. He asked that resuscitation be delayed as long as possible, adding, bizarrely, that 'the car needs oil in the gearbox'.

With Ward unconscious in St Stephen's Hospital, the jury found him guilty on two counts of living on immoral earnings. He died on 3 August, without regaining consciousness. Even after he was dead, the newspapers kept vilifying him.

There were only six mourners at Stephen Ward's funeral and only two wreaths. One came from his family. The other was from Kenneth Tynan, John Osbourne, Arnold Wesker, Joe Orton, Annie Ross, Dominick Elwes and Penelope Gilliatt. The card on it read: 'To Stephen Ward, victim of hypocrisy'.

When the Denning report was published in October 1963,

it was an instant best-seller, selling over 4,000 copies in the first hour. It, too, laid the blame squarely at the door of Stephen Ward, who was in no position to answer back.

Profumo, left political life and threw himself into charity work, for which he was awarded the CBE in 1975. He remained married to Valerie Hobson. Christine Keeler was jailed for six months for contempt of court for failing to appear at the trial of Johnny Edgecombe. Her autobiography *Scandal* was published in 1989 and was made into a successful movie.

Mandy Rice-Davis wrote a series of novels, became a film actress, opened two clubs in Israel and married a millionaire. George Wigg became chairman of the Horse Race Betting Levy Board and later pleaded guilty to soliciting for prostitutes in Soho.

Watergate

Until the presidential follies of Bill Clinton, it was a safe bet that Watergate was going to be the political scandal of the 20th century. It involved break-ins, coverups, slush funds, dirty tricks, black lists, presidential paranoia, illegal taping and deleted expletives. As a result, Richard Nixon became the first – and, so far, only US President to be forced to resign from office.

The causes of the Watergate scandal lay deep in the character of Richard Nixon. Born in small-town California, he saw himself as the perpetual outsider. Even when he was President, he thought that the Eastern Establishment and the liberal big city press would stop at nothing to get him. He may have been right. Few politicians have been more hated and feared than Richard Nixon.

Nixon started off on the wrong foot. As a young congressman, he sat on the House Un-American Activities Committee and was pivotal in the downfall of Alger Hiss, an official with the State Department revealed, falsely, many believe to be a Soviet spy.

Being conspicuously on the right of the party, he was picked as running mate to the liberal-leaning Dwight Eisenhower in 1952 to balance the ticket. This provoked an immediate scandal when it was alleged that he controlled a secret slush fund set up by wealthy Californian businessmen. Nixon responded by going on television – still a relatively untried medium – and made his famous 'Checkers' speech. In it he protested his innocence. He claimed that instead of going around in fur coats, his wife Pat wore a good old-fashioned cloth coat. The only gift his family had ever received, he assured viewers, was a puppy dog called Checkers and he was darned if he was going to give that back. It was a bravura performance and earned him the sobriquet, among opponents at least, of 'TrickyDicky'.

After two terms as vice-president, Nixon was nominated to be Eisenhower's successor, although with little enthusiasm from Eisenhower himself. However, he narrowly lost the 1960 election to John F. Kennedy, possibly as a result of Democratic ballot-stuffing in key districts. Although Kennedy was an Irish Catholic, in Nixon's eyes he was everything he hated – moneyed, an Easterner, a writer, an intellectual and a Harvard man.

In 1962, Nixon was decisively defeated when he ran for the governorship of California. At a press conference the following day, he told reporters: 'For 16 years, you have had a lot of fun. Now you won't have Nixon to kick around any more because, gentlemen, this is my last press conference.'

But he was wrong. He got a further kicking when he and his campaign manager, H.R. 'Bob' Haldeman were fined for using unfair campaign practices. Even so, his appetite for power was unsated.

After the Republican Barry Goldwater was routed by the

incumbent Lyndon Johnson, Nixon set about re-establishing himself as a leading figure in the party. In 1968, he won the Republican nomination once again. This time he had luck on his side. Johnson's popular domestic policies were completely swamped by the nation's catastrophic involvement in the Vietnam War and Johnson refused to run again. The assassination of Robert Kennedy robbed the Democrats of their natural leader, and the assassination of Martin Luther King that year sparked race riots. The Democratic convention in Chicago degenerated into a running battle between Mayor Daley's brutal police and the peace protesters and civil rights activists. Nixon claimed to speak for the 'silent majority' and promised to bring back law and order. He also stole what was left of the Democrats' clothes. The Democratic nominee, Hubert Humphrey, although a man of impeccable liberal credentials, had been vice-president in the Johnson administration and was thus tainted by the war. Nixon, however, promised to end the war, bringing 'peace with honour'. He won by a landslide.

But Nixon was not a peacemaker by instinct. He stepped up the war, extending into neighbouring Laos and Cambodia. This was illegal. War could only be declared by Congress. But Nixon figured that even if this did not bring the victory the Pentagon promised him, it would help bomb the Vietnamese to the bargaining table.

To conduct such a clandestine policy under the very eyes of the Eastern Establishment required the utmost secrecy. There were few people in Washington he could trust. Nixon surrounded himself with other outsiders, men who had not held public office and had no political ideas above the acquisition of power for its own sake.

Haldeman, a former public relations man, became the White House Chief of Staff, who controlled access to the President. Nixon's former law partner and 1968 campaign manager, John Mitchell, became Attorney General.

Another PR man and a friend of Haldeman, John Ehrlichman, became the Assistant for Domestic Affairs.

Nixon felt the danger of domestic sedition most keenly due to the growing opposition to the Vietnam War. But he also mistrusted such a natural ally as the FBI Director, J. Edgar Hoover, and tried to sack him more than once. Hoover had been head of the Bureau since its inception in the 1920s. He had a power base of his own and was not to be shifted. Nixon saw him as a rival and a threat.

Even more, Nixon mistrusted the CIA for what he saw as its Ivy League pedigree and its history of accommodation with America's enemies. He set up his own private intelligence capability, responsible only to the White House.

Then there were the Democrats. In 1970-71, he set up a number of projects to bug political opponents and harrass the press. The operations were overseen by Nixon's appointment secretary Dwight Chapin, press secretary Ron Ziegler, Haldeman's aide Gordon Strachan and White House attorney Don Segretti – all of whom had been members of a student club at the University of South California called the Trojan Knights, which specialized in stuffing ballot boxes and other election tricks.

Opposition to the war entered the mainstream when, in June 1971, the *New York Times* began publishing the 'Pentagon Papers'. These were a secret history of the war in Vietnam and contained damaging information about America's involvement, particularly Nixon's illegal incursions into Laos and Cambodia. The source was Daniel Ellsberg, a former intelligence analyst at the Pentagon.

Nixon's response was to set up a `special investigations unit' to collect information on Ellsberg and his links to the Democrats, especially to Ted Kennedy, who threatened to run for president in 1972. Wrapped in the mantle of his two dead brothers, he would have made a formidable opponent.

The unit was quickly dubbed the 'plumbers'. Ehrlichman

was in charge and his aide Egil Krogh Jr ran the unit from Room 216 in the Executive Office building next door to the White House. It had a staff of about 50 in all. The senior men included National Security Council staff lawyer, David Young, and Nixon's own special counsel and action man, Charles Colson.

Colson recruited E. Howard Hunt, an ex-CIA man who had been involved in the abortive CIA invasion of Cuba that was thwarted at the Bay of Pigs. He was joined by former FBI agent and assistant district attorney, G. Gordon Liddy.

Their first object was to smear Ellsberg. On 3 September 1971, Hunt and Liddy stood guard as three of Hunt's Cuban contacts burgled the office of Ellsberg's psychiatrist.

Liddy was plainly a man who could be relied on so in December 1971, White House counsel John Dean picked him to work under John Mitchell and Jed Magruder at the Committee to Re-Elect the President, known by the wonderful acronym CREEP. Liddy's job title was General Counsel, but his job was 'political intelligence-gathering.' On 27 January 1972, he outlined a plan called Operation Gemstone to Mitchell, Magruder and Dean. In the forthcoming election, he aimed to wage a campaign of sabotage, blackmail, kidnapping, break-ins and electronic surveillance. It would cost a cool $1 million.

Although Mitchell rejected the plan as too expensive, Liddy was authorized to put a scaled-down version of Gemstone into effect, with a budget of just $250,000. The first operation was to be a break-in at the campaign headquarters of Senator George McGovern, who had emerged as the front-runner for the Democratic nomination that year. It was a failure. But that same night, 26 March 1972, Liddy, Hunt and their team of Cubans broke into the Democratic National Committee offices in the Watergate building. James W. McCord, CREEP's 'security co-ordinator', installed two wiretaps. In the nature of things, only one of the wiretaps worked and it produced little more than secretarial chitchat.

The 'plumbers' decided to have another go on the night of 16 June 1972. It ended in disaster. An alert night-watchman called the police who arrested five intruders on the sixth floor of the Watergate building. They were carrying bugging devices, walkie-talkies and substantial sums of money. They gave false names, but on interrogation quickly admitted their true identities.

The five men were James McCord, which tied the break-in to CREEP; former CIA agent Bernard Baker; Frank Sturgis, a US-born mercenary who had fought both for and against Castro; and two Cubans, Virgilio Gonzalez and Eugenio Martinez, a locksmith. Liddy, Hunt and Alfred C. Baldwin, a former FBI agent, were nearby supervising the operation and got away.

These men may well have staged this break-in on their own authority. But the chain of command ran back via Strachan and Krogh to Haldeman and Ehrlichman, the President's closest advisers, and via Mitchell to the President himself.

Nixon claimed that news of the break-in came to him while he was on holiday in Key Biscayne, Florida. His reaction was that bugging the headquarters of the Democratic National Committee was stupid – 'anyone who knew anything about politics would know that the national committee headquarters was a useless place to go for inside information on a presidential campaign,' he wrote in his memoirs.

When the five burglars were arraigned in court on 17 June, they identified themselves as `anti-Communists' and McCord whispered 'CIA' to the judge. Press reports identified McCord as the security co-ordinator of CREEP, but Mitchell issued a statement saying that McCord had been hired merely as a temporary security consultant who had been let go a month before.

The story would have ended there, but for two young reporters at the *Washington Post* – 29-year-old Bob Woodward and 28-year-old Carl Berstein who discovered that address books found on two of the burglars contained the name of E. Howard Hunt.

On 20 June 1972, the *Washington Post* reported that Hunt worked as a consultant to Charles Colson, Nixon's own special counsel. This linked the break-in dangerously close to the President.

The White House was rattled. The internal phone directories were recalled and amended to disguise the fact that Hunt had an office there. John Dean told Hunt to get out of the country, which he did – briefly. Liddy melodramatically offered to stand on a street corner where he could be gunned down.

Dean devised complex cover stories to prevent the operation being traced beyond Liddy and up the chain of command. Hush money was paid to the burglars. The cover-up was in full swing.

But there was another wild card. Baldwin who had probably been an FBI plant, told the FBI that Hunt and Liddy had been involved. Nixon had to be informed. Fatefully, on 23 June 1972, Nixon and Haldeman discussed the possibility of using the CIA to block the FBI's enquiries.

Hunt and Liddy had to be sacrificed, but the trial of the 'Watergate Seven' was scheduled for January 1973, conveniently after the November election. As it was, Nixon romped home. The Democrats were in disarray. In July they had to drop their vice-presidential candidate, Thomas Eagleton, when it was revealed that he had been hospitalized three times for 'nervous exhaustion and fatigue'. Their presidential nominee, George McGovern, was an anti-war candidate. But, since Nixon was only months away from a negotiated end to the American involvement in the Vietnam War, it seemed sensible to let him finish the job.

At the trial, McCord and Liddy both pleaded not guilty, but at the last minute Hunt changed his plea to guilty. Throughout the hearings, the judge, John Sirica, was irritated by the government prosecutors who seemed to be handling the defendants with kid gloves. The trial passed off without anyone, outside the seven conspirators, being implicated and all seven were convicted of conspiracy, burglary and illegal wiretapping.

However, press stories, largely in the *Washington Post*, continued to link the conspirators to the White House and it was beginning to become clear that the Watergate break-in was only part of a wide programme of electoral dirty tricks. On February 1973 the Senate voted to set up a committee under Senator Sam Ervin to investigate irregularities during the presidential campaign.

FBI director J. Edgar Hoover had died in May 1972. Nixon wanted the acting director, L. Patrick Gray, to be confirmed as his replacement. So while the Ervin committee sat, Gray went before the Senate Judiciary Committee. There he revealed that the FBI had failed to interview key witnesses in the Watergate case and that he had allowed the President's counsel, John Dean, to sit in on interviews of White House personnel.

This put the spotlight on Dean, the man who had co-ordinated the cover up. He was called to testify to the Ervin committee, but refused. Nixon had already made it clear that he would not let White House staff testify on the grounds of executive privilege. Ervin warned that White House staff were not nobility or royalty. If they failed to comply with subpoenas, he would recommend that the Senate issued warrants for their arrest.

On 23 March, Judge Sirica handed down savage sentences on the Watergate conspirators – 20 years for Liddy, 35 for Hunt and 40 years for Barker, Conzalez, Martinez and Sturgis – more than they would have expected for murder in the District of Columbia. However, Sirica made it clear that these sentences were provisional and would be reviewed in the light of how much they co-operated with Ervin's committee.

McCord was not sentenced at that time. Instead, Sirica read a statement from McCord, admitting that political pressure had been applied for him to plead guilty and keep quiet. The defendants had perjured themselves, he said. They knew that others involved in the Watergate operation had not been identified at the trial. He was released and given immunity to subsequent prosecution.

On 26 March, McCord told the *Los Angeles Times* that both Magruder and Dean knew of the Watergate break-in in advance. Dean was beginning to get rattled. He warned Nixon that there was 'a cancer close to the presidency, and it's growing', Hunt was now demanding more money, otherwise he would tell what he knew about the Ellsberg break-in and bring Ehrlichman down.

By 8 April, Dean was talking to the prosecutors via his lawyer. Haldeman and Ehrlichman were pressuring him to persuade Mitchell to take the rap for the break-in, hoping the buck would stop there. Meanwhile, Magruder was talking to the prosecutors, telling them that Mitchell and Dean had coached him to commit perjury as part of the cover-up. He also outlined Liddy's Gemstone plan and confirmed that hush money had been paid to the burglars.

Under pressure from the prosecutors, Dean gave way, implicating Haldeman in the hush-money payments and Ehrlichman in the destruction of incriminating documents removed from Hunt's safe.

Nixon summoned Dean to the Oval Office. Dean expected to be hauled over the coals, but Nixon was surprisingly cautious in his choice of words. For the first time, Dean began to suspect that conversations in the Oval Office were being taped.

Nixon wanted Dean to resign, citing his 'involvement in the Watergate affair'. When Dean refused, Nixon removed executive privilege from White House staff, hoping to force Dean's hand. If his testimony to the Senate committee resulted in his prosecution, only the President could offer him executive clemency. However, this move had the opposite effect on Dean. He now sought to make a deal with the prosecutors, telling what he knew in exchange for immunity from prosecution. He told the press that he was not willing to be 'a scapegoat in the Watergate case' and spent the rest of his time in the White House, gathering all the incriminating material he could put his hands on.

But a scapegoat is exactly what Nixon intended Dean to be. On 26 April, the White House leaked a story to the columnist Jack Anderson, saying that Mitchell and Dean had known about the break-in from the outset. They had orchestrated the cover-up and the payment of hush money. Dean had misled Nixon over the matter and Ehrlichman and Colson had laboured to discover the truth. This would not wash.

The following day, Patrick Gray resigned as acting head of the FBI, after newspaper reports revealed that he had burnt documents from Hunt's safe, given to him by Ehrlichman and Dean.

On 30 April 1973, Nixon went on TV and admitted there had been a cover-up – 'an effort to conceal the facts from the public, from you and from me'. The break-in, he said, had been a 'senseless, illegal action'.

'The easiest course would be for me to blame those to whom I delegated the responsibility to run the campaign,' he told the American people unblinkingly. 'But that would be a cowardly thing to do. In any organization, the man at the top must bear the responsibility. I accept it.'

As to the cover-up, he had received 'continuing assurances' from those investigating the matter that no one in the White House was involved, up until 21 March. Now he was going to have to accept the resignations of Haldeman and Ehrlichman – 'two of the finest public servants it has

been my privilege to know'. There was, he said, 'no implication whatsoever of personal wrongdoing on their part'.
He pointedly did not give the same assurance when he
announced the resignation of John Dean.

'I will do everything in my power to ensure that the
guilty are brought to justice,' he said solemnly. 'There can
be no whitewash at the White House.'

No one believed him.

In an effort to draw a line under the scandal, Nixon was
fulsome in his praise for everyone in sight, including the
'vigorous free press'. Woodward and Bernstein were singled out for an apology by White House press spokesman,
Ron Ziegler, for the vilification he had previously heaped
upon them.

But the scent of blood was now in the air. If Haldeman
and Ehrlichman knew about the cover-up, surely Nixon
must have known, too. And if he was willing to sacrifice
two of his closest advisors, he must be fighting for his very
survival.

The following day, the Senate passed a unanimous vote
calling on the President to appoint a Special Prosecutor.
This was to be Archibald Cox. He was professor of law at
Harvard. Worse, he was a Kennedy man.

By now it was clear that the Watergate 'plumbers.' had
also been behind the break-in at Ellsberg's psychiatrist's.
Charges against Ellsberg of theft, conspiracy and espionage for the leaking of the 'Pentagon Papers' were dismissed on the grounds of 'government misconduct'.

The task in hand now was to tie the Watergate break-in
and the subsequent cover-up to Nixon himself. The Ervin
committee, now staging televised hearings, were asking
one central question. As Senator Howard Baker put it:
'What did the President know, and when did he know it?'

McCord told the committee that a Treasury Department
official, John J. Caulfield, had brought him an offer of
clemency 'from the very highest levels of the White

House' in exchange for his silence at the Watergate trial. Caulfield testified that the offer had come from Dean, not Nixon.

Haldeman and Ehrlichman also blamed Dean. Along with the President, they had scarcely given Watergate a thought during the summer of 1972. It was up to Dean to keep them informed.

Dean came out with guns blazing. He told the committee that Nixon kept an enemies list. People on it were to be targeted for harassment by the FBI and the Internal Revenue Service. Dean denied that he had been employed by Nixon to investigate who was responsible for the Watergate break-in. Rather, he was to find out what the FBI and the Justice Department had discovered and to come up with 'plausible scenarios' to obscure White House involvement. He testified that as early as September 1972, Nixon had known of his cover-up activities. And, most damning of all, at a meeting on 21 March with Haldeman present, he said that Nixon had assured him that there was 'no problem' raising a further $1 million to buy the continuing silence of the Watergate burglars.

Dean was then asked whether he was `fully aware of the charges you have made under oath against the highest official of our land'. He replied: `I realize it's an almost impossible task, it's one man against another. And it's not a very pleasant situation.'

But Dean was lucky. It was not just one man's word against another's. On 16 July 1973, one of Haldeman's aides told the committee that Nixon had a system for taping the conversations in his private offices. Both the Senate Investigating Committee and Special Prosecutor then issued subpoenas demanding access to those tapes.

At this point, Nixon considered destroying the tapes. But that, he concluded, would look like an admission of guilt. He also thought that the tapes could still be of some use to him. They gave him a hold over others who, like Dean, might turn against him. He also thought that he still had some degree of control over the tapes and their release.

On 29 August 1973, Judge Sirica ordered Nixon to hand over the tapes of eight specified conversations. He refused, although he eventually conceded that he would hand over a summary of the specified tapes. These would be authenticated by John C. Stennis, a partially deaf senator from Mississippi. In exchange, Archibald Cox was to make no further attempts to gain access to the tapes. Cox refused. In response, Nixon abolished the office of Special Prosecutor and ordered the Attorney General, Elliot Richardson, to sack Cox. Both Richardson and his deputy resigned. Cox had to be sacked by the third in line in the Justice Department, Solicitor General Robert Bork.

The reaction to this high-handed action was overwhelming. Millions of letters and telegrams of protest poured into Washington. Congress considered impeachment for the first time. This became a genuine possibility on 10 October when the demagogic vice-president, Spiro Agnew, resigned after pleading *nolo contendre* – no contest – to charges that he had accepted millions of dollars in bribes from engineering contractors when he had been Chief Executive of Baltimore in the early 1960s. In his place, Nixon appointed the dull but safe Gerald Ford.

This move sealed Nixon's fate. No one would have removed him if Agnew was going to take over. But Ford seemed a decent alternative.

On 23 October, Nixon surrendered the tapes that Sirica had asked for. He was now isolated. He had lost all his top advisors and dared speak to no one. Even his new White House Chief of Staff, General Alexander Haig, was seen as a man loyal to the all-powerful Secretary of State, Henry Kissinger, rather than to Nixon. Kissinger was one of the few top men in the Nixon administration to come through with his reputation more or less unsullied.

Although Nixon had taken to brooding alone in the White House, on 17 November he gave a press conference. It was another mistake. Emotionally, he told the assembled journalists: 'I am not a crook.' It was a phrase that would become the derisive chant of the demonstrators who came to taunt him.

Things went from bad to worse. On 21 November, White House counsel J. Fred Buzhardt had to deliver the embarrassing news that the first 19 minutes of the first tape Sirica had subpoenaed had been wiped. It was from 20 June 1972, Nixon's first day back in the White House following the Watergate break-in. The story was that Nixon's long-serving secretary, Rose Mary Woods, had accidentally erased it. This was later shown to be impossible, but no one believed it anyway.

This was the straw that broke the camel's back. The House of Representatives then voted 401 to 4 for the House Judicial Committee to begin drawing up a bill of impeachment. Haldeman, Ehrlichman, Strachan, Mitchell and Colson were all indicted by a Grand Jury for conspiracy, perjury and obstruction of justice.

Nixon made one last bid to hold on to office. He offered to release to the Judiciary Committee all the tapes that the Special Prosecutor had demanded. And he admitted the broad outline of the conversation he had had with John Dean on 21 March. But this only whetted their appetite. They demanded more tapes. Instead, he offered to release transcripts of the tapes they asked for and others that, he assured the nation on television, would prove that he had no prior knowledge of the break-in and no knowledge of the cover-up, until the conversation with Dean on 21 March. The transcripts would be edited for relevance and national security considerations, and senior members of the Judiciary Committee would be able to check the tapes to ensure their accuracy.

On 30 April 1974, a 200,000-word transcript was released

to the public. It did him no good. They clearly showed that Nixon had discussed misleading scenarios and hush money – though he claimed he was simply thinking out loud. Prudish supporters were shocked by the 146 gaps marked 'expletive deleted'. Others were appalled by the rambling nature of his thought processes which were sometimes reduced to a series of incoherent grunts.

And the transcripts, bad as they were, did not even tell the whole truth. The Judiciary Committee found a number of passages that had been incorrectly transcribed, and published its own version – transcribed, it said, using superior audio equipment. For example, the Judiciary Committee's version has Nixon telling Dean on 22 March to 'get on with the cover-up plan', whereas the White House version contains the rather less damning 'get off the cover-up line'. And in some places, key passages discussing the cover-up were missing from the White House version altogether.

Nixon was all but finished, when Judge Sirica revealed that when Haldeman et al had been indicted on 1 March, Nixon had been named as a co-conspirator, but an indictment had not been handed up because no one was sure if you could bring a criminal indictment against a sitting president. Despite the now familiar misgivings about the impeachment process, the House Judiciary Committee's hand was now forced. Three articles of impeachment were passed. Even so, Nixon still had his supporters in Congress, particularly in the Senate, and the outcome of the impeachment procedure was far from certain.

The killer blow came from the Supreme Court which, in a unanimous decision, ordered Nixon to hand over even more tapes to be used in the Haldeman conspiracy trial. On one of those tapes was a conversation from 23 June 1972, in which Nixon had ordered Haldeman to try to get the CIA to block the FBI's investigation into the origin of the money the Watergate burglars were carrying. Nixon had kept the existence of this conversation secret, even from his own attorney. It was what everyone had been looking for from the beginning the 'smoking gun'. Here was the chief law officer of the United States using the machinery of government to block a criminal investigation. It was a clear case of obstruction of justice.

When Nixon told Buzhardt, Haig, Kissinger and his counsel James St Clair, they urged him to resign. Although Nixon admitted that portions of the tape were 'at variance with certain of my previous statements' he protested that `the record, in its entirety, does not justify the extreme step of impeachment'. Congress did not agree. After a private briefing, Republican leaders told Nixon that 425 of the 435 members of Congress would vote for impeachment and that only a dozen senators would vote against his conviction.

The following day, 8 August 1974, Nixon made a speech trumpeting his foreign policy achievements, but announcing that he was going to stand down because 'it has become evident to me that I no longer have a strong enough political base in the Congress'. The day after that, he formally resigned and Gerald Ford became the first US president not to have been elected either as president or vice-president.

After only a month in office, Ford granted Nixon a 'full, free and absolute' pardon. This cooked his goose. Some of his staff resigned in protest and Ford was voted out of office in 1976.

The Prisoners Left Behind

The Watergate scandal covered up another, more serious, scandal created by the Nixon White House, that did not come to the attention of the American public until 1985 with the release of the film, *Rambo: First Blood Part Two*. In the movie, Vietnam veteran John Rambo returns to South-east Asia to rescue American prisoners of war held there more than 10 years after the US's ignominious withdrawal in 1973. But it is not only the Vietnamese he has to fight. He also faces the opposition of the CIA, Department of Defence and even the US government itself, which had been covering up the fact that they had left American prisoners behind in Communist hands after the end of the war.

Rambo was not the first film to suggest this. There had been a series of them, including one called *Missing in Action*. The missing prisoners were known across America as MIAs, in the mistaken belief that they had been listed as 'missing in action' during the war.

In the 1980s, polls showed that between 73 and 85 per cent of Americans believed that their government had left prisoners behind in Vietnamese hands. But the government denied it. Indeed, in 1978, the Carter administration had officially declared dead any men listed as 'missing' or 'prisoner' during the war, who had not returned home. So what was the truth?

To discover that, you have to go back and look at the whole conduct of the war. America's war in Vietnam began with the Gulf of Tonkin incident, when the US government claimed that the US *Maddox* was attacked by three Vietnamese gunboats in the Gulf of Tonkin. It is debatable whether this incident ever happened, but Congress passed the Gulf of Tonkin Resolution, which funded the war.

Officially, the war was contained to Vietnam itself, but secretly the Americans fought in neighbouring Laos and Cambodia, too. On the ground in Vietnam, America, with its overwhelming technological superiority, falsified enemy casualty figures to Congress who had to foot the bill. This falsification of intelligence was a key factor in America's defeat in the Vietnam War. It also cast doubt on the US's own casualty figures.

Although Vietnam veterans claimed that comrades who had been listed KIA killed in action – were, in fact, prison-

293

ers, they could not prove their case. It was non-commissioned officers at America's National Security Agency, who first discovered what was happening. The NSA, one of America's most secret intelligence organizations, eavesdropped on Vietnamese military communications. They discovered that American airmen shot down over Communist-held territory were being segregated as soon as they were captured. Ordinary pilots were taken to the camps around Hanoi. Those who had special skills – backseat electronic warfare officers, the crews of the brand new F-111, those who had been on space programmes, or men with special qualifications were flown into the Soviet Union. No airman shot down over South-east Asia was ever returned from the USSR.

Men who were badly injured were sent to the medical facilities in Shanghai, in China. Others were used as slave labour on installations of strategic importance. Since the war between North and South Vietnam continued after the Americans withdrew, these men could not be handed back. They knew too much.

Throughout the Vietnam War, the people of the Communist North were told that prisoners of war were valuable. Leaflets explained that downed American pilots would be exchanged for factories, hospitals, schools and money.

This was no empty boast. The Vietnamese had already beaten the French in 1954. US intelligence documents from the American war, 1965-73, show that large numbers of French prisoners were still being held then. But the French were prepared to deal. Year after year, they paid millions of dollars to get their prisoners back. The last French prisoner was returned from Vietnam in 1976.

After the Tet offensive in 1968, it became obvious that the war in Vietnam was unwinnable. President Lyndon Johnson announced that he would not stand again as president; he halted the bombing of the Communist North and began peace talks in Paris.

From the beginning of the talks, the Vietnamese asked for reparations. After all, they argued, they had not attacked America. America had attacked them and devastated their country.

Promising to end the war, Richard Nixon became president in 1969. Instead, he went on the, offensive, upping the bombing of North Vietnam, Laos and Cambodia. More airmen were captured. Since action in Laos and Cambodia was illegal, it was not possible for the American administration to admit that prisoners had been taken there. The ground war was also extended into Laos and Cambodia. This was too much for the American people. Students and other demonstrators threatened to bring the country to a standstill and Congress repealed the Gulf of Tonkin Resolution, starving the American war effort of money.

The Nixon administration had to make what it dubbed 'peace with honour' quickly. In the Christmas offensive of 1972, the Nixon administration even tried massive new bombing strikes on Hanoi to force the Vietnamese to make a settlement.

The Paris Peace Accords, ending the US involvement in the war, were signed on 27 January 1973. They specified that there would be an 'exchange' of prisoners of war. The problem was that since no war had been declared (American involvement in South-east Asia was merely a 'police action'), the Geneva Conventions had not been observed and no prisoner of war lists had been exchanged during the hostilities.

When the North Vietnamese eventually produced a list, it contained less than half the number of names the Americans had expected. In fact, men whom the Americans knew the Vietnamese were holding – their names and pictures had appeared in Communist newspapers and propaganda films – were not on the list. The Americans could complain, but there was nothing they could do about this discrepancy. Public opinion was so against the war at this time that the US delegation in Paris had no leverage.

Even more glaringly, none of the more than 600 men the US knew had been captured in Laos appeared on the lists. When the Americans asked what had happened to them, the Vietnamese said to ask the Laotians. Since, officially, there had been no war in Laos, the Americans could not do this.

However, they did halt their troop withdrawals from Vietnam until the North Vietnamese cleared up the Laotian anomaly. Eventually, the North Vietnamese came up with nine men from Laos. But they were held throughout their captivity by the North Vietnamese. No one captured by the Lao Communist guerrillas, the Pathet Lao, was ever returned.

Men captured in Cambodia were simply written off. No one, it was assumed, could have survived Pol Pot's Khmer Rouge. However, there were more problems with the prisoner returns in South Vietnam.

The Paris Peace Accords had specified an exchange of prisoners. The Viet Cong, the communist guerrillas in South Vietnam mustered the Americans they held in order to exchange them for men of theirs that the Americans held. But the Americans returned no one. They had either killed the Communists they had captured, or had given them to the anti-Communist South Vietnamese, who had killed them. So the Viet Cong simply held on to the Americans they had captured.

The Hanoi government also knew that the war had not been won on the battlefield. It had been won on the TV sets of America. Images of burning children and napalmed villages had changed the world's mind about the war.

Returnees were given a special nutritious diet so they looked good. The US authorities, expecting large numbers of burn cases and amputees among the downed airmen returned, put all the hospitals in the USA on alert. But the beds remained empty. Every American prisoner of war who stepped off the plane back into the USA in a whirlwind of publicity was fit and well.

A quick analysis of those returned showed that the highly trained backseaters were missing. Returned prisoners also asked where their comrades in captivity were. The government asked them to be patient. The matter was in hand.

Indeed it was. The Nixon administration secretly promised the Vietnamese $3.25 billion for the return of the other prisoners. The problem was that such an expenditure had to be approved by Congress. By then, President Nixon was embroiled in the Watergate scandal. He had no clout with Congress and could not get the funds.

But the Nixon administration's one triumph was the end of the Vietnam War. It could not reveal that it had been short-changed at the peace talks. So the officials simply ignored the problem.

When President Carter came to power he wanted to heal the wounds left by the divisive Vietnam War. He tried to open diplomatic channels with Vietnam and declared the missing men dead.

However, boat people fleeing Vietnam brought news of Americans still being held. In 1981, within weeks of taking office, President Reagan received a telegram from the Vietnamese, asking for $4 billion for the return of American prisoners. Instead, President Reagan authorized a number of Rambo-style raids into Vietnam and Laos. They were unsuccessful.

After the fall of Communism in Russia, President Boris Yeltsin admitted that American prisoners captured in Vietnam had turned up in the former Soviet Union. America was still trying to reopen diplomatic relations with Vietnam. To clear the air, the US Senate set up a Select Committee to investigate.

In 1994, hidden in a thousand-page report, the committee found that American prisoners had indeed been left behind in Communist hands after the Vietnam War. But the committee concluded that they were all dead now – though it could produce no evidence showing how and when they had died. Nor could it explain the evidence that showed American prisoners were still being held by the Vietnamese in remote areas of Laos, which they occupy.

So what happened to the men? One of them, a US Marine named Bobby Garwood, returned in 1979, six years after the American withdrawal. He had been taken prisoner in 1965 and held in a number of PoW camps in North Vietnam.

In 1968, he was being moved when the truck carrying him stopped so that the driver could have a rest. Garwood saw tall, white men working in a field and approached them. They spoke French. Garwood knew that the French war in Indochina had ended in 1954. Fourteen years later, French prisoners were still there. The Vietnamese were serious when they told him: 'We can keep you forever.'

Garwood began to co-operate. He fixed jeeps and did other odd jobs. But he made himself a little too useful and, in 1973, he was not returned. Between 1973 and 1979 he often saw other American prisoners like himself.

In 1979, the Vietnamese economy was strained. Garwood persuaded his jailers to take him to Hanoi where, as a foreigner, he would be able to buy cigarettes that they could sell on the black market. On one of these trips he managed to slip a note to an official of the World Bank. He informed American authorities, who did nothing except complete the procedures, declaring Garwood dead. But Garwood's story broke on the BBC.

The US government was forced to ask for Garwood back. The Vietnamese denied having him, but eventually handed him over. The Americans immediately arrested him on four capital charges. His court-appointed lawyer advised him not to mention the other men he had seen at his court martial. He was found guilty on just one charge – collaborating with the enemy – fined the exact amount of his back pay and dishonourably discharged from the Marine Corps.

The fate of American prisoners after the end of the Vietnam War can have come as no surprise to the US authorities.

While investigating what had happened to American PoWs from the Vietnam War in 1990, the Senate Foreign Relations Committee looked into the fate of prisoners from previous wars. It was discovered that German prisoners from World War I had been taken into Siberia. Some remained there all their lives. During the Allied Intervention into Russia in 1919, British and American prisoners had been taken by the Communists and never returned.

During the Korean War, members of the UN forces fighting under US leadership were seen being transported under guard across the border from China into the Soviet Union. Others remained in China where there is evidence that they were used as guinea pigs in biological warfare experiments.

In 1953, when the Korean War ended, the American press was full of stories about the 954 US prisoners who had not been returned. One hundred and fifty-one British prisoners shared their fate. But since nothing could be done to put pressure on the Communists to return them, the matter had to be quietly forgotten about.

Even more shocking was the fate of British and American PoWs from World War II, when the Soviet Union was one of the Allied powers. As Russian troops swept across Eastern Europe, Allied prisoners of war `liberated' from the camps were not repatriated. Some 20,000 American and 30,000 British servicemen found themselves in Soviet labour camps, along with large numbers of Frenchmen, Belgians and Dutchmen. Naturally, millions of Germans and Japanese shared their fate.

Since a Cold War existed between the Soviet Union and

the West for the next 45 years, nothing could be done to get them out. During the occasional thaw – as in 1953, when Stalin died – some men were able to get out. They were initially held for 'debriefing' by the authorities and released on conditions of secrecy. Years later, when they have spoken out, no one has believed them.

Gladstone and Disraeli

William Ewart Gladstone was one of the greatest parliamentarians of the 19th century. Like Lloyd George, he diced with scandal all his life. On several occasions his addiction to prostitutes almost brought him down, but he somehow always emerged unscathed.

In the 19th century, the streets of London were awash with prostitutes. Despite the stifling strictures of Victorian values, it was not uncommon for gentlemen to seek the company of ladies of the night. Although he was married, Gladstone made no secret of his vice. He would even bring young prostitutes that he had picked up on the streets, back to 10 Downing Street, even though other members of the cabinet begged him not to.

Apologists pointed out that Gladstone was a fierce moralist and a lay preacher. Some contended that all he did with his 'erring sisters' was to read them an uplifting passage from the Bible. Indeed, he did manage to guide some of the young women he brought home into honest employment. However, Gladstone admitted in his own diaries that his motives were partly, at least, 'carnal'.

He began visiting prostitutes when he was a young man at Oxford in the 1820s. Tormented by guilt, he would scourge, himself afterwards. But this did not seem to stem his appetite as he writes of returning to sin 'again and again'.

He married in 1839. It did not help. In 1843, when he joined Robert Peel's government as President of the Board of Trade, he wrote in his diary that he was 'fearful [of] the guilty sin of returning again and again in forms ever new but alike hideous'. Conscious of his position, he avoided prostitutes initially. Instead, like many another Victorian gentleman, he indulged in pornography. But by 1851, his diary shows that he was visiting a prostitute named Elizabeth Collins regularly sometimes every other day. Afterwards, he notes, he always scourged himself. This continued when he became Chancellor in 1852.

And there were others. A man named William Wilson saw Gladstone picking up a prostitute near Leicester Square and tried to blackmail him. Gladstone handed over the blackmail demand to the police and Wilson went down for 12 months' hard labour.

There had been another brush with scandal with a courtesan named Laura Thistlethwayte. They exchanged passionate letters and he visited her regularly, both in her London town house and in her cottage in Hampstead. But Gladstone grew wary when she began showering him with gifts to the point that he feared her extravagance would ruin her husband, Colonel Thistlethwayte.

As prime minister, Gladstone had a close friendship with the Prince of Wales' mistress, the actress Lillie Langtry. And in the 1870s there were rumours that he was having an affair with Madame Olga Novikov, who advised him on Russian affairs.

However, he could not give up prostitutes. In 1880, when he was 70, he was still visiting brothels on what he called 'rescue work. The situation became more ticklish in 1882, when the threat of assassination over the Home Rule Bill meant that he had to have a 24-hour police guard. Lord Rosebery, then a junior minister in the Home Office, warned him of the danger of some lowly paid policeman taking advantage of the situation and selling the story to the press. It did no good. Three months later the Tory MP, Colonel Tottenham, saw Gladstone talking to a lady of the night and decided to make some political hay in the House with it. Gladstone answered Colonel Tottenham's allegations with studied dignity.

'It may be true that the gentleman saw me in such conversation,' he said. 'But the object was not what he assumed or, as I am afraid, hoped.'

He survived. But even this close call did not stop him. In July 1886, his private secretary, Edward Hamilton, warned him that another blackmailer was at work. Gladstone promised Hamilton that he would stop, but his diaries record that he was still seeing prostitutes in 1892, although they may have accosted him rather than the other way around.

In 1896, two years before his death, Gladstone sought to set the record straight. He wrote a Clintonesque statement and sent it to one of his sons, Stephen, who had become a clergyman. In it, Gladstone said that he had 'not been guilty of the act which is known as that of infidelity to the marriage bed'.

As we know from President Clinton's case, that leaves an awful lot of room for misbehaviour. When one young prostitute came home with him for a second time, he wrote that he had 'certainly been wrong in some things and trod the path of danger'.

Maybe he just liked to watch. Some of the girls called him 'Glad-eyes'; others called him 'Daddy-do-nothing' – but he was 82 when he gave up visiting whores. His reputation, though, was far more formidable.

'Gladstone founded the great tradition,' ran one obituary, 'in public to speak the language of the highest and strictest principle, and in private to pursue and possess every sort of woman.'

Gladstone's great political rival was, of course, Benjamin Disraeli who is reputed to have said to Gladstone: 'When you are out saving fallen women, save one for me.'

Disraeli, too, had his fair share of scandal. As a young

man eager to make his way in the world, he borrowed heavily in order to buy into gold and silver mines in South America and to start up a newspaper with his friend, John Murray. However, a stockmarket crash in 1825, when Disraeli was just 21, wiped him out and the newspaper, which he could no longer afford to finance, collapsed after six months.

Left with massive debts, Disraeli wrote a novel about the collapse called *Vivian Grey*. It was so thinly fictionalized that it drew threats of a duel from Murray. The duel never took place, but it brought such notoriety to the book that Disraeli could pay off enough of his debts to keep going.

Disraeli then had a nervous breakdown and, to escape his remaining creditors, went off on a tour of the Middle East. He returned a changed man. Always a dandy, he was now positively effeminate, dressing in green velvet trousers and ruffles. He spoke openly at dinner parties of his passion for the East and, according to the painter Benjamin Haydon, 'seemed tinged with a disposition to palliate its infamous vices... sodomy'. Disraeli's biographer Jane Ridley concurred.

'Bisexuality came as naturally to Disraeli as did Tory Radicalism,' she said.

He then had a series of affairs with older women, some of whom were married. His affair with Henrietta Sykes became a public scandal. She was much older than him and had been married for 11 years to the ailing Sir Francis Sykes, who was the father of her four children. Her letters to Disraeli were signed 'your mother'.

Despite the gossip, they were seen out together at parties and the opera. Her husband turned a blind eye because he was having an affair with Clara Bolton at the time. Clara was another of Disraeli's former lovers. She was jealous and encouraged Sir Francis to break up the affair. He did so, but soon after he found his wife in bed with Disraeli's successor. In a fit of pique, he kicked her out of the house and placed a notice in the newspapers, advertising her adultery and causing a scandal that tainted Disraeli along with everyone else involved.

How much the scandal harmed him it is hard to say as he seemed completely unelectable anyway. Voters did not appreciate his dandified dress, and his Jewishness counted against him. On the hustings he was greeted with cries of 'Shylock' and he was pelted with chunks of rotten pork and ham.

When he was elected for Maidstone on his fifth attempt, there were accusations that he had offered bribes to the electorate. This was a common enough practice, but Disraeli outraged the voters of Maidstone by not paying up.

He handled the resulting scandal by making even more scandalous allegations against his chief critic, a Maidstone lawyer called Charles Austin. Austin sued. Disraeli went to court where he apologized effusively. His court costs were paid by the latest woman in his life, Mary Anne Wyndham Lewis, the widow of his late rival for the Maidstone seat. It was a masterly stroke. This fresh scandal eclipsed the bribery allegations.

Mrs Wyndham Lewis was 12 years older than Disraeli. And she was rich. They married. But even his wife's fortune was not enough to discharge his debts. He left Maidstone and stood for Shrewsbury in 1841. It had a smaller electorate and consequently fewer voters to bribe.

Realizing his plight, his rivals for the seat plastered Shrewsbury with posters detailing his debts. They amounted to £21,000. Handbills pointed out that Disraeli needed to stay in Parliament, otherwise he would go to debtors' prison.

But the voters of Shrewsbury took no notice and soon found their MP making his way to the top of the greasy pole of the Conservative Party. However, the Conservatives were kept out of power by another scandal.

At the age of 79, the Liberal leader Lord Palmerston was cited in the divorce case of the attractive 30-year-old Mrs O'Kane. Disraeli said that it was a pity that this had got out because Palmerston would sweep the country. With the unofficial party slogan 'she was Kane and he was able', Palmerston won by a landslide.

Disraeli had to compete with this. After his wife died in 1872, he began romantic liaison with two sisters, Lady Bradford and Lady Chesterfield, which he maintained until his death in 1881. In office, Disraeli bought the Suez Canal without the backing of Parliament. During a recess, he borrowed the money from the Rothschilds and bought the shares belonging to the ruler of Egypt, the Khedive Ismail Pasha. Fortunately, when Parliament reassembled they saw that it was a tangible asset to Britain and approved the purchase.

Rainbow Warrior

The French have fewer scandals than most other countries for two reasons. Firstly, it is expected that any man with a position in society would have at least one mistress, so to discover that a politician has fathered an illegitimate child is no scandal. Secondly, there are strict privacy laws, which prevent the details of a person's private life being aired in the press. This is why French scandals tend to centre around military matters.

The French are particularly proud of their nuclear- bomb. When everyone else in the world had given up testing them, the French still took great pride in blowing up small islands in the Pacific. This did not sit well with the environmentalist organization, Greenpeace. In 1985, it sent its ship *Rainbow Warrior* to harass the French military, who were planning a nuclear test on Mururoa atoll in French Polynesia.

On 10 July 1985, *Rainbow Warrior* was preparing to set sail from Auckland harbour when there was a terrific explosion on board. One crew member died in the blast and the ship sank. It soon became clear that the explosion had been caused by a bomb.

Two days later, New Zealand police arrested Alain and Sophie Turenge who had been seen 'acting suspiciously'. They claimed to be Swiss tourists, but telephone numbers found on them connected them to the French Secret Service. They turned out to be two French agents named Alain Mafart and Dominique Prieur.

President Mitterand was informed, but he did nothing, hoping that the affair would blow over. It didn't, so on 8 August, when fresh revelations were imminent, he ordered his Prime Minister, Laurent Fabius, to instigate a rigorous inquiry under Bernard Tricot into what Mitterand called this 'absurd and criminal affair'. Naturally, the inquiry would leave no stone unturned and Tricot was ordered to track down those responsible, 'no matter how high their status'.

After just two and a half weeks, Tricot reported back. Five agents including Mafart and Prieur, he said, had been sent to New Zealand to gather information about Greenpeace's intention, and he had no reason to believe that they had overstepped their brief.

'Everything I have heard and seen makes me certain that, at governmental level, no decision was taken to damage the *Rainbow Warrior*,' he said.

Few were convinced that he had really got to the bottom of the matter. Meanwhile, journalists began their own investigations. On 17 September, *Le Monde* published a story saying that a third team of agents, whom Tricot had not been told about, had planted the bomb on the *Rainbow Warrior* and escaped undetected. The Minister of Defence, Charles Hernu, who had ordered the surveillance of the Greenpeace vessel, had apparently either approved the

306

bombing or, at the very least, failed to prevent it. The Chief of the General Staff and the head of the Secret Service were both implicated; and President Mitterand's own military advisor had approved the funding of the operation.

Hernu repeatedly denied that the attack had been ordered by his department. Then he changed his tune. It had been ordered by his department, he admitted, but the truth had been concealed from him personally. On 20 September, he was sacked. The head of the French Secret Service was also removed for refusing to answer questions.

On 23 September, Laurent Fabius conceded that the agents who had blown up the *Rainbow Warrior* had indeed been following orders. He offered compensation to the family of the Greenpeace photographer who had died, and to the government of New Zealand. However, the French government refused to return the agents who had actually done the bombing to stand trial. So the New Zealand authorities tried Mafart and Prieur for being party to the plot. They were found guilty of manslaughter and sentenced to 10 years. The French were outraged. They threatened to bar New Zealand butter from the European Union.

New Zealand backed down. A deal was brokered under which Mafart and Prieur would serve three years on an isolated atoll in French Polynesia. In return, France would pay compensation and make a public apology.

France did not live up to its side of the agreement. In 1987, the Chirac government repatriated Prieur without New Zealand's consent. On the eve of the 1988 election, Mafart was returned home, too, contrary to the agreement.

New Zealand protested and the matter went to international arbitration. In 1990, the panel brought in a split decision. France, it said, was wrong to have returned Prieur early, but conceded that it was too late to send her back into exile. In lieu of compensation, France was ordered to establish a fund to promote peace and understanding between the two countries.

Journalists continued to look into who ordered the sabotage. In 1987, Hernu admitted responsibility for conducting an `action of the State' against *Rainbow Warrior*, but he maintained to his death, in 1989, that he was a scapegoat that had been sacrificed by his colleagues. Indeed, there was no evidence found that he ordered the bombing in as many words. However, on a memorandum by a senior admiral on the effects of Greenpeace's activities on the nuclear test programme he underlined the word 'forestall'.

Although the money for the operation came from the Elysee Palace, no 'smoking gun' was found to link the sinking of the *Rainbow Warrior* to President Mitterand. However, many people believe that authorization for such an operation could have come only from the very highest level.

P-2

The Italians' political scandals are more often connected with the Mafia and with the Catholic Church. And that is exactly what they got in 1981 when they discovered that a mysterious lodge of Freemasons called P-2 – *Propaganda Due* – was acting as a state within a state. Not only were its leaders prominent members of the establishment, some had links to organized crime. And one of them Robert Calvi – was known as 'God's banker' because he organized the financial affairs of the Catholic Church.

During the 1970s, Italy was plagued by left-wing terrorism. P-2 posed a threat from the right which Italy's Prime Minister, Giovanni Spadolini, called a 'creeping coup'. No one can be sure just how much of a threat it was. That the lodge was a government-in-waiting may well have been one of the grander delusions of its head, Licio Gelli. It mainly used its political influence to secure favours and cut through red tape. Businessmen used P-2 as a way of fixing up contracts and dealing with Italy's labyrinthine bureaucracy.

In fact, few of the members knew what was going on. Gelli and his deputy, Umberto Ortalini, were highly secretive. They held their initiation ceremonies in anonymous hotel rooms and it was only when the scandal broke and the membership lists were published, that members discovered who the other members were. Although they came from all political parties, ranging from the socialist PSI to the neo-Fascist MSI-DN, members tended to be rightward leaning. Gelli himself held dual Italian-Argentinian nationality and had been a friend of Argentine dictator, Juan Perón.

Freemasonry has long been entwined with Italian politics. During the 19th century its secret network and anti-clericalism made it the perfect vehicle for Italian nationalism, which culminated in the unification of the country.

The Masonic lodge P-2 had been in existence for a long time. It was part of the Grand Orient rite of the freemasonry. However, when Gelli took over in the 1970s, it was expelled, and when the scandal was revealed orthodox Freemasons denied any connection.

The existence of P-2 only became known to the public in 1981, when investigating magistrates in Milan were trying to untangle the affairs of the disgraced Sicilian financier, Michele Sindona. Sindona had used the contacts he had made through P-2 to build a financial empire. He was an expert in evading Italy's banking laws – having set up foreign companies, through which money could be laundered. One of his P-2 contacts was Roberto Calvi.

Calvi was born into a Catholic family in Milan in 1920. At the age of 26, he joined the Ambrosiano bank, rising to become its head in 1975. It was around that time he joined P-2. The Sindona empire was already in ruins by then. Sindona had skipped the country in 1974 to avoid arrest on charges of fraud and false accounting and Calvi picked up the pieces. Banco Ambrosiano quickly became the biggest private bank in Italy. Much of its growth was on paper only though. Calvi transferred money at lightning speed between companies, artificially inflating their share price. In the process, billions of lire left Italy illegally for accounts in Switzerland, Peru and Argentina. Calvi was secretive, a law unto himself. No one else in the bank knew what was going on and no one in charge thought to ask – just as long as Calvi continued making money.

One of the major clients Sindona introduced to Calvi was the Instituto per le Opere di Reglione – the Institute for Religious Works, the Vatican bank. Calvi's involvement with IOR earned him the nickname, 'God's banker'. The IOR's head, Archbishop Paul Marcinkus, allowed Calvi access to massive amounts of cash and turned a blind eye to his activities. This was because Calvi's money laundering techniques allowed the Catholic Church to support, for example, the banned Polish trade union Solidarity. But Calvi was just as happy using the Vatican's money to invest in Communist-controlled companies and in other enterprises that the Church would certainly not have approved of.

The Bank of Italy was investigating Ambrosiano. But the national bank was itself involved in a scandal in 1979, and the investigation was proceeding at a snail's pace. A number of people who got in Calvi's way were gunned down in Mafia-style shootings. Pope John Paul I's mysterious death after just 30 days on the papal seat was even attributed to Calvi. The new pontiff had threatened to clean up the Vatican's financial affairs.

Although Sindona had escaped arrest in Italy in 1974, he was not so lucky in New York in 1979. Arrested for fraud and for staging his own kidnapping, he was sentenced to 25 years. The authorities began looking into his Mafia ties. An informant mentioned Sindona's connection to Gelli. Gelli's office was raided by the customs police. In a briefcase, they found files detailing P-2's activities and the names of its 962 members. These included media barons, businessmen, judges, two serving cabinet ministers, a former head of the civil service, the chief of the general staff, the head of military intelligence, the past and present head of the customs police and banker Roberto Calvi.

It was clear that P-2 had not just used its influence and inside knowledge, but had also used blackmail and extortion as a means to its ends. It was also implicated in the Bank of Italy scandal of 1979 and the 1980 bombing of the railway station at Bologna by a neo-Fascist group.

The Christian Democrat government immediately set up a commission of inquiry into the activities of P-2. But with two of its own ministers members of the lodge, this had little credibility. The Christian Democrat's coalition partners withdrew their support and the government fell – not an unusual event in Italy. The new prime minister was Giovanni Spadolini, leader of the Republican Party. This was the first time since 1945 that Italy had had a prime minister who was not a Christian Democrat. .

P-2 was branded a secret society, and thus outlawed under the Italian constitution. The head of the customs police and his chief of staff were arrested for their part in an oil tax evasion scam, fined 50 billion lire each and sentenced to seven years in jail. The military chiefs were reshuffled. Directors of radio and TV news were sacked; the editor of the influential newspaper *Corriere della Sera* resigned. The owners of the *Corriere della Sera* Rizzoli group were under investigation. The company's senior executives were P-2 members. Angelo Rizzoli and the managing director, Bruno Tassan Din, were arrested and charged with fraud and concealment of debt. Their interests in the firm were later seized by the authorities. Rizzoli had been used as a front by Calvi, whose company, La Centrale, had a 40 per cent stake.

Calvi was arrested and charged with the illegal export of

currency, He was found guilty, fined 16 billion lire – some £8 million – and sentenced to four years in jail. Out on bail pending appeal, he went back to work at Ambrosiano. The bank had lent some $774 million to foreign subsidiaries that could not be recovered. A further $1.3 billion had disappeared, after being lent to Panamanian registered front companies.

The Bank of Italy wrote to Calvi, demanding that he inform his fellow directors of the bank's true position. When he did, he lost the support of the board for the first time. On 10 June 1980, Calvi disappeared from his flat in Rome. At first, it was feared that he had been kidnapped. His disappearance shook what was left of the bank's credibility and the UK's Midland Bank and others forced Ambrosiano's overseas network into liquidation.

Using a forged passport, Calvi had fled to London with Flavio Carboni, a Sicilian building contractor with Mafia connections, and Silvano Vittor, a small-time smuggler who acted as Calvi's bodyguard.

On 11 June, Calvi booked into a cheap hotel in Chelsea. He stayed in his room, making frantic phone calls to his family and business associates. On the night of 17 June, he went out, seemingly on his own. The next morning he was found dead, hanging by a rope from some scaffolding beneath Blackfriars Bridge. In his pockets there were bricks and £7,000, mainly in lire and US dollars.

Initially, his death was thought to be suicide. But it seemed improbable that a 62-year-old man would go to the trouble of clambering out across scaffolding and weighing himself down with bricks before hanging himself when he could have killed himself in his hotel room. However, there were no marks of violence on his body. How he died remains a mystery, and an open verdict was recorded by the coroner's court. Elaborate theories about ritual Masonic killings have been advanced. Murder was an obvious possibility. But Calvi had so many enemies that the Metropolitan police hardly knew where to start and, with Italy still reeling over the P-2 scandal, the Italian authorities were less than helpful.

On the day Calvi died, his devoted secretary, Graziella Corrocher, was killed when she fell from the fourth floor of the Banco Ambrosiano building. Appalled by his fraud, she left a note saying that she hoped Calvi 'be cursed a thousand times for the harm he has done to everyone at the bank, and to the image of the group we were once so proud of'. Clearly, she knew nothing of what her boss was up to.

The authorities were still trying to unravel what had happened when Gelli was arrested in Geneva, trying to withdraw $55 million from a Swiss bank account. The money had come from one of Banco Ambrosiano's foreign subsidiaries. Suspicious bank staff called the police. Gelli was in disguise. He was immediately jailed for travelling on a false passport. But before he could be extradited back to Italy, where he faced charges of political conspiracy, criminal association, extortion and fraud, he escaped from his maximum security Swiss prison with the help of a warder, who drove him across the French border to a waiting private jet.

The Ambrosiano bank collapsed, putting its 4,200 employees out of work. Ten of the bank's directors and officials were convicted of illicit share dealing and contravention of foreign exchange controls.

But Archbishop Marcinkus went unpunished, even though he was on the board of several of Banco Ambrosiano's overseas companies and the Panamanian front companies where $1.3 billion had gone missing. Some of Ambrosiano's subsidiaries were found to be owned directly or indirectly by the IOR, but where the money went to the authorities never discovered.

Italy's Treasury Minister, Beniamino Andreatta, accused the Vatican of being responsible for the collapse of Banco

Ambrosiano, and IOR officials were forced to stay within the confines of the Vatican City, afraid that they would be arrested if they set foot on Italian soil.

In an effort to rebuild the relationship between the Catholic Church and the Italian government, the Pope set up a joint commission of inquiry. But the Church remained as secretive as ever. In May 1984, the Vatican agreed to pay 109 creditor banks some $250 million of the $1.3 billion outstanding, in recognition of its 'moral involvement' in the scandal. However, the IOR refused to accept responsibility and the Vatican only handed over the money when the banks agreed to drop their claims for any other outstanding debts.

I Was a Drug Smuggler for the CIA

Panamanian strongman General Manuel Noriega worked for the CIA. But when the CIA discovered that he was a double agent, also providing intelligence to Cuba and to the Soviet Union, it used his connections with drug barons in Florida to bring him down. But to make the arrest it had to stage a full-scale invasion of Panama.

The country of Panama had been founded in 1903 by a break-away province of Colombia. The US government backed the succession so that a sympathetic government there would allow it to build the Panama Canal.

Born in a poor *barrio* of Panama City in 1938, Noriega joined the army and rose swiftly through the ranks of the National Guard. In 1969, he foiled a coup against the then dictator, Brigadier-General Omar Torrijos, and was appointed head of military intelligence. In 1981, Torrijos was killed in an air crash. Noriega was appointed commander of the Panamanian Defence Forces and *de facto* head of state. He then used his powerful military intelligence network to subvert the opposition, and to blackmail and intimidate the electorate. When that failed, he simply stuffed the ballot boxes.

In 1987, allegations came to light that Noriega was involved in drug smuggling. The US Senate passed a resolution, asking him to step down while the allegations were investigated by the CIA. Noriega's second-in-command, Roberto Dia Herrera, broke ranks and accused him of murdering Torrijos, conspiring to murder the opposition leader, Hugo Spadafora, and rigging the 1984 elections. Herrera quickly found himself out of a job.

Federal grand juries sitting in Miami and Tampa issued indictments against Noriega. They accused him of turning Panama into one 'vast criminal empire', a staging post for the Colombian cartel that was smuggling drugs into the USA. Noriega, they estimated, had made $4.6 million from this racket.

The US applied economic sanctions against Panama. The nominal head of state, President Eric Delvalle, a Noriega appointee, announced that Noriega had been sacked, but the Panamanian Legislative Assembly promptly sacked Delvalle, too. The resulting election was declared null and void when it became clear that the results were running against Noriega.

Then the army turned against him. Rebel troops held Noriega captive in the headquarters of the Panamanian Defence Forces for four hours, until troops loyal to Noriega surrounded the building. Leaders of the abortive coup were executed some say by Noriega personally – and the army was purged.

Although US troops from the Canal Zone had offered the rebels some assistance, Congress now criticized the administration for not doing more. On 15 December 1989, Noriega had himself officially declared President by the Panamanian National Assembly and declared that

Panama was at war with the USA. This was not a good move.

The following day an off-duty US Marine was killed by a Panamanian soldier. Another US soldier was beaten up and his wife threatened.

On 20 December, the USA invaded. Some 9,500 troops were airlifted in from the USA to join the 3,500 already stationed there. US tanks rolled out of the Canal Zone. The Americans destroyed the headquarters of the Panamanian Defence Forces and seized key installations. For the first time in its history, the Panama Canal was closed.

The following day, the Pentagon announced that resistance had been crushed. The US had lost 23 men. Nearly 300 Panamanian troops had been killed and 1,500 taken prisoner. The number of civilian dead stood at 230. Although sporadic action continued for several days, the USA congratulated itself on its victory. However, Noriega – whose arrest had been the object of the invasion – was nowhere to be seen.

Four days later, it was discovered that he had taken refuge in the papal nunciature in Panama City and was claiming sanctuary. The Americans insisted that the papal authorities hand him over. The Vatican said they would not. US troops tried to force him to surrender by playing loud rock music outside the nunciature day and night. It worked. Two weeks after the invasion, Noriega walked out and was arrested by the US authorities.

He was flown to Miami where he was arraigned on drug-smuggling charges. A legal battle ensued. Noriega's defence claimed that the manner of his arrest was illegal and the coverage of the invasion made it impossible to get a fair hearing.

Some $20 million in Noriega's bank accounts world-wide were frozen. This sparked more actions in foreign courts. Some of the money was later unfrozen so he could pay his spiralling legal bills.

Noriega himself threatened to release documents that would be embarrassing to the CIA. It came up at the hearings that the CIA had indeed used Noriega to spy on his own people. Noriega also claimed that he had delivered Exocet missiles to the Argentines during the Falklands War on the orders of the CIA.

Nevertheless, in April 1992, he was found guilty on drug smuggling charges. His position was hardly enhanced by his wife, who was arrested during the trial for stealing buttons off designer clothes. Noriega was jailed for 40 years.

Iran-Contra

The Iran-Contra scandal was a much more serious scandal than Zippergate and a bigger scandal than Watergate. It was clear that numerous illegal acts had been ordered by the President. However, the 70-year-old Ronald Reagan – who was diagnosed as suffering from senile dementia when he left office – said that he could not remember a thing. And, terrifyingly, everyone believed him.

Iran-Contra began with a scandalous revelation in the Lebanese magazine, *Al Shiraa*, on 3 November 1986. It said that President Reagan's National Security Adviser, Robert McFarlane had secretly travelled to Tehran and supplied the Iranian government with military equipment. This was scarcely credible. Since the Islamic revolution in 1979, Iran had been an international pariah. President Reagan himself had called the Islamic Republic a 'terrorist state' and supplying arms to Iran was illegal.

However, on 4 November 1986, the speaker of the Iranian parliament, Hojatolislam Hashemi Ali Akbar Rafsanjani, confirmed that it was true, but claimed that the American delegation had been arrested, detained in their hotel for five days, then expelled. The Iranian government could hardly admit to dealing with America, whom they cast as the 'Great Satan', either.

It was soon clear that there was more here than met the eye. In the Lebanon, it was said that the object of the arms deal was the release of David P. Jacobsen, a US hostage held by a pro-Iranian faction in Beirut. The US routinely condemned bargaining for hostages. Then it was revealed that the secret dealings with Tehran had not ended with Bob McFarlane's resignation the previous December. The new National Security Adviser, Vice-Admiral John M. Poindexter, had continued the trade through an official of the National Security Council named Oliver North.

Ten days after the story first broke, President Reagan was forced to admit publicly that the US government had secretly sold `defensive weapons and spare parts' to Iran. But this was not a deal for hostages, he said. It was a covert operation designed to encourage moderate elements in Iran; and it was working. President Reagan boasted proudly: 'Since US government contact began with Iran, there's been no evidence of Iranian government complicity in acts of terrorism against the US.'

Three days later, Secretary of State George Shultz flatly contradicted this. By that time, the White House was in a state of confusion. Reagan issued a statement claiming that no third country was involved in this arms deal. This was almost immediately contradicted by a White House statement saying that Israel had been involved.

The following day, 20 November, Attorney General Ed Meese was called in to investigate. Just five days later, Meese announced that Poindexter had resigned and North had been dismissed when it had been discovered that profits from the deal – some $10-30 million – had been diverted to aid the right-wing rebels in Nicaragua known as the Contras.

It was no secret that the Reagan White House backed the Contras, who were trying to overthrow the left-wing Sandinista government in Managua. But Congress had specifically banned any aid to the Contras, so North was breaking the law. Worse, Meese discovered that Poindexter knew of North's activities and so did McFarlane, but only after he had left office. The obvious question was that, if the President's National Security Adviser knew North was breaking the law, did the President know as well?

Unfortunately, when Meese uncovered the Contra dealings on 23 November, he did not seal North's office. That wasn't done until the press started baying for blood on 25 November. In the intervening two days, North and his secretary, Fawn Hall, spent day and night shredding documents.

Reagan sought to rescue the situation by appointing Senator John Tower of Texas to investigate the role of the National Security Council in the affair. As head of the National Security Council – assuming he was awake at their meetings Reagan should have known what was going on. This did not satisfy Congress, which pressured Reagan into appointing an independent council to investigate the scandal. Then Congress set up its own joint House-Senate committee to look into it.

The problem was that despite the Watergate fever on Capitol Hill, there was not very much to look into. Everything was known in the first few weeks. Apart from Poindexter and North, the only other casualty was White House Chief of Staff, Donald Regan. He resigned after the Tower Commission report said that 'he must bear primary responsibility for the chaos that descended upon the White House'. Ironically, it was Regan who had sought to alert the President to the problem. He later claimed that his plan to handle the crisis was overruled by the President's wife, Nancy, on the advice of her astrologer.

However, the investigation into the Iran-Contra scandal revealed deep divisions within the administration. Secretary of State George Shultz and Secretary of Defence Caspar Weinberger had both warned against selling arms to Iran at an early stage and had believed that the deal had been cancelled on their advice. The CIA grew cold on the operation because of the shady middlemen employed to broker the deal. One of them, expatriate Iranian Manucher Chorbanifar, even failed a CIA lie detector test. So the only people left to put the plan into operation were the NSC staff and the ever-compliant Colonel Oliver North.

President Reagan had been elected to power over Jimmy Carter's mishandling of the 1980 Iranian hostage crisis. North – a gung-ho military man knew that his Commander-in-Chief was coming under similar pressure over the number of hostages being taken in Lebanon, just as he knew that Reagan backed the Contras, despite the liberals' opposition in Congress.

It came out during the hearings that North had had a nervous breakdown during the Vietnam War and was something of a fantasist. The whole Iran-Contra operation was characterized as a renegade plan by North, his side-kick Major-General Richard V. Secord and Secord's Iranian-born business partner, Albert Hakim. Secord had had a chequered career, resigning from the Defence Department when the FBI discovered his business connections to rogue CIA operative, Edwin Wilson, who had been jailed for 52 years for selling arms to Libya.

Donald Regan told the Tower Commission that President Reagan had only approved the weapons shipment retrospectively. Reagan himself said that he could not remember, but when Bob McFarlane said that he had approved the shipment as early as 1985, Reagan stood corrected. He told the American people: 'A few months ago I told the American people I did not trade arms for hostages. My heart and my best intentions still tell me that is true, but the facts and the evidence tell me it is not. What began as a strategic opening to Iran deteriorated in its implementation into trading for hostages.'

Poindexter pointed out that this was the opposite of the

truth. His memo on the affair, which was signed by the President on 5 December 1985, talked only of trading for hostages. The first reference to the trade being a 'strategic opening' occurred only in a memo of 17 January 1986. Unfortunately, the documents concerned had been shredded. But whichever the case was, at the very time that North and McFarlane were flying arms into Tehran, the USA was trying to shore up an international arms embargo against Iran. Since 1984, Iran had been on the State Department's list of countries that supported terrorism, a country it became illegal to export arms to under the Diplomatic Security and Anti-Terrorism Act that Reagan signed into law in August 1986.

But all this was becoming too complicated for the public to follow, particularly because of the involvement of Israeli intelligence and competing factions in Tehran. So the interest turned to the Contra end of Iran-Contra in a search for the 'smoking gun'. But this end was messier still. Aid to the Contras had been banned in 1984 by the Boland Amendment, when it was discovered that the CIA had been mining Nicaraguan harbours. If it could be shown that Reagan had used the money from the arms shipment to Iran to send aid to the Contras, deliberately thwarting the will of Congress, it would be a very serious matter indeed.

However, Poindexter and North said that they did not think that the Boland Amendment applied to them, only to the CIA. And Poindexter said that he never told the President about sending support to the Contras.

'Although I was convinced that we could properly do it and the President would approve if asked,' Poindexter said, 'I made a very deliberate decision not to ask the President so that I could insulate him from the decision and provide some future deniability for the President if it ever leaked out...

'On this whole issue,' Poindexter announced, 'the buck

stops with me.'

North said that he had never communicated directly with the President about the matter. He had sent some memos to Reagan via Poindexter, but they had not been acknowledged and North had put his copies through the shredder. Reagan told *Time* magazine that North was 'a national hero'.

Also in the firing line was William Casey, head of the CIA. He was eager to break free of the shackles applied to the agency by Congress after the House had investigated its activities in the aftermath of Watergate. It was then that the CIA's successful plot to overthrow the government of Salvador Allende in Chile and its ludicrous attempts to assassinate Fidel Castro came out. But Casey could hardly argue that the Boland Amendment did not apply to the CIA.

Casey claimed that he only knew of the diversion of funds to the Contras after Meese had told him. However, before he could testify, Casey was struck down with a brain seizure on 5 December 1986 and died in May 1987. Bob Woodward, one of the *Washington Post* reporters who had unearthed the Watergate scandal, said that Casey had told him on his deathbed that the CIA had been involved from the start. Casey's wife spiked his guns, saying that Woodward had never been anywhere near her husband's bedside.

However, when Oliver North was hauled in front of the Congressional Committee in July 1987, he told the same story as Woodward. He said that Casey had envisaged the arms-for-Iran deal financing, not just the Contras, but any other activity for which they did not want to ask Congress for funding. The Boland Amendment, naturally, had caused him some problems, but they had both agreed that if anything should go wrong North would be the fall guy.

America watched the televised hearing riveted as Ollie North wrapped himself in the flag in front of the

Congressional Committee. He was a soldier just doing his job. After all, the Contras he funded were 'freedom fighters'.

When George Shultz referred to him as a 'loose cannon,' at the NSC, North looked directly into the eyes of the congressmen and said: 'That wasn't what I heard while I worked there, people used to walk up to me and tell me what a great job I was doing.'

However, it turned out that North and his cronies were not as selflessly patriotic as they made out. The deal had made some $48 million in all. Albert Hakim had $8 million, which he was unwilling to surrender. Secord resisted all requests by the US government to look into his Swiss bank accounts. The committee noted that he drove a Porsche and owned a private jet. North himself had had a $16,000 security fence, paid for by Secord, installed around his house. When the scandal broke, he readily accepted back-dated invoices for the work.

With the NSC, which had effectively been making foreign policy, now in disgrace, Secretary of State Shultz seized the opportunity to reassert the power of the State Department, which had known of the Iranian arms deal only when officials read about it in the Lebanese press. Now assured the ear of the President, he fulsomely acknowledged the Constitutional authority of Congress and the Boland Amendment on behalf of the administration. Caspar Weinberger did the same thing for the Defence Department, saying that he had only learnt of the arms deal through the intelligence service of another government.

The Congressional Committee's report blamed North, McFarlane and Poindexter. Although the President was ultimately responsible for allowing a 'cabal of zealots' to take over, it stopped short of accusing him of complicity or any impeachable offence. A minority report issued by the Republican members of the committee concluded that

there was 'no systematic disrespect for the "rule of law",
no grand conspiracy and no administration-wide dishonesty or cover-up'. The Republicans were still smarting
from Watergate and did not want to see another of their
number go that way.

However, someone had to pay the price. McFarlane, a
broken man who attempted suicide in 1987, pleaded guilty
to misleading Congress when he had said that North was
not sending aid to the Contras. He got a small fine and two
years' probation. This was part of a plea bargain with the
Special Prosecutor. He turned state's evidence against
North, Poindexter, Secord and Hakim, who faced a port-
manteau of charges, which included conspiracy, fraud and
embezzlement but no charges relating to gun running.

Although the Special Prosecutor wanted the four to be
tried together, the judge ruled that they must be tried separately. North would go first. President Reagan continued
to make nice noises about North's high motives. but the
White House refused any help. In response, North refused
to be the fall guy. He demanded that the administration
hand over documents relating to various intelligence operations and gave notice that he intended to call President
Reagan and Vice-President George Bush as witnesses at
his trial. This forced the Special Prosecutor to drop some of
the more wide-ranging conspiracy charges.

The trial was a tedious affair, unearthing no new evidence. North's defence was that he had been obeying
orders, or thought he was obeying orders, when he sent
money to the Contras. After 13 days of deliberation, the
jury agreed. They found North not guilty on the nine most
serious charges, including conspiring to conceal the funding of the Contras from Congress. However, they found
him guilty of shredding government documents, falsifying
records and accepting an illegal gratuity in the form of the
security fence. A penitent North was given a suspended
three-year jail term and 1,200 hours of community service,

and fined $15,000. This got George Bush, who was now President, off the hook. Had North been jailed, Bush would have come under a great deal of right-wing pressure to pardon him.

With his exaggerated sense of patriotism, North had become a right-wing icon and was being mooted as a congressional candidate by the Republicans. But due to the nature of his offences, the judge banned North from running for public office.

Secord and Hakim pleaded guilty to minor charges on a plea bargain and were given two years' probation and a fine. Hakim also promised to hand over $7.3 million worth of profits from the deal, which he had stashed in a Swiss bank account. Poindexter was sentenced to six months' imprisonment, largely on the testimony of North, who said that he had supervised the arms shipment in November 1985, although he had told Congress that he had only found out about it in January 1986.

North's convictions were eventually overturned. The Archbishop of Canterbury's special envoy Terry Waite, who had been sent to Beirut as a hostage negotiator, was taken hostage himself. Eventually, the hostages were released and the Sandinistas were defeated in an election.

Evita

Thanks to Andrew Lloyd Webber, the whole world knows that Argentina's most famous First Lady was once a prostitute. But if that was not scandalous enough, her husband, Juan Domingo Perón, was eventually kicked out of office for being a paedophile.

Perón was born in 1895 in Lobos, a small town about 60 miles southwest of Buenos Aires. His parents were Creole and unmarried. At 15, he was sent to military school, where he had his first sexual experiences with prostitutes.

'In the era when we were boys,' he said, 'we weren't accustomed to going to social parties, and it would not have occurred to us to go to a home and make love to a family girl.'

At the age of 33, he married a respectable school teacher. They had no children and after 10 years of marriage his wife died.

In 1939, he was posted to Rome as military attaché and he was very impressed by Mussolini and his methods. Travelling extensively throughout Germany, Hungary, Austria, Spain and Portugal, he concluded that Fascism worked. But he would never have been able to put what he had learnt into practice without the help of his second wife, the celebrated Evita.

Born Marma Eva Duarte in the small town of Los Toldos in 1919, she was the daughter of the wealthy local landowner, Juan Duarte, and his mistress of 15 years' standing, Juanita Ibarguren. When Evita was seven, her father died and her mother was left to fend for herself. She made ends meet by running an *amoblados* or 'love hotel'.

The prospects for young girls in a dusty pampas town like Los Toldos were bleak. At the age of 14, Evita agreed to sleep with the small-time tango singer, Jose Armani, if he would take her the 150 miles to Buenos Aires. Later, she claimed her first lover was the far more famous singer, Agustin Magaldi.

When she first arrived in Buenos Aires, Evita had little choice of career. She became a prostitute and modelled for pornographic photographs. But she was burning with ambition. Five feet five, with brown eyes and bleached-blonde hair, she was determined to become an actress. At the age of 15, she became the mistress of Emilio Kartulovic, publisher of the movie magazine, *Sintonia*. Kartulovic had all the contacts she needed. Evita soon turned her attention to the impresario, Rafael Firtuso, owner of the Liceo theatre. He cast her in one of his productions, which was sent out on a provincial tour. The play was called *The Mortal Kiss*, a rousing melodrama about the evils of promiscuity – sponsored by the Argentine Prophylactic League in response to Argentina's soaring illegitimacy rate.

On her return to Buenos Aires, Evita landed a number of small parts in lacklustre Argentine movies. To make ends meet, she would spend her evenings in clubs with wealthy businessmen. Her nights would often end in one of the city's numerous love hotels and a ride home in a cab with an extra 50 pesos in her purse.

Evita's big career breakthrough came when she got on the radio. She quickly became queen of the soaps and appeared on the covers of the radio listings magazines.

In June 1943, a number of ambitious officers, including Juan Perón, staged a military coup. With her eye on the main chance, she began bedding the Minister of Communications, Colonel Anibal Imbert. Showing off in front of her fellow actresses in the rehearsal room of Radio Belgrano, she phoned Government House and spoke to President Ramirez, who invited her to dinner. The owner of Radio Belgrano promptly upped her salary from 150 pesos a month to 5,000. She was going up in the world.

Colonel Imbert moved her out of the rough Boca district into a smart apartment off the fashionable Avenida Alvear. When an earthquake destroyed the town of San Juan in January 1944, Evita persuaded him to stage a benefit concert for the victims to be broadcast nation-wide. Of course, Argentine's favourite soap star would be guest of honour.

Also present was Juan Perón, the rising strongman of the new regime. He arrived with Argentina's loveliest movie star, Libertad Lamarque, on his arm. But when Libertad stood up to do a bit at the microphone, Evita slipped into the empty chair beside him. The 48-year-old Perón already had a reputation for liking young girls. Evita was already 24, but she knew how to please a man and it took little effort to seduce him.

A few days later, Evita marched into Perón's apartment and evicted his teenage mistress. Perón had let it slip that he and a few like-minded officers were plotting to oust the civilian president. They planned to put Fascism into action without making the mistakes they thought Mussolini had made.

Evita was convinced that Perón could be the leader of the coup this time, if he had her help. And she moved into his apartment block to keep an eye on him. She realized that the traditional source of popular power in Argentina was the gauchos, the cowboys who had once inhabited the pampas and had now migrated to the shanty towns around the cities in search of work. As Minister of Labour, Perón was in a perfect position to mobilize their support. He introduced a minimum wage, sick leave, paid holidays and a bonus payment every year before Christmas. On the back of his growing popularity, Perón formed the *descamisados*, a paramilitary organization modelled on Mussolini's blackshirts.

His growing popularity among the poor brought a swift reaction. Moneyed interests forestalled his coup with a coup of their own. Perón, by then Vice-President and Minister of War, was arrested. Evita quickly rallied the labour unions. Hundreds of thousands took to the streets in protest. On 17 October 1945, Perón was released. Together, Perón and Evita were taken to the presidential palace where he addressed a crowd of 300,000. It was more of a coronation than a coup. A few days later, they were married.

Now President, Perón used his powers to conceal the sordid details of Evita's past. The pornographic photographs she had posed for were collected and destroyed. The regime invested a good deal in her popularity. Although she dressed in jewels and furs, she was portrayed as a woman of the people. In posters, she appeared as the Virgin Mary, the personification of Perónist beauty.

But many were not fooled. Argentinian poet and leading opponent of the regime, Jorge Luis Borges, said: 'Perón's wife was a common prostitute. She had a brothel near Junin. And it must have embittered him, no? I mean, if a girl is a whore in a large city that doesn't mean too much, but in a small town on the pampas, everybody knows everybody else.'

One day, when protesters taunted her while she was riding in an official car with an elderly Italian admiral, she turned to the admiral and said: 'Do you hear that? They are calling me a whore.'

He said: 'Yes, I quite understand. I haven't been to sea for 15 years and they still call me an admiral.'

However, Evita did try to legalize prostitution and regulate the red light district. At the same time, she used her women's welfare organizations to siphon off millions of pesos into her Swiss bank accounts.

While she boasted that her husband rewarded her work with just 'a kiss on the forehead', it was said that she maintained her position in the regime by using her womanly wiles on a network of men. The Perón regime used torture to suppress political opponents and the collection of rebel leaders' testicles that Evita kept on her desk was used to intimidate those who came to petition her.

In 1947, Evita made a trip to Italy where she made love to Aristotle Onassis in his villa on the Italian Riviera. Afterwards, she made him an omelette and he gave her a cheque for $10,000 for charity. He said later that it was the most expensive omelette he had ever eaten.

Moving on to Rome, she was greeted by crowds shouting 'Perón, Perón' and giving the straight-armed Fascist salute outlawed since the War. The riot police were sent in.

Evita died of cancer of the uterus at the age of just 33. Her death plunged Argentina into mourning. Moves were even made to have her canonized. Sadly, her husband could not live up to her virtuous image.

He was now 56, but his taste for teenage girls had not diminished. He began to take an inordinate interest in the Union of Secondary School Students, especially its young female members. There were branches in every school and young girl recruits were sent to luxurious 'recreational centres' where they entertained high-ranking government officials. Teams of doctors were on hand to cope with venereal diseases and unwanted pregnancies.

At Perón's private recreational centre, he would while away the hours watching teenage girls swimming or playing basketball. At least one of them, 13-year-old Nellie Rivas, became his mistress.

Nellie was the daughter of a worker in a sweet factory and slept on a sofa at the end of her parents' bed. One day, at the Union of Secondary School Students, she was told that she would be having lunch with the President. More lunches followed. Soon she moved into the love nest he had built in the basement of one of his villas. It had mirrored walls and white bearskin rugs on the floor.

As well as making love to her, he would teach young Nellie the rudiments of culture. He offered to send her to Europe to learn about the world but she said she did not want to leave him.

'The very thought of leaving the residence brought me to the brink of madness,' she said later.

Rumours about Perón's underage mistress soon spread. With the economy in ruins, stories that Perón was staging orgies with young girls in the presidential mansion spread. Many thought he had besmirched the memory of the saintly Evita. Supporters deserted him in droves. Deposed, Perón had to seek refuge on a Paraguayan gunboat that had put in at Buenos Aires for repairs. Before it took him into exile, he scribbled one last note to Nellie.

'My dear baby girl,' it read, 'I miss you every day, as I do my little dogs... Many kisses and many desires. Until I see you soon, Papi.'

Perón was tried in *absentia* in a military court for paedophilia. Their torrid correspondence was read out and subsequently published. His reputation in ruins, Perón was stripped of his rank for 'conduct unworthy of an officer and a gentleman'.

Summing up, the judge said: 'It is superfluous to stress the horror of the court at the proof of such a crime committed by one who always claimed that the only privileged people in the country were the children.'

Nellie was sent to a reformatory for eight months, then went into exile with her parents in Montevideo. The new regime had Evita's remains dug up and sent to Italy, where they were hidden to prevent them becoming an object of veneration.

Perón himself was in exile in Spain when he met and married his third wife, Isabel Martinez, an Argentinian dancer. In 1971, there was yet another coup in Argentina. This one promised a return to democracy and, as a gesture of reconciliation, Evita's remains were returned to Perón in Spain.

In 1973, Perón returned to Argentina to run in the presidential elections with his wife as his running mate. They romped home, but Perón was already dying. His widow succeeded him into office in 1974, but she could not hope to live up to the image of Evita. In a last-ditch attempt to rally support, she had Evita's remains flown home from Spain and interred next to her husband's in a crypt in the presidential palace.

In many eyes, this seemed only to confirm her illegitimacy. In 1976, the Air Force seized power. Isabel was held under house arrest for five years. In 1981, she was banished back to Spain, where she died in 1985.

Imelda Marcos and the Scandal of the Shoes

Imelda Marcos, long-serving First Lady of the Philippines, will always be known for the 3,000 pairs of shoes she left behind in Manila when she and her unscrupulous husband, Ferdinand, were driven from power in 1986. However, these are a symbol only of the scandalous self-indulgence of a regime that had systematically robbed the National Bank of billions and had the temerity to gun down the opposition leader, who was returning from exile, in front of a planeload of journalists.

Ferdinand Marcos was born in Luzon in 1917. In his highly fanciful autobiography, *Rendezvous with Destiny*, he claimed that he had distinguished himself as a highly decorated resistance leader during the War, against the Japanese. In fact, he had collaborated with the Japanese, but that did not matter: as President of the Philippines, he could give himself any decoration he liked. Not only that, as a fervent anti-Communist and one of America's few allies during the Vietnam War, he forced the Americans to award him the US Medal of Honour, as well as a vast amount of foreign aid, even though they knew the truth.

As a politician, Marcos had already done the seemingly impossible. He had got himself elected to Congress after being convicted of murder. Jailed for killing a political opponent, Marcos had used his incarceration to study the law. He had passed the bar exams and argued his own case in front of the Supreme Court. There he got lucky. The chief justice himself had been convicted of murder at the age of 18 and had successfully argued his case in front of the Supreme Court. Marcos walked free.

Marcos first met Imelda when he gave an address at her high school in Tacloban, on the island of Leyte. Although she was one of the island's powerful Romualdez clan, her side of the family was poor. For a time, they had lived in a car port and, as a child, she had gone barefoot – which might explain why she needed so many shoes later on.

At 16 she was a considered beauty. She fell in love with Victoriano Chan, the heir of a wealthy Chinese family. They considered her unsuitable. Then she was pursued by a rich saw-mill owner, Dominador Pacho. To escape his attentions, she fled to Manila with just five pesos in her purse.

She got a job in a bank, where one of the customers was Ferdinand Marcos. He paid her no attention. However, the editor of the Sunday supplement *This Week* noticed her and put her picture on the cover of the magazine's Valentine Day's issue. Suddenly, she was a star, and welcome at the Manila home of her kinsman, Congressman Daniel Romualdez. There, she was courted by an up-and-coming young politician named Benigno Aquino. But when he learnt of her humble origins, he dropped her.

In an attempt to make her way in the world, she entered the Miss Manila competition. Her family, who were strict Catholics, were shocked. They assumed that she would have to sleep with the judges. Presumably she didn't, as she lost to 20-year-old Norma Jimenez from Pangasinan province.

Realizing her mistake, Imelda appealed to Mayor Arsenio Lacson, who was well known for his wide-ranging sexual interests. It was said that he took 'Chinese tea' every afternoon with two Chinese girls thoughtfully provided by a constituent; a case of two for tea, perhaps?

When Lacson tried to overturn the judges' decision, it was assumed that Imelda was his latest conquest. However, the judges stuck by their original choice for Miss Manila, so Lacson simply named Imelda the 'Muse of Manila'. Both girls went forward for the Miss Philippines' contest, but neither won.

Imelda consoled herself by becoming the mistress of Ariston Nakpil, one of Manila's wealthiest men. Unfortunately, he was married.

It was then that she met Ferdinand Marcos once more at an ice-cream party. He began pursuing her. The following week, when she took off to Baguio with two girlfriends, he followed with a marriage licence that he had already signed just in case.

A religious girl, Imelda would go to Mass each morning. Ferdinand would sit beside her and tell her how golden their future would be together. She did not believe him, until he took her to see his bank deposit box, which contained the best part of $1 million in cash. They had a small private wedding conducted by a justice of the Peace. From meeting to marriage it had taken just 11 days. Her wedding ring had 11 diamonds set into its white gold, one for each day of their courtship.

Imelda thought her father would be angry about the marriage, but he took to Ferdinand immediately and forgave his daughter – provided they had a proper church wedding. Marcos did better than that. He arranged a wedding in the cathedral in Manila in the presence of the President of the Philippines, Ramon Magsaysay. Imelda wore a couture gown, comprising acres of white satin and tulle, embroidered with seed pearls and sequins. Among the 3,000 guests at the reception in Malacanang Park, across the river from the presidential palace, were numerous senators and congressmen. The wedding cake was a model of the Congress building.

'It was a very political wedding,' said Imelda's sister, Conchita.

The Marcoses had a very public honeymoon in Baguio. This was vital since there was already one Mrs Marcos. Her name was Carmen Ortega. Four years before his marriage to Imelda, Ferdinand had offered to sponsor Carmen for the Miss Press Photography contest. When she became his full-time mistress, he moved her into the house he shared with his mother, Doña Josefa. Marcos even announced their forthcoming nuptials in the press. Neither a civil nor a church wedding ever took place, but around Manila she was known as Mrs Marcos. Even Imelda knew her as such. Marcos had once brought her into the bank where Imelda worked to withdraw $50,000 for a shopping trip to the USA and had introduced her.

Donia Josefa considered Carmen her son's real wife. Imelda was merely a political mistress in her eyes. At the time, Marcos was planning to run for the Senate. He needed the backing of the Romualdez family, both politically and financially.

This fact was brought home painfully to Imelda. While they were away on their honeymoon, Marcos had Carmen and their three children moved out of the family home into a larger house in the suburbs. Imelda would now move in with Marcos and Doña Josefa. If the associations with Carmen there were not bad enough, the house was on Ortega Street. Imelda insisted that they sell up and move immediately. Marcos and his mother refused.

Worse, Marcos continued to see Carmen. Imelda paid her a visit and insisted that Carmen stop seeing her husband as she was destroying her happiness. Carmen said that it was Imelda who was ruining her happiness. At the time, Carmen was pregnant with Marcos's fourth child.

Imelda was now between a rock and a very hard place. In a Catholic country like the Philippines, she had no chance of an annulment, so there was no chance of making another lucrative match. She had no money of her own, and she could not stop her husband seeing his mistress.

Imelda had a nervous breakdown. Marcos sent her to New York for treatment. She spent three months in Manhattan's Presbyterian Hospital, but no amount of therapy changed the situation. She must either leave her husband and return to a life of penury, or bite the bullet.

There was only one thing a good Catholic woman could do. She flew back to the Philippines by way of Portugal, where she visited the shrine of Our Lady of Fatima and prayed for fertility. She gave birth to her first daughter, Imee, during Marcos's congressional campaign the following year. Two years later, their second child, Bong Bong, was born. Their third child, Irene, was born during Marcos's 1959 senatorial campaign.

Imelda suffered migraines and other recurring psychiatric symptoms, but she clung on. By the time Marcos was running for the presidency in 1965, Imelda was warming up the audience at his political rallies with stirring, patriotic Filipino songs. During that campaign Imelda emerged as a political figure in her own right, but she was still unused to the rough and tumble of political life. When the opposition circulated a nude photograph of her, claiming that it came from Marcos's private collection, she collapsed in a state of shock. Marcos supporters insisted that Imelda's head had been superimposed on another woman's nude body.

For Imelda, the best revenge was to be installed as First Lady in the Malacanang Palace. Nevertheless, Imelda remained unsure of herself and demanded inordinate deference from all those around her. When the Beatles turned up in Manila in 1966, she invited them to come and perform in the Malacanang Palace. They respectfully turned down the invitation, but invited her to come and see their public concert like other Filipinos. Imelda took this as an insult. They found themselves unceremoniously expelled from the country. As they left, they were punched and kicked by Imelda's hired thugs on the way to their plane.

The nude photo scandal had revealed a weakness in Imelda that political enemies sought to play on. The Governor of Negros, Alfredo Montelibano Jr, installed a two-way mirror in the lavatory of his hacienda. When Imelda came to his house for a party, he invited a number of guests into a back room to watch the First Lady pee. He took a photograph, which was circulated. Benigno Aquino kept a copy in his wallet until shortly before he died.

Marcos modelled himself on John F Kennedy and Imelda was only too happy to play Jackie. Like Kennedy, Marcos liked to show off his pretty young wife. He was also an inveterate womanizer. This was still painful for Imelda and it was politically dangerous for Marcos. In 1969, he began showing an interest in Gretchen Cojuangeo, wife of Eduardo Cojuangco, who controlled the Philippines' multi-million-dollar sugar-producing corporation. Imelda was determined to put a stop to the affair. She wrote Gretchen a note. Although what it said has never been revealed, when Gretchen read it she could not stop weeping.

Cojuangco took another approach to keep Marcos away from his wife. He suggested that Marcos's dire book, *Rendezvous with Destiny*, was feature film material. He had contacts in Hollywood and set to work immediately.

In *Rendezvous with Destiny*, the fearless guerrilla fighter claimed that his Filipino-American lover, Evelyn, had sacrificed her life to save his, by stopping a Japanese bullet meant for him.

A producer at Universal was employed to recruit girls to audition for the part of Evelyn. One of them was an actress called Dovie Beams. When she arrived in the Philippines, Marcos seduced her. He installed her in a house in the Green Hills suburb and claimed that he had been sexually estranged from Imelda for years. She was frigid and suffered, he said, from 'virginitis'.

Things went swimmingly until Dovie discovered Marcos was still seeing Carmen Ortega, who was now pregnant yet again. Dovie began recording their love-making sessions and when Marcos took her to the presidential palace while Imelda was away, Dovie searched his desk and took documents.

Imelda grew suspicious and began to have them followed. Marcos insisted that Dovie move out of the house
in Green Hills and into a hotel. She later discovered that
Marcos had given the house to Carmen Ortega, as he had
planned all along.

Dovie was determined to get even. Marcos had bought a
Polaroid camera and began taking pictures of their love
play. He also asked her for a lock of her pubic hair. She
consented to give him one, provided he gave her a lock of
his. She sent this with a collection of the photographs, the
tapes and the documents to the USA for safekeeping.

By then, Marcos was getting tired of her. He told Dovie
that she had been miscast for the role of Evelyn and he
wanted to audition some new actresses. She packed her
bags and flew back to California.

She later returned to the Philippines on the pretext of
making a travelogue. She was given $10,000 to buy silence.
Although she took it, she insisted that her silence was
worth more like $100,000. When that was refused, she
asked for $150,000. That night, she was grabbed by the
secret police and taken to a house where Marcos was
awaiting. There was a row. He tried to make up with her.
She spurned him and was beaten up and tortured by the
secret police.

When they allowed her to go to the bathroom, she gave
them the slip and called a friend in Los Angeles, who contacted influential people Dovie knew in the USA. One of
them was former movie actor, Ronald Reagan, then
Governor of California. He called the State Department
while Dovie checked into a private clinic under a false name.

Meanwhile, Imelda had learnt about everything and had
her cohorts combing the island for Dovie. The American
ambassador turned up at Dovie's bedside with an offer
from Imelda – $100,000 tax free if she kept quiet. But things
were not going to be quite as easy as that. Dovie told the
ambassador about the incriminating evidence she had on

Marcos and said that she believed her life was in danger.

The US ambassador realized that the only way to keep Dovie safe was to make the scandal public. He arranged a press conference. Dovie spilt the beans, referring to Marcos throughout as 'Fred' so that journalists could report the story without falling foul of the recent restrictions preventing the publication of anything critical of the President. She even played one of the tapes that featured bedsprings creaking, murmurs, moans and a man's voice crooning an Ilocano love song, which the whole of the Philippines knew was one of Marcos's favourites. Pirated versions of the tape were soon changing hands at $500 a time.

When the students at Manila University got hold of a copy, they looped the tape and played it over and over on the University radio station. Everyone's favourite section was the part where Marcos begged Dovie to perform oral sex on him. Even the troops sent to shut down the radio station could not keep a straight face. Senator Benigno Aquino, tongue buried firmly in cheek, called for a congressional investigation.

Imelda was now fighting mad. The US authorities had to spirit Dovie out of the Philippines. She was taken to Hong Kong, where the British Secret Service held her in protective custody for five days.

Back in the USA, Dovie published an account of the affair called *Marcos' Lovie Dovie*, which included some of the nude Polaroids. Mysteriously, the books vanished from the bookshops. Even the Library of Congress's copy went missing.

When Imelda cooled off, she realized that she now held the whip hand. If she dumped Marcos now, he would be finished. She told him that she would not ask for a divorce, provided he gave her everything she wanted – everything. He had no choice. He wrote an open cheque. It was then that the shopping started in earnest.

But it was not enough for Imelda to be personally

wealthy. She wanted respect. She was First Lady of a small poverty-stricken state. For her to be anything in the world, the Philippines would have to raise its profile. She planned to stage a Manila Film Festival, which she hoped would rival the glamour of Cannes. As part of the project, she planned a 100,000-seater stadium, the construction of which fell badly behind schedule.

To speed up its building, she demanded that the structure be erected before the concrete floor had dried. Predictably, the upper floors collapsed, killing 168 building workers. Imelda simply ordered their remains to be concreted over so that building work could begin again, before their relatives had time to collect their corpses.

Marcos continued his womanizing ways, starting an affair with the wife of a US Navy officer, jeopardizing Filipino-American relations. There followed a liaison with the Filipino singer, Carmen Soriano. Imelda caught up with her in San Francisco in 1970. Arriving at her apartment with her financial adviser, Ernesto Villatuya, Imelda insisted that Carmen sign a declaration promising never to go to bed with Marcos again. When Carmen refused, Imelda took a swing at her. She ducked and Imelda floored Villatuya. Soon after, he was made President of the Philippine National Bank, a position he held until 1972.

With Marcos and the national exchequer in her pocket, Imelda roamed the world as the Philippines' roving ambassador. In Libya, she claimed that Colonel Qaddafi made a pass at her, but to friends she confided he was gay. There were gay rumours about Imelda, too. She travelled everywhere with Cristina Ford, wife of Henry Ford II, and it was said they were lovers. Others say that she went to bed with the permanently tanned actor George Hamilton. And why not? Everyone else did.

According to the Philippines' constitution, the President can hold office for only two four-year terms. In 1973, Marcos considered putting up Imelda as his successor, thereby holding on to the reigns of power for eight more years. But with Imelda constantly away on state-sponsored shopping sprees, he felt she might leave a power vacuum. Instead, he declared martial law.

Popular frustration soon turned to violence. At an open-air awards ceremony, one of the recipients lunged at Imelda with a cane-cutting blade. She instinctively protected her breasts and was slashed on both forearms. The would-be assassin was slaughtered on the spot by her bodyguards.

The assassination attempt had a profound effect on her. She called in voodoo advisers to protect her from hostile spells. Old clothes were hoarded and no personal items were thrown away, lest they fall into the hands of those plotting against her. She began wearing a scarf around her neck to ward off the danger of decapitation. And she surrounded herself with handmaidens, whom she called her 'blue ladies' because they were dressed identically in a traditional Filipino *termos* with a blue sash. They were hand-picked for their loyalty and owed their elevation from the grinding poverty that was now engulfing the country solely to Imelda.

Imelda travelled around the world in her private jet, which had a bathroom with gold fittings. She carried with her an entourage of freeloading socialites, supping on champagne and caviare. On one shopping trip that took in New York, Copenhagen and Rome, she spent more than £3 million. Admittedly, that did include a £2-million Michelangelo. And she bought some bath towels costing £8,000. After her plane took off from Rome, Italian air traffic control received a message from the pilot asking permission to return. Fearing some life-threatening technical problem, the air traffic controller asked what the problem was.

'We have no cheese,' said the pilot.

Wherever she stayed, there was a standing order that the hotel would furnish her suite with £500 worth of flowers.

Whenever she returned to the Philippines, Manila airport was closed down, the red carpet was rolled out and the local school-children were turned out to cheer and wave.

At home, she was hardly more frugal. She had a plane-load of sand flown in from Australia when she decided that the natural Philippine sand around her summer house wasn't quite the right shade of white. The entire 5,000 sq ft basement of the Malacanang Palace turned into her private wardrobe. Along with her breathtaking shoe collection she had 1,500 handbags, 35 racks of fur coats, 500 brassieres – one bullet proofed – and 1,200 hand-sewn designer dresses, each of which had been worn only once.

When the Philippine ambassador in London failed to get her an invitation to the wedding of Prince Charles and Lady Di, she sacked him. In 1983, she tried to outdo the splendour of St Paul's with the wedding of her daughter, Imee. New façades were put on the houses around Manila Cathedral to make them look like seventh-century Spanish colonial homes. For the reception, she hired a luxury liner to house the 500 guests. The entire beanfeast ran out at £7 million. And this was in a country that was practically bankrupt.

But it was not these excesses that brought the Marcoses down, it was sexual jealousy. Since Marcos had introduced martial law, the Leader of the Opposition, Benigno Aquino, had fled into exile in the United States. Ronald Reagan was now in the White House and the Americans were beginning to get a little worried about the dictatorial methods of Ferdinand Marcos. To placate the Americans, Marcos called elections. The US government insisted that Aquino be allowed to return to the Philippines so that he could stand, and they brokered a deal with Marcos. However, they had counted without Imelda. Still smarting from her rejection 30 years earlier, she ordered that Aquino's feet should never again touch Philippine soil. When he flew into Manila airport with a plane-load of journalists, Imelda's henchmen shot him as he came down the steps of the plane.

Ferdinand was horrified. He knew his number was up. In desperation, he blamed the assassination on rogue elements in the army and fixed the presidential election. Strikes and public demonstrations followed. The media slipped its yoke and the Philippines teetered on the brink of anarchy.

Somehow the Marcoses clung on. In 1986, Ferdinand called another election, again to placate Washington. This time he faced Benigno Aquino's widow, Corazon. He claimed victory but it was plain that he had won only by ballot rigging. There was an international outcry. Hundreds of thousands of people took to the streets of Manila. They stood in the path of tanks and Marcos's troops in a demonstration of 'people power', while the Marcoses were airlifted to safety in Hawaii.

Once order had been restored, the new government under Cory Aquino began to untangle the web of corruption the Marcoses had left behind, and discovered that an estimated $10 billion was missing from the treasury.

Apart from the money the Marcoses had squandered on high living, the rest seemed to be in Switzerland. But after interminable court battles the Swiss were prepared to return only about $2 million.

The Aquino government had more luck in the USA. There, the courts were prepared to freeze the Marcoses,' assets. The US authorities maintained that the Marcoses had broken US laws by transferring Philippine government money into private accounts on US soil. Ferdinand and Imelda failed to answer subpoenas to appear before a Grand Jury in New York, and in October 1988 they were indicted under the Racketeer-Influenced and Corrupt Organizations Act.

Ferdinand Marcos never stood trial. He had long suffered from lupus and his health had deteriorated since he had been ousted. He was excused the trip to New York for his arraignment. Imelda appeared alone. She was charged with stealing a mere $200 million from the Philippines and illegally investing it in the United States. She was also charged with fraudulently obtaining loans from the USA and obstructing justice. Pleading not guilty, she was released on $8.5 million bail.

In September 1989, Ferdinand Marcos died. Cory Aquino refused permission for his body to be returned to the Philippines for burial.

In March 1990, Imelda stood trial in New York. Her co-defendant was Saudi arms dealer, Adnan Khashoggi, an old pal of the Marcoses and reputedly the richest man in the world. He was charged with fraud and obstructing justice by helping Imelda hide some of her ill-gotten gains.

The prosecution accused Imelda of systematically looting her country. The charges related particularly to four skyscrapers that the Marcoses had bought in Manhattan between 1981 and 1983 as a nest egg should something go wrong in Manila. When the US authorities froze the Marcoses' assets in 1987, it was alleged that Khashoggi drew up bills of sale and backdated the purchase to 1985.

The prosecution called 95 witnesses. One of them was Oscar Carino, the manager of the Philippine National Bank's branch in New York. He claimed that when Imelda was in town, she used the National Bank like her own 'personal piggy bank. He regularly delivered up to $100,000 in cash to her hotel room as loose change for her shopping sprees. When state investigators examined the books, they found unreimbursed withdrawals totalling over $22 million.

The defence called no witnesses. Instead, Imelda's attorney, the flamboyant Gerry Spense, who wore a Stetson and cowboy boots in court, delivered a *tour de force*. He focused the jury's attention on the 3,000 pairs of shoes. This was not as extravagant as it may seem, he pointed out. Shoe manufacturers regularly deliver dozens of free samples as courtesy. Most of them did not fit.

It was true, he said, that Imelda 'may have been a world-class shopper, but she was also a world-class decent human being who was guilty only of loving her husband'. The jury acquitted both defendants of all charges.

With a personal fortune estimated at $7.5 billion – every penny obtained honestly, she says – Imelda went on to become queen of the chat shows. Her defence was her beauty.

'They call me corrupt, frivolous,' she said. 'I would not look like this if I were corrupt. Some ugliness would settle on my system.'

Interviewers are too polite to point out that her beauty is fading.

Slowly, the courts in Switzerland and the USA ordered the return of some of the money the Marcoses had embezzled. More went to the victims of torture and human rights abuses and to the families of the estimated 10,000 killed during Marcos's presidency. Imelda's jewellery and shoes were auctioned off, but she still had plenty of money left to buy more.

Imelda kept Ferdinand's body on ice in Honolulu until 1993, when she was allowed to return it to the Philippines for burial. She then stood in the presidential elections, but stood down after being accused of cheating. However, she was elected to the House of Representatives in 1995.

The Flower Child First Lady

Pierre Trudeau was the first French-speaking Prime Minister of Canada. He served from 1969 to 1979, and again from 1980 to 1984. Although a Liberal and progressive, he defeated the French-speaking separatists who wanted Quebec to secede.

No scandal there then. That's true, but when Trudeau came to power he was a handsome and eligible bachelor. On holiday in Tahiti, he met Margaret Sinclair, the daughter of a wealthy politician. She was 29 years his junior and, in the spirit of the time, a flower child. They married in 1971.

Everything was fine to start with, but it gradually became clear that Margaret Trudeau was not going to settle into the life of a politician's wife. She remained, at heart, a flower child, and wanted a career of her own.

She became a photojournalist and, in 1977, while Pierre was baby sitting in Ottawa, she travelled the 240 miles to Toronto to photograph the Rolling Stones who were on tour. As much photographed as photographing, Margaret Trudeau sported a tight-fitting blue boiler suit. She danced to the Stones' music and sat at Mick Jagger's feet as he sang.

It was also noted by the press that she had turned up to the concert in Jagger's limousine. She spent the night in their hotel in a room next to Keith Richards, who had recently been charged with drug offences in Canada. She was also seen hanging around the hotel corridors in a white bathrobe, and seemed happy to pose for photographs with the band.

The Rolling Stones' drummer, Charlie Watts, summed up the feelings of most Canadians when he was heard to comment: 'I wouldn't want my wife associating with us.'

The next night she attended another Stones' concert, arriving with Jagger in his limousine once more. Afterwards, she went to a party with Jagger and Richards that lasted until 7 a.m.

But it did not end there. Margaret Trudeau followed the Stones to New York like some groupie. By that time, she seemed to have developed a closer relationship with guitarist, Ron Wood. On the foreign exchange markets, the Canadian dollar dropped one and a half cents.

Even the Stones were embarrassed by the affair. They were still trying to live down their disastrous gig at Altamont, where a young black man named Meredith Hunter was stabbed to death within feet of the stage by the Hell's Angels the Stones had hired as security.

'The last thing in the world the Stones want is any scandal, any crazies,' said their press spokesman, Paul Wassermann. 'Their whole energy is needed for new albums. Jagger and the others are in New York for specific things. Mrs Trudeau and the group have completely different interests in New York.'
Jagger himself simply shrugged off the growing scandal.

'We just had a passing acquaintance for two nights,' he told the media. 'She just wanted to be introduced. Princess Margaret wanted to be introduced in London. Lee Radziwill followed us. These ladies are charming to have around. There is no question of anything more.'

But it did not look like such a small thing the other side of the 50th parallel.

'Someone should control the lady,' said one Toronto newspaper, pointing the finger at the Premier. 'It is unacceptable for the wife of the Prime Minister to be cavorting with a group like the Rolling Stones. Most of them have, at one time or another, been involved with drugs.'

Embarrassed by the situation, Margaret Trudeau was defiant. Instead of meekly returning home, she went to stay with Princess Yashmin Khan, the daughter of Aly Khan and the movie star Rita Hayworth.

'I don't want to be a rose in my husband's lapel,' she said. 'I've had enough. After six years, I abdicate.'

What made the scandal all the more embarrassing was that Trudeau was awaiting an official visit from the British Prime Minister, James Callaghan, and the Foreign Secretary, David Owen, both of whom were bringing their wives. Margaret was persuaded to return home. She arrived the day before the official visit, wearing dark glass-es. But the following day, she refused to entertain Mrs Callaghan and Mrs Owen, while their husbands held high-level talks.

This provoked a blazing row and things were thrown. Two days later, Margaret appeared with a black eye.

'Pierre said I deserved a good spanking,' she explained. 'He belted me. But that night we made love and it was wonderful. I don't think it had ever been so good before.' Or again. They separated. After a half-hour meeting at an airport, it was decided that Pierre should have custody of their three children. Margaret moved to New York where she set up as a freelance photographer, using her maiden name, Margaret Sinclair.

The Prime Minister's office issued a brief statement: 'Pierre accepts Margaret's decision with regret and both pray that their separation will lead to a better relationship between themselves.'

Margaret's name was soon linked with those of King Hussein, Senator Edward Kennedy and Ryan O'Neal. She had a brief career as a movie actress, then published her autobiography, *Beyond Reason*, just in time to embarrass her husband at a general election.

It repeated all her greatest *faux pas*, like the time she sang a dreadful song of her own composition to the President of Venezuela's wife at the state banquet in Caracas. During an earlier general election, she had turned up at her husband's hotel in the middle of the night, grubby and barefoot, and had demanded to be taken to the Prime Minister's suite.

She had shocked the guests at a formal dinner in Washington by wearing a micro-miniskirt. Unfortunately, she had had a ladder in her tights. At a New York luncheon, she had inflicted herself so gauchely on Princess Margaret that the normally sociable royal had frozen her out.

She proudly announced that she had shown her tits to

Prince Charles. She had tried to get him to come over to Paris when she was on a photo assignment there, but when he had called her hotel he had asked for Margaret Trudeau. The feisty Mrs Trudeau had checked in as Ms Sinclair.

But it was her flirtation with drugs that scandalized her husband's Liberal Party more than anything.

'Of course, I smoked marijuana in Morocco,' the flower child announced proudly. And, although she said that she steered clear of hard drugs, she admitted: 'I still smoke marijuana from time to time.'

Canada may be a laid-back place, but it's not that laid-back.

Victorian Values

The governments of Margaret Thatcher were dogged by scandal. Although she prided herself on her adherence to 'Victorian values', she surrounded herself by those who did not. Or if they did, it was to those values that meant one out of every four women in Victorian London was a prostitute.

The first casualty was Sir Nicholas Fairbairn, whom Mrs Thatcher appointed as Solicitor General for Scotland. In October 1981, the 47-year-old MP's 34-year-old ex-girl-friend tried to commit suicide in spectacular fashion. The press said that the spurned lover had been found hanging from a lamp-post outside Fairbairn's London home. She denied this, saying: 'I wouldn't even have the energy to climb up a lamp-post.'

However, she admitted the affair. It had begun when she was a secretary in the House of Commons and he was still married to his first wife, Elizabeth McKay. He had wooed her with red roses, passionate love letters and proposals of marriage. Unfortunately, on the last item, he did not come through.

When the scandal broke over Christmas, Mrs Thatcher had no comment to make on whether Sir Nicholas's values were Victorian or not. It was, she said, 'a private matter' between 'two single people'.

The press pursued Fairbairn to Fordell Castle, his Scottish home. They found the drawbridge up and camped outside. Eventually, the laird appeared in a blue and white dressing gown. They had got the story the wrong way round, he told them. It was the lady who was the ardent suitor, not he. It was she who had suggested marriage.

Fairbairn had only just survived this scandal, when he walked right into another one. In January 1982, he decided not to pursue the prosecution of three Glasgow youths in a controversial rape case. Unfortunately, he announced his decision in the *Glasgow Daily Record* the day before he told the House of Commons. MPs will not stand for this discourtesy. The next day, Fairbairn was summoned to 10 Downing Street. Mrs Thatcher already had his letter of resignation drawn up. She handed him a pen and said: 'Sign here.'

He showed no bitterness, later describing Thatcher as 'probably the warmest and kindest human being that those who have met her have ever encountered'. Fairbairn was probably happier on the back benches where he could spend more time 'making love, ends meet and people laugh' – the hobbies he had once listed in *Who's Who*.

One of his greatest laughs came from his parliamentary put-down of Edwina Curry, who was embroiled in the salmonella-in-eggs controversy at the time. He rose to remind the Honourable Lady that she had once been an egg herself and Members on both sides of the House regretted that it had been fertilized.

In October 1982, Fairbairn was back in the headlines when he was cited in a divorce case. Unrepentant, he furiously attacked the press's hypocritical moral crusades. He told *The Times*: 'Scandal may be good copy, but it adds nothing to the integrity of our institutions. I do not think they were any worse, indeed I think they were probably much better, when those who ruled us were known, and seen to have healthy sexual liaisons with many mistresses and lovers.'

Mrs Thatcher's reaction was not recorded.

In 1983, Mrs Thatcher lost another of her favourites to sexual scandal. Cecil Parkinson was the golden boy of Tory politics in the early 1980s and Mrs Thatcher had been grooming him as her successor.

'In some ways, he seems too good to be true,' said *The Times* in October 1981. 'Tall, handsome, charming and likeable... the perfect constituency MP, intelligent without being intellectual, self-made, brilliantly supported by a politically committed wife – is there no flaw?'

There was – a fatal one.

Born in 1931, the son of a railwayman, Parkinson went to Royal Lancaster Grammar School and won a scholarship to Emmanuel College, Cambridge. In 1955, he met Ann Jarvis, daughter of a wealthy building contractor. When they married in 1956, her father set up Parkinson with his own building firm in Stockport. From these humble beginnings, he became a millionaire with homes in Hertfordshire, Pimlico, Cornwall and the Bahamas.

He entered Parliament in 1970 and was quickly seen as the model Thatcherite man. In her first administration in 1979, Mrs Thatcher made him Minister of State for Trade. In 1981, he became Chairman of the Conservative Party and, in 1982, Chancellor of the Duchy of Lancaster. This brought him into the cabinet, and during the Falklands War, he was one of the inner cabinet that engineered the Argentine defeat.

Everything was right on track until 9 June 1983, when as Party Chairman, he delivered her a landslide victory. A few hours before they were seen together waving to glee-ful supporters from the upstairs window of Conservative Central Office, Thatcher had offered him any job in her cabinet that he wanted. She knew he had always hankered after the Foreign Office, but instead of asking to be appointed Foreign Secretary, he admitted to a 'serious personal problem.'

In 1971, Parkinson had begun an affair with Sarah Keays, a House of Commons secretary. The affair had continued until July 1979, when she went to Brussels to work for Roy Jenkins, who was then a commissioner for the European Community. When she returned to London in October, the affair had resumed. They were nearly discovered. One night his car was stolen from outside her house in a Southwark muse. It was recovered, but since his ministerial red boxes had been in the car, he had had to own up to the Home Secretary, Willie Whitelaw. Whitelaw was supportive.

'There but for the grace of God go many of us,' he said.

A month before the 1983 election, Keays announced that she was pregnant. Parkinson told Thatcher that he could hardly expect to be in her cabinet under these circumstances.

'Mrs Thatcher was immensely sympathetic, not at all censorious,' Parkinson wrote later. Rather than Foreign Secretary, she offered him the more junior post of Secretary of State for Trade and Industry until the dust had settled. As to the baby, Mrs Thatcher 'was sure that as sensible people we could sort it out'.

While Parkinson and his wife went off for a well-earned rest in their holiday home in the Bahamas, journalists from the *Daily Mirror* began pursuing the heavily pregnant Sarah Keays, demanding to know whether Parkinson was the father.

While on holiday, Parkinson decided to stay with Ann, his wife of 27 years and mother of his three grown-up daughters. This put paid to his political career. As we know, politicians who divorce their wives and marry their paramours can keep their jobs – even if they are Foreign Secretary, as Robin Cook proved in Tony Blair's administration. Those who stay after having erred are often forced out.

When he returned to England, Parkinson broke the news to Keays. There was a row and they agreed that all future communication should be via their solicitors.

It was then that Sarah Keays' father took a hand. He wrote to Mrs Thatcher, warning her of an imminent public scandal. In preparation, Parkinson stepped down as Party Chairman on 14 September. The then unknown John Selwyn Gummer took over.

On 5 October 1983, the satirical magazine, *Private Eye*, ran a gossip piece saying: 'Why was Cecil Parkinson asked to step down as Tory Party Chairman? I can assure readers that it had nothing to do with his marital difficulties which have recently raised eyebrows in Tory circles. Now comes the news that Parkinson's fun-loving secretary Ms Sarah Keays is expecting a baby in three months' time.'

Although libel writs were issued and the magazine paid out damages, the damage had been done.

Parkinson issued his own statement that day at 11.45 p.m. It read: 'To bring to an end rumour concerning Miss Sarah Keays, and her family, I wish, with her consent, to make the following statement. I have had a relationship with Miss Keays over a number of years. She is expecting a child, due to be born in January, of whom I am the father. I am of course making financial provision for both mother and child. During our relationship I told Miss Keays of my wish to marry her. Despite my having given Miss Keays that assurance, my wife, who has been a source of great strength, and I have decided to stay together and to keep our family together. I regret deeply the distress I have caused to Miss Keays, to her family and to my family.'

353

Mrs Thatcher made no comment, again saying it was a 'private matter'. The press reaction was generally favourable. Parkinson had done the right thing, he had stayed with his wife and he had provided for his ex-lover and their child.

'Men who tell the truth and face their responsibilities are, in my view, far more worthy of public office than men who take the easy way out,' wrote Mary Kenny in *The Times*. 'I trust Cecil Parkinson more for having done the brave thing.'

The editorial in *The Times* agreed with Mrs Thatcher that it was a 'private matter'. *The Daily Telegraph* even suggested that the problem would be best solved with an abortion.

The public was sympathetic, too. Parkinson's office received 16,000 letters of support and 46 against.

In confessional mode, Parkinson went on the BBC's flagship current affairs programme, *Panorama*. For the moment, he would stay on in office. But 'if ever I ceased to be an asset and become a liability, and the Prime Minister felt so, then of course I would leave immediately,' he said.

But hell hath no fury like a woman scorned. And Sarah Keays was not just scorned, her ambitions had been thwarted. She, too, had set her heart on a political career. She had stood unsuccessfully as a councillor in Southwark and had been runner-up in the selection for the Conservative candidate in the nearby constituency of Bermondsey.

When a by-election had been called in Bermondsey, the candidate whom the constituency party had selected could not run. They had asked Conservative Central Office whether they should then take the runner-up – Keays – or start the selection process all over again.

The decision had fallen to Parkinson, who could hardly declare an interest. If he had opted for the former, he would have been open to charges of nepotism; if he had chosen the latter, he risked alienating his lover. As it was, he had decided that Bermondsey should reselect. They did, and chose a young man called Robert Hughes.

In fact, Parkinson had done Keays a favour and saved her from a very unsavoury campaign. Bermondsey was a rock-solid Labour seat and the Labour Party had selected as a replacement for the sitting Member, Bob Mellish, who had died, a young Antipodean firebrand named Peter Tatchell. During the hustings, Tatchell was outed as a homosexual, which did not sit well with the working-class voters of Bermondsey. The Liberal candidate, Simon Hughes, had romped home and the Conservatives had never stood a chance.

After Parkinson's statement, Keays bided her time. She waited until he went to the Conservative Party conference at Blackpool the following week. He delivered a low-key speech, but he garnered enough applause to believe that the party would, if not condone what he had done, at least forgive him.

It was then that Keays blew him out of the water. She issued the following statement:

'I agreed for the sake of my family that we would not discuss with the press the statement made by Mr Parkinson last week. I hoped that it would not become necessary for me to say anything. However, I now feel that I have a duty to do so.

'On Friday, October 7, *The Times* said that."Mr Parkinson had made a sad and silly blunder". Like the government, the editor believes that this should have remained a "private matter".

'For *The Daily Telegraph* (Monday, October 10) "the moral logic is that a quiet abortion is greatly to be preferred to a scandal". I was not aware that political expediency was sufficient grounds for an abortion under the 1967 Act, quite apart from the fact that I could not have contemplated it.

'On Monday night, in spite of the understanding expressed in his statement, Mr Parkinson saw fit to answer questions about the matter in a much publicized *Panorama* programme. It appeared from that programme that the Prime Minister had been kept fully informed and that the statement issued by Mr Parkinson contained the full facts.

'The full facts have not been made public. Press judgements and public opinion have been influenced by inadequate information, speculation, and the Government's desire to restore Mr Parkinson's position – as someone else put it, to "rehabilitate" him.

'1. It had been implied that I tried to trap Mr Parkinson into marriage;

'2. that I sought to destroy his reputation; and

'3. that the matter should have remained private.

'The last presumes that I should hide from public view and declare on the baby's birth certificate "father unknown", so casting further doubt on my reputation and denying the child his fundamental right to know the identity of his father.

'According to the view expressed in *The Telegraph*, I should have sacrificed my baby's life for Mr Parkinson's career and the Government's reputation.

'I wish therefore to make known the following chronology of events:

'1. My baby was conceived in a long-standing, loving relationship which I had allowed to continue because I believed in our eventual marriage. It has been suggested that Mr Parkinson only asked me to marry him after I became pregnant, when in fact he first did so in 1979.

'2. In May, when I knew I had to accept the fact that he was not going to marry me, I could not deny my baby his right to know the true identity of his father.

'3. I did, however, implore Mr Parkinson, during May and early June, to inform the Prime Minister because his name and mine were sufficiently linked in political circles for speculation to be inevitable and it was essential that the Prime Minister was made aware of the situation before forming her new Government. He would not agree to this.

'4. On polling day, Mr Parkinson sought a reconciliation and asked me to marry him. I gladly accepted. He said that he was about to see the Prime Minister to inform her of our relationship and to tell her that he would be getting a divorce in order to marry me. That evening he told me he had so informed her.

'He also told other members of my family his intention. He asked me to give him time to arrange matters and to leave my job at the House of Commons, which I did at the end of June. I and my family assured him of our full co-operation and that we would give him such time as he needed.

'5. On August 5, Mr Parkinson went on holiday abroad with his wife and family, having reassured me of his intention to marry me.

'6. On August 23, I was visited at my London home by reporters from the *Daily Mirror* who demanded to know if it was true that I was pregnant by Mr Parkinson. At that very same moment others from the same newspaper called on my father and sister.

'Later that night, as I was driving a girlfriend to her home, I was pursued by two cars which I believed to be driven by reporters from the *Daily Mirror,* who tried to force me to stop and one of their cars collided with mine. I had to take refuge in Rochester Row Police Station.

'7. On August 24, I informed Mr Parkinson, who was still abroad, of the incident with the *Daily Mirror*. I assured him that neither I nor any member of my family had told them anything, but I was concerned that the press would shortly confront him.

'He advised me to leave London, which I did, and he said he would speak to me again on his return to England the following week. He gave me no indication that matters between us had in any way changed.

'8. On September 1, Mr Parkinson asked me to meet him secretly in an office in London, where he informed me that he was not going to marry me after all. Later that day I telephoned him to say that I thought it essential that he should inform the Prime Minister.

'9. I subsequently instructed solicitors with a view to Mr Parkinson and myself issuing a joint statement. In the ensuing weeks it became clear that other newspapers were pursuing the story and that it was being talked about in political circles.

'10. On Wednesday, October 5, when I was informed of what had been published in *Private Eye*, I telephoned Mr Parkinson and told him that if he did not issue the statement which solicitors had been discussing for some weeks, that I would be obliged to defend myself.

'Press comment, government pronouncements, and continued speculation about this matter have put me in an impossible position. I feel that I have both a public duty and a duty to my family to put the record straight.'

That, of course, was only Sarah Keays' side of the story, but it was damning. The timing was perfect, too. Publication of the statement would coincide with Mrs Thatcher's victory speech at the party conference, when Parkinson was sure to be on the rostrum by her side. *The Times* sent a copy of the statement to the Imperial Hotel, Blackpool, where the Parkinsons and the Thatchers were staying. After reading it, Parkinson walked the few yards to Thatcher's suite. They talked for about 15 minutes, then, at 2 a.m., he resigned. He was replaced by Norman Tebbit, his one-time deputy at Hemel Hempstead Conservative Association.

The following day, Parkinson was noticeably not at Thatcher's side when she gave her victory speech. He and his wife had already left for Hertfordshire. Thatcher made some last-minute amendments to her speech. Although she praised 'the man who so brilliantly organized our campaign", she did not name him.

On New Year's Eve 1983, Sarah Keays gave birth to an 8 lb 3 oz girl she named Flora. Parkinson did not visit the mother or the child, but issued a statement wishing his daughter 'peace, privacy and a happy life'. Although Parkinson was criticized for denying his daughter any contact, Sarah Keays revealed on the radio that the child was handicapped and said that the publicity attendant on any visit from her father would be cruel and confusing for her.

But that did not mean that she was not going to have her pound of flesh. By 1985, things had cooled sufficiently for Mrs Thatcher to consider having Parkinson back in her government. But on the eve of the 1985 Conservative Party conference, Keays serialized her autobiography in the *Daily Mirror*, banishing him to the political wilderness once more.

In the 1987 election, Parkinson was returned with an increased majority and Thatcher felt that she had an electoral mandate to return him to the ranks of her ministers. She gave him the junior cabinet post of Energy Secretary. Two years later, he was made Transport Secretary, but he had lost his sparkle. The scandal had knocked the wind out of his sails. No one mentioned him as a potential leader again. He quit the cabinet when Margaret Thatcher stepped down in 1990. He did not stand again in the 1992 election and was elevated to the Lords.

In his autobiography, *Right at the Centre*, he devotes just seven pages to 'The Keays Affair'. One only wishes that Sarah Keays had done the same.

Then followed a couple of gay scandals for the

Conservative government. Michael Heseltine's Parliamentary Private Secretary, Keith Hampson MP, was arrested by a plain-clothes police officer in a gay club in Soho and charged with indecent assault.

Although Hampson resigned his position as Heseltine's PPS, he insisted that he had done nothing wrong. He had accidentally brushed the policeman's thigh, he said. And he had only been in the club because he had been drunk. He said he had downed five pints of beer before completing a speech for Heseltine then, with time to spare before meeting his wife, he had chanced upon the Gay Theatre in Berwick Street, which promised a non-stop male strip show. Naturally he went in.

This story was somewhat undermined by the club's manager, Russell McCleod, who said mischievously that Hampson was a regular client, along with a number of other MPs.

Hampson's wife claimed that her husband was a red-blooded heterosexual and, despite calls for his resignation, he decided to tough it out. At the trial, the policeman said that Hampson had grabbed his buttocks with one hand and his groin with the other.

In his defence, Hampson wheeled out former Speaker of the House of Commons, Lord Tonypandy, as a character witness. The judge, if no one else, was impressed. He told the jury that to say that Hampson was a homosexual was 'absurd and unthinkable'. His story about finding himself in a gay club was plausible since 'the history of mankind is littered with the debris of men who have acted more stupidly than anyone else would have thought possible at the time'.

Nevertheless, the jury came back after five hours and said that they could not agree on a verdict. The Attorney General, Michael Havers, then stepped in. Due to the widespread publicity the case had received, it would not be possible to stage a retrial. So a verdict of not guilty would be recorded. Hampson stayed on as an MP and co-ordinated Michael Heseltine's bid for the leadership in 1990.

Conservative MP Harvey Proctor's sexuality first became apparent in 1981 when he locked his long-standing boyfriend, Terry Woods, out of his Fulham flat. Woods shot his mouth off to journalists. *Private Eye* ran the story and soon the newspapers began a hue and cry.

Proctor claimed that the allegations against him was 'a campaign of political character assassination'. He had certainly made himself a target. He voiced right-wing views about immigration, and was generally viewed as 'one of the Thatcher praetorian guard'.

The trail went cold until 1986, when *The People* ran a story about a young male prostitute who claimed that Proctor had employed him for spanking sessions. The paper alleged that Proctor paid rent boys £35 a time to spank them while he watched by-election results on the television.

Although Proctor had previously sued *The People* and won – when the paper had falsely claimed that Mrs Thatcher was refusing to call Proctor 'my Honourable Friend' – this time he did not sue. The paper then ran a six-week campaign against Proctor, during which it was claimed that he had used an underage boy for sex who had tape recorded their spanking sessions. The rent boy concerned was 18, but it is clear from the tape that he told Proctor he was over 21. The newspaper handed over its evidence to the police.

Even with an election looming on the horizon, Proctor managed to secure the backing of his constituency party~

Then the *Daily Mirror* broke the story that on a trip to Morocco, a naked Arab youth had been found under Proctor's bed in his hotel room. Proctor protested that the youth concerned was 25 and he was not naked – at least not at the time he was found. That story had hardly died down when Terry Woods found himself locked out of Proctor's flat again, this time clad only in his underpants.

The police, led by Chief Superintendent Marvin, then began a series of raids on his flat. These were unfailingly attended by a gaggle of journalists. On 11 May, the day the Prime Minister announced the date of the 1987 general election, Proctor was charged with four counts of gross indecency.

With the election campaign now underway, Proctor had no alternative but to resign. His solicitor, Sir David Napley, pointed out that although Proctor had believed that all the rent boys he employed were over 21, some had not been. In homosexual cases, the reasonable belief that someone was not underage was not enough. Proctor pleaded guilty and was fined £1,450 with £250 costs.

Even then the scandal did not die down. When Chief Superintendent Marvin retired from the Serious Crime Squad, he sold his story to *The Sun*, which happily printed more sordid details of Proctor's private life.

However, his colleagues rallied around. Michael Heseltine, Tristan Garel Jones, Tim Yeo and Neil Hamilton – both of whom came to grief in the Major government – helped him set up a high-class menswear shop in Richmond called 'Proctor's Shirts and Ties' When it featured in a Spectator cartoon with a sign saying 'Shirtlifters will not prosecuted', Proctor bought the original and proudly displayed it in the store.

Not all scandals during the Thatcher years centred around sex. One concerned the conduct of the Falklands War and the fate of the Argentine cruiser, *General Belgrano*, which had been sunk by the British nuclear submarine, *Conqueror*, on 2 May 1982 with the loss of some 370 lives.

In December 1982, veteran backbench MP, Tam Dalyell, published a book called *One Man's Falklands*. In it, he alleged that the government's decision to sink the *Belgrano*, also sank any peaceful resolution of the conflict. The day before the sinking, Dalyell maintained, the leader of the Argentine junta, General Galtieri, had agreed to withdraw from the Falklands under a peace plan brokered by Peru. The Thatcher government knew this and went ahead anyway. What's more, the *Belgrano* was outside the 30-mile exclusion zone the British had declared around the islands, and it was heading back towards its home port. Even so, the Ministry of Defence claimed that the cruiser 'posed a major threat to our ships'.

When the President of Peru confirmed that the Argentine junta had indeed been on the point of accepting the peace plan when they had received news of the sinking, 150 Labour MPs asked for a full inquiry. For the government, Cranley Onslow, Minister of State at the Foreign and Commonwealth Office, insisted that Peruvian proposals had only reached London, via Washington, three hours after the *Belgrano* went down.

Interest was revived when Dalyell revealed that he had some leaked documents showing that a secret internal inquiry, ordered by the Secretary of State for Defence, Michael Heseltine, had confirmed his accusations.

An assistant secretary at the Ministry of Defence, Clive Ponting, was charged with offences under the Official Secrets Act. In court, he freely admitted handing classified material to Dalyell, but he argued that Dalyell was 'a duly elected MP and a man of considerable integrity who had been systematically mislead', and it was 'in the wider interests of Parliament to be told how it had been misled and how the government was now proposing to mislead it.' Ponting was acquitted.

In 1985, a Commons Select Committee issued a majority report, which said that the sinking of the Belgrano was justified. Four Labour MPs issued a minority report, which said that the government had tried to cover up 'a hasty and unjustifiable decision to risk many lives and possible disaster in order to ensure the life of an administration which itself was palpably negligent'.

It is now generally conceded that Dalyell was right. But the war was long over and victory had returned Margaret Thatcher as one of the most popular prime ministers ever.

After the Falklands War, the Thatcher government adopted a decidedly gung-ho approach. In 1984, the Deputy Chief Constable of Greater Manchester, John Stalker, was asked to investigate whether the Royal Ulster Constabulary had adopted a 'shoot-to-kill' policy to combat terrorism in Northern Ireland.

In September 1985, he submitted an interim report, saying that such a policy was in operation and that seven senior RUC officers should be prosecuted for conspiracy to murder and for attempting to pervert the course of justice. Stalker suddenly found himself on an enforced leave of absence, while he was investigated for unspecified allegations unrelated to Ulster. His place on the 'shoot-to-kill' inquiry was taken by Colin Sampson, Chief Constable of West Yorkshire, the same man who was also charged with the investigation of Stalker.

The allegations against Stalker amounted to his long-standing friendship with Manchester businessman, Kevin Taylor, who was allegedly an associate of known criminals. Sampson recommended that Stalker appear before a disciplinary tribunal. The Greater Manchester Police Authority rejected Sampson's report and reinstated Stalker, but he had had enough and resigned from the force.

Meanwhile, following the Stalker-Sampson report on the 'shoot-to-kill' policy in Northern Ireland, the Attorney General Sir Patrick Mayhew told the House of Commons that no RUC officers would be prosecuted, despite the fact that the Director of Public Prosecutions for Northern Ireland had concluded that there was evidence that there was a conspiracy to pervert the course of justice. The Attorney General said that national security considerations and the public interest must have priority. No RUC officers faced disciplinary procedures.

Kevin Taylor was eventually cleared of fraud charges and John Stalker was exonerated.

One place where there certainly was a 'shoot-to-kill' policy in action was Gibraltar. Three IRA terrorists – Daniel McCann, Mairead Farrell and Sean Savage – were shot by members of the British secret service, after the Spanish police had warned that they intended to car-bomb the changing of the guard ceremony outside the governor's house on Gibraltar.

The IRA confirmed that the three were part of an 'active service unit.' However, the car they had parked outside the governor's residence did not contain a bomb and the three people killed were found not to be carrying guns.

A 140lb bomb, bomb-making equipment, timing devices, ammunition and false passports were found in two other cars the three had rented on the other side of the border. Nevertheless, the Irish government said that it was 'gravely perturbed' at the gunning down of three unarmed Irish citizens. Amnesty International described the killings as 'extrajudicial executions.'

An inquest held in Gibraltar concluded that the three had been unlawfully killed. Six secret servicemen, identified only by the letters A to F, appeared at the inquest behind a screen. They maintained that their intention had been to arrest the three but, fearful that they might detonate a car bomb by remote control, had shot them.

More disturbing were witnesses who said that they had seen McCann and Farrell put their hands up before they were shot, or that they were shot while they were lying on the ground.

Thames Television's award-winning *World in Action* programme had first opened up the story. In Mrs Thatcher's reorganization of independent television, Thames lost its franchise to the anodyne Carlton. Some suspected that it was part of a vendetta.

The Thatcher government's fearful attitude to the truth came to world attention once more with the scandal surrounding the publication of the book, *Spycatcher*.

The book was the memoirs of Peter Wright, a long-serving member of the British intelligence outfit, MI5, who had retired in Tasmania. In it, he alleged that Sir Roger Hollis, head of MI5 from 1956 to 1965 was a Soviet double agent, that MI5 officers and others had plotted to remove Prime Minister Harold Wilson from office, and that the organization was generally treacherous, bungling and incompetent.

Spycatcher could not be published in Britain due to the Official Secrets Act. Its publication in America could not be prevented, but when Wright tried to publish it in Australia the British government obtained an injunction.

The British Cabinet Secretary, Sir Robert Armstrong, was sent to Australia to make the case for the government. He argued that Wright owed a duty of confidentiality to the Crown; that the book would put at risk the lives of other intelligence officers and their families; that it would damage liaisons with other friendly intelligence services since confidentiality could not be guaranteed; and that it would aid the enemies of Britain.

In March 1987, the court found in favour of Wright and publication. It ruled that although Wright was bound by a duty of confidentiality, most of what was in the book was not confidential since it had been published elsewhere. Disclosure of the other information, it judged, was not damaging to the UK or MI5. The court also found that since the Australian security forces liaised with the British, publication in Australia was in the public interest. That way, people could judge how competent MI5 was. The British government appealed, and lost. *Spycatcher* went on sale in Australia in October 1987.

The British government continued to fight the battle

against *Spycatcher* in the British courts, however. From 1986 to 1988, the government had obtained injunctions against *The Guardian, The Independent, The Sunday Times* and the *London Evening Standard* in an effort, often not very successful, to prevent them publishing extracts from the book.

In February 1988, the Court of Appeal ruled that the government could not maintain a permanent ban on publication of material from the book, now that it was being published world-wide. The court pointed out that the government had not gone to such great lengths to prevent the dissemination of more important material in other books and TV programmes. But with typical Thatcherite grit, the government took the *Spycatcher* case all the way to the House of Lords – and lost. However, their Lordships noted lamely that the members of the security services did have a life-long obligation of confidentiality, as enshrined in the Official Secrets Act.

But it was not just the Tories who involved themselves in sex scandals in the 1980s. The 33-year-old firebrand George Galloway, who ousted the SDP's Roy Jenkins from his Edinburgh Hillhead constituency in June 1987, also managed to land himself in hot water.

But the scandal over 'Gorgeous George' began with certain financial irregularities. Before being elected, Galloway was head of the charity, War on Want. Although his flamboyant management brought in a massive 25 per cent increase in revenue, there were questions over his expenses. However, in March 1987, the auditors cleared him of any impropriety, dishonesty or bad faith.

After he was elected, some of War on Want's executive members went to the Charity Commissioners, who again cleared him of any wrongdoing but recommended tightening up the procedures. Galloway agreed to repay £1,720, including £525 to attend a 'World Marxists Review' seminar in Athens and £850 in minicab fares to take him to work and back.

BBC Scotland then attacked his running of the charity. He hit them with a libel writ for six-figure damages and called a press conference. This was an ill-judged move. Journalists began to question him on his sexual conquests during his all-expenses paid trip to Greece for a seminar that grappled with the Horn of Africa. Galloway was unrepentant.

'I spent lots of time with women,' he said. 'I actually had sexual intercourse with some of them.'

Such candour earned him the headlines: 'Gorgeous George: I bonked for Britain' and 'My Sex Orgy – By MP'.

This did not please his wife, who was at home in Scotland with their five-year-old daughter, nor his girlfriend who lived with him in his one bedroomed flat in London's East End. Two days later, this arrangement hit the headlines, too. His domestic affairs, Galloway protested, had never been a secret.

But there were more clouds on the horizon. A Channel 4 documentary accused Galloway and three other Labour MPs of illegally transferring funds from three of Dundee's Labour social clubs into the coffers of the Labour Party. However, a police investigation found that one of the club's managers was responsible for the missing money.

Nevertheless, his local party executive passed a vote of no confidence in him. However, Galloway managed to get himself reselected and re-elected. He also won massive libel damages from the *Daily Mirror*.

Ron Brown MP was another loony left-winger from Edinburgh. The Parliamentary Labour Party knew it was in for a rough ride from the first moment he arrived in Westminster. In his maiden speech, which are by tradition noncontroversial, Brown declared a class war on Mrs Thatcher.

In 1981, when the Russians invaded Afghanistan Brown flew over to congratulate the invading forces, stopping for a photo opportunity by a tank. Frequently suspended from the House of Commons, Brown took his fight against Mrs Thatcher to the streets. When she visited Glasgow in 1982 he lunged at her and shouted: 'You're not welcome here.' He was fined £50 for a breach of the peace.

If his Afghanistan trip had not made him unpopular enough with the Labour leadership, in 1984 he went to visit Colonel Qaddafi, only months after WPC Yvonne Fletcher had been murdered outside the Libyan Embassy in London.

In 1988, Brown tried to emulate Michael Heseltine and swing the ceremonial mace. But he fumbled and dropped it. Asked whether he had been drunk, he said: 'I'd only had a pint of Younger's Tartan. The bloody thing was heavier than I expected.'

He offered to get the Amalgamated Engineering Union, who sponsored him, to mend it. The union dropped its sponsorship. The following day he refused to read an apology that he had agreed with the Speaker, 10 times. Three times the Speaker ordered him to leave the chamber and he refused. Eventually, a burly Labour whip bundled him out. He was suspended from the Commons for 20 days and Labour withdrew the whip. A private prosecution of criminal damage was later brought against him, but the Director of Public Prosecutions put a stop to it.

The night the PLP upheld the decision to withdraw the whip, Brown was caught naked in a shower with a woman at the House of Commons. The woman, Brown's researcher, Norma Longden, denied shouting: 'I want your baby.'

Brown said that Longden had wandered into the men's shower room by mistake and denied having an affair with her.

'I may be bonkers but I wasn't bonking,' he told the press. 'Because I drop the mace, I also drop my trousers?... I can assure you that at my age, 47, I have sex weekly – very weekly according to my wife. My credentials certainly leave something to be desired. That's why I keep my trousers up.'

A few weeks later, he denied rumours that Longden was pregnant by him.

'It would be physically impossible,' he said. 'A doctor can examine me if he wishes.'

In January 1990, Brown appeared at Lewes Crown Court, charged with theft and causing £800 worth of criminal damage to Longden's flat in St Leonards. He admitted having a three-year affair with Longden that had ended the previous March. Longden claimed that Brown was seeking a reconciliation when he turned up at her flat on the way back from the TUC conference at Eastbourne, blind drunk. Brown went berserk and she fled with her new boyfriend. When the police arrived, Brown had gone, leaving the one plaintive word 'love' scrawled across a mirror in lipstick.

Brown said that he had only dropped by the flat to pick up some documents and tapes. The damage, he said, was caused by Longden's new boyfriend who threw things at him.

The trial lasted six days. Brown was acquitted of theft, but fined £1,000, with £2,500 costs for criminal damage. He was also ordered to pay £628 compensation. Brown supped champagne with his wife on the courtroom steps to celebrate what he claimed was a 'moral victory.'

In Edinburgh, his local party secretary said: 'People here think he's a bit daft but at least he's a bit daft on behalf of us and they are prepared to forgive him.'

They weren't. The rest of his constituency party turned against him and deselected him. He fought them in the courts all the way up to the Court of Sessions, Scotland's highest civil court, but still lost. In the 1992 general election, he stood as an independent and trailed home second to last, trounced by the official Labour candidate.

Later, it was disclosed that Brown had had a long association with the KGB controller in London and Soviet double agent, Oleg Gordievsky. Brown admitted passing on information about Labour colleagues, but only things that the Soviet spy could have 'read in *The Beano'*. Sadly for Brown, any sensitive information would have been passed to MI5, too, and may well have reached the ears of Mrs Thatcher.

One of the other left-wingers with Ron Brown on the Afghanistan trip was Allan Roberts, Labour MP for Bootle. When he got back, *Private Eye* ran a story about another less publicized trip the MP had taken to Berlin, the previous Easter.

The rogue MP had visited a gay bar called the Buddy Club. According to Roberts's companions, he had been supping at the bar when a man in an SS uniform had approached him and asked him what his name was. Roberts said: 'Allan.'

Nein,' shouted the SS man. 'It is Rover.'

Then he had attached a dog lead to the studded collar the MP for Bootle was already wearing around his neck. Roberts was then dragged around the floor and while the other S&M fans looked on the SS man had flogged him. When he had finished, Roberts, who was bleeding profusely, reportedly said: 'That was beautiful, baby.'

Next stop was the hospital, where he had left without paying the bill.

Roberts told his constituency club: I was a bit drunk.... it is true that I was in the club, but the suggestion that I was dressed in a dog collar and whipped is complete and utter rubbish.'

He said that he had fallen over and cut himself. So he had gone to hospital, where the wound required one stitch. However, the doctor who administered the treatment told *Private Eye*: I declined to administer any sutures as the swelling was so great that additional damage could have been caused.'

The magazine also detailed the MP's injuries. They

included 'deep lacerations to the back, buttocks and genitalia, apparently caused by a belt buckle'.

Roberts said that he had neglected to settle the bill because he had thought that there was 'an arrangement between the NHS and Germany'. Fortunately, Tory right-winger, Charles Irving, MP for Cheltenham and Chairman of the House of Commons Catering Committee, happened to be in Berlin 'by coincidence' and paid the bill for him.

This was not the first time Roberts had been involved in such antics. The outrageous parties at his Manchester home were legendary. Once, when Roberts was giving a speech to Manchester City Council, it was noticed that the MP, who usually waved his arms about when he spoke, kept his right hand firmly in his pocket. When a fan rushed up to shake his hand, he was shocked to discover a pair of handcuffs dangling from Roberts' wrist. The MP said 'f***ing key' and left.

Roberts, resented the intrusion into his private life and successfully sued both *Private Eye* and the *News of the World* when they reported, falsely, that he was being investigated by the police for sexual offences.

On the other hand, he liked to flaunt it. He turned up for an election night party at the American embassy with a number of friends in leather gear. They were thrown out after one of their number stood on the bar and denounced Ronald Reagan as a homophobe.

If the Conservatives can do it, and Labour can do it, so can the Liberals. That's what Paddy Ashdown proved in 1987. Although happily married to the mother of his two children, the MP for Yeovil took a leaf out of Lloyd George's book – and many another MP who gets elected – and had an affair with his secretary, Tricia Howard.

Had it been known about at the time, it would certainly have damaged his chances of becoming party leader. But he managed to keep it quiet.

Three years after the brief affair, Mrs Howard began

divorce proceedings. Terrified that his name might come up in court, Ashdown called his solicitor, Andrew Phillips. Phillips made a note of their conversation in case action was needed later, locked the note in his safe and forgot about it.

In January 1992, his office was burgled. The note fell into the hands of Simon Berkowitz, an ardent Thatcherite who believed in private enterprise and standing on your own two feet. He offered the note to the *News of the World*, initially for £5,000. When they showed interest, he upped the price to £20,000. They refused to pay. Instead they tracked down Tricia Howard.

When reporters turned up at Mrs Howard's Wiltshire home, she called Ashdown, who in turn called Phillips. It was only then that Phillips discovered that his *aide memoire* was missing.

He obtained an injunction to stop the media publishing the note, since it had been obtained by a criminal act. But Ashdown knew the story was bound to come out. Seizing the initiative, Ashdown held a press conference and confessed all. *The Sun* quickly dubbed him 'Paddy Pantsdown.', but otherwise he emerged unscathed. In fact, his approval rating climbed quite sharply afterwards.

A former captain in the Royal Marines, Ashdown had carefully cultivated his 'action man' image. A toy manufacturer rushed out an Ashdown model in army fatigues. They offered a free sample to Mrs Howard. She declined, preferring, one supposes, the real thing.

Back to Basics

John Major should have known better. When he told the Tory Party conference in October 1993 that he wanted to go 'back to basics' he unwittingly delivered the kiss of death to his government, which was eventually driven from office after an unprecedented series of scandals.

He made it perfectly clear what he meant by 'back to basics'. He said that he wanted his Conservative government to stand for 'a country united around those old, common-sense British values that should never have been pushed aside'. This was greeted with rapturous applause by the blue-rinsed delegates.

But under John Major, the Conservative Party had already weathered three scandals. The first occurred in March 1992, when Alan Amos MP, the teetotal anti-smoking campaigner who favoured birching for criminals, got caught in the bushes at a homosexual cruising spot on Hampstead Heath. He denied being gay, but admitted to indulging in 'a childish and stupid act'. Nevertheless, he was pilloried by the press, whom he accused of muckraking. After all, he had not even been charged with anything, let alone tried and found guilty.

It made no difference. The *Daily Star* said: 'Amos is a teetotaller, opposes abortion, and brands smoking a "dirty, dangerous and anti-social habit". Hopefully he is now questioning his judgement in wandering around at dusk, at a place which has been turned into a no-go area for decent families by perverts practising what many people – even smokers – would call another dirty dangerous and anti-social habit. His downfall must be sad for him. But he should not try to tar us with his own muck.'

His Hexham constituency party turned on him and Amos was forced to resign.

The next scandal was a real shocker. It concerned David Mellor, a close friend of the Prime Minister's and a fellow Chelsea fan. John Major had appointed Mellor his Secretary of State at the new Department of Heritage, which was quickly dubbed the Ministry of Fun. It soon became known that the 43-year-old minister, who was married with two children, did not leave his portfolio in the office.

Part of his brief was to handle Sir David Calcutt's report on press intrusion into individual privacy. A Privacy Bill had already been mooted and Mellor had warned Fleet Street that it was drinking in the 'last chance saloon'. But it soon appeared that Mellor was imbibing there himself.

The Minister of Fun was having his own private spot of fun with 31-year-old actress, Antonia de Sancha. This was extraordinary hubris since Mellor had been introduced to de Sancha three years earlier by *Private Eye* journalist, Paul Halloran.

De Sancha was the only child of a Spanish father and a Swedish-born mother, who had both died shortly after they split up when she was in her mid-20s. She made her living as a topless model and bit part actress. Her starring role was in a soft-porn film called *The Pieman*, where she played a one-legged prostitute who pays the pizza-delivery man in kind.

It took some time for the affair to develop, but by June 1992 they were lovers. Antonia wrote to her Swedish grandmother saying: 'I am having a marvellous time at the moment. I have met a wonderful politician. I am very happy.'

But she was already concerned about the possibility of exposure. Nosy neighbours, she feared, might spread gossip. Confiding her fears to a friend, she borrowed his flat in Finborough Road, West London, as a temporary love nest. The flat was bugged. Soon, tapes of Mellor complaining that his nights of passion with the young actress were exhausting were being touted to the *News of the World*.

Early in July 1992, Mellor had a call from Sir Tim Bell, PR consultant and former government spin doctor. He informed Mellor of the story and the evidence that the *News of the World* had. Mellor denied that he was having an affair and expressed surprise that a newspaper could handle tapes that had been recorded in such an underhand fashion. This was just the sort of thing that his Privacy Bill would stamp out.

The moment that Bell was off the phone Mellor phoned de Sancha and told her to keep her mouth shut.

Although they were not entirely convinced by Mellor's denials, the *News of the World* put publication on hold. *The People* had no such reservations. On Saturday, 18 July 1992, Mellor was tipped off that *The People* were going to run the story the next day. He phoned the Prime Minister and tendered his resignation.

John Major refused to accept it. He said he would stand by his friend and he saw no conflict between his current plight and his handling of the Calcutt Report. But the press did. The very man who was threatening to shackle them had been caught with his pants down. What's more, because of Antonia de Sancha's career, they had plenty of juicy pictures to illustrate the story with.

Soon, Antonia was besieged by the press. Mellor had to distance himself. He issued the obligatory statement saying: 'My wife Judith and I have been experiencing difficulties in our marriage. We want to sort the situation out for the sake of each other and especially for our two young children.' And there was the photocall with Mellor and his wife and children smiling outside the in-laws, before going in for a cosy family lunch. From a man demanding privacy, this reeked of hypocrisy.

By an unfortunate coincidence, the *Desert Island Discs* radio programme that Mellor had recorded earlier went out that weekend. Mellor's father-in-law, Professor Edward Hall, decided to attack his daughter's errant husband in the media.

'If he'll cheat on our girl, he'll cheat on the country;' he said.

In an effort to defend herself, Antonia de Sancha employed the publicist Max Clifford to handle the press for her. Soon the press was full of stories that Mellor liked to make love in a Chelsea strip and that he indulged in toe-sucking as foreplay.

Clifford sold the serialization of de Sancha's story to *The Sun*. They even mocked up the tawdry scene for their readers, complete with the mattress on the floor where the couple had first made love, the bottle of cheap white wine and the lurid red silk bedclothes.

Although Mellor had become a laughing stock, he may have survived this. But more serious allegations came to light. Mellor and his family had holidayed in the Marbella home of Mona Bauwens, daughter of one of the founders of the Palestine Liberation Organization. While they had been there, Iraq had invaded Kuwait and the PLO had backed Saddam Hussein. Mona Bauwens sued *The People*, which carried the story for casting her as a 'social outcast and leper'.

Although the court case failed, it kept Mellor in the limelight. Valiantly, he fought on. He made endless rounds of TV studios and even took the time to attend the National Press Fund's annual reception.

'I was going through a quiet patch so it was good of you to invite me tonight,' he told them.

But his sense of humour did not save him. He admitted that he had behaved foolishly but insisted that what he had done was not a resigning matter.

'Who decides who is to be a member of the British Cabinet, the Prime Minister or the Editor of the *Daily Mail*?' he asked defiantly.

The answer was, of course, the Editor of the *Daily Mail*. With the newspapers against him, Tory backbench support began to go soft. John Major then had no choice but to accept David Mellor's resignation, despite a letter of support in *The Times* signed by many senior figures in the arts whose work he had championed in his ministerial post.

It was a case of 'From toe-job to no job', as *The Sun* so succinctly put it.

There was no chance of him returning to office either.

Two years later, the *News of the World* discovered that he had abandoned the wife who had stood by him and was having another affair – this time with Lady Penelope Cobham, a former adviser at the Department of Heritage. Mellor divorced his first wife and married her. He later went on to build up a successful career in the media.

Norman Lamont fell from power because ultimately, as Chancellor of the Exchequer, he had to carry the can after the pound had been forced out of the European Exchange Rate Mechanism, costing the country millions of pounds. But by that time he had already been involved in more than his fair share of scandals. As Mrs Thatcher's Trade Secretary, he had once appeared in the House of Commons with a black eye, the result of walking into a door, he said.

Daily Mail gossip columnist, Nigel Dempster, told another tale. He said that the 43-year-old minister, who was married with two children, had paid a latenight visit to the £350,000 Bayswater home of glamorous divorcee, Olga Polizzi, daughter of Lord Forte. Unfortunately, wealthy art dealer Richard Connolly was already there. The result, Connolly confirmed, was the minister's shiner.

After Lamont became Chancellor, the *News of the World* discovered that he had asked a local estate agent to rent out the basement of his Notting Hill home. Unbeknown to Lamont, the new tenant was a freelance 'sex therapist', soon universally known as 'Miss Whiplash'. She denied being a prostitute, although admitted dressing in a number of specialized costumes to administer domination to her clients and stripping naked to perform massage.

Lamont said he knew nothing of her activities and, if the allegations were true, promised to evict her. *The Sun* thoughtfully provided him with a guided tour of the 'vice den', detailing the facilities that he, as landlord, was providing to the sexually deprived of West London. And Lamont, good to his word, kicked her out.

But five months later, the newspapers spotted that the

Treasury had provided £4,700 towards the £23,000 legal bill Lamont had run up over the eviction. The rest had been stumped up by 'Tory benefactors'. The Treasury protested that it had paid only for the cost of handling the press enquiries generated. Lamont was a government minister and he would not have incurred these costs if he had been a private citizen. The Tory benefactors turned out to be, not wealthy individuals, but Conservative Central Office. Lamont had not done anything wrong, but it provided another opportunity to rake over the coals of Miss Whiplash.

After the debacle of Britain's withdrawal from the ERM, the papers were out to get Lamont. *The Sun* reported that he had done a bunk from a Brighton Hotel without paying the bill. In fact, his bill, along with those of several other Tory ministers, had been forwarded to Central Office.

Then *The Sun* revealed that he paid his credit card bills late and had received five warning letters from Access – hardly a record of prudence by a Chancellor of the Exchequer. Lamont protested that this was a private matter. *The Sun* responded with 'Threshergate'. Lamont's Access card had last been used at a branch of the off-licence chain, Thresher's. The assistant manager of the branch, in a seedy part of Paddington, said that Lamont had used the card there to buy a bottle of champagne and 20 cigarettes. The Treasury responded by showing the press the Chancellor's credit card receipt. It showed that he had used to it two buy three bottles of wine in a branch in salubrious Marble Arch.

Although Norman Lamont could claim, with justification, that there was a conspiracy in the press to bring him down, he condemned himself out of his own mouth. In October 1992 he said he could see 'the green shoots of economic spring,' while everyone else was still feeling the winter chill of recession.

A week after Black Wednesday, when Britain pulled out

of the ERM, he casually remarked to a reporter that he had been 'singing in the bath'. He had not meant this as any sort of economic comment – he said his wife had complained about his singing – but that was how it was taken.

In May 1993, there was a by-election in Newbury and Norman Lamont was wheeled out to talk about the government's economic successes. During a televised press conference he was asked which he regretted more – seeing green shoots or singing in the bath? He replied flippantly: '*Je ne regrette rien.*'

The Tories lost the by-election and Lamont lost his job.

When John Major used the phrase 'back to basics', he meant health, education and law and order, along with his Miss Marple image of England as a country full of warm beer and spinsters' bicycles passing the cricket pitch on the village green to the sound of church bells. But the press mischievously interpreted it to mean a call for the Tory *jihad* on sexual immorality. Soon his ministers were lining up with sordid sex scandals.

Transport Minister Steven Norris was the first to go. Married with two children, the 48-year-old minister was said to have not one, but five mistresses. His wife, admiral's daughter Vicky Cecil-Gibson, lived in her own house in Berkshire and was fully aware that her husband was a weekday Romeo.

The 1993 'back-to-basics' Tory Party conference was scarcely over when Norris announced that his marriage was now over and he intended to marry 45-year-old *Times* political reporter, Sheila Gunn, his mistress of three years' standing. It was then revealed that he had been two-timing her with 40-year-old Harpers & Queen executive, Jennifer Sharp. Then there was 46-year-old sales executive, Lynn Taylor, who had met him at a party at his Newbury home seven years earlier and had taken over as his mistress from a lady surgeon who had been Norris's lover for the eight years before that. Then out of the woodwork came the inevitable House of Commons secretary, 29-year-old Emma Courtney. She had been dating Norris for 12 months and was 'devastated' to discover that he had not been giving her his undivided attention. However, when the dust settled, they managed to patch it up.

In happier times, Norris would have stayed on. He had done no wrong and was admired by both the press and his colleagues, not least for his sexual prowess. Major did not sack him, but the 'back-to-basics' ground swell at constituency level resulted in an effort to deselect him. He saw that off, but later announced that he would not stand again in the next election.

Environment Minister Tim Yeo, it was said, was so pro-family that he had two of them. On Boxing Day 1993, the press revealed that he had a six-month-old love child with Julia Stent, a Tory councillor in the London borough of Hackney and, now, a single mother.

Mrs Diane Yeo was a proper Tory wife and stood by her husband. John Major declared that Yeo's love life was a private matter and the errant MP headed off on holiday with his wife and their two grown-up children. But while they were sunning themselves in the Seychelles, the back-to-basics mullahs were baying for his head, led by his local Tory mayor, Mrs Aldine Horrigan.

Yeo returned home like a criminal, hiding on the floor of the family car to avoid the press. Just as David Mellor had done, Major insisted weakly that it was he who decided who was in the government – not the tabloids. But this time Tory activists took a hand. The officers of his constituency party refused to support him and he resigned as a minister, bitterly blaming Mrs Horrigan. Ten days later though, a meeting of the full constituency party backed him, even after it was revealed that he had sired another illegitimate child when he was a student at Cambridge.

Yeo was later seen lunching with his mistress, Julia Stent, at Langan's Brasserie and his wife said that she received hate mail for her loyalty to her husband.

Even while the Yeo affair was unfolding, John Major lost another minister, Lord Caithness, a junior transport minister, after his 40-year-old wife killed herself. The newspapers deduced that Caithness had told his wife that weekend of his close acquaintanceship with glamorous divorcee, Jan Fitzalan-Howard.

One Tory wife who did not stand by her man was Italian-born Silvana Ashby. She told *The Sunday Times* that her husband, David Ashby MP, had left her because of 'a friendship with another man'. Ashby denied that he was gay, but admitted that he had shared a hotel bed with another man when he had been on holiday in France. They had shared the bed, he said, merely to save money.

The other newspapers happily sniped away at Ashby. But when *The Sunday Times* announced that he had also shared a bed with a young man in Goa – which was not true – Ashby sued. *The Sunday Times* apologized for the Goa story but refused to withdraw the allegation that the MP was a homosexual, a liar and a hypocrite.

At the ensuing libel trial, Ashby's wife Silvana took the stand as *The Sunday Times*' key witness. She insisted that, when they had separated after 28 years of marriage, her husband had admitted to her that he was a homosexual.

Ashby himself insisted that he had not had sex with his wife for four years because he was impotent. His Harley Street physician, Dr Lewis Sevitt, told the court that he had been treating Ashby for the condition but there had been no improvement. His bedmate in France also testified that they had not had sex.

But *The Sunday Times* had a surprise witness. *Times* journalist Andrew Pierce had seen Ashby in a well-known gay pub in Chelsea. He gave a vivid description of it, pointing out that no one could have been under any illusion that he was not in a hang-out for homosexuals.

The jury found in favour of the newspaper. After the

judgement his wife tried to hug him, but he shrugged her off. Already a casualty at Lloyd's, Ashby was ruined. He did not, however, resign his seat in the House of Commons. He then cast the decisive vote against the government in the Labour amendment to the Housing Bill, which would let the surviving partner of a homosexual couple inherit the tenancy in the event of the death of the other. For his constituency party, this was the final straw. They deselected him. He railed against the press and 'homophobes' in the constituency party. It was at this point that he decided to come out, and announced on Radio 5's *Out This Week* programme that he was proud to be a gay MP – even though he was soon to be an MP no longer.

In January 1994, the *News of the World* announced that church-going bachelor Garry Waller, MP for Keithley, had been kicked off the books of a posh dating agency for claiming that he was unattached. In fact, the 48-year-old Waller had a long-term girlfriend and a love child by – yes – a House of Commons secretary.

'Back to basics' then took a dip into black comedy. On 7 February 1994, young high-flying Tory backbencher, Steven Milligan, was found dead in his Chiswick flat by his Commons secretary, Vera Taggart. Naked except for a pair of black stockings and suspenders, he was trussed up with electrical flex. There was a black bin liner on his head and a satsuma jammed between his teeth.

The police investigated his shady private life and discovered that he was another MP who enjoyed the service of a posh dating agency. Although the circumstances of his death were considered unusual, foul play was not suspected.

Apparently, Milligan was indulging in an esoteric sexual practice that involves restricting oxygen to the system. The precise details remain sketchy, although apparently someone at the BBC had some internal knowledge. An internal memo was circulated which said: 'We can now say that he was wearing women's clothing, we can say he had a plastic bag on his head, and we can mention that he was bound with flex. But on no account mention fruit.'

Don't try this at home. How very back to basics.

Six days after Milligan's body was discovered, the papers broke the story of an affair between Tory MP Hartley Booth and his 22-year-old House of Commons secretary. Although he claimed that it was an innocent infatuation, as a Christian and a pro-family campaigner, he admitted hypocrisy. He resigned as the Parliamentary Private Secretary to Foreign Office Minister, Douglas Hogg, whose wife Sarah was the Downing Street adviser responsible for the 'back to basics' campaign.

In May, it was reported that Michael Brown, Tory MP for Brigg and Cleethorpes, had been on a Caribbean holiday with his 20-year-old boyfriend. Brown resigned, not because he was gay, but because the homosexual age of consent was still set at 21. It would only be reduced to 18 that autumn.

In March 1995, the second wife of junior civil service minister, Robert Hughes, discovered that he was having an affair with his House of Commons secretary. He did the decent thing and tried to sack her. She threatened to take him to an industrial tribunal. He persuaded her not to and she went to the *News of the World* instead.

A few weeks later, the *News of the World* announced that the Conservative MP for Bury St Edmunds, Richard Spring, had enjoyed a three-in-the-bed love romp with a Sunday school teacher and a pension fund manager. He resigned as Parliamentary Private Secretary to the Northern Ireland Secretary.

Next, Rod Richards resigned from the Welsh Office when an affair came to light with Julia Felthouse, a public relations officer 20 years his junior. Married with two children, Richards was another keen supporter of the family who found himself all over the pages of the *News of the World*.

Not that the Tories were the only ones at it. A *News of the World* headline turned hard-line working class Labour MP Dennis Skinner from 'The Beast of Bolsover' the name parliamentary sketchwriters had saddled him with – to the 'The Beast of Legover'. The object of his affections was his House of Commons researcher, Lois Blasenheim.

Skinner's wife was 61, a working class Northern lass who lived in their semidetached council house in the Derbyshire village of Clay Cross. His lover was 47, an American heiress living in Carlyle Square, Chelsea, where her neighbours included Felicity Kendal, David Frost and the Duchess of Portland.

The Beast of Bolsover had long boasted his no-nonsense attitude by claiming that he did not even have a passport. It came out that his mistress was teaching him to drive. The working class Northern boy had been corrupted at last.

Skinner had long lived a separate life from his wife. But the situation was made all the more ludicrous by the furtive nature of his new relationship. Instead of walking straight up to his mistress's front door and ringing the bell, he would go to her house in disguise and lurk in the bushes outside. Then, at a pre-arranged time, she would let him in.

Apart from this amusing interlude, the Tories kept up their torrent of sex scandals right up until the 1997 election. In the last gasp of the dying government, Piers Merchant, the 46-year-old Tory MP for Beckenham, claimed he was set up when *The Sun* photographed him canoodling in the park with 17-year-old Soho nightclub hostess, Anna Cox. Merchant, who had been married for 20 years, claimed that Ms Cox was merely helping him with his campaign.

Meanwhile, the Chairman of the Scottish Conservative Party, Sir Michael Hirst, stepped down following allegations that he had had a homosexual affair with civil servant Paul Martin, who had been involved with Michael Brown, MP for Brigg and Cleethorpes. Conservative candidate Allan Stewart also stood down – after allegations of a friendship with a woman he had met in a clinic where they were both being treated for alcoholism.

But all this was icing on the cake for New Labour whose candidates, by comparison, looked like choir boys.

Tory Sleaze

With the myopia of hindsight, it might be imagined that Tory sleaze was a condition that affected only the Major government. In fact, it has a long and dishonourable tradition.

Reginald Maudling was Chancellor of the Exchequer when the Conservatives lost power in 1964 and he used the financial expertise he had gained at the Treasury to enrich himself during his time in opposition. After he lost the leadership battle to Edward Heath in 1965, he began taking on directorships. Obviously, a former Chancellor of the Exchequer on the board did a company no harm. Within months, he was earning £20,000 a year, four times his ministerial salary. By the end of the 1960s, he was a name at Lloyd's and a prominent banker, as well as a board member of numerous companies. He owned a home in the country, as well as a Regency house in Belgravia.

But his wealth did not just come from what he earned. As a former Chancellor, he knew the tax system well. He also knew how to get around it. One of his directorships was with Peachey Properties, a company run by a dubious businessman named Eric Miller. Maudling was anxious to avoid income tax and wanted to protect his two homes from the new capital gains tax that the Labour government was proposing to introduce. He offered to work as a consultant for Peachey Properties, but waived his fee. In exchange, Peachey would buy the freehold on his country house. This was already in Maudling's wife's name; he held a lease on the property from her. Peachey would then make repairs and improvements to the house. The deal was worth a year's salary in advance, tax free, to Maudling and was of no commercial advantage to Peachey.

Through Eric Miller, Maudling met the architect John Poulson. His practice was the largest in Europe and he earned over £1 million a year in fees. The tax man saw little of that as a Conservative MP and tax expert had set up an umbrella company as a tax shelter.

Poulson used a number of corrupt practices to secure business and get around bureaucratic constraints. These included building houses for prominent civil servants. He was also in cahoots with corrupt local politician, T. Dan Smith, a prominent figure in the Labour Party in the North of England.

Together they set up a number of public relations firms that employed local councillors. In return, the councillors would put council building projects Poulson's way. Poulson and Smith also had a wide range of contacts politically, socially and in the freemasons. These were all encouraged to give Poulson work, in exchange for free holidays, accommodation, mortgages and other fringe benefits.

The nest of corruption worked because the Labour Party faced no serious opposition in most northern cities. The political network was entrenched and television and the expansion of the national newspapers had enfeebled the local press.

Poulson wanted to expand overseas, and he hired Labour MP Albert Roberts and Conservative right-winger John Cordle to front the organization. But he was still looking for a big name when Eric Miller introduced Poulson to Maudling.

Maudling became chairman of Poulson's overseas operations. Poulson also employed Maudling's son on a
healthy salary and gave £8,000 a year to a theatre charity
that Maudling's wife ran. It was also agreed that when
business started booming, Maudling would be allowed to
buy shares.

But boom it did not. Although in a series of trips to the
Mediterranean and the Middle East, Maudling was able to
open doors for Poulson, only one was converted into a
contract. The Maltese government was building a hospital
on the island of Cozo. It was partially funded by the
British, and Maudling used his influence to win the contract.

Poulson's solicitor put another opportunity Maudling's
way and introduced him to Jerry Hoffman, head of the
Real Estate Fund of America. REFA was an offshore investment company, which promised to generate massive tax-
free profits out of international property speculation.
Hoffman wanted big names to front the company and
offered Maudling a seat on the board. Maudling accepted,
waiving his fee for 250,000 shares in the venture.

Solely on the strength of Maudling's name, two banks
invested in REFA – only to discover, to their cost, that the
whole thing was a scam. Hoffman and his associates were
taking investors' money and putting down deposits on
real estate. They then charged commission and handling
fees on the full purchase price. This made Hoffman and his
friends rich, while giving the impression that the company
was much larger than it really was.

Maudling denied actual involvement in the activities of
REFA and later claimed never to have attended a board
meeting. But in 1969, when the press started investigating
REFA, Maudling pulled out.

In 1970, the Conservatives were returned to power and
Maudling became Home Secretary. He resigned his con-
sultancy with Peachey and stepped down as chairman of

Poulson's overseas companies. By this time, Poulson was running into difficulties. His corrupt practices effectively front-loaded his contracts, leaving him with increasing cashflow problems. To ease his liquidity problems he simply forgot to pay the taxman. It would all come tumbling down.

In 1972, Poulson filed for bankruptcy. Maudling's name was mentioned during the hearings and he complained stridently. But when the Metropolitan Police Fraud Squad began investigating, Maudling resigned. This, he said, was merely because, as Home Secretary, he was nominally responsible for the police. He made it clear that if he had held any other position in the government, he would not have stepped down.

The police enquiries resulted in a number of corruption trials. These revealed how deeply Maudling was involved. His house was still owned by Peachey Properties. And although he had stepped down from the board of REFA when it began to get flak in the press, he had left the company a great testimonial, saying it was a brilliant concept with a great future. He even held on to his REFA shares for another year, in the hope of capitalizing on what he saw as a 'little pot of gold'.

When the new Labour government came into power in 1974, it promised to tighten up the parliamentary rules on Members' business interests. But MPs look after their own. There was little criticism of those who had had dealings with Poulson, probably because members of both parties were involved. In 1976, the Attorney General announced that the criminal investigation into Poulson's affairs was at an end.

But then a damning article in *The Observer* forced the government to set up a Select Committee to investigate the involvement of Cordle, Roberts and Maudling. Cordle came in for the most criticism. When numerous trips to West Africa had borne no fruit, Cordle had written to

Poulson justifying his fee. In this letter, he mentioned that he should be paid because he had taken part in a debate in the House of Commons 'largely for the benefit of Construction Promotion', one of Poulson's firms. This was considered a contempt of the House and Cordle resigned.

All three were criticized for failing to declare an interest at the appropriate time. Roberts complained about being lumped together with Cordle and Maudling, as he had only 'transgressed in shallow waters'. Maudling was also criticized for being less than completely frank in his resignation letter of 1972.

In the debate that followed the publication of the committee's report, Edward Heath described Maudling as an 'honourable man'. Maudling continued to deny any wrongdoing. He was consigned to the backbenches and died in 1979.

Keith Best, the Conservative MP for Anglesey, was the first casualty of the Thatcher administration, when he subscribed over-enthusiastically to the privatisation of British Telecom.

At the age of 34, he had joined the government as PPS to the Welsh Secretary, Nicholas Edwards, and seemed to be something of a rising star.

The £4 billion sell-off of British Telecom in 1984 was the government's first privatization and they were delighted by its success. The list of those who had made share applications ran to 51,000 pages and the magazine *Labour Research* began the laborious business of checking through them to see if any Conservative MPs had their fingers in the cookie jar.

The rules of the privatization were that any one individual could make only one application. *Labour Research* found Keith Best's name. They also found that of Keith Lander Best and a Lander Best. Not only had he used three different variations on his name, he had used four different addresses – including that of his widowed mother –

and six different bank accounts. As a result, he bought six times as many shares as permitted for £6,240, making a clear profit of £3,120.

When the story broke in April 1987, Labour called for Best's resignation and arrest. The Leader of the House of Commons, John Biffen, struck back, describing Labour's demands as 'sanctimonious and distasteful'. Best defended himself, saying that he had not made applications in false names, only variations on his real name. He had made multiple applications, he said, because he was afraid that the sell-off would be over-subscribed and he would miss out.

It was then revealed that he had also made multiple applications in the Jaguar cars sell-off, although this was not illegal. His eager dealings in Mrs Thatcher's other sell-offs – of the TSB, British Gas, Britoil, Cable and Wireless, Enterprise Oil and British Aerospace – all came in for investigation.

In the face of this barracking, Best announced that he would donate the profits from his share dealings to charity. He stepped down as a PPS and said he would not seek re-election at the forthcoming election. The Labour MP Brian Segmore was not satisfied, claiming his resignation was 'political expediency at the expense of parliament. Labour leader Neil Kinnock turned the guns on the rest of the government, saying he was 'waiting to see if we get a sermon on moral values from Norman Tebbit in the next few days; he has fallen strangely silent.'

Labour Research then discovered that another Conservative MP, Eric Cockham, Member for Ludlow, had bought more than his share of British Gas shares. He claimed that they were for his grandchildren. He, too, said that he would not stand at the forthcoming election. The Crown Prosecution Service said that he would not be prosecuted.

Best was not so lucky. In October 1987, Best pleaded not

guilty at Southwark Crown Court and wept in the witness box. It did no good. He was found guilty and sentenced to four months in jail and fined £3,000, with £1,500 costs. After an unpleasant weekend in the hospital wing of Brixton Prison, the prison sentence was dropped, but the fine was increased to £4,500.

Best seems to have learnt his lesson. He moved into charity work and became head of the Immigration Advisory Service.

'Cash for questions' did not begin with the John Major government either. John Browne, Conservative MP for Winchester, blazed the trail in 1970 when he asked a number of seemingly innocent questions about the freezing of certain Middle Eastern assets at Prime Minister's Question Time.

It was only later that *The Observer* and the TV documentary series *World in Action* discovered that, at the time, he was working on a study of the subject for the Saudi Arabian Monetary Agency, which was paying him $88,000 – more than an MP's annual salary.

Browne was also an early exponent of 'cash for access'. He was on the payroll of a firm of Lebanese consultants keen to make contacts in Number 10. They paid him an annual retainer of £2,400, which he failed to declare. Not that he needed the money. He had already hit the headlines with his divorce from his wife of 18 years. She was the daughter of a shipping magnate and he had walked away with a £175,000 settlement.

Although Browne married another heiress, he went back to court to pick up the £65,000 his ex-wife still owed him. She played to the press, clutching a suitcase full of clothes, claiming they were her only possessions. She threw herself on the mercy of the court, saying she had already forked out £200,000 – £110,000 to her ex-husband and £90,000 in legal fees. If she paid any more, it would leave her destitute. Her histrionics did not work and she narrowly escaped going to jail. But the press was sympathetic and dubbed Browne a cad. In response, he tried to introduce a Privacy Bill. It was laughed out of the House.

When the Select Committee looking into *The Observer*'s 'cash-for-questions' allegations found against him, Labour demanded Browne's resignation. He refused to step down. His constituency party deselected him. Mrs Thatcher chastised him from the dispatch box and the Leader of the House, Sir Geoffrey Howe, proposed that he be suspended from the House without pay for 20 days. The motion was unanimously carried.

Browne condemned his treatment by the House as a 'show trial'. The press, he said, were conducting a 'venomous witch-hunt' against him because of 'my divorce, my Privacy Bill and the recent Select Committee report'. He wrote an open letter to his constituents, alleging that he had been pushed out to make way for a minister. And he sought the Attorney General's advice on whether he could bring a case under the UN Convention of Human Rights.

Later, when he won a Commons ballot, he addressed the House at great length on the huge injustice that had been perpetrated on him by all and sundry. When he sat down, the Labour MP John Fraser summed up the feelings of the whole House by describing Browne as 'a public schoolboy, Guards officer, banker, MP – and whinger'.

Browne then seemed to lose the plot totally. He began wearing an oversize top hat, which he took off only when he stood to speak, apparently as some protest over the Ministry of Defence's failure to pay compensation to an ex-Guardsman who had lost his legs. It caused much amusement when a fellow MP sat on the hat and, later, when Browne accidentally sat on it himself.

At the next election, he stood as an independent – and lost.

Northern Ireland Minister, Michael Mates, gave his friend Asil Nadir a £20 watch at a party to celebrate the Cypriot businessman's 52nd birthday. It was a much-needed present. Nadir's Polly Peck empire was under investigation by the Serious Fraud Squad and Nadir's £3,500 Blancpain watch had been confiscated by the SFO during one of its raids.

But Mates made a stupid mistake. He spent £32 having the words 'Don't let the buggers get you down' engraved on the back.

Three days after his birthday, Nadir jumped bail, which had been set at £3.5 million, and fled to his house in Turkish-controlled Northern Cyprus. Turkish occupied Cyprus is not recognized by the British government and has no extradition treaty with the UK. The press and politicians alike tore into the runaway businessman. Nadir responded by praising Mates's 'unflinching help'. This turned the spotlight on the minister.

When the gift of the watch was revealed, Mates shrugged it off as a 'lighthearted gesture'. But his support for the man who had pulled off one of the biggest frauds in history ran deeper than that. One of Nadir's advisers was a constituent of Mates's and, with the help of Nadir's defence counsel, Mates had written three letters to the Attorney General accusing the SFO of running a witch-hunt against Nadir. Mates insisted that he was within his rights to do so.

John Major, as always, rallied around, saying that Mates's resignation had neither been sought nor offered. The minister clung on. It was then revealed that Nadir had given the Conservative Party £440,000, although his companies owned millions. Party Chairman Sir Norman Fowler said that the gift was stolen money and would be returned.

Nadir was now claiming from Cyprus that there was an establishment conspiracy against him. The press gave little credence to the allegations of the bail-jumping entrepreneur, but the press had a problem. Fraud cases are often so complex that juries, even after months of detailed testimony, are none the wiser. Explaining Nadir's crooked deal-ings to tabloid readers is next to impossible. Mates was a much easier target.

It was soon discovered that Mates's contact with the Nadir empire had continued, even after Nadir had absconded. He had borrowed a car from Nadir's public relations adviser for his estranged wife and he had been seen dining with him.

Eventually, Mates resigned – not, he said, because he had done anything wrong, but because his continued presence in Major's government was embarrassing the Prime Minister.

In a barnstorming resignation speech, Mates attacked the SFO for trying to put pressure on the judge in Nadir's case. Nine times the speaker warned him that he was intruding into matters that were *sub judice*. This is academic since, at the time of writing, Asil Nadir shows no inclination to return to the UK to stand trial.

In the very week Tim Yeo and Lord Caithness resigned for not following 'back to basics', Alan Duncan MP was embroiled in a scandal for showing a little too much good old-fashioned Tory private enterprise.

He had taken advantage of the government's right-to-buy scheme to purchase, not his own council house, but the one next door to his Westminster home. His neighbour, long-standing tenant Harry Ball-Wilson, took advantage of the £50,000 discount he had accrued. Duncan then bought the freehold off him and did up the dilapidated property. His ultimate intention was to extend his home through into the next-door building when his sitting tenant passed on.

The deal was perfectly legal. Indeed Mr Ball-Wilson was enjoying a holiday in Hawaii on the proceeds when the story broke. However, as far as the papers were concerned, it was a case of a Tory MP profiting from Tory policies – in other words sleaze.

By 1994, the Conservatives' 'back to basics' campaign was in tatters. But, although catching pro-family Tory MPs bed-hopping was fun, the newspapers wanted something more substantial to get their teeth into. It had long been suspected that John Browne was not the first, nor the last, to take cash for questions. *The Sunday Times*'s Insight team decided to investigate.

Posing as a businessman, a *Sunday Times* reporter offered 10 Tory MPs and 10 Labour MPs £1,000 to ask a question at Prime Minister's Question Time, which then took place twice a week in the House of Commons. Two of the Tories, David Tredinnick and Graham Riddick, both Parliamentary Private Secretaries, accepted.

When the newspaper published its scoop, Tredinnick denied the charges. The next day, *The Sunday Times* released a tape of Tredinnick asking for the cheque to be sent to his private address. Riddick, too, had accepted a cheque, but had had second thoughts and sent it back.

Although MPs accused *The Sunday Times* of entrapment, the Chief Whip Richard Ryder suspended them as PPSs. The Committee of Privileges suspended them for two weeks and fined Riddick £900 and Tredinnick £1,800. However, the Press Complaints Commission upheld Riddick's complaint that *The Sunday Times* had used unacceptable methods to lure the MP into wrongdoing.

But more sleaze was about to hit the fan. Northern Ireland Minister, Tim Smith, resigned when it was revealed that he had been paid by Mohamed Al-Fayed to table helpful questions during the Egyptian businessman's battle to take over Harrods. But the Tory Trade Minister, Neil Hamilton, denied similar allegations and issued a writ for defamation against *The Guardian*, which had pointed out that he and his wife had stayed for a week in the Ritz Hotel in Paris, which Al-Fayed owned. They had run up a bill of over £3,000, which had been settled by the management.

Hamilton claimed that he had stayed in the hotel as Al-Fayed's guest, much the same as he would in a private house. On a visit to a biscuit factory in his constituency, he emerged with his wife Christine by his side, holding a biscuit.

'I must remember to declare this in the Register of Interests,' he quipped.

Soon after, he compared his hounding by the press to that of John Major, who had issued a writ against the subversive magazine *Scallywag* when it falsely alleged that he was having a torrid affair with a Downing Street caterer. How Major could have claimed that this allegation damaged him was never tested in court. For one fleeting moment, he almost looked interesting. Plainly, that was the last thing he wanted. Nor did he want to be reminded of the case and he promptly sacked Hamilton from the government.

Hamilton, who at first had been gung-ho about his defamation case against *The Guardian*, inexplicably dropped it. Senior Tories, including the Prime Minister, urged him to stand down. More allegations of sleaze were hurled at him. He admitted accepting £10,000 as a lobbyist. But still his constituency party in Tatton backed him, claiming he was the victim of a media smear campaign. However, in the 1997 general election, the whitesuited, whiter-than-white BBC foreign correspondent, Martin Bell, stood against him as the 'anti-corruption candidate'. Hamilton was booted out, but continued, feebly, to try to clear his name.

However, during its investigation into Hamilton and his stay at the Paris Ritz, *The Guardian* had hooked a bigger fish. Jonathan Aitken, Chief Secretary to the Treasury and once tipped as a future Prime Minister, had also been staying there. His £1,000 bill for two nights had been paid, the paper said, not by Al-Fayed, but by a Saudi businessman named Said Mohamed Ayas, who was staying in a £2,000-

a-night suite in the hotel.

Aitken claimed that the bill had been settled by his wife, in cash, and he went on the offensive. In the House of Commons, he called for an end to 'sleaze journalism'.

It was true that *The Guardian* had used underhand tactics to obtain a copy of Aitken's bill. The newspaper had mocked up a fax purporting to come from Aitken's office, using House of Commons' headed notepaper requesting a copy of the bill. The Editor of *The Guardian*, Peter Preston, was hauled over the coals. He resigned from the Press Complaints Commission and was kicked upstairs at *Guardian* Newspapers.

The Independent then renewed the onslaught. It reported that a company on whose board Aitken sat had been exporting arms to Iran, via Singapore, in contravention of an international arms ban. When the Granada TV programme, *World in Action*, repeated the allegations, Aitken called a press conference. He denied everything and turned on his accusers.

'If it falls to me to start a fight to cut off the cancer of bent and twisted journalism in our country with the simple sword of truth, and trusty shield of fair play, so be it,' he said. 'I am ready for the fight.'

He resigned from the government and sued *The Guardian* and Granada TV.

Meanwhile, the *Sunday Mirror* reported that he had had a fling with a prostitute 15 years earlier. His wife, Aitken said, had forgiven him. Later, a love child he had sired with a friend of the family emerged.

By the time he emerged from the Law Courts, Aitken's simple sword of truth and trusty shield of fair play looked decidedly battered. It came out during the libel trial that his wife had not paid his bill at the Ritz. She had not even been in France at the time and Aitken had asked his wife and daughter to perjure themselves to back his story. His case collapsed, leaving him with massive costs. He later admitted perjury and attempting to pervert the course of justice.

In the meantime, John Major's government which seemed riven from stem to stern with immorality, corruption and sleaze, was swept from power. Tory sleazemasters could draw only one shred of comfort from their election defeat. Alan Clark was returned to Parliament as Conservative Member for Kensington and Chelsea. The former Defence Minister was a serial adulterer who had told all in his scandalous diaries. He had also admitted his involvement in government wrongdoing over the Matrix-Churchill affair, where the government allowed businessmen to be prosecuted for illegal arms exports even though, via the Secret Service, it had approved it.

All The President's Women (And Men)

Even Alan Clark's scandalous confessions could not match the sordid details teased out of Monica Lewinsky by Special Prosecutor Ken Starr in his best-selling Starr report. But it is worth remembering that President Clinton was not the first president to be involved in a sex scandal.

The first president, George Washington, set a dizzying standard that few presidents have come close to equalling with the 'Washerwoman Kate Affair'. While the father of the nation was busy fighting the British during the War of Independence he had a congressman procuring for him, so that when he returned from the front there was a young woman waiting to administer the comforts of love. Among the congressman's hand-picked comforters was Kate, who was not a washerwoman herself, but the washerwoman's daughter.

The story broke in the *Boston Weekly News-Letter*. It was

picked up by the *Gentleman's* Magazine in London and became the basis of a Broadway play they must have had big billboards. Washington had a reputation as a serial womanizer. His first lover was an Indian squaw. He went on to have a long affair with the wife of his best friend. During the War of Independence, he took an active interest in the daughters of the household wherever he was billeted.

Among the Revolutionary forces, the French General Lafayette set the tone by bedding the wives of fellow officers. General Lee smuggled girls into Valley Forge, and the distraught wife of the disgraced Benedict Arnold would run around Washington's headquarters naked. Only Washington himself could comfort her.

Much of this was known at the time and used in the propaganda war. Rumours were spread that Washington had many mistresses, both black and white. Since he had no legitimate children it was even said that Washington was a woman in drag. However, there were persistent rumours that two of his staff officers were, in fact, his illegitimate offspring. Washington himself fondly imagined that he might one day start a family if his wife Martha died and he had a new young wife.

Washington's interest in women continued throughout his presidency. Love letters written by the first president to the wife of a former mayor of Philadelphia came to light in the 19th century. And, according to the distinguished historian, Arnold Toynbee, Washington died of pneumonia after catching a chill in the unheated slave huts during a passionate encounter with a black woman.

Thomas Jefferson, who became the third president of the United States, fathered a second family with his slave girl, Sally Hemings. Although some historians have sought to hush this up, at the time the press indulged in the sort of feeding frenzy we see today.

When his father-in-law died, Jefferson had inherited the

old man's slaves. One of them, Sally Hemings, was, in fact, Jefferson's half sister-in-law. Like many Southern gentlemen, the old man had made free with his slaves.

After Jefferson's wife died, he was sent to Paris, where he enjoyed an affair with the artist, Maria Cosway, and a number of other married women. When Jefferson's daughter, Mary, came to Paris, 14-year-old Sally travelled with her as her companion. It was there that the affair began.

When Jefferson was recalled to the USA, he urged Sally to stay in France as a free woman. But she returned with. him to Virginia, as a slave. She was already pregnant and went on to bear him five children. This was no secret. When Jefferson entered the White House in 1801, his former friend, the rabble-rousing Scots journalist James Callender, rounded on him in the *Richmond Recorder*. First, he revealed Jefferson's youthful indiscretion with a married woman. When that did nothing to dent Jefferson's credibility, Callender attacked Jefferson's ongoing relationship with his 'black Venus'. He wrote that, in Virginia, Jefferson maintained his 'black wench and her mulatto litter'. He kept another 'Congo harem' in the White House, it was said.

Jefferson went about his business and weathered the storm. He went through with the Louisiana Purchase, doubling the size of the United States at a stroke and opening its expansion to the west. Callender died drunk, in penury. After Jefferson's death, Sally and her children were freed.

During the 1828 election, it was revealed that Andrew Jackson had married bigamously. His wife's divorce had not been finalized when they were wed. Jackson was a lawyer; he should have checked. The press had a field day. Although Jackson won the election, his wife Rachel died of shame before he entered the White House.

President John Tyler's wife, however, died after he entered the White House. Within months Tyler was wooing the 'Rose of Long Island' Julia Gardiner, a model who advertised soap. Tyler fought off a challenge for her hand from his sons and they married. Tyler was 54; Julia was 24. During his honeymoon, the press pitied the President his 'arduous duties' and urged him to take rest – from the cares of office. The couple had seven children.

Gossip concerning the President's homosexuality was rife during James Buchanan's tenure of office in the late 1850s. His room mate in Washington was William Rufus De Vane King, Vice-President under Franklin Pierce. King was variously known as 'Mrs Vice-President', 'Miss Nancy', Buchanan's 'better half', 'Mrs B' and 'Auntie Fancy'. And smirking references were made to 'Mr Buchanan and wife'.

James Carfield also seems to have had a gay affair, before joining one of the many 19th-century sects in America that encouraged free love. His political career survived an affair with an 18-year-old journalist on the *New York Times* and, during the 1880 election, the allegation that he had slept with a prostitute in New Orleans. He was shot four months after taking office and died, leaving his widow to defend his reputation.

During the 1884 election, Grover Cleveland was forced to admit that he had fathered an illegitimate child. He was also a draft dodger, having paid a young Polish immigrant $150 to fight in the Civil War in his stead.

Cleveland won the election because his Republican opponent, James G. Blaine, was even more corrupt. Then the 49-year-old Cleveland went on to marry his 20-year-old ward while in office. The press pursued them on their honeymoon, watching the couple through telescopes, while editorials speculated on what a man of Cleveland's age and girth could be doing with a pretty young thing.

Scurrilous pamphlets alleging 'bestial practises' lost Cleveland the 1880 election. But he returned to the White House, with his popular young wife, in 1885. They had five children.

The lugubrious President Woodrow Wilson was a serial adulterer. His first wife died while he was in office and Wilson began pursuing a wealthy widow, Mrs Galt. When he asked her for her hand in marriage, Washington gossips quipped that Mrs Galt was so shocked she fell out of bed. The affair hit the rocks when one of Wilson's former *amoretti* published his love letters. Wilson tried to limit the damage with a sickeningly schmaltzy press release.

More trouble ensued when the *Washington Post* made one of the greatest typos in history. When President Wilson presented his fiancee at their first formal engagement, the *Post* reported: 'The President spent much of the evening entering Mrs Galt.' It meant to say 'entertaining Mrs Galt'.

Warren Harding could just about qualify as America's first – and only black president. He had a Jamaican grandfather. His racial origins, which he never denied, were a major issue in the 1920 election.

This helped distract attention from his compulsive womanizing. His, wife caught him in *flagrante delicto* with a young woman in the coat closet in the Oval Office. Had he not died after two years in office, he would almost certainly have been brought down by the drunken orgies he attended with chorus girls in a house on H street. His wife tried to salvage his reputation by burning his papers, but Nan Britton, the underage mother of his illegitimate child, wrote a book called *The President's Daughter*. The Society for the Suppression of Vice tried to stop its publication, until campaigning journalist H.L. Mericken of the *Baltimore Sun* rode to the rescue.

But Harding's corrupt administration was known for a much more famous scandal. Known as 'Teapot Dome', it was billed in 1923 as the 'Crime of the Century'. In 1909, President Taft had created three huge petroleum reserves for the Navy, as a hedge against future shortages. One. of the richest was at Teapot Dome, Wyoming. As soon as Harding came to office, his Secretary of the Interior, Albert

Fall, took control of the reserves from the Secretary of Navy and began selling off drilling rights for suitable kick-backs. The lease at Elk Hills, Nevada, went to the multi-millionaire, Edward Dohney, who sent his son to deliver a $100,000 'cash loan' to Fall. In return, Dohney expected to double his $100 million fortune.

The Teapot Dome contract would go to Harry Sinclair, who was already worth an estimated $300 million. Sinclair was a generous man. He had bailed out Fall's struggling ranch in New Mexico, giving him six prime heifers and a young bull. When Sinclair received his lease in April 1922, he handed over $200,000 in liberty bonds and $100,000 in cash. It was money well spent. When rivals tried to muscle in on Sinclair's concessions, Fall sent in the US Marines.

Naturally, people began to comment on the Secretary of the Interior's newfound wealth. His ministerial salary was a mere $12,000. Harding stood by him.

'If Albert Fall isn't an honest man, I'm not fit to be President of the United States,' he said.

Fall knew Harding well and did not find these words a comfort. He resigned as Secretary of the Interior, saying he had done all he could do in the job. Harding proposed to appoint him to the Supreme Court, but Fall declined, per-haps fearing an investigation into the source of his wealth during the Senate confirmation proceedings.

Half-a-dozen of Hardings other cronies, known as the Ohio Gang, were under investigation, when in June 1923, President Harding set out on a 'voyage of understanding' across America. In San Francisco, he ate some tainted crab meat and died in the Cow Palace Hotel with his wife by his side. It was soon rumoured that his wife had poisoned him to save him from impeachment.

Franklin Roosevelt sailed closer to the wind than any president in history. Always a ladies' man, during World War I when he was Secretary of the Navy, he seduced his wife's social secretary. When Eleanor found out, she said she would stick by him, provided he gave up his mistress. He said he would. This was a lie and he continued seeing her for the rest of his life.

Roosevelt took this accommodation with his wife as *carte blanche* to take other lovers. But when Eleanor took a lover, threatening his chances in the 1932 election, he got one of his own mistresses to seduce his wife's lover, in order to prevent a politically devastating divorce.

By the time Roosevelt entered the White House, Eleanor had turned lesbian. The press made veiled references to Eleanor's strange 'companion', the cigar-smoking, Bourbon-swilling AP reporter, Lorena Hickok, whose sexual proclivities were no secret. However, during the Depression and then the War, Roosevelt was seen as America's saviour. The press were happy to keep quiet about the Roosevelts' sex lives, just as they made no mention of the fact that the President was wheelchair-bound as the result of polio.

During the crucial days of World War II, Roosevelt and his mistress lived uneasily in one wing of the White House, while Eleanor and her lesbian lover occupied the other. Roosevelt hated his wife's sapphic liaison but there was nothing he could do about it.

One sex scandal did rock the Roosevelt White House, however. Under Secretary of State, Sumner Welles, Roosevelt's envoy to Hitler, Mussolini and then Churchill, was entrapped propositioning a Pullman porter. Roosevelt tried to hush up the affair, but J. Edgar Hoover leaked it, forcing Welles from office.

Roosevelt died in the arms of his lover at their retreat in Warm Springs, Georgia. She packed and fled before he was cold, leaving Roosevelt's reputation untarnished.

President Eisenhower's wartime affair with his army driver, Kay Summersby, was well known by the press. They were often photographed together in wartime Britain and on trips to North Africa, but when he returned to the

USA to pursue his political career, he abandoned her.

She hinted at the affair in her 1948 book, *Eisenhower Was My Boss*. And when he ran for office in 1953, she threatened to spill the beans to *Look* magazine. The affair caused a lot of sniggering during the election, but it was only in her autobiography, *Past Forgetting: My Love Affair with Dwight D. Eisenhower* in 1972, that she revealed the full details of the affair.

John F. Kennedy's prodigious sex life is now well known. He always sailed close to the wind. During World War II, Kennedy was kicked out of US Navy Intelligence when the FBI taped him in a hotel room with Danish beauty queen, Ingrid Arvad, a known Nazi sympathizer who, J. Edgar Hoover claimed, was a former mistress of Hitler. Kennedy was transferred to the Pacific where he became a war hero.

His behaviour was extraordinarily reckless. During the Cuban Missile Crisis, when the world hovered on the brink of nuclear war, JFK was in the cabinet room in the White House discussing whether to press the button when a pretty young secretary came in. Kennedy turned to his Secretary of Defence, Robert McNamara, and said: 'Bob, get me her name and her phone number. We may avert war tonight.'

As with Roosevelt, the press covered up for him. Plenty of hints were made about his affair with Marilyn Monroe and the others. A *Newsweek* reporter walked into Kennedy's hideaway in Palm Springs during the 1960 election to find actress Angie Dickinson relaxing on Kennedy's bed. Nothing was published.

Even more scandalous stories were hidden away. Kennedy, the first Catholic president, was a divorcee when he married Jackie. He had married Florida socialite Durie Malcolm in 1947. Kennedy also had daily reports of the Profumo scandal delivered to the Oval Office, marked for his eyes only. He had been involved with some prostitutes in London and was frightened that he might become embroiled.

Lyndon Johnson was even more blatant. He flaunted his infidelity in front of the press, even boasting that he had celebrated signing the equal rights legislation into law by having sex with a black girl in the Oval Office.

'I had more women by accident than Kennedy had on purpose,' he bragged memorably.

In fact, Johnson had only got into the White House because of sexual blackmail. As a senator in Washington, he had lived next door to FBI boss, J. Edgar Hoover, and had borrowed FBI files as his bedtime reading. He knew about Kennedy's wartime affair with Ingrid Arvad.

When Johnson lost the Democratic nomination to Kennedy at the 1960 convention in Los Angeles, Kennedy was not going to put him on the ticket as his running mate. Johnson went to see Kennedy and threatened not only to ruin his clean-living image but also to lose him the Jewish vote. Kennedy capitulated.

'Lyndon, I'm 43 years old,' Kennedy said. 'I am not going to die in office, so the vice-presidency doesn't mean a thing.'

Johnson said: 'I looked it up. One in four presidents dies in office. I'm a gambling man, and this is the only chance I've got.'

Alongside his general promiscuity, Johnson maintained a second family in Texas and he had regular sex sessions in the Oval Office with a female reporter from the *Washington Star*.

When Johnson stepped down, JFK's brother Robert Kennedy ran for the presidency. It was only after he was gunned down in a Los Angeles hotel during the primaries that it was revealed that he, too, had had an affair with Marilyn Monroe, after his brother had finished with her.

The Kennedy clan continued its scandalous saga, which had begun with paterfamilias Joe Kennedy, prohibition bootlegger and one-time lover of Gloria Swanson. With

JFK and RK dead, Edward Kennedy was next in line for the presidency, but his chances died in 1969.

On the night of 18 February 1969, he took off from a party on Chappaquiddick Island, off the coast of Massachusetts, with a young campaign worker, Mary Jo Kopechne. After missing a turning, he skidded off a narrow bridge into the water. He managed to get out of the car. Mary did not. He claimed to have dived repeatedly in an attempt to rescue her from the car, but the surging tidal waters made rescue impossible.

He ran back to the party, avoiding a house only 200 yards from the bridge. Without telling the other partygoers, he returned to the bridge with two friends, Joe Gargan and Paul Markham. They, too, dived on the car, fruitlessly.

Gargan and Markham then returned to the party while Kennedy swam across to Edgartown on the mainland. They assumed he had gone to get help. Instead, he went back to the hotel where he was staying and changed into dry clothes.

The following morning, he again failed to raise the alarm. After drinking a cup of coffee and chatting to other guests, Gargan and Markham came to get him and, together, they took the ferry back to the island.

By this time the tenant of the house near the bridge had called the police. Edgartown Police Chief Jim Arena arrived. Seeing the car in the water, he called for help. Police diver, John Farrar, turned up 25 minutes later. He found the body of Mary Jo Kopechne in the back seat of the car. She was uninjured and had survived, Farrar reckoned, in an air pocket for about an hour before drowning. Had he been called straightaway, Farrar said, she would have lived.

When Kennedy and his two friends arrived back on Chappaquiddick Island, they heard people talking about the discovery of the car. They turned right around and took the ferry back to Edgartown. Kennedy went straight to the police station and reported the accident. Chief Arena had already discovered that the car in the water was registered to Kennedy and was looking for him.

Kennedy told the police that he had not reported the accident earlier because he had been dazed. In court, he pleaded guilty to leaving the scene of an accident and failing to report an accident. He later admitted that he had delayed in the forlorn hope that 'the sense of guilt would somehow be lifted from my shoulders'.

Although Chappaquiddick was not the end of his political career, it was the end of his presidential hopes. When it was mooted that he would stand for the nomination against the desperately unpopular Jimmy Carter in 1980, the *New York Post*, freshly purchased by Rupert Murdoch, brought Chappaquiddick up relentlessly, pushing home the point that, if it were not for Ted Kennedy's presidential ambitions, 29-year-old Mary Jo Kopechne would still be alive.

In Washington, Kennedy's womanizing became legendary. He was once caught making love to a waitress in a restaurant. Bedsheets with his life-size portrait printed on them went on sale. His reckless behaviour came into the public spotlight again when his nephew, William Kennedy Smith, was accused of rape after his Uncle Ted had taken him out on a drinking spree.

Kennedy then had to sit through the conformation hearings of Clarence Thomas with a straight face. Anita Hill, a one-time legal employee of Thomas, charged Thomas with sexual harassment. During the 107-day hearing, which was televised, she claimed that he boasted of the size of his penis, accused her of putting a pubic hair on her Coke can and talking, at length, about a porn movie called Long Dong Silver. Thomas was confirmed as a Supreme Court Justice by the narrowest margin ever – 52 votes to 48.

In 1999, Kennedy also sat through the senatorial trial of President Clinton, without once crying out 'good on you

Bill'. But then he was in distinguished company. The Senate's oldest member, 90-year-old Strom 'Sperm' Thurmond, had married a 22-year-old beauty queen at the age of 66. Three years later, she was carrying their first child. He claims to have a permanent erection. In the US Senate, the story is that Thurmond keeps a baseball bat in his office so that when he dies, the undertaker can beat his member down to close the coffin lid.

Lyndon Johnson's successor, Richard Nixon, was so deeply mired in the political sleaze of Watergate that his sexual misdemeanours were overlooked – except by his archenemy, J. Edgar Hoover. Before he became president, Nixon had been filmed by British Intelligence having sex with a young Chinese woman in Hong Kong. She was thought to be a Communist agent.

The pictures came into Hoover's hands, which explains why Nixon could never sack him – although he tried twice. Nixon's Chinese woman turned up in the USA for his inauguration. She settled in California, not far from Nixon's home in San Clemente.

President Jimmy Carter caused a scandal by not having sex. During the 1976 election campaign, he told *Playboy* magazine: 'I have looked on a lot of women with lust. I've committed adultery in my heart many times.'

Bill Clinton would probably not think that that counted.

Ronald Reagan lived the feckless life of a Hollywood movie star. While planning to marry the pregnant Nancy, he forced his attentions on 19-year-old Selene Walters, whom he picked up in a Hollywood night-club.

'They would call it date rape today,' Walters told the author Kitty Kelly.

Butter would not melt in his First Lady's mouth either. In the White House, Nancy Reagan masterminded the 'Just Say No' campaign. But *Spy* magazine said that when she was an actress, she gave the 'best head in Hollywood'.

During the 1988 election, it was alleged that George Bush

had had a longterm affair with Jennifer Fitzgerald, an aide on his vice-presidential staff. The allegation came from US Ambassador, Louis Fields, who had arranged private accommodation for Bush and Fitzgerald on a trip in 1984. He claimed 'first-hand knowledge of the affair'.

In the 1988 election, the rules were changed, thanks to Democrat hopeful Gary Hart. He was a youthful candidate in the JFK mould. A young Republican voter summed up the situation, when she said: 'My heart is for Bush, but my bush is for Hart.'

Hart made a fateful mistake though. When he was accused of having an extramarital affair, he challenged the press to catch him out. And catch him they did. Reporters from the *Miami Herald* spotted 29-year-old jeans model, Donna Rice, creeping out of Hart's Washington town house one morning when Hart's wife Lee was away. Later they were pictured fooling around on a yacht aptly called *Monkey Business*. Hart abandoned his campaign.

Hart's legacy was that the media dropped their self-imposed restrictions on reporting on the private lives of presidents and presidential candidates, which had been in operation since Franklin Roosevelt's administration. If it had not been for Gary Hart, there would have been no Zippergate. No one would ever have heard of Monica Lewinsky, that stained dress or her novel way of enjoying a cigar.

New Labour

New Labour came into power in Britain in 1997 with a squeaky clean image. Within months, Foreign Secretary Robin Cook, while pursuing an ethical foreign policy, was found to be shacked up at home with his secretary. Under instructions from the Prime Minister's press secretary, Alistair Campbell, he dumped his longstanding wife,

Margaret, and married his lovely mistress Gaynor.

Eighteen months in, the government had its first casualty, Welsh Secretary Ron Davis resigned after an incident on Clapham Common that had nothing to do with a homosexual pick-up. It was merely an error of judgement.

Next, the Agriculture Secretary Nick Brown was outed, as was the Trade Secretary Peter Mandelson – although the BBC was not allowed to say so. Everyone held their breath, expecting another outing not a million miles away from Number 10.

Wronged wife and woman scorned, Margaret Cook then savaged the errant Foreign Secretary with a scandalous autobiography, but she failed to damage him politically. In fact, Cook benefited from what has become known as the 'Clinton effect'. Suddenly the cheating Foreign Secretary's approval rating shot up in the polls. Before Margaret Cook's blistering attack he had been dismissed as a gingerbearded gnome. Afterwards, people suddenly saw the mischievous twinkle in his eye. *Sun* readers said they wanted to go to bed with him. He was Lothario who could down a bottle of brandy in one go and still bed 12 mistresses.

There was a minor 'cash-for-access' scandal, then along came the big sleaze. Peter Mandelson, the spin doctor responsible more than anyone for the election of New Labour, had borrowed £375,000 from Paymaster General, Geoffrey Robinson, the very man his department was investigating for irregularities over off-shore funds. They both resigned, soon to be followed by Treasury spin doctor, Charlie Whelan, who was thought to have leaked the story on the orders of Chancellor of the Exchequer, Gordon Brown, as part of a vendetta against Mandelson. The Blair government seemed to be living up to the dizzying standards of its predecessors. Meanwhile, the Tories were trying to clean up their act when Conservative MEP Tom Spencer was caught smuggling drugs and gay porn into the country.

At least Tony Blair can stand tall though. His international reputation for integrity was bolstered by his close relationship with... President Clinton.

A scandalous deja-vu hit the headlines once more when Peter Mandelson, after being re-instated into the cabinet as Secretary for Northern Ireland, dealt a second blow to Tony Blair. Mandelson's inability to tell the truth, particularly in the public's gaze, became his downfall again. Mandelson was asked to leave the government for an incredible second time in January 2001 after lying about significant cash donations to Labour's 'Dome' project. Mandelson allegedly played a significant role in obtaining passports for the two Indian Hinduja brothers in return for a significant sponsorship sum for one of the Dome's attractions. After lying to the press and to Labour's press secretary, Alastair Campbell, Tony Blair had no choice other than to accept Mandelson's resignation from the cabinet.

Rock'n'Roll Scandals

Led Zeppelin

'Led Zeppelin', Jimmy Page once said, 'is a stag party that never ends.' If ever a band was born to party until one or all of its participants keeled over it was Zeppelin – a rocking, rolling, careering orgy spiced with stories of black magic rituals, shotgun weddings and wakes.

Page was the frail former child prodigy guitarist who put Led Zeppelin together after his band, The Yardbirds, fell apart in 1968. Linking up with session bassist John Paul Jones and a brace of Midland neanderthals, Robert Plant on vocals and drummer John 'Bonzo' Bonham, he set about re-interpreting the delta blues in a hard rock context. Zeppelin played at deafening volumes to record-breaking audiences. For a while in the Seventies they were outselling The Rolling Stones at the ratio of three albums to one.

Through all this success they made merry, causing all sorts of astonishing rumours of backstage peversions to reverberate round Europe and America. Tales of massive orgies with willing female participants abounded.

The two stories that began to circulate like dogs on acid during their first American tour in 1969 (the Brits had rejected them as blues pilferers without talent or finesse) were sordid and thrilling, respectively.

The first was that never in the history of human conflict had so much semen been implanted in so many by so few. They were in essence the groupie's Godsend. Two of them – fresh out of the Midland murk, not too knowledgeable but willing to learn; the other two – wise-ass London musicians worldly and cynical enough to indulge in the eagerly-proffered bodies of young America.

The other rumour had its roots in probably the most baffling phenomenon in the history of blues music. It concerned Robert Johnson, a young Mississippi blues singer and guitarist in the years leading up to the Second World War. Johnson had left his hometown as a fairly unconvincing talent, and certainly no genius, and returned almost a year to the day later as a possessed, electrified magician. Those who had known him were in no doubt. In accordance with the beliefs of the time, Johnson had sat down by the crossroads on a moonless night, met with the Devil himself and sold his soul in return for money and fame. He prospered for a while, wringing songs of magnificent tortured splendour like '32-20 Blues' and 'Love In Vain' from his occupied soul. But attempts in 1938 to locate him and put him on a national radio show proved fruitless. Johnson had been murdered by a jealous husband, struck down by poison tantalizing on the lip of fame.

Jimmy Page was known to be fascinated by Satanism. He was an authority on Aleister Crowley, the Great Beast, 666, the English Beelzebub, the Wickedest Man In The World. His interest in the occult seemed more informed than that of a mere dilettante. Obsessed by Crowley, the eccentric mountaineer-turned-mystic who strived for a plateau of sexual and narcotic gratification, Page went so far as to purchase Crowley's former temple, Boleskine House, overlooking Loch Ness. This was a brooding, sinister place, reputedly haunted by the ghost of a man who had been beheaded there. In 1970 Page became laird of Boleskine. The king of the colossal riff was putting in his bid for magus status.

Right from the off, everything about Zeppelin spelled big. From their sound, a Page-produced holocaust of guitars and drums, to their gargantuan manager, Peter Grant, to the hordes of dazed and confused Quaalude-guzzling teenagers who patronized the band, to their own appetites for more, more, more, Zeppelin went further than any band had dared to go.

They picked up widespread notoriety on their second

American tour for an incident in Seattle in which a groupie was allegedly battered about her naked body with a dead shark, before having pieces of it inserted into every available orifice. Their former road manager, a libertarian karate-expert named Richard Cole, whose thirst if anything exceeded that of his charges, explains what really happened.

'The true shark story was that it wasn't even a shark. It was a red snapper and the chick happened to be a fucking red-headed broad with a ginger pussy, and that is the truth. Bonzo was in the room but I did it. And she loved it. It was like, "You'd like a bit of fucking, eh? Let's see how your red snapper likes this red snapper!" That was it. It was the nose of the fish, and that girl must have come 20 times.

Later on that same tour they were joined by a journalist named Ellen Sander, who was filing a report for *Life* magazine. She wasn't to know it but a book had been opened on which of the entourage would bed her first. When she left the tour she went to say goodbye. She was almost raped in the dressing-room, only the unexpected chivalry of Peter Grant saving her at the last moment. She did not write the story at the time, but later she wrote a barbed account of life with the 'animals'.

Page's attitude towards women had remained shadowy. As liberal as the others where groupies were concerned, he nevertheless used Cole as his go-between. A likely target would be informed that Mr Page would be interested in making her further acquaintance. On one occasion Page joined the rest of the band in erotic contemplation as one of the famous Plastercasters was gang-banged in a tub of warm baked beans.

Referring once again to Crowley he said, 'Crowley didn't have a very high opinion of women and I don't think he was wrong.'

In 1972 he began a long affair with a 14-year-old

American model, Lori Maddox.

'You'd hear a lot,' she says, 'about Jimmy being a sorcerer or wizard and like that. I think he's got a lot of power in his own little way. Sometimes when we were making love and it had been going on for *hours*, it was like being in a magic spell.'

Crowley had developed the knack of 'sex magick', the prolonging of the sexual act, delaying orgasm indefinitely to produce a drug-like trance.

The other members of Led Zeppelin were finding exciting uses for their hotel rooms. At the Tokyo Hilton Richard Cole and John Bonham sliced their rooms to shreds with samurai swords. In a Nantes hotel Robert Plant was informed that there was no milk on the premises. In retribution two floors were flooded with fire hoses and the toilets were jammed.

They soon found out that the best fun could be had from launching huge hotel televisions out of top-floor windows and watching them smash in balls of blue electric flame on the street below. Or, at conveniently coastal hotels, by throwing them into the sea. Once John Paul Jones took a TV apart and glued it back together again in expert fashion – on the ceiling.

The inspiration behind this mayhem, and quite often the violence that resulted, was John Bonham. Bonham was an awesome drinker who missed his wife and family. On the Zeppelin private plane, *Starship*, he made a hopeless attempt to molest one of the stewardesses. Richard Cole pulled him off and calmed the girl down, and then told the assembled gentlemen of the music press that not one word of the incident was to reach their news desks.

Bonham became so chronic an alcoholic that a doctor had to be brought on tour to look after his bowels. If they travelled by road the vehicle had to have an in-built toilet.

He also had a deep mistrust of the press. While Page laughed off the bad reviews Bonham could not understand why Zeppelin were not universally acclaimed. Approached one night in a Los Angeles bar by a writer from *Sounds*, who introduced himself as a fan, Bonham lifted the man by his lapels and screamed into his face. 'I've taken enough shit from you cunts in the press!'

On another occasion, also in LA, he went into a bar and ordered 20 Black Russians. Swigging down half of them he paused only to punch a female publicist who had been 'looking' at him, then returned to the bar to drink the other ten.

But perhaps the most daring Bonham escapade came in 1976, on the eve of the release of the *Presence* album. Bonham was at a Deep Purple concert on Long Island. During a particularly boring instrumental interlude he staggered on stage, watched by stunned roadies, and announced into a free microphone: 'I just want to tell you that we've got a new album coming out called *Presence* and it's fucking great. And as far as Tommy Bolin [Purple's guitarist] is concerned, he can't play for shit!'

The first sign that things were going to be terrible for the rest of Zeppelin's existence came in August 1975. The car carrying Robert Plant, his wife Maureen, who was driving, their children and Jimmy Page's daughter smashed into a tree in Rhodes after skidding on one of the island's treacherous roads. Maureen Plant suffered a fractured skull, her husband a broken ankle and elbow, and the children various broken limbs. Plant was told not to attempt to walk for at least six months.

It's been said that at this point Plant sobered up. He put part of the blame for the accident on Page's black magic dabbling. Plant denies this, but another associate of Page's, the American film director, Kenneth Anger, who was also a devotee of Crowley, saw fatal flaws in the guitarist's application of Crowley's dicta. For not only was Page, Anger reckoned, less than halfway to understanding the master's work, but his heroin habit was depleting his resources. Crowley had been a monster of a man and heroin Page was a mere will o' the wisp, becoming incoherent and brittle. That was the difference.

By now Page was not the only heroin dependant. Bonham was well past the stage of flirtation and most of the road crew were hooked as well.

Back at Boleskine House the vibes were getting out of hand. A caretaker had killed himself, and his replacement had gone mad.

In July 1977 the greatest tragedy of all happened. Robert Plant's five-year-old son Karac died of a freak respiratory complaint. With this latest calamity for the Plant family to deal with the stories began to buzz: there was a curse on Zeppelin; Page had got it all horribly wrong; he had displeased his masters and now they were telling him about it.

Somehow the mystical musical glue that keeps bands together worked its spell on Zeppelin and they made one more album, the lacklustre *In Through The Out Door* in 1979. But then came the next tragedy and after this there could be no more.

It was 24 September 1980, John Bonham, on his way to a rehearsal at Page's Windsor house, stopped off at a pub for lunch. He washed down his sandwiches with sixteen vodkas. At the rehearsal which followed he continued to drink prolifically until he could no longer play. The rehearsal mutated into a party, with Bonham drinking vodka after vodka until he passed out. He was carried to a bedroom and left to sleep it off.

The next morning he would not respond to wake-up calls and when they turned him over they found that he was blue. The rock drummer extraordinaire, the man who played drum solos with his fists, had died at the age of 31.

Quite apart from any in-band fears of communal retribution for Page's irresponsibility in the past, it was obvious that Led Zeppelin was finished as a band. A statement to this effect appeared in the press in December of 1980.

And there it all stopped. Until the crazy summer day in 1985 when Bob Geldof persuaded the remaining three members back on to a stage with a guest drummer to help the Live Aid cause. The music they proceeded to play was an uncultured shambles, but it was nice to see them back doing it.

And then came 1988's surprise. At the 40th birthday celebrations for their former label, Atlantic Records, they reformed with John Bonham's 16-year-old son Jason on drums. Everyone assembled agreed that, if you closed your eyes, it was just like listening to the ruthless paramilitary clout of his old man.

Prince

Nothing can be said with any degree of finality about Prince Rogers Nelson. His legend is as tricky as one of his guitar solos, his image as carefully applied as his make-up. Only two things are sure: he is small, and he is strange.

Prince has been recording since 1977, when his first album, *For You,* was the subject of mild amusement by virtue of its lyrical content. A credit to God on the sleeve seemed pretty out of place among some fairly blatant tributes to the sexual acts. However, paradoxically, sex and religion appear to have no problems co-existing on a Prince record. Between them they have constituted nearly all of his inspiration and a peek at his stage show will confirm that he draws equal pleasure from both.

His present superstar status – the only two non-political black Americans as famous as him are Mike Tyson and Michael Jackson – is not the transient affair that most rock stars enjoy. There seems no question of Prince ever becoming obsolete. There is probably no way he'll even be out of date. And one look at his prolific output since 1983, when the double album *1999* opened the commercial floodgates, suggests that he isn't even close to running out of ideas. What seems much more likely, if he *is* to fade from the limelight, is that internal traumas and massive self-doubts will be the causes. For, at the moment, Prince – quite simply – seems to believe that he is God.

It started to get heavy in 1984. The reason may have been the invisibility of Michael Jackson, for although the Jacko chart input was still spectacular, the album *Thriller*, from which all the singles were being culled, was by then two years old, and people were getting impatient for new product. They found a man called Prince, who had been releasing records of a highly sexual and exciting nature for several years, and who appeared to be approaching some kind of creative watershed. They sat back and were prepared for disappointment. Most of them are still waiting for disappointment. Prince simply will not slow down.

The sexual content of his lyrics is phenomenally high, thanks to albums like *Dirty Mind* and *Controversy*, which between them dealt with a whole array of spicy subjects such as oral sex, incest and masturbation. When he was not singing about the peripherals he was singing about the original. 'Sex-related fantasy is all my mind can see,' he sang.

It was this attention to detail that won him the wrath of the 'Washington Wives' – the Parents' Music Resource Center, or PMRC – who found a wealth of pornographic imagery in his lyrics. Song such as 'Darling Nikki' (specimen lyric: 'I met her in a hotel lobby / Masturbating with a magazine') and 'Let's Pretend We're Married' (easy to surmise) were singled out for the special rage of these custodians of taste, although what all these middle-aged women were listening to when Little Richard and Jerry Lee Lewis were singing remains anyone's guess. Prince's tendency to have a bed on stage with him just in case of

424

emergencies must have peeved them even more.

And it was not just the Washington Wives who were after him. The Moral Majority had seen the regular 'thanks-to-God' sleeve notes and could not reconcile this apparent devotion with the lustful lyrical pyrotechnics.

Prince hysteria came in 1984 with the release of the *Purple Rain* film and soundtrack. It rivalled Jackson's *Thriller* as the best selling album ever in vinyl form, and secured the attention of tabloid newspapers everywhere in celluloid form. This new freaky 5ft 2 in (157 cm) star was perceived to be a dynamic and resonant influx in a rather unexciting year. The press resolved to stick around. Unfortunately, Prince had decreed in 1982 that he would never give another interview again, as long as he lived, ever. It messed around with his heart rate or something. For want of fact, fiction became the necessity.

Britain at large got its first chance to see Prince in January, 1985, at the annual BPI awards. When he was announced he stood up in an outrageous purple get-up and walked behind his minder Chick Huntsberry – a human megalith – to the stage. The fact that the audience was made up of fellow performers, none of whom, one presumes, had any intention of attacking him, did not deter him from keeping them all at a very safe distance. Once on the stage he approached the microphone and mumbled something incoherent about God and traipsed off.

Holly Johnson of Frankie Goes To Hollywood made a joke at his expense at the same awards and the whole gathering seemed relieved to be able to vent their spleen in laughter at this strange young American. The next day Prince had made the papers. His behaviour was called 'extraordinary'. Prince announced that he wouldn't ever be coming to Britain again because people had not shown him enough respect.

Prince has always been a loner, musically. While he is

quite happy to sponsor groups with one of his songs he tends to record his own records himself, playing all the instruments and doing all the singing. He was probably the only major American artist not to appear on the star-studded USA for Africa single 'We Are The World'. Even Bob Dylan had been persuaded to cough a line or two but Prince was nowhere. Likewise, at the 1985 American Music Awards, he refused to join in on the 'We Are The World' sing-song, thereby getting up the backs of many who saw the Lionel Richie/Quincy Jones project as much more sacred than any one artist.

His prima donna antics were very soon the subject of much mirth. His twitchy face, sort of a cross between Jimi Hendrix and Charlie Chaplin, was ridiculed on puppet shows and unkind conjecture about his sexual proclivities was spread about.

When, in March 1985, he announced that he was retiring from live shows and going off 'to look for the ladder', a sizeable portion of the musical population believed this to be a good time for the straitjacket to be applied. What he meant, as became clear later in the year, was that he was going to look for 'The Ladder'. This was a lofty concept articulated in his much-maligned 'psychedelic' album, *Around The World In A Day*. He delivered the tapes of this record to Warner Bros accompanied by an entourage that Gloria Swanson in *Sunset Boulevard* would have been grateful to grace. He then sat on the floor surrounded by flowers while the WB boffins got to grips with the product. It all sounded very ominous – and would it sell?

The move towards *Sgt. Pepper*-type psychedelia confounded all those who had discovered him at the time of *Purple Rain* and expected something similar as a follow-up. But the move towards *Purple Rain* itself had disturbed all those who had stuck with Prince since the saucy post-card era of the late Seventies. It all pointed to one conclusion: clearly, Prince could not be second-guessed. At least

426

the *Around The World* album was consistent in one factor: there was the legend 'all thanks 2 God' (Prince is the worst speller since Slade) on the sleeve.

This album had been credited to 'Prince And The Revolution'. The Revolution was not so much a group as a family of friends and girlfriends whom he could call on to play specialist parts. His chain of girlfriend/backing singers has included Vanity, Apollonia (with whom he starred in *Purple Rain)* and Sheena Easton, the chirpy Scots chanteuse who shot to fame thanks to Esther Rantzen's philanthropic TV show 'The Big Time'. She reputedly left him because he never spoke to her. Instead, he expected her to communicate with him by means of ESP.

Aficionados were less than overwhelmed with his next album, *Parade* (1986), although the single taken from it. 'Kiss', was hailed as a masterpiece. In March of that year two Princian bodyguards were sentenced to two years' probation, fined $500 and ordered to do 100 hours of community work for beating up some photographers who had tried to take pics of the puny maestro.

Th singer's behaviour reached off-the-wall saturation level. He made a movie called *Under The Cherry Moon* which was universally reviled, some of the reviews actually descending to prolonged abuse. He started work on a new musical project which became the legendary lost album, or 'The Black Album'. This was first mentioned in the Warner Bros soon-come list in 1986, then mysteriously withdrawn. Bootleg tapes circulated, however, and it certainly sounded like a fine album. An explanation as to why it was held back eventually came from the man himself, in a surprisingly cogent and articulate statement sent to Warner Bros. Here is one paragraph.

'Spooky Electric must die. Die in the hearts of all who want love. Die in the hearts of men who want change. Die in the bodies of women who want babies that will grow up with a New Power Soul Love Life Lovesexy – the feeling u get when u fall in love, not with a girl or boy but with the heavens above. Lovesexy – endorphin. Camille figured out what 2 feel. Glam Slam Escape – the Sexuality Real.'

What would appear to be going on here is that Prince is having alter-ego problems. He has divided his psyche into two opposite trends. There is Spooky Electric, the lustful urchin in search of cool women and cheap thrills. And there is Camille, who only cares about the future of the world.

Having sorted that little problem out, Prince toured Britain to great acclaim in 1988. His album *Sign of The Times* was deemed 'a bit more bloody like it' from all quarters and he was once again in the ascendant.

Still, the best stories come from the fizzy days. Of how he wrote to Miles Davis, the greatest living jazzman and a fan of Prince's, warning him that his popularity was on a noticeable downstroke and that, should he wish to reverse this trend, he really ought to come over and hang out with Prince.

Prince signed the letter 'God'.

The Rolling Stones

With the cool detached precision of a dedicated user-abuser Keith Richards dips the tiny spoon in the bag and brings it up to his nose. His risky-gypsy features contort and, one sniff later, the norm is resumed. He passes the bag across to the journalist.

The journalist accepts, mute, thrilled to be co-opted on to the board. He fumbles at first and hopes to God the great man hasn't noticed his lack of expertise. Seconds later he is in the lap of the Gods, artistically licensed, jack-plugged, coked to the eyeballs. He has taken cocaine with Keith Richards.

A few minutes later the process is repeated. And again,

a few minutes after that. Eventually the journalist is running on a dangerously combustible level, a mass of speeding heart, mind and limbs. His cheeks – if only he could feel them – are so hollow they are almost concave.

Richards lets him get on with it for an hour or so. Then he sidles across with some of his notoriously Grade A heroin (streets are for singing about, not for scoring on) and the man from the music press passes out in a blank, luxurious swoon on the plush Chelsea carpet.

Keith Richards' long-lived relationship with drugs has been well documented. His lifestyle would have destroyed lesser mortals years ago. But the reason Richards continues, in his own cavalier way, to exist its because he is a connoisseur. Denying that he has a problem with drugs, 'only a problem with cops', he has been the subject of spectacular, salacious rumours: he has his blood changed twice a year; he never sleeps; he can't remember the Seventies, any of it.

And following the rumours, in quick succession, the predictions: he'll be dead in a year; he'll be dead in an hour; he'll drop dead on a stage, in the middle of one of his legendary bastardised Chuck Berry solos. And the bandit grin on what remains of his middle-aged face will vanish and one famous quote will hang in the air.

'If they take the fun out of this life, I'll *leave.*'

It was an ambition of pure intent. The Rolling Stones would be a faithful and exciting testimonial to the electric blues, fashioned by their original leader Brian Jones in the musical styles of Elmore James, Muddy Waters and Chuck Berry.

Harangued by the trad jazz set and ignored by most of their own generation on their inception in 1962, they built up a strong following in R&B clubs and were approached by a young, flashy fix-it merchant by the name of Andrew Oldham who was armed with something of a reputation (having done publicity for Brian Epstein's NEMS company), an eye for a scoop, a literary style purloined from Anthony Burgess's *A Clockwork Orange,* and a Decca recording contract. Under his guidance The Stones had their first hit in 1963.

The Stones' line-up divided neatly into three factions. The first was the Mick Jagger-Keith Richards axis. Cajoled by Oldham into writing original material for their first album, they began spending more and more time together, re-establishing the friendship they had had as small boys in Dartford, Kent.

The second, and most clearly defined, was the rhythm section of Bill Wyman and Charlie Watts. With no say in the proceedings and no superstar aspirations, they lurked at the back of the stage, hunched over their respective instruments.

This left on his own the most complex member of the group – Brian Jones. Jones had founded the band in his own likeness – dedicated, talented, sneering, mischievous, artistic, raffish and almost dangerously heterosexual. Banished from the streets of his home-town, Cheltenham, Gloucestershire, for impregnating two girls by the age of 16, he lived for just three things: clothes, R&B and stardom. Visually the most striking of the band, he was also the most prodigiously talented, being able to play practically any instrument in the band. But he had many personality problems beneath the surface.

'Brian was brought up in the worst possible way,' Keith Richards has said. 'He had a very good education, was very clever at school, but somewhere along the line he decided he was going to be a full-time professional rebel, and it didn't really suit him. So that when he wanted to be obnoxious, he had to really make an effort, and having made the effort, he would be really obnoxious. I don't want to be too hard on Brian. He was a very difficult person.'

Increasingly erratic, struck down on occasions by

chronic asthma attacks and just generally a liability, Brian began – ever so subtly – to be phased out. Interviews were handled by Mick and Keith. Brian was never considered as a possible songwriter. Pills and drink conspired to hospitalize him. As early as 1965 his doctor told him he would be dead in a year if he didn't stop drinking.

In September of that year Brian met Anita Pallenberg, a woman who would have an incalculable influence on the lives of at least three of The Stones over the course of the next ten years. A major European model-turned-actress, she was attracted first to Brian because of all The Stones he was the only one who bothered to speak to her. He even spoke a little German, her native language. Now with three illegitimate sons (the last two of which in an act of gratuitous mischief he had christened by the same name, although he preferred to refer to the third by the nickname 'Broad Bean Head'), Brian invited Anita to live with him in London. She became his lover, his spiritual adviser and even, in a certain light, his exact double – a fact which did not escape seasoned Brian-watchers. She persuaded him to be photographed wearing an SS uniform, stamping on a doll with his jack-boots. The photo caused a furore in the British press.

Earlier that year The Rolling Stones had experienced the first in what would prove to be a long line of court visits. It transpired that on an evening in March a chauffeur-driven Daimler had stopped at a service station in East London and out of it had stepped a 'shaggy-haired monster'. The monster was Bill Wyman and his mission was the immediate location of a urinal. Informed that it was out of order he summoned reinforcements from the Daimler and eight or nine people jumped out. Mick Jagger pushed the garage-owner out of the way with the words 'we piss anywhere man', and he, Brian Jones and Wyman proceeded to empty their bladders in a line, against the wall of the forecourt. They were found guilty of 'insulting behaviour' and fined £3 each.

The predictably outraged headlines in the tabloid press were easily laughed away but the sheer weight of press opinion directed against them should have told The Stones what to expect. One day in early 1967, nauseated by countless rumours of sordid drug frenzies and bacchanalian orgies to which none of them had been invited, the combined forces of journalistic and detective talent on the *News Of The World* decided that it was about time something was done about The Rolling Stones.

The most obvious solution was to catch them in the drug-taking act. It was well known that they indulged with chilling frequency in marijuana, and it was strongly believed that pills were involved too somewhere along the line. There was a rumour about a new drug of awesome hallucinogenic power called LSD which a very cosmic British group had been caught taking.

Therefore, further incensed by the refusal of The Rolling Stones to observe a quaint British custom – that performers on Sunday Night At The London Palladium shall congregate at the end of the programme on a revolving stage and wave cheerily to the audience – the *News Of The World* went out to get itself a story.

It got it all wrong.

It started promisingly enough. Mick Jagger came into the club where the reporters were waiting, consented to be interviewed and pleaded guilty to all the charges. Yes, he took marijuana, it was great. Yes, he took acid, that was even better.

In gleeful capital letters it was spelled out. The *News Of The World* had caught Jagger bang to rights. Except that in its hurry to get the story the newspaper had forgotten to check the names with the faces. It was not Mick Jagger they had been talking to but Brian Jones, whose insouciance was legendary.

It is quite likely that the story would have stopped right

there, in a garbled report of hilariously righteous prose and mangled facts, had not Mick Jagger been booked to appear on the Eamonn Andrews Show on the Sunday the story broke.

Questioned about the matter he announced that it was all a lie and that a libel writ against the newspaper would be issued. When they heard this, the *News Of The World* set out to fix The Stones once and for all.

It has never been established where the tip-off came from. The facts are that at Keith Richards' country house in Sussex a group of 11 people including Richards himself, Mick Jagger along with his girlfriend, Marianne Faithfull, George Harrison and his wife, and a few close friends and hangers-on assembled for a weekend party. Jagger, who despite his 'confession' to the *News Of The World* had not yet tried LSD, was intrigued by reports from close friends, and one of their number, David Schneidermann, (the self-titled 'Acid King'), had come equipped with a leather attaché case full of it.

Sunday passed in quiet relaxation, tripping on acid and touring the nearby countryside. Harrison and his wife left and the guests returned to watch TV.

A knock came at the door.

When the police busted Richards' house they found all but one – Richards' servant – lying in a giggling zoo of long hair and pillows: Richards was laughing, asking them to be careful not to ruin the patterns on the carpet; Marianne Faithfull was dressed in nothing but a fur rug; the Acid King's case of LSD was on the floor in full view; Robert Fraser, an art dealer and friend of Richards', was a heroin addict and had plenty of it in his pocket as well as some uppers and some hashish.

It looked bad for most of them but Jagger, having no drugs in his possession, was sure he had no cause for alarm. It would later come out in court that Marianne Faithfull had treated the raid as a hug joke, flashing to the

policemen and making remarks about 'dykes' when a
policewoman tried to search beneath the rug she was
wearing. She had earlier deposited four amphetamine
uppers in a green velvet jacket of Jagger's, and forgotten
about them. Jagger, faced with the evidence, made the
most gallant gesture of his life by admitting that they were
his, but added that he had been prescribed them. He even
named the doctor.

The Stones were not believed. Richards was sentenced
to one year's imprisonment for allowing marijuana to be
smoked on his premises. Fraser got six months for possessing heroin and amphetamines. Jagger, who burst into
tears when his sentence was announced, received three
months.

Of course there was more to the court case than a list of
drugs followed by a verdict. Maximum mileage was
obtained from Faithfull's near-naked condition, plus the
thought-provoking fact that she was 'apparently enjoying
the situation' and 'in merry mood'. Rumours of astonishing bestiality and decadence have plagued The Stones
since but none has been so fascinating and hard to dispel
as the rumour that swept Britain during that court case –
that when the police raided the house Mick Jagger was on
his knees, his enormous Michelin Man lips licking a Mars
Bar embedded in Marianne Faithfull's vagina.

Outrage greeted the sentences. William Rees-Mogg,
then editor of *The Times,* risked prosecution by comment-
ing on a *sub judice* case. In his editorial, which he entitled,
'Who Breaks a Butterfly on a Wheel?', a quotation from
William Blake, he condemned the sentences and more per-
tinently the atmosphere of smug, narrow-minded righteousness with which they had been arrived at.

Meanwhile the Acid King had disappeared off the face
of the earth. It is now widely believed that he was
employed to set up The Stones, since he escaped prosecution – ludicrously, since he was laden with LSD – although

the *News Of The World* categorically denied having hired him.

On appeal the jail sentences were quashed although Jagger's conviction stood. His sentence was commuted to one year's conditional discharge. Later that day, heavily sedated and barely comprehensible, he faced the *World in Action* TV cameras in a debate chaired by Rees-Mogg in which he denied himself to be anything other than a musician.

Brian Jones had intended joining the party that weekend. However, in a rare burst of musical activity, he had been working on a soundtrack for a new film which would star Anita Pallenberg. He escaped the raid by hours. And walked straight into another one.

It was astonishing in a way that it took so long for the Brian Jones debut bust to happen; he was notoriously lax in habit and behaviour, decadent in public as well as private, living in a frantic netherworld of clubs, alcohol and narcotics. Tony Sanchez, 'Spanish Tony', his nasal attaché, was employed exclusively as his minder. 'The only reality Brian wanted was oblivion,' he says.

Jones was busted at his London flat and charged with possession of cocaine, methedrine and cannabis resin. On bail, he began to see a psychiatrist. He was sentenced to concurrent prison terms of nine months and three months.

On appeal, and on the recommendation of the psychiatrist, this was commuted to a £1,000 fine and he was put on probation for three years. The last of those three years would prove to be unnecessary.

Following a second bust in May 1968. Brian plunged into a state of almost psychotic despair. Convinced that the other Stones were plotting to replace him (if he was imprisoned this time he would miss the next tour and there were rumours that Eric Clapton was about to disband his group Cream), he succeeded in kicking all his drug dependencies but hit the bottle with a vengeance. His weight shot up, his blond hair looked thick and unwashed and his face became bloated. In a display of extreme – reporters at the time said unprecedented – leniency he was fined £50 and told not to be so naughty again.

Later that year he bought Cotchford Farm in Sussex. It was a child's idyll, the house where little Christopher Robin had frolicked as a boy while A. A Milne wrote about him and his funny friends Eeyore and Winnie the Pooh. These days the house boasted a large swimming pool.

Exasperating everyone with his now totally unreliable personality (he was no longer playing on Stones records, aiming his acoustic guitar at a microphone that, had he looked closer, he would have seen was not plugged in), Brian was asked to leave. In May 1969 he agreed not to be a Rolling Stone any longer. In the early hours of 3 July he went for a swim in his pool and remained in the water until his lifeless body was discovered and dragged out. He was 26.

Three days later Mick Jagger walked on to a stage in Hyde Park in what looked like an obscene transvestite out-fit. He instructed the quarter of a million expectant fans to 'cool it' for a minute and proceeded to quote Shelley in a poetic tribute to the man who had founded The Rolling Stones, given them their name, direction and early image, and died in a swimming pool purchased with their riches.

Hundreds of white butterflies were released into the air, white, virginal and beautiful, they were to be the ultimate tribute. Most of them had died, however, suffocated in their boxes.

That winter The Stones toured America in what would prove to be the epitome of the rock 'n' roll nightmare. They antagonized and alienated journalists and fans alike with their exorbitant ticket prices and irritating tendency not to play until they had exhausted the contents of the drugs cabinet. And eventually, at Altamont, the spirit of freedom and optimism of the late Sixties perished for all time to the tune of one of their songs.

Altamont, those with a sense of irony have observed, was supposed to be a gift. A way of saying thank you – and, it is just conceivable, sorry – to the kids of America who had followed the hectic events of the blockbusting tour. At the Altamont Raceway, a stock-car racing track in California, The Stones, pressurized by complaints of excess and contempt to their audience, decided to give a free festival. The Grateful Dead, who knew the area and were famous for their free shows, advised them that the local Hell's Angels would make admirable security guards, putting the sheen of good vibes and self-control on the whole show.

This seemed fair enough. The Stones hated having the police at their gigs and anyway the London Hell's Angels had policed Hyde Park in subtle and laudable fashion earlier in the year. Jagger and Richards probably admired the image of the Angels too; irrepressible rogues, life's true wanderers, cinematic rebels, locked in a fraternity of women, drugs and booze.

It had been a traumatic year. Woodstock's example of goodwill and communal nudity had been tarnished by violence at other copycat festivals. Drugs had got out of hand; political groups were muscling in; Manson was slicing people up in the name of rock 'n' roll; and songs about revolution were being taken just a little too literally for their authors' liking.

Jagger, who wrote about war, Satan and the Boston Strangler, was bringing a noticeable edge of sinister evil to his performances. Richards was increasingly fuelled on heroin. The whole thing was getting a little scary. Altamont, it was hoped, would cool everybody down.

The toll of four deaths seems, in retrospect, incredible. The official film of the event, *Gimme Shelter*, shot under conditions of extreme danger by the Maysles brothers, tells a dark, nasty tale: at first menace and bad karma as people

freak out on site and Jagger is attacked by a kid; then sporadic violence as Hell's Angels lose their tempers at the
freaks. Members of Jefferson Airplane are threatened and
beaten up by the very people they believed should be running the country.

The Stones come on stage about eight hours later than
scheduled. Word has it that Jagger thinks he will look more
impressive in the dark. Angels are by now laying into anyone who looks at them the wrong way. Pool cues fly, kids
exit bleeding and Jagger steps up to address his party
guests. 'Brothers and sisters,' he exhorts them in his weird
Home-Counties-meets-Truman-Capote twang, 'just cool
out now ...' His voice sounds flat, powerless and not a little concerned. The stage is only a few feet high and there
are Angels milling around, looking at him with the abattoir eyes of drugged, drunken animals.

The set breaks down again and again. 'Cats' are urged
to 'cool it' or the band will 'split'. The argot impresses no-
one. People are terrified, seriously afraid for their lives.
The hundreds of thousands of dazed hippy kids are seeing
the beautiful vision explode in hues of black and red at the
hands of a few greasy Hell's Angels who have been given
$500 worth of free beer on condition that they do not fling
the empty cans at the stage.

The murder of Meredith Hunter happens, not as was
widely believed at the time, during 'Sympathy For The
Devil', although a murder nearly did take place during
that song ('we always have something very funny happen
when we play that song'). It is while new guitarist Mick
Taylor is negotiating the chords of 'Under My Thumb' that
the tall black boy in the gaudy green suit makes a desperate leap for safety. Hounded by Angels for being black and
grinning a lot, as well as being in the company of a white
girl, he flashes a gun. He is stabbed once, twice, then disappears in a melée of skulls and crossbones. Attempts to
revive him prove fruitless when the blood begins to seep

through the green jacket. The Stones play on.

The morning after, it was generally felt that the day had been something of a success. Although four had died (apart from the murder of Meredith Hunter there had been three accidental deaths) there had been an equal number of births, lots of people had been privileged to hear some great music (it is reckoned that The Rolling Stones played one of their finest gigs at Altamont) and after all nobody had had to pay to get in.

Then the true reports started filtering in. Nobody had been born at Altamont. It had been a day of destruction and fear. A few Hell's Angels' motorbikes had been knocked over and the stoned, naked freaks had paid the penalty.

The Rolling Stones were condemned in the press for their gross conceit and superstar hubris and especially for their lack of contrition.

Rolling Stone magazine, which had taken its name from the group, was scathing in its criticism, with Jagger being singled out, scorned for his helplessness in the face of real demons.

Whereas The Beatles' innocence had manifested itself merely in disastrous business ventures and Lennon-inspired follies, The Stones, getting meaner and meaner, riding on the fiery wings of 'Sympathy For The Devil', 'Midnight Rambler' and 'Street Fighting Man', were challenging the skulls and the bones to react. And in the warm, sticky twilight the words of the song that defined evil in 1969, as sung by a 26-year-old from Kent, echoed round the Altamont Raceway: 'I'll stick my knife right down your throat, baby. And it *hurts.*'

With Brian Jones's 'death by misadventure' verdict had come the inevitable raised eyebrows. He went for a swim at midnight? And nobody saw him drown? Wasn't he supposed to be a first-rate swimmer?

Suicide had been ruled out. Everyone who saw him

during his last few days alive remarked on how happy he had seemed, how he had all sorts of plans for forming a new blues band dedicated to his new Mississippi visions.

In 1983 the *News Of The World's* magazine printed the revelations of a close friend of Jones who reportedly had proof that the guitarist had been murdered by drug-dealers whom he had double-crossed several years previously. The story, frustratingly enough, was written in time-honoured what-if format.

With Mick Taylor on guitar The Stones hit the Seventies in cavalier fashion. They were now writing their finest rock 'n' roll, songs of thrilling rhythmic power like 'Brown Sugar', 'Bitch' and 'Loving Cup'. Their 1972 double-album *Exile On Main Street* is arguably the greatest rock album of all time.

However, the Richards-Jagger songwriting duo were becoming more and more estranged. Jagger, whose former girlfriend Marianne Faithfull had left him after a failed suicide attempt in Australia, was now married to Bianca Perez Mora Macles, a Nicaraguan gossip-columnist's dream whose physiognomy was uncannily similar to his own.

Richards, who had rescued Anita Pallenberg from the fists of Brian Jones one night in Morocco, was holed up in a French mansion, hooked on heroin, becoming increasingly scornful of Jagger's jet set existence.

As it turned out, the Seventies would not be over-kind to any of them. Jagger's marriage collapsed in acrimony and his bank account came dangerously close to collapsing in alimony. In the event, Bianca got $1 million, having claimed twelve and a half. Jagger took up with model Jerry Hall and resumed his life of highly-mannered controversy, always cautious not to go too far.

His ex from the Sixties was having a bad time. Marianne Faithfull was as deep in the heroin morass as it is possible to get – scoring on the street, living rough, frequently waking up in a cell. Somehow she pulled herself out by the roots and forged a critically-acclaimed solo career as a cracked-voiced singer of painful vulnerable laments.

Mick Taylor left in 1974. He hadn't even smoked before meeting The Stones. He was now a heroin addict. When John Phillips of The Mamas And The Papas visited him in 1976 he found him still battling the drug:

'I got his address from a friend, went over to Taylor's place, and knocked. He peeked through a hole in the door. We had met before but he didn't recognize me. I told him what I wanted but he snapped, "I haven't played a guitar in two years", and shut the peephole.'

The nightmare of Keith Richards and Anita Pallenberg was gathering speed. Informed that he would not be allowed into the United States to participate in The Stones' tour of 1975 if his blood showed any trace of heroin, he entered a Swiss clinic. The rumours at the time were disarmingly blunt – Keith Richards was having his blood changed. His friend and dealer, 'Spanish' Tony Sanchez, recounts that Richards was delighted at this new states of affairs.

'It doesn't matter if I get hooked again now,' he is reputed to have said. 'I can give it up any time I like without any bother.'

Richards had subsequently scoffed at the blood-change stories. The truth, he maintains, is slightly less glamorous: he underwent excruciating cold turkey withdrawal treatment.

Whatever happened, he did get hooked again, and in February 1977 it seemed to be all over. Stopped at customs at Toronto airport, Anita was found in possession of hashish. Three days later the hotel room she shared with Richards was raided. As well as cocaine they found an ounce of pure heroin. This was enough to put him away for life.

It seemed pretty clear that The Rolling Stones were finished. Taylor had been replaced by the less acclaimed guitarist, Ron Wood, Wyman was muttering about leaving and their lead guitarist and backbone was about to be convicted on a charge of trafficking smack. 'Could This Be The Last Time? asked one newspaper.

Twenty months later, Richards was released on condition he play a charity concert for the blind. The Canadian government, stunned by photos of the Prime Minister's wife, Margaret Trudeau, in the company of The Rolling Stones, and appalled by the fact that – yet again – a Rolling Stone was going to get away with it, appealed. Richards walked away cackling.

And Keith is clean today. Remorseless, flippant, even proud of his past, he plays on, crafting his inimitable five-string chords that no chart can accommodate, siring indirectly a whole legion of lookalikes, think-alikes and act-alikes. Totally underestimating the famous Richards constitution, however, they shoot up, fall down, burn out.

A blank generation of minor league rock musicians has sprung up in his wake, and the master looks like outliving them all.

He split from Anita Pallenberg, said to be a witch, weaving strange, malignant spells over all who crossed her. None of that seems to matter now. Bloated and beaten, she met the courts yet again in 1980 when a teenage boy shot himself at her house.

Her former lover has yet to die on stage. It probably won't happen – falling asleep during 'Fool To Cry' was the closest he's ever come – just as the much-vaunted Stones reunion tour probably won't happen. One day a quiet breath will fade to nothing and the tributes will start to flow for the rock 'n' roll genius who left friends, lovers and enemies strewn along the bloody roads in his tireless odyssey for the good time to end them all.

Janis Joplin

'I wanted to smoke dope, take dope, lick dope, suck dope, fuck dope, anything I could lay my hands on I wanted to do it ... Hey, man, what is it? I'll try it. How do you do it? Do you suck it? No? You swallow it? I'll swallow it.' – Janis Joplin, 1970, a few months before her death.

Janis Joplin had the blues, and didn't she let the world know about it. If pain had a singing voice, it would sound a lot like the Joplin howl. Straight from the gut she sang, via her tortured soul and her broken heart. Even a line like, 'Oh Lord won't you buy me a Mercedes Benz' scorched in tones of raw hurt, symbolic of all the fine things in life Janis could not have – simple things like a pretty face, a loving husband, and maybe a couple of kids to make tomorrow something to look forward to.

In the 27 years of her life, tragically curtailed when she became yet another victim of heroin, she proved beyond any doubt that Sophie Tucker was in no way the *last* of the red hot mammas.

She came out of Port Arthur, Texas – an All-American, small, backward, fiercely proud, intermittently violent, thoroughly racist town of about 60,000 inhabitants, none of them like Joplin.

She shocked and delighted her parents with her sharp intelligence and precocious painting ability. She could read before she started school. Indeed, even in her bleakest hours of how-can-they-love-me self-doubt, even after the unqualified triumphs and unmitigated disasters, there was never a book very far away. It was an unfair myth that Janis Joplin was rescued from a life of mundane manual work by rock 'n' roll.

As she grew up, her fate was gradually sealed. Completely lacking the demure, cleavage-clenching pretti-ness of your average Southern belle (and possessing a terrible complexion), she became the focus for horrible abuse at her school. That, and a tendency to hang out with the boys, would shape her life. It would be a major heartbreak for her that men were perfectly content, willing even, to be seduced from the safe distance of a stage when she sang, but, once the show was over, she went home alone while they retreated into the arms of girls designed with more conventional ideas of beauty in mind.

Displaying a serious alcohol problem as early as the age of 17, she was admitted to the local hospital and subsequently saw a psychiatrist. It was clear that flight was necessary.

So off to Los Angeles she went, then to Venice Beach, and on her return to Port Arthur it was noticed by everyone that Janis was now a fully-fledged wildcat, combining a manic, head-on, hard drinking charm with a Californian-inspired beatnik lifestyle.

Her drinking habits changed. Out went the beer, in came the hard stuff. Crossing the Sabine River into the much funkier state of Louisiana she and her male friends would embark on trawls of sleazy bars, risking the madness and violence, scoring free drinks off the regulars.

In 1962 Janis entered the University of Texas. She immediately took up with a like-minded ghetto crowd, one of whose main passions was folk music. Janis was singing now. Her voice underwent several changes until she found her style (a whining bluegrass yodel was attempted but didn't sound right), and eventually her whisky voice slid into a bluesy Bessie Smith groove for the barking, pleading phrases that would become her trademark.

As ever, an undercurrent of depression was starting to taint the good times. In a display of slightly cruel humour the students of the university nominated her as the 'Ugliest Man on Campus'. Crushed by her irredeemable unpopularity, she upped and left, for San Francisco. It would be a long time before she returned.

In San Francisco her boozing habits got more and more extraordinary. Sipping almost constantly from a Bourbon bottle, she was also not averse to hanging out on street corners, shooting the breeze with chronic winos. She recognized fellow refugees when she saw them.

Another characteristic of San Francisco in the early Sixties was the ubiquity of speed. Janis dived in, eager to embrace the drug of the street, and it is quite likely that she tried heroin too. She moved to New York in 1964 and spent the summer shooting speed. Returning to San Francisco she began to deal to finance her own addiction, becoming increasingly strung out. Finally, in May 1965, she went to a San Francisco hospital and declared herself to be insane. Suspicious of her ragged appearance, they turned her away. Now, living with a shady character whose habit matched her own, her down-ride gathered pace. Aware that this ride had only one way out, Janis managed to pull herself together before it was too late.

She returned to Port Arthur to a life of long-sleeved dresses, parental chats and tense, unfamiliar conformity. There was a desperate attempt to wean herself off speed. She managed it thanks to a scrupulous routine of college and family occasions, and also a firm belief that she was to be married to the slumped figure that had shared her San Francisco nightmare. That particular illusion was well and truly shattered when the hapless wretch arrived at the Joplin house and announced that he was 'splitting'.

The rejection was taken seriously. All that kept her from heading back to oblivion was the belief that somewhere deep down in her soul was a sweet homely little housewife just waiting to be given the chance.

In her feast of anxieties she began to consider that relations with women might be slightly less painful. An ardent desire to get close to someone – anyone – added to a genuine sense of gratitude when somebody made even a tentative sexual gambit in her direction, meant that lesbian/straight differentials went by the board, fogged by her all-consuming need for the human touch. To the outside world it looked repulsive, but Janis Joplin cared little for public opinion; there was never any question of a prospective partner being asked to fill out an application form.

The ephemeral blasts which constituted her sexual encounters were in their own squalid way nothing more sinister than compressed love affairs – only casual, trivial and meaningless when she awoke the following morning, feeling nothing.

But at least she was singing again. Eschewing the saccharine tones of Joan Baez, which is certainly what the Port Arthur audience expected from a 'chick' singer, she hit the blues notes with a passion. Some success came her way, however, and in time a call came from San Francisco – there was a band up there who needed exactly a chick of her nature, could she drop everything ...?

The band was Big Brother And The Holding Company, a fairly rudimentary but deafening loud blues outfit whose unerring ability to hit four different wrong beats instead of one good one was made irrelevant by the fact that they were all out of tune anyway. However, slamming down sledgehammer blues behind Janis Joplin, they sounded almost great. She moved in with the band and the rollercoaster started to shudder in anticipation.

She had now been clean for a year. Holed up in the beautiful hippie household, however, when every guitarist had a girlfriend and she was the only one on her own, she began to feel real loneliness. Also, she was one of only two not doing speed. At last her resolve snapped. Temptation got the better of her and the habit came back.

One thing that she never embraced, being utterly terrified of its unpredictable flashes and psychological squeezes, was LSD. When somebody slipped her an acid-laced drink she made herself vomit rather than tremble her way through a much-feared trip.

That particular idiosyncrasy aside, her own emotional and physical needs coincided conveniently with the prevailing ideas of the hippie community, do what you enjoy and enjoy it while you're doing it. Then, when you've finished doing it, do it again.

Her "hard-livin', hard-loving" exterior endeared her to the Hell's Angels – she would later dedicate an album to them – and they appreciated the competition she provided. Even concern among close friends that she was being made a fool of did not distract her from the riotous arm-wrestling fights with the Angels.

In June 1967 an event happened that changed the lives of Big Brother And The Holding Company, and made an overnight star of their loud, bluesy singer.

The Monterey Festival was an incredible triumph. Playing twice by public demand, they won over the huge audience and made the pages of every national publication with a double-spread to spare and an interest in youth culture. The film made of the festival, *Monterey Pop*, shows a mesmerizing Joplin performance of 'Ball And Chain'. At the end of the song the camera picks up Cass Elliott of The Mamas And The Papas. There is no sound, but you don't need to be told that she is breathing the word 'wow'.

The rollercoaster was moving Dylan's manager Albert Grossman signed them (significantly, a personal dislike of heroin and the people who use it made him include a clause in the contract stipulating that the deal was off at the first sniff of smack). While the press acclaim reached mayhem level, Janis proved difficult to locate. She was down in Mexico, having an abortion.

The publicity became fame and the fame became madness. Not only was Janis's every move being monitored by the press, she was also receiving free advice. The gist was: that band had got to go.

It was certainly true that no-one looked further than Janis when Big Brother played. Her self-destructive streak and pent-up frustration manifested themselves in magnetic performance, her voice spelling out the rage in stuttering phrases punctuated by hair-tossing and fist-clenching. She looked and sounded on the verge of bitter tears.

Nobody was in any doubt about her talents, but the band was getting worse and worse reviews as writers dredged newer and fresher insults from the depths of the thesaurus. The official split came in August 1968 and Janis, guilty as hell, was now a solo singer.

Motivated by a dubious marriage of Southern Comfort and heroin (which she had been taking behind Grossman's back) she put together a band which would variously be called Kozmic Blues, The Janis Joplin Revue and Main Squeeze. Some critics judged them to be absolutely terrible, totally incompatible with Janis's voice, and some depressing audience figures resulted.

Around this time she overdosed on heroin and had to be slapped back to life by two friends.

Her stage performances had become very raunchy, and profanities rife as she spun her lewd stories of sexual abandon. Towards the end of 1969 the Kozmic Blues tour reached Florida, scene of Jim Morrison's notorious audition for *Hair*. Janis, irritated by old-fashioned auditorium rules that prevented people from dancing and enjoying her show, used 'vulgar and indecent language' at a show in Tampa to get her point across. She was fined $200 and her reputation as a far-from-safe bet increased.

She attempted to kick heroin the following month, December, but failed. A few intellectual conversations with her specialist on the nature of obsessive behaviour were not much use in the real world. There was an element of superwoman about her boasts – she shot this, she drank this amount, she slept with all these guys – and her ego was in an eggshell state. On the one hand, she knew she was unique, she was the greatest. On the other hand, she liked to hear people say it.

Her reactions to heroin were pretty abnormal. Instead of it draining her sex drive, which is what it's famous for, it seemed to fuel it, and her constitution enabled her to withstand days when heroin was not available. She never shot up before a show, but she definitely did so afterwards, trying to maintain the comfort and warmth of perform-ance. It did not necessarily work. 'On stage I make love to 25,000 people,' she was famous for saying. 'But I'm going home alone.'

In a once-and-for-all effort to come off the drug she went to Brazil for a vacation, where, apart from a motor-cycle accident, she had a great time. Clean, in the compa-ny of a caring man, seriously happy in Rio, she neverthe-less scored smack the minute her plane touched down in Los Angeles. Surrounded by fellow addicts, spongers, leeches and outright thieves, she was hopelessly lost.

Convinced that she was destined to marry the American football star Joe Namath, whom she had met only once, she slumped deeper into a junk morass, emerg-ing only when her best friend and flatmate walked out in disgust.

She split up the Kozmic Blues band shortly afterwards and formed her final and best band, Full-Tilt Boogie. To complete the image she brought a problem of full-tilt alco-holism that saw her seek psychiatric help in the middle of 1970. However, that ended in failure – her analyst only told her what she already knew, that she'd have to change her lifestyle.

What she *did* change was her name. From then on she took to calling herself 'Pearl', the title of a future LP. In Pearl was entrusted the sacred rites of performance – the imploring screech of rejection and betrayal that gave voice to the clenched fists, the bottle by her side, the manic danc-ing – while Janis got on with the serious business of trying desperately to come off heroin. But, disillusioned with straightness and bored with life, she talked of suicide or, at the very least, a massive re-appraisal of her new drug-free existence. Fascinated by the live-fast die-young legend of blues singer Bessie Smith, she started to consider herself one of the doomed ones, destined never to see 30.

The very real possibility that she would get married – and quit having to always sing the blues – arose in the summer of 1970, during which Janis gave sobriety a chance and appeared to mellow out considerably. But it only took one short separation from her fiancé to bring on the loneliness and she started to mess with heroin again in September, while she was recording what would be her final album. The death of Jimi Hendrix could not shake her out of it; not even dire predictions of moons in Scorpio could shake her out of it. And, following a huge injection of heroin at her Hollywood hotel, she blacked out, fell, hit her head and died sometime in the early hours of 4 October 1970.

The official cause of death was accidental overdose of heroin. It was pointed out that, after months of liberation from the drug, her tolerance level would have been very low.

The tributes were oddly muted. Everyone seems to have seen it coming. Her fellow musicians in the San Francisco community were almost flippant about it, muttering inane platitudes and defending heroin to the end. A typical yeah-well-life-goes-on quote came from The Grateful Dead's organist Ron 'Pigpen' McKernan, himself a disciple of the bottle. He planned a tribute of the most personal kind. 'When I get a few days I'm gonna sit and get *ripped* on Southern Comfort.'

Unfortunately Pigpen probably did just that, several thousand times over. He died, a shrivelled alcoholic cartoon of his former burly self, of acute liver failure, stomach haemorrhages and internal organ wastage, in March 1973. He was aged 27, exactly the same age in death as Janis Joplin.

Boy George

The story of how Boy George went from being unequivo-
cally the smash hit of 1983 to the tabloid stooge of 1986 to
the sad cabaret artist of 1988 is, if nothing else, a cautionary tale in media manipulation.

George Alan O'Dowd trod the usual path of the true
rock 'n' roll rebel/victim. Expelled from school for insub-
ordination, he drifted into an underground London society of drag artists, performance artists and piss artists. He
was by no means the most outrageous of them, but he was
easily the most talented. His voice was assured and soulful, and he made the transition from merely going to clubs
to actually appearing at them when he was snapped up by
Malcolm McLaren as co-singer for the band Bow Wow
Wow. This was not just a safety measure against the band's
teenage singer Annabella quitting, but also a testament to
George's striking looks and voice. While he was in Bow
Wow Wow he called himself ' Lieutenant Lush'.

Worries over McLaren's influence led to his departure
from the band. Besides he had ideas of his own, and soon,
with the addition of Jon Moss, Roy Hay and Mikey Craig,
an interesting multi-coloured funk-toting four-piece.
Culture Club, was conceived. The end result was probably
nowhere near as cynical as it looked. But the happy mix of
colours and images, to say nothing about the rumours concerning exactly who if any in the band was gay, got the
word around. After a couple of minor hits they had a huge
number one success in 1982 with the song 'Do You Really
Want To Hurt Me'.

The music press had been courting him for years, since
his arrival on the club scene, but when the daily tabloids
were faced for the first time with the unashamedly
androgynous George, the results were predictable: 'Is It A
Her? A Him? Or Is It Neither?' .'Mister (Or Is It Miss?)

451

Weirdo' ... He even won the nauseating Nina Myskow Wally Of The Week Award.

When they found out that he was not a freak and indeed had not only a mind of his own but the vocabulary to express it, their claws retracted a good deal. The tabloids even began to interview George, drawing supposedly outrageous quotes from him about how he preferred a cup of tea to sex. He was hardly ever out of the pop gossip columns. The greatest tribute a singer can receive – the *Daily Mirror* Personality Of The Year Award – adorned his mantelpiece for two years in a row.

And all the while hordes of lookalikes – mostly girls, for some reason – followed him in every conceivable fashion style. The records he made with Culture Club – 'Time (Clock Of The Heart)', 'Church Of The Poison Mind', 'Karma Chameleon' – outdid each other on the dance-floors and in the charts, and his got-it-flaunt-it style even provoked comment from Princess Margaret ('Who's that over-made-up tart?').

The problem only started when the hits stopped, when George ceased to be the charming vamp in flagrant delicto and began to look vulnerable. By 1986 Culture Club were finished. A string of mediocre records and a blatant lack of number one singles convinced the fickle teenage armies that more exciting thrills lay elsewhere, and George went the way of The Bay City Rollers and Adam Ant before him. Forced to rely exclusively on musical content, he was found wanting. The tabloids hissed a little and sat back waiting for the first mistake.

George had made anti-drug statements in the past and had persuaded most people that he was much too happy in the high life to mess with narcotics. So it was a genuine shock when the story of his heroin addiction broke in the pages of the *Daily Mirror* in June 1986. The George-as-junkie headlines were given even more lurid life by the fact that the information came from his brother. George had also given an interview to John Blake, writer of the *Mirror's* pop column, in which he let slip a few indiscretions. Now there was not only a George-on-heroin scandal, there was an O'Dowd-family-at-war scoop as well.

The detective work of Britain's second favourite daily paper was completed by the police, and in the second week of July Boy George was arrested and charged with heroin possession. Later that month he was found guilty, and fined £250.

The nightmare continued. The following month an American musician, Michael Rudetski, aged 27, died at George's Hampstead home. He was to have been a crucial integer in the Boy George comeback plan, being a master of the Fairlight computer. The inquest found traces of heroin and methadone in his blood.

A fortnight later George's friend Marilyn (Peter Robinson), who had been arrested in the same police operation – Operation Culture – was freed on heroin possession charges when the prosecution offered no evidence. The same week saw Radio One DJ's criticizing a song called 'Some Candy Talking', by the Jesus And Mary Chain, because it was 'obviously' about heroin ...

And still it would not stop. December saw a young employed man named Mark Golding, 20, collapse and die, this time at George's flat in Paddington. Again, heroin and methadone were found in his blood.

George disappeared, embraced Buddhism and seemed to be last year's news – used and rejected by his teenage fans in the manner of The Bay City Rollers, Kajagoogoo and Nik Kershaw – when suddenly there came news that he had cleaned up and was ready to stage a comeback.

The comeback was quite surprisingly successful. Releasing a cover version of David Gate's slushy but tuneful 'Everything I Own', George made it back to pole position in the charts. And he had another number one record later in 1987 as a member of 'Ferry Aid'. Now this was ironic. In an effort to raise money for the families of victims of the Zeebrugge ferry disaster, many of whom had won the trip through their competition, *The Sun* set up a super-group of media alumni, including various EastEnders characters, Page 3 girls, newsreaders and Paul McCartney. And Boy George, who perhaps had reason to hate the tabloid press more than any living human being, accepted the invitation.

Sadly, the comeback faltered on the third or fourth single. It remains to be seen how George O'Dowd will survive the Nineties as a worldly-wise, once-proud musician.

Jimi Hendrix

On 18 September 1970, Jimi Hendrix, the man who did more than anyone to erase the barriers between black and white music, took several sleeping tablets. The normal dose for the pills he used is one half. Hendrix died after inhaling his own vomit.

The sordid circumstances of his death were a shocking conclusion to a life which, since early 1967, had been phenomenally successful. There were those who remember him as a sad man, perhaps even a manic depressive (a song called 'Manic Depression' appears on his first album, *Are You Experienced*). Eric Burdon of The Animals claimed at the time of Hendrix's death to be in possession of a Hendrix poem which bore traces of a suicide note. Observers at close quarters of his astonishing guitar could perceive scars on his wrists where the slash marks of the past had attempted to heal.

Like the best legends. Hendrix's death is much better documented than his birth. The most likely date is 27 November 1942, which would have put him at 27 when he died. The *Rolling Stone* obituary had him as 24. Other publications have suggested that he could have been born in the late Thirties. Whatever the date, the location was Seattle, Washington. He learned to play guitar when he was ten, holding it upside down to compensate for his left-handedness.

After a brief spell in the US Airborne Paratroopers (he was discharged with a back injury) he began to tout for work, playing with The Isley Brothers and Little Richard among others. He quickly won a reputation as a virtuoso, although his stage act was not yet the petroleum-fuelled extravaganza that would make him the smash hit of Monterey and Woodstock.

One night he was discovered playing in a New York club by Chas Chandler, the bassist with The Animals (Chas later went on to manage Slade, thereby embodying the spirit of bathos), and was persuaded to go to England. Chandler was convinced – correctly, as it turned out – that Hendrix's gifts would be better appreciated in the some-what smaller pond. Returning as a mighty fish in 1967, he had to persuade the Americans that he was one of them and not some crazy English eccentric.

Chandler put him in touch with two English musicians, Noel Redding (bass) and Mitch Mitchell (drums) and the trio began to play gigs as The Jimi Hendrix Experience. The vibe spread through the underground that a new gui-tar genius was performing all sorts of tricks and making the local heroes look pretty humble.

His wild looks and psychedelic apparel, in tandem with the raw heat of his music, had a sensational effect on audi-ences. When he played a mundane song like 'Wild Thing' he injected it with a sense of swooping hysteria, played guitar with his teeth, behind his back, between his legs, and eventually actually set fire to the poor instrument to howls of anguish from the fretboard.

He made great records too – 'Hey Joe', 'Purple Haze', 'The Wind Cries Mary', all perfectly in synch with the Summer of Love and the mindblowing decisions of stoned youth. Europe bowed to him and his success in many countries came literally overnight.

When the Jimi Hendrix Experience played at the Monterey Festival in 1967 it was, incredibly, the band's US debut. They went on stage and immediately defined the event – cool, loud, colourful and ebullient. The lighter fluid came out at the end and up went the guitar. How he must have grinned when The Who passed him on their way to the stage – the world's most notorious destroyers of expensive electronic hardware just about usurped by a frizzy-haired unknown.

His records became more and more adventurous. His third album, *Electric Ladyland*, which achieved some renown quite unconnected with the music when the punters saw the bevy of totally naked women who adorned the cover, was a wonderful tour de force. But there was dissension in the ranks of The Experience, especially from bassist Noel Redding. Hendrix had always written and sung the songs, and was wont to produce them too, but on the cover of *Ladyland* there was an additional credit to Hendrix for 'direction'. Redding, possibly feeling himself relegated to teaboy status, rebelled and the result was the break-up of the band.

Hendrix formed a new trio, which he called The Band Of Gypsies, with the help of Billy Cox (bass) and Buddy Miles (drums). Gone were the flash pyrotechnics, in came some serious guitar studies. Hendrix only played two concerts with the band. The second was stopped midway through by the man himself, who announced to the audience, 'I'm sorry but we're not quite getting it together', and walked off.

When he died in September in London he had only released four official studio albums. Thereafter a flood of material from the Hendrix vaults saturated the market, a lot of which was woefully half-finished. One track which certainly was finished was the single 'Voodoo Chile' which provided him with his only (posthumous) UK number one.

The legend lives in other places than record racks. Everyone who made his acquaintance was flabbergasted by his drug intake. 'He was the heaviest doper I ever met', said Eric Burdon. He did not hide this fact. On trial for possession of heroin in Toronto in 1969, he argued that he had been the dupe of a generous fan. However, he admitted that he had mused most drugs. He was acquitted.

Most people's abiding memory of Hendrix is the terrific butchery he perpetrated on 'The Star Spangled Banner' at the Woodstock Festival in 1969. The story goes that, when he was through hacking at the sacred song of America, the audience were in such stunned catatonic silence that the ensuing applause which can be heard on the record and film of the event had to be edited in later.

His guitar innovations live on in the efforts of more meagre talents and his stage mayhem all looks pretty tame in the cold light of the late Eighties. But while he burned, the music and the smell were of molten gold, and God knows he was a voodoo chile.

Brian Epstein

The young Brian Epstein had been a failure at school, a failure in the army and a failure at acting. That he was suddenly a success at business surprised and delighted his family. He had taken over the record department in the Liverpool branch of the family NEMS store. He built it into one of the North's most important record stores.

Everything was going swimmingly until one day a young man named Raymond Jones came into the store and requested a record that Epstein had never head of – 'My Bonnie' by Tony Sheridan, notable for being the first Beatles recording. Epstein prided himself on being the first to hear about new records but he was totally unaware of

The Beatles, even though they shopped at his store and he had probably seen them and served them.

He resolved to find out more about them. Therefore, one night he went to a local club called The Cavern where he had learned they would be playing. Swiftly locating a quiet corner where the cut of his suit and the brevity of his hair would not be noticed, he checked out The Beatles. He was immediately struck by their casual attitude and attire, and he saw a raw quality to the music that persuaded him to introduce himself to the band. There was something else, too. Epstein, whose sexual relations had been as doomed as his army career, was a homosexual and, to put it bluntly, he fancied them, especially the callow John Lennon, who was quite clearly the loudest, rudest and most outrageous musician he had ever come across.

Impressed by Epstein's enthusiasm and sweet-talked by his acumen, The Beatles agreed to be managed by him and he secured them a record deal with Parlophone after impressing the equally well-spoken George Martin, their future producer.

During the year 1962-63 Epstein became emperor of a recording syndicate that would make him one of the wealthiest figures in rock music. Having seen The Beatles spectacularly hit the upper reaches of the British charts, Epstein busied himself with a host of equally garrulous Liverpudlian wide boys. Gerry And The Pacemakers became history makers when their first three singles all reached number one, a feat unequalled until Frankie Goes To Hollywood in the Eighties. Billy J. Kramer, and his backing group The Dakotas, were an immediate success with a Beatles tune. And Priscilla White, the cloakroom attendant at The Cavern, became a star in the Epstein firmament when he renamed her Cilla Black; and a lifetime of nasal laughs and blind dates had been kickstarted into action. The stable in its entirely was a huge triumph, but it was The Beatles to whom he kept returning.

But the pressures of top-level involvement and the constant worries over 'his' boys and girls meant no sleep for Brian. His personal life was a mess of unfinished business and emotional dead-ends, and the attitude of The Beatles was invariably cold and cutting. However, when a split was mooted, the band stood by him and threatened to break up themselves rather than lose their manager.

Beatlemania reached the States, the Ed Sullivan Show kept juvenile crime off the streets of America for an entire hour, and Epstein's throne sparkled a little brighter with each catchy hit record. When The Beatles were awarded MBEs by Harold Wilson's forward-looking government it was Princess Margaret who asked if MBE stood for Mr Brian Epstein.

However, Epstein was not generally in a laughing frame of mind. His life was a succession of brief encounters punctuated by large intakes of barbiturates and amphetamines. Depression plagued him all day, and insomnia all night and, what was worse, The Beatles were outgrowing him. They had already decided to stop playing live – there was no point, nobody could hear them and only about 40 people could see them – and concentrate on the astonishing music they were getting out of the studio. Epstein's few attempts to influence the band's musical direction ended in humiliation, usually at the hands of Lennon.

After the last live show given by The Beatles, in San Francisco's Candlestick Park, Epstein attempted suicide, stricken by the emptiness of the future. His projects after the Beatles 'retired' were mixed and he took little pleasure in them. Eventually he entered a clinic where his condition was diagnosed as a mixture of depression, exhaustion and insomnia. The pessimism remained even after he left the clinic, and in August 1967 he died of an overdose of sleeping pills. He had been too depressed to remember how many he should take, so he had taken them all.

Iggy Pop

'I've been spit at, I've been slugged, I've been egged, I've been hit with paper clips, money, cameras, brassieres, underwear, old rags, and with expensive garments and belts and things. I've been hit with, well, a slingshot. Yeah, you just get used to it after a while.'

Play word games with the legend of Iggy Pop and you are liable to arrive at any or all of the following: a self-destructive lunatic; a messiah of sleaze; a poet; a drug-ravaged true survivor (just); a highly articulate and literate artist in the Warholian social realism mould; a drinking buddy of David Bowie's; the man who introduced spitting into the rock 'n' roll context, thereby providing legions of future British punks with a reason to live; the king of the whole damn slum.

Iggy Pop started life in a normal world, born James Osterberg on 21 April 1947. Suffering as a child from severe bronchial asthma he was molly-coddled all the more because of his tiny frame and babyish features. Even today, at 5 ft 1 in (155 cm) and despite the excursions to hell and back, Iggy still looks like a petulant kid.

Rock 'n' roll provided a cool outlet for his exhibitionist talents, and he started off playing drums for a local Michigan school band, The Iguanas, whence came the first half of his nickname.

After avoiding the draft by registering at the army barracks wearing nothing but a huge erection and claiming to be a homosexual, he formed The Stooges in Detroit in 1968. The line-up was completed by three like-minded square pegs, and they set about their native land with barely-controlled visceral glee.

Jim Morrison of The Doors had opened up whole new avenues of performance with his leather-clad whirling and regaling of the front rows. But Morrison was like a lounge lizard compared to Iggy.

For whereas The Doors perceived themselves as an intelligent and passionate blues group caught up through no fault of their own in distasteful displays of censorship and crowd control, The Stooges, although undeniably a far less popular group, were quite simply a violation of every prevailing rock 'n' roll dictum in the late sixties. Namely, that ye shall sing and play in tune: that the songs ye play shall have some degree of recognizable harmony, however scant and short-lived; and that ye shall at all times cater for and respect your audience, some of whom have paid good money to see you.

On vinyl, which basically amounted to three studio albums between the years 1969 and 1973, plus a live recording from which the passing of time could never wrestle the smouldering sense of violence, what The Stooges played was a fierce slovenly nowhere-bound doomed guerrilla guitar noise. This was laden with some marvellously basic wah wah effects and Iggy's primeval lyrics, most of which were dedicated to the pursuit of that all-important first sexual conquest.

Live, in the flesh, The Stooges, were, according to one's taste, one's worst nightmare or wildest dream come to life. While the neanderthals in the band laid down the basic uncompromising gonzo grunge, Iggy turned somersaults, contorted his short-arsed frame into terrible spastic statues, threw himself head first at the stage and screamed into the microphone. When he was done doing that he would slam the mike against his lips until the blood started to flow, scrape the mike stand against his puny body until the blood became a river (screaming all the while) and bang his head on the stage.

Then he would turn on the audience. Spotting a likely victim – preferably a couple – he would jump up on their table and launch horrifying screams of pure hatred in their faces. If this failed to provoke a reaction other than

461

stunned incomprehension he would smash the microphone into his mouth again, and bleed all over the table.
As a final party-piece, he would pick up the candle that
had stood on the (by now vacated) table, brandish it like
Neville Chamberlain, and slowly tilt it so that the hot wax
dripped all over his chest.

'Aaaaauuuuuggghhhhh,' he would scream. 'Aaaauu-
uggghhhhh.' And nobody could be quite sure if it was a
cry of pain or simply the next line of the lyrics.

The few people left in the audience would invariably
come out with shrewd observations on the lines of, 'If he
had done that 200 years ago he'd have been locked up.'

The compulsion that drove Iggy on was also driving
him to indulge in drug feasts. Once, showing extraordinary nerve, he entered the offices of Elektra Records and
demanded $400 to buy cocaine.

He also emulated Jim Morrison by exposing his genitals
on stage, although the authorities never seemed to care
what a glorious loser like Iggy Pop got up to in the heat of
the moment.

In 1971, when their record company rejected the tapes
for their third album, The Stooges combusted. Hooking up
with David Bowie, who would become his friend/men-
tor/lifesaver, Iggy embarked on phase two of The Stooges,
even more demented than the first.

Unfortunately The Stooges mark two had a bad time of
it, and a soul-destroying American tour so depressed them
that confrontation was inevitable. After receiving a beating
from a Michigan gang-member at one gig, Iggy went on
local radio and challenged the entire gang to come to the
evening's show and do their worst.

The recording of the consequences later became a cult
album, *Metallic KO*. Despite the atrocious lo-fi production
quality one can easily make out the sound of missiles hitting the stage, and Iggy provides a superb running commentary:

'Our next selection tonight for all you Hebrew ladies in the audience is entitled "Rich Bitch"... hey, I don't care if you throw all the ice in the *world* ... you're paying five bucks and I'm making ten thousand, baby! So screw ya!

'Well, well, ladies and gentlemen, thank you for your kind indulgence. I'm proud to present a song that was co-written by my mother entitled, "I've Got My Cock In My Pocket". One – two – *fuck you pricks!*

'Aaaah, it'll all be over soon ... (to female catcalls) I won't fuck you when I'm working. Anybody with any more ice cubes, jelly beans, grenades, eggs, they wanna throw at the stage, c'mon. You paid your money so you takes your choice, you know ... (Having introduced the band), and let's not forget your favourite well-mannered boy! The singer, let's hear it from the singer! I *am* the greatest Thanks for the egg. Do we have any more eggs? Ah, you missed, c'mon, try it again, c'mon! Listen, I've been egged by better than you. Is it time for a riot, girls? rii-iooottt!!! Lightbulbs too? Paper cups? (Huge crash) – Oh my we're getting violent ...'

Since the gory glory days Iggy has spent time in a mental hospital, on coke, on smack, on a golf course, and of course on stage. And while his albums aren't quite the devastating pillages of old, he's still the incomparable showman when the lights go down and the amps hit ten.

A footnote: at the 1988 Reading Festival many of the performers, including Meat Loaf and Bonnie Tyler, were assaulted by missiles and bottles of liquid of dubious extraction. Iggy Pop, the most bottled man on the entire bill, did his set to nothing more violent than thunderous applause.

Alice Cooper

The kid was adamant, 'You *suck!*' he berated Alice Cooper. Alice, who was born Vincent Furnier, a minister's son from the *right* side of the tracks (for a change), grinned and could not find it in his heart to disagree. He bent down so that his face was level with the heckler's and began to chant the word 'suck' over and over again.

The kid thought for a moment about his rejoinder.

'You *still* suck!' he cried.

That was 1970, when the love/hate relationship between America and the phenomenon known as Alice Cooper was at its most ambivalent. Before that they just hated him. Now, even in virtual middle age, they love him.

Alice Cooper was a Frank Zappa acolyte, trained in the use of shock tactics and rock 'n' roll attrition, who eventually outdid his teacher in the project of disgusting, unnecessarily gross images. If ever a performer deserved hanging it was Alice Cooper. Realizing this, he brought his own gallows on stage with him.

The decision to offend was probably made early on in Furnier's life when he saw The Rolling Stones and what they were getting away with. He formed a band of long-haired reprobates that toured the Michigan area to almost unanimous hostility, playing slab-like angst anthems over which Alice/Furnier howled his untutored vocals. The name Alice Cooper, he claimed, came from a ouija. The spirit they had contacted wanted to speak to 'Alice Cooper'. When asked who that meant, the spirit replied that it was Vincent Furnier.

In 1969 they met Shep Gordon, who became their manager. The circumstances gives some idea of the seriousness of the concept. Alice Cooper and band – they were bracketed as a collective entity, as though as much depravity could not exist in just one man – had reached Los Angeles

and were playing a prestige gig at a club there. When Alice
was a few songs into the set, something about the menacing leather gear, the whips, the realistic baby dolls that
were slaughtered, the live chickens that got molested, the
mock hanging of ringleader Alice for all these crimes, the
incessant fondling of of a morose-looking boa constrictor
and the stage blood everywhere inspired the audience en
masse to get up and leave. As Gordon put it, 'When I saw
2,000 people walk out on them, I knew I had to manage
them.'

Alice admitted that the act was '60 per cent' contrived.
His guitarist at the time put his finger on why people were
so distressed: 'Towards the end of the act people start to
realize that it's not going to stay on stage.'

The basis of the act has always been the execution of
Alice Cooper for various sins. This execution has come in
numerous forms. The gallows became a guillotine, which
in turn became the electric chair. And in order for this to
work, it is clear that some suitably nefarious deeds have to
be perpetrated first, so that Alice is seen to deserve this
punishment. Hence the baby mutilation, the chicken
killing, the debauchery.

Yvonne the boa constrictor was his slippery partner in
crime, casting her beady eyes over her master's mis-
deanors. The Freudian symbolism may have been lost on
the less intelligent youth who packed out his shows all
through the Seventies, but Alice thought it through. It was
inspired theatre and it smacked of danger.

This was because the boundaries of definition between
Alice Cooper and Vincent Furnier tended to be obscured
once Alice took the stage. Rather than acting out a part –
which would have been perfectly acceptable in the bogus
glam era – he actually *became* Alice. The crimes were simulated on stage, but they were real in his mind. And
although he invariably jokes about it now, it must have
been hell on earth coming off stage and finding oneself

back in the real world again. No wonder he became a chronic alcoholic.

The real world tried to catch him out. In 1974 a boy in Canada mimicked the mock hanging act and died. To his credit, Alice dropped the act. But Alice Cooper was becoming a threat to the internal welfare of Vincent Furnier, and in 1977 he sought medical assistance to try to keep his liver. He claimed never to have been sober from 1974 to 1977 and to have regularly put away forty cans of beer a day. His dry-out was a resounding success and Alice became something of a caricature from that point on.

Once people realized that Alice was a put-on the albums stopped doing as well, and Alice was courted as a kind of survivor-celebrity. He was a pretty good golf player, so he got invited to play pro-celeb tournaments. He even appeared on the gameshow, Hollywood Squares, in full make-up.

While the group Kiss – of even less musical know-how and even more shock appeal – won the appreciation of Alice's erstwhile armies of teenage fans, the man himself mellowed on vinyl and even got a little introspective. The ironic thing is that, had they thought about it, his admirers would have seen far more outrageous success in playing golf with Bob Hope and annoying the heart of America at source, than in singing some loud brazen music to a few thousand already-converted kids.

Alice returned to the stage, with a show that lacked all the menace of the early ones but intensified the humour. Yvonne had been put out to grass, so her place was taken by Arnold (the boa constrictor), if anything an even more natural performer.

And every time he tours all the ingredients are still there. They just seem funnier now (are we all getting older?). The audience knows when to scream in ecstacy and when to scream in terror. There is no trouble. But perhaps Alice thinks back to the days of 1969, to the skin-of-the-teeth getaways.'

'A motorcycle gang rushed the stage in Michigan and tried to kill us,' he told a reporter in '69. 'It was great but we felt we had to get out of there.'

Lou Reed

From the moment he wrote a pop song called 'Heroin' and instantly doomed his then-band The Velvet Underground to a career totally unassisted by radio play, Lou Reed has probably offended more people more frequently than any other contemporary rock musician. His gruesome antics and supposed uncontrolled worship of every malevolent chemical have been exaggerated in the past – not least by the master storyteller himself – but the desire to appal has always been there at the back of his dark, cruelly witty mind.

Like Iggy Pop – perhaps even more so – Lou Reed is a man of extreme intelligence and articulacy. He can talk about himself far better than any writer can write about him. Even the greatest rock writer of them all, Detroit's Lester Bangs, was forced to admit defeat and join his hero in nothing more intellectual than a glorified drinking contest.

An early RCA press release from 1973, the year when Lou Reed had a surprise hit with the single 'Walk On The Wild Side', notes that most people were only then getting to hear Reed's music for the first time. His original band, The Velvet Underground, have without doubt influenced more British bands than anyone else in history. (They all get it hopelessly wrong, if you want to be like The Velvet Underground you jettison *all* influences and do your own thing with a scatting vengeance.) However, by virtue of the fact that Reed was writing, and boasting about having written, songs dealing with such non-Top 40 phenomena as hard drugs, sado-masochism, murder, prostitution and some mysterious den of depravity known casually as The Factory, which turned out to have Warholian connotations, America left them well and truly alone.

They had been formed in 1965 in New York by Reed. Other founder members were his buddy from university, Sterling Morrison on guitar, and a guy named John Cale who played bass but was a classically trained pianist and viola player. Cale had played with legendary underground avant-garde classical composer La Monte Young, doing such crazy things as bringing a plant onstage and screaming at it until it died, and taking part in piano marathons that were supposed to leave you emotionally drained at the end.

Reed himself had been a difficult child and at one stage his parents made him undergo electro-shock therapy for depression. His wealthy, upright family got him into Syracuse University, where he studied English under the poet Delmore Schwartz, a carefree bohemian alcoholic/paranoid whose hatred of pop music Reed later made reference to by dedicating The Velvets' song with fewest lyrics, 'European Son', to him. Lou Reed was by this time a drug taker of cavalier habits. He used heroin overtly and was eventually asked to leave.

After a dead-end job writing imitation pop songs to order for Pickwick Records (his best effort was 'The Ostrich' which introduced a new dance – you put your head on the floor and get your partner to step on it) The Velvets began to take shape. Very coolly at first, not really making any headway, until Andy Warhol turned up one night. This was the night. The Velvet Underground's sound proved to be substantially at odds with the requirements of New York's unhip club proprietors. Play that song – 'The Black Angel's Death Song' – one more time, they were told, and you're fired. The next night, they opened their set with it, drawing its spectacular viola rushes and speedy, uneasy lyrics out over 10, 15 minutes. Sure enough they were fired.

Warhol moved in, started to direct their career and introduced them to Gerard Malanga, the man with the whip who made The Velvet Underground's early performances a visual as well as an aural thrill. They also met Nico (real name Christa Paffgen) who was a European model of quite disconcerting beauty who had had a child by the French actor Alain Delon. In the end scant details emerged about her except that she was German, had appeared in Fellini's *La Dolce Vita* and had a stunning Teutonic whisper of a singing voice. Reed sat down to write some songs for her (Nico eventually came to live in England, having left The Velvets in 1968, and made several classic solo albums. A committed heroin addict, she died in 1988 on holiday in Spain. Death was attributed to heart failure.)

The first Velvet Underground LP was only noted that at the time (1967) for its weird cover – with the picture of an unpeeled banana. It was a Warhol idea and he signed it just in case people did not get the picture. Unpeeled sleeves are now almost priceless.

The music disappeared without trace. American music in 1967 meant Jefferson Airplane and The Grateful Dead, both of whom Reed loathed, and songs of vague, half-baked brotherly love. The black core of authenticity which featured in all The Velvets' songs of the street was the exact antithesis of the San Francisco hey-man-like-what's-happenin' types. In typically deadpan style, the LP came accompanied with its own bad reviews on the gatefold sleeve.

Their second LP, *White Light/White Heat*, was, if anything, even less enthusiastically received by the pop populace, although critics in certain quarters saw a vulnerable beauty to its spewing feedback-toting contents. Its longest and scariest song, 'Sister Ray', was a 17-minute epic the like of which nobody had ever heard: to an increasingly

frazzled backing noise of organ, guitars and barely audible
drums Reed recounts a tale of oral sex, murder, drag
queens, heroin injection and orgies of sex and violence.
The casual listener might just be able to decipher Reed's
flat voice mentioning something about 'sucking on his
ding-dong'. It was the ultimate one-take song.

The Velvet Underground became a marginally less
interesting band in 1968 when Reed fired Cale, and the LPs
they made until their combustion in 1970 were highly
melodic, almost spiritual in tone.

Reed's solo career got off to an inauspicious start with a
decidedly ropey eponymous album. But his 1972 effort,
the David Bowie-produced *Transformer,* was a great success and all of a sudden Reed found himself catapulted
into the front rooms of the western world on delivery of a
hit single, 'Walk On The Wild Side'. The song was a memorable juxtaposition of a suitably languid bass line and a
résumé of events at Andy Warhol's Factory. The people
mentioned in the song – Holly, Candy, Jackie and Joe –
were erotic freaks on the periphery of the art scene. To
judge by Reed's song they were already lost souls by the
time they made it to New York.

The song was a big hit in Britain, winning constant airplay, which was a source of much mirth in the hip press –
the foils at the BBC couldn't be too au fait with US slang, it
was said, or else they would surely have baulked at the
line, 'But she never lost her head/Even when she was giving head'. And if nothing else, at least 'Walk On The Wide
Side' got feminine shaving mentioned in a song for the
first time.

The sight of Lou Reed was still something that the public at large were not adequately geared for, however, and
the image was becoming more and more uncompromising. The odd transvestite reference in the song was compounded by Reed's propensity for eyeliner. In the early
Seventies he and David Bowie (and to a lesser extent Brian

Eno of Roxy Music) crossed a great many barriers with regard to androgyny in rock.

Bisexuality fascinated Reed, just as it did Bowie, and, like Bowie, Reed liked to write about it. And, like Bowie, he was married. The edges blur on many of his songs; it's not clear if the relationship he is alluding to at a given point is straight or gay. He relished the confusion, and in interviews he slipped in additional teasers, intimating that the two topics that interested him most were devil worship and suicide.

The awful pain of listening to the entire contents of *Berlin,* the 1973 album on which Reed's concerns with self-destruction, dope, bad sex and suicide gelled horrifically, tends to detract from its more straightforward, *musical* strengths. Listening to Reed recount the squalid tale of Caroline, the beautiful junkie slut whose artistic aspirations die like butterflies by the Berlin Wall, and her loser husband Jim, is an unsettling, almost voyeuristic experience. As the couple's kids are taken away by the authorities and Caroline kills herself in desperation, the listener concedes that this is the single most depressing record ever made. This record probably killed off the cosy drag image, showing Reed to be an expert on more than just matters chemical.

The album also saw the nervous breakdown of its producer, Bob Ezrin, who made the terrible mistake of trying to keep up with Reed. His habits steered him toward total collapse.

The brilliance of *Berlin* was not widely acknowledged. In fact, the record was savagely panned for its indulgence (how can one write about suicide and *not* be indulgent?) and the attacks took personal form. Most writers agreed that Reed's lowlife trawls were a bit distasteful. Well, sure. And the album's closing song is not called 'Sad Song' for nothing. But, one of them conceded, at least it was good to see Lou writing about heterosexuals again.

One of the problems people had with the record – and others made by Lou Reed – was the attitude of the artist. His famous deadpan drawl, a 'monotone of nuances' as one writer put it, adopts a dispassionate, purely journalistic stance. Not pro, not anti, just *there*. And for him to paint a musical picture of a crumbling marriage and a decaying life in which hopes of reconciliation and rejuvenation are not even entertained was clearly to invite antagonism.

More ill feeling was encountered on the *Berlin* tour. An overriding sense of violence became the reality of personal assaults, as Reed laid his menacing street voodoo on the audiences. His fans, recently swayed to the cause in the wake of 'Walk On The Wild Side' and certainly in no sober state to consider Reed as a bona fide artist, behaved like idiots and thugs, believing that this was expected of them. As for the man himself, stage performances became extraordinary exercises in self-loathing. All done up in whiteface, lipstick, eyeliner and leather, he stalked the stage as his second-degree heavy metal band played havoc with the subtleties of 'Heroin' and 'Sweet Jane'.

The subtext suggested that Lou was lost and sure enough the image altered drastically in a matter of weeks. The hair was shaved off to accommodate a Swastika clipped into the remaining blonde thatch; he looked pipe-cleaner thin and he didn't blink – no once.

1974 saw him take up with the notorious Rachel, a half Mexican transsexual whose undeniable delectability was slightly undermined by the quarter-inch stubble that shadowed his/her face. A lifetime of reformatories and prisons made Rachel the perfect companion for Reed. The resulting tour, during which he promoted his *Sally Can't Dance* album (the reason Sally couldn't dance was because she was dead, of a drug overdose), had Reed peroxide his hair, put on some nail varnish, shed another perilous few pounds, highlight the iron cross and depress every critic who saw the show.

Typically, the critics' wrath was compensated for by the antics of the dumb Quaalude quorum who yelped their way through 'Heroin', lazily overlooking its lyrical skill and assuming it to be something between an artist's tribute to his muse and an ideal for living.

The whole sorry business reached its stultifying conclusion in December 1974. 'Heroin' became a party piece, a vehicle for a true moronic showbiz gimmick in which Reed produced a syringe, wrapped the microphone cord tight around his arm to bring up a vein, and simulated the act of injection. At least it was *assumed* he simulated it. Later Reed claimed never to have shot heroin, although the methamphetamine in his bloodstream presumably didn't get there by accident.

There was deep concern about his welfare. Sometimes he was violent and unhinged. Other times he just did not seem to be there at all. Talking backstage with Mick Jagger at a Madison Square Garden gig, he was asked if he had ever played there before. 'How the fuck should I know?' he replied.

In 1975 Lou Reed shocked, flummoxed and appalled his few straggling disciples with the release of an album ominously entitled *Metal Machine Music*. The reviews of *Berlin* were as nothing compared to the outburst of sheer visceral hated directed at the 64 minutes and four seconds of *Metal Machine*.

Lou doesn't exactly play on it; no-one does. And he doesn't sing; there aren't any words. What you get is just over an hour of shrieking electronic fury in the form of a non-stop drone, a couple of bleeps and the odd motif of a tune. The album was not, it must be stressed, played for laughs. Nor was there a surfeit of rib-tickling when Reed acolytes purchased the record in their local shop. Copies were returned in droves and RCA, who had actually been thinking of releasing it on their classical Red Seal label, were forced to make an apology. Reed defended the album

in strong terms, calling it 'the closest I've ever come to perfection; it's the only record I know that *attacks* the listener'.
It certainly attacked the poor wretches who forked out the
hard-earned cash for it and sat wondering if may be there
had been a fault at the pressing plant.

He also indignantly refuted rumours that sides three
and four were merely sides one and two backwards, something suggested by the fact that each side lasted exactly 16
minutes and one second.

This whole question of recording, for posterity and
judgment by one's peers, what seems at the time to be a
good idea typifies Lou Reed's career, it is a career unparal-
leled in its variety (only Marlon Brando's acting career,
with its troughs of garbage and peaks of genius, comes
close), and the zenith and the nadir are so far apart that
one forgets what each looks like and they keep getting
mistaken for each other. Now, years later, as the act of a
madman, or an incorrigible drug fiend, or simply an artist
who wasn't very together, *Metal Machine Music* makes
sense. Once you have been written off as a completely
unreliable chemist's shop there isn't much you can do to
shock people Rock 'n' roll as a two-fingered gesture is
quite often the only recourse.

Lou wasn't finished.

After a brace of decent rock 'n' roll returns to form, he
made a live album called *Take No Prisoners*. There aren't
many live albums like it, certainly not in the rock context.
Lenny Bruce fronting The Doobie Brothers might have
made something similar. Amid a torrent of foul language
and off-the-cuff observations he takes verbal revenge on
the press.

Ironically, the two critics he chooses to badmouth,
Robert Christgau of *Village Voice* and John Rockwell of the
New York Times, were actually fans. But neither had been
too chuffed with Lou's vinyl indiscretions in the past, and
both had laid into *Metal Machine Music*. Reed asks

rhetorically what Christgau gets up to in bed and wonders if he might be a 'toefucker'. Rockwell fares a little better, although Reed gives him a hard time for calling him 'Mr Reed' in his articles.

He starts to sing 'Walk On The Wild Side' and comes in on the wrong beat. 'I have no attitude without a cigarette,' he says. 'I'd rather die of cancer than be a faggot. That wasn't an anti-gay remark. Coming from me that's a compliment. It's like going to bed with a brontosaurus, it's out of style.'

In another selected outburst he declares, 'I do Lou Reed better than anybody, so I thought I'd get in on it.'

It was once pointed out that the quicker you say 'Lou Reed' the closer it sounds to 'lurid'. Fair enough, he has documented activities and personalities that less honest writers would gratefully leave alone. But anyone who can sum up a character, a philosophy, a life force, maybe even an entire generation in one line has got to be considered a major contributor to the human controversy. For the record, that line goes, 'You know some people ain't got no choice and they could call their own, so the first thing that they see that allows them the right to be, they follow it. You know it's called ... back luck.'

David Bowie

In April 1971 a strange record hit the shops of Britain. Not overwhelmingly strange in content, although the music was forbidding and dark and the lyrics showed a strong fascination with mental illness. What was strange about it was the cover. It was a photo of a man in a dress.

To be precise, it was a photo of David Bowie in a dress, lounging on a couch with one hand stroking his hair and the other holding a playing card. The dress was one of six that he had bought from a hip London boutique. The album was called *The Man Who Sold The World* and it was not a huge commercial success.

The music world had already heard of David Bowie by 1971. As a veteran of various R&B and mod bands during the mid-Sixties he had earned some renown as an okay singer and fair saxophonist. He had also had a top five hit in 1969, with the weird death-in-the-capsule song 'Space Oddity'.

By the time the newspapers caught up with him in 1971-72 Bowie had tired of the obscurity in which his life threatened to remain. On the wings of a spectacular publicity campaign spearheaded by his manager Tony De Fries, Bowie urged to look, talk, act and dress like a star. Eventually, pop music being what it is, he became a star. The outrage, however, the love of the good scam and the memorable quote, they had all been implanted several years previously ...

David Robert Jones was born in January 1947 in Brixton. A member of a large, interweaving family, he was attached as a child to his half-brother Terry, who was ten years older than him.

The family was noted for the streak of schizophrenia which paralysed first David's grandmother, then his aunt and finally his half-brother. Fears that he too may be afflicted with the illness led him to reject his family at the first opportunity; he has also claimed to be terrified of psychiatrists.

At the age of 15 David had a fight with a school friend in which the muscles in his left eye were irreparably damaged. The pupil would not close, and to this day his eyes are oddly unmatched: one is blue, the other grey and the pupils vary substantially in size.

A more lurid schooldays escapade concerns his early sexual experiences. 'It didn't really matter who or what it was with,' he has said, 'as long as it was a sexual experience. So it was some very pretty boy in class in some school or other that I took home and neatly fucked on my bed upstairs.'

David had been playing guitar at school and had taken saxophone lessons from the noted jazz saxophonist Ronnie Ross (who would much later play the sax break on Lou Reed's 'Walk On The Wild Side', a Bowie co-production). In 1962 David joined his first group, The Kon-Rads and had a preliminary bash at song-writing.

Leaving them to join The King Bees, one of whom, George Underwood, was the same chap who had injured David's eye in the school playground, he started out on an R&B imitation trip, singing in a pseudo-black style. That was exactly what The Rolling Stones were doing, and people were certainly taking notice. A record deal resulted, although the song itself was a flop.

Linking up with a budding authentic R&B combo called The Manish Boys he continued to pursue the American dream, and built up a strong support with his audiences. Dominating the group right from the off, he also took care of the interviews, one of which was with Cliff Michelmore on 'Tonight'. David was defending the civil rights of long-haired men everywhere. 'For the last two years we've had comments like "Darling" and "Can I carry your handbag" thrown at us and I think it just has to stop now.'

It was with The Manish Boys that his 'camp' stage act started to alienate the provincials in the audience, and quick exits from greaser ballrooms were often necessary.

Eventually, the failure of Manish Boy vinyl to set the world alight precipitated David's departure and in 1965 he joined a viable professional recording outfit called The Lower Third. His split from them in January 1966 was brought about by a failure amongst group members to realize who exactly was the star of the show. David Jones became David Bowie and from now on any people he played with would be very definitely his backing band.

A few mod excursions came and went, as did several record deals, until at last the Bowie composition 'Space Oddity', the story of Major Tom's hassles with the circuits, struck oil in 1969, the year of Neil Armstrong. The song was a huge success at the time and an even bigger one when it was re-released in 1975.

The songs Bowie was now writing were entertaining themes of darkness, evil and insanity. Scared of LSD because of its links with mental instability and schizophrenia, and living in close proximity to Terry, he started to genuinely experiment with his lyrics, asking huge, unanswerable questions and coming up with great responsive shrugs like: 'I'd rather stay here/With all the madmen/For I'm quite content/They're all as sane as me.'

That song, 'All The Madmen', was one of the tracks on the controversial-cover album, *The Man Who Sold The World*.

By now Bowie was married, to Angie Barrett, a fiercely free-thinking American girl whose curriculum vitae included her expulsion from college for having an affair with another female student and the intriguing fact that when she and David Bowie met for the first time, they were both sleeping with the same person.

In Angie, Bowie had a willing partner in crime and slowly the great stardom and world domination started to gain momentum. The whole thing gelled when Tony De Fries came on the scene, a man whose ruthless ambition matched Bowie's own, and whose business acumen would be the perfect counterpart to the artist's rock 'n' roll excesses.

The first hint that this might be a brilliantly productive partnership came on a trip to New York in 1971. Urged by De Fries at all times to think 'star', Bowie travelled first-class and behaved like Mae West after a particularly anxious hour in front of a mirror. He got to meet Elvis, Lou Reed and Iggy Pop, and elements of all these diffuse performers would be meshed together in the single most ingenious musical creation of the Seventies, Ziggy Stardust.

Ziggy would be an alien who comes to earth and is hailed as a rock stair. The album which came out in 1972, *The Rise And Fall Of Ziggy Stardust And The Spiders From Mars*, was an undeniably fine record, but it was the concerts that were thrown to promote it which secured, then and for all time, David Bowie's reputation as one of the most extraordinary characters in rock 'n' roll.

Before all that, however, one more media master-stroke was needed.

In an interview with *Melody Maker* David Bowie became the first rock star to admit to being gay. 'I'm gay and always have been,' he said, 'even when I was David Jones.' Asked why he wasn't wearing his woman's dress, he sighed, 'Oh dear, you must understand that it's not a woman's, it's a man's dress.' The article was published with a Bowie song title as its headline: 'Oh You Pretty Thing'. All of a sudden every journalist in the land wanted to talk to David Bowie.

The Ziggy tour electrified Britain. Working as bizarre intergalactic duo, Bowie and his lead guitarist, former Hull municipal gardener Mick Ronson, played off each other, Bowie simulating fellatio on Ronson's guitar, Ronson pouting away like a coquettish French maid.

The tour wound up at the Royal Festival Hall, at a Save The Whale benefit. The ensuing press was ecstatic. There was just one thing – De Fries had denied the press access to Bowie for the foreseeable future. He was, after all, just too big a star to be messing around with hacks, right? The public were left starved of Bowie so that the merest hint of activity was liable to lead to mass hysteria. Meanwhile Bowie was beginning his jet set period, being driven everywhere in limos, protected by gigantic bodyguards. The product was being marketed, and the market was drooling in expectation.

Anything with Bowie's name on it would do. Career-reviving Bowie productions for Mott The Hoople, Lou Reed and Iggy Pop kept him busy during 1972. On a gruelling tour of the States, during which he collapsed with exhaustion, the line between Ziggy and the frail, artistic performer whose job it was to 'play' him every night was beginning to blur.

After a disastrous show at Earl's Court and a monstrously long British tour, Bowie made the following announcement at Hammersmith Odeon on independence Day, 1973. 'This has been one of the greatest tours of our lives, and of all the shows on this tour this particular show will remain with us the longest because not only is it the last show in the tour, but it's the last show we'll ever do.' The audience, stunned and hurt, launched into a spontaneous wail of 'Noooooooo!!!!' and some even began to cry.

Bowie was not retiring as such. He was merely getting rid of one of the problems. Unable to be totally sure who was David Bowie and who was Ziggy, he killed the alien off. The guest list at the party after the show gives some indication of the status that the Bowie phenomenon had attained – the Jaggers, Tony Curtis, Ryan O'Neal, Peter Cook and Dudley Moore, Elliott Gould, they all came to pay their respects to the prettiest star of all.

'I became Ziggy Stardust,' he said later. 'Everybody was convincing me that I was a Messiah ... I got hopelessly lost in the fantasy.'

Bowie, deadened by years of hassles with musicians, did not baulk at sacking the Spiders From Mars, his backing band, when the tour finished. He kept Mick Ronson, had a quick rethink, and entered the next phase, the horror of 1984 and the apocalypse that caused it.

The album that resulted, *Diamond Dogs* (on which Bowie usurped Ronson and played the guitar parts

himself), is an edgy, almost visual document in music of
Orwell's famous novel. The show that promoted it was a
theatrical tour de force. The cityscape around him may
have been disintegrating, but he was creating new music,
new drama. But there was one ingredient that was making
the trip an especially risky one.

Shattered from his ridiculously heavy schedule and the
physical exertions on stage, Bowie began to use cocaine.
People around him noticed stark changes in personality
when he was taking coke – and he seemed to become
hooked pretty quickly. 'I had more than a passing relationship with drugs.' He said later. 'Actually I was zonked out
of my mind. One winter's day, three days before
Christmas, a friend pulled me over to the mirror and said,
'Look at us both ... if you continue to be the way you are at
the moment you'll never see me again, you're not worth
the effort.' After that I locked all my characters away forever.'

The drug-ravaged Bowie was now a gaunt, hollow-
cheeked stick insect for all to see. He was subsequently to
describe the years 1975-76 as 'probably the worst year or
year and a half of my life'. Ironically, some of his most
compelling music dates from precisely that period, with
the 1976 album *Station to Station* being a strong contender
for his best ever album.

He had broken free of De Fries in early 1975, sick of the
constant pressures of stardom, and De Fries got one of the
most lucrative pay-offs in legal history. There was even a
proviso that De Fries heirs could claim royalties from sales
of Bowie albums made between 1972-82 in the future from
Bowie heirs. But David Bowie had finally bought freedom.

One of the first things to do to clean his act up was
move out of Los Angeles, the city he had inhabited since
Diamond Dogs. Calling it 'the most vile piss-pot in the
whole world ... the scariest movie ever written,' he suggested in 1980 that the place 'should be wiped off the face

of the earth.'

With the help of his aide/manager Corinne Schwab and his friend and rival in drug overload, Iggy Pop, Bowie underwent something of a transformation on his 1976 'Thin White Duke' tour, coming across as a cool Sinatra type, aloof from his audience, bathed in white light. The shows had a strong European flavour, influenced at least as far as the set was concerned, by impressionist film-directors and surrealist painters. He was also getting heavily into Brecht, the German dramatist, and, more disturbingly, architects of Nazi propaganda such as Albert Speer, who had designed the Nuremberg Stadium in such a way that Hitler's position in the centre would be highlighted by white light.

Around this time Bowie was invoking Hitler in interviews, at first with tongue firmly wedged in cheek ('I think I might have been a bloody good Hitler. I'd be an excellent dictator. Very eccentric and quite mad'). But then it got a bit more serious. 'I believe very strongly in fascism. People have always responded better under a regimental leadership. He also called Hitler 'one of the first rock stars'. And Britain, he believed, 'could benefit from a fascist leader. After all, fascism is really nationalism.'

The nightmare intensified in May 1976 when Bowie arrived in London for some Wembley shows. Emerging at Victoria Station dressed in a brown shirt, he was ushered into a black Mercedes Benz. He stood up to greet the people who had flocked to see him and was snapped in midwave. The photograph which resulted was damning and explicit – there, in all his puerile trash rock glory, was David Bowie giving the Nazi salute. The image lingered for many years, despite protestations that it was only a harmless wave, and that anyway it was all done with irony, and besides it was during a way mixed-up period of his life, and what's so bloody serious about a bit of rock 'n' roll theatre anyway?

Then Bowie went to live in Berlin, where he recorded his *Low* album and worked on Iggy's *The Idiot*. He took inspiration from the Berlin Wall, did some shopping and sailed around the various Strassen without being recognized. The *Low* album, perfectly titled, stands as his most depressive work ever. Some of the songs he could not even bring himself to write lyrics for. The reviews were scathing. One writer called it 'an act of purest hatred and destructiveness', another 'Hunnish'.

In 1980 the stormy and irregular marriage between Bowie and his wife Angie ended in divorce. It was an acrimonious business, with great amounts of money being at stake, as well as the custody of their child, Zowie (he later expressed the understandable wish to be addressed as 'Joe').

Angie had been displaying signs of erratic behaviour for a while. She had attacked her lover, guitarist Keeth (sic) Paul, and attempted suicide a couple of times. David told the court she was an unfit mother and a drug addict. In the end she got a large settlement and he got custody of his son.

In 1983 he returned to the arena with the upbeat, optimistic *Let's Dance* album and a string of sell-out concerts. The image was scrupulously clean, the conversations peppered with tributes to his son and he revealed that he went to bed at ten and got up at six.

In January 1985 his half-brother Terry committed suicide by throwing himself under a train near the mental hospital where he had been living on and off since 1969. Bowie went a message to the funeral. It read: 'You've seen more things than we could imagine, but all these moments will be lost, like tears washed away by the rain.'

The David Bowie of the late Eighties is not, it has to be said, a very interesting figure. At Live Aid he delighted the audience by dedicating his song 'Heroes' to the children of the world, and by hammering it up on video in a duet with

Mick Jagger of the old Motown classic, 'Dancing In The Streets'. But the dangerous charges of the past are not working any more, and the songs are not the mysteries of the inner sanctum that made, say, *Hunky Dory*, such a great record. Drug-free, sane and happy, David Bowie sings his old songs in concert now as if they were written by a slightly wacky young nephew. See what you make of this, he smirks, as 'Rebel Rebel' starts up, reminding us of what a wide and mighty ravine separates art and artifice.

Ozzy Osbourne

In the entire sphere of rock 'n' roll, no character exists like John 'Ozzy' Osbourne. At no point along the circumference can anyone of a similarly irresponsible persuasion be found; and to go off at a tangent, never have so many appallingly pithy one-liners emanated from such a mundane music-maker. As a writer/singer/seer Ozzy is outclassed in every single department. As a performer/superstar/presence, however, he sets the agenda.

This is the man who added the final flared vocal to the Black Sabbath harangue, the man who came out of various booze and cocaine binges cackling and demanding more, the man who defecated in a hotel life and sought to ease the manager's apoplexy by assuring him, 'It's all right, mate. I'm a resident.'

He was born in Aston, Birmingham, in December 1948 and his early career embraced house burglary and slaughterhouse menial work. He took to the abattoir with relish and showed a propensity for separating animals from their heads that was never really to desert him. The burglary was not quite so successful and he spent some time in prison after a botched robbery attempt. Drifting around towards the end of the Sixties he found himself more by accident than design in a local band variously called Rare

Breed, Polka Tulk and Earth. The other members, Tony Iommi (guitar), Terry 'Geezer' Butler (bass) and Bill Ward (drums) were similarly disenfranchized young men with a love of basic blues and booze. Eventually the quartet renamed themselves after one of their better songs, Black Sabbath.

Black Sabbath – or The Sabs as most playgrounds in the western world swiftly dubbed them – was an extraordinary concept, almost menacing in its simplicity. Rather than perfect any degree of virtuosity, which was what other self-styled heavy rock bands of the era were doing (Deep Purple, Led Zeppelin), and rather than adhere to a traditional blues outline, as Jethro Tull, Free and Fleetwood Mac were attempting to do, Black Sabbath resorted to brute force. There would be one riff per song, agonizingly intense; there would be waiting lyrics about war, death, paranoia, night and darkness. They were rejected by fourteen record companies. Somehow, however, a record crept out on the Vertigo label and to a chorus of critical scorn the first Sabbath album scaled the charts and became a hit. It would later be commonplace for Black Sabbath to release an album to the immediate and damning reactions of the rock press, but to the manifest delight of the Sabbath army of loyal followers. The appeal of the group was always a mystery to those who could not see it, but irate letters of defence from fans assured the press that the key adjectives were 'strange', 'mystical' and 'eerie' and the key noun 'graveyard'.

The nose of Sabbath on stage was enhanced by the anti-social antics of its lead singer. Singing about madness, he would pretend to be out of his mind. Singing about death and damnation, he would make like he was the Devil. The kids of America, who had gone for Led Zeppelin for their ability to fuse heavy metal and elementary psychological concerns, went customarily ape for Sabbath and pretty soon the new world of drugs, orgies and lakes of alcohol presented itself. When it did, it was not turned away.

Osbourne quickly left behind the LSD experiences and moved over to the comfort of cocaine. On their 1972 US tour they did their best to outdo the similarly engaged Zeppelin and Rolling Stones by indulging more for indulgence's sake than any real physical need. Braving the uncertainties of the social disease they entertained floods of groupies and showed liberal gung-ho when offered a new drug thrill. And when the evenings got a bit boring, they would liven them up by setting fire to their drummer, Bill Ward. One time guitarist Tony Iommi poured lighter fuel over Ward's legs and set them alight. Ward needed medical attention.

Strangely enough, this did not lead to Sabbath having to scour the Musicians Available ads for a new drummer. Instead, the rift was between Iommi and Ozzy Osbourne. Iommi was exhibiting a peculiar reluctance to join in the revelry backstage and occasionally admonished Osbourne for his cheerful excess. Osbourne, in retaliation, used to go off stage for a cigarette during Iommi's guitar solos.

Events took a turn for the worse in 1976 when Black Sabbath had their first flop. They had never been a 'singles' band – their only hit single had been 'Paranoid', which they had not attempted to follow up – but they took pride in mammoth album sales. With *Technical Ecstasy*, it was universally decided, they had made a prime bummer. This intrigued the critics, who could not see any difference from previous records, but slagged it off anyway.

Osbourne was now well embedded in cocaine, sick of constant touring and management pressure. One day he snapped and blasted all his farmyard chickens to pieces with a shotgun.

He left Black Sabbath in November 1977 and soon afterwards checked into a mental asylum. By January 1978 he was back in the band, supposedly recuperated. The ensuing album, *Never Say Die*, was arguably the worst of the band's entire career, although it did spawn a hit single (the title track) and thus enabled new legions of Sabbath fans to see their heroes on 'Top Of The Pops'.

The next time, he was sacked. In the summer of 1979 he was replaced by the tiny US singer Ronnie James Dio and, as far as anybody who cared was aware, that was the last we would ever hear from Ozzy Osbourne.

The immediate future was spent consuming as much cocaine and drink as his burly frame could handle. A lifeline was only provided by the intervention of Sharon Arden, daughter of the legendary terrifying manager/impresario Don, whose Jet Records offered Ozzy a contract.

And sure enough Sharon (to whom Osbourne is now married) was able to sort her charge out well enough for him to audition and hire some backing musicians, two of them well-travelled and hardly adventurous journeyman, the other the exciting American guitarist Randy Rhoads. The band, called Blizzard of Ozz, made a self-titled album and it was fairly typical stuff, apart from one interesting moment – a song called 'Suicide Solution' – which would haunt Osbourne in later years.

The Ozzy name, it was feared, had been too long out of the public consciousness, so a little publicity was needed Therefore, a CBS Records convention was chosen as the best place for some Osbourne theatre of the nauseating kind. He was equipped with some white doves, which he produced at the appropriate moment. Then, to the horror of those present, he bit the head off one of them, splattering blood over his trousers, and grinned amiably.

The immediate result was his banishment for all time from the CBS building and the real threat of being thrown off the label. Osbourne now launched himself on an unsuspecting world as the Man Who Eats Whatever You Care To Throw At Him. And so it was that, during a concert of much projectible-lobbing and mirth, Osbourne found himself the recipient of a rubber bat. He raised it to his lips and sank his teeth in ... oops, not a rubber bat. A real bat.

The joke that circulated at the time was 'Did the bat have to get rabies shots?' Osbourne, of course, did and he did not enjoy the experience. However, a toning-down of his act was not the answer and so mock dwarfhanging, offal-catapulting and other atrocities took place with regularity whenever the Ozzy Osbourne roadshow came to town.

His biggest mistake, as far as the States was concerned, was to relieve himself in a spot in San Antonio, Texas, without checking out the lie of the land. When confronted by an outraged local, he realized that he had urinated on the Alamo. This defilement of Texans' most scared heritage got him fined and banned him from the district for all time. Soon the Humane Society urged the banning of his shows; meanwhile Osbourne announced his intention to wet the steps of the White House next.

The Osbourne of old has mellowed now – a spell in the Betty Ford Clinic has helped – and aside from the odd hiccup like getting a mouth full of glass when a mirror-shattering trick went wrong during the shooting of a video, his life is almost content. The only major danger came when a young American boy took his life after listening repeatedly to the Osbourne song 'Suicide Solution'. The boy's parents sued him for damages, but the Los Angeles Supreme Court found him not guilty, with the impressive and not totally reassuring quote, 'Ozzy's music may be totally objectionable to many but it can be given First Amendment protection too.'

Elvis Presley

Make no mistake – if there had never been an Elvis Presley, this book would not exist. Which is not to say that Presley's increasing odd behaviour leading up to his premature death at the age of only 42 can be entirely explained by the pressure which he felt as the King of

Rock, but the expectations of others clearly contributed to his tragic belief that he was infallible, immortal and in a word, Godlike.

When Elvis made his first records for Sam Phillips's Sun label in Memphis, he was a truck driver without prospects, living in a house that was little more than a shack. His father was a convicted criminal who was charged with forgery after altering the figures on a cheque he was given from $4 to $40 in 1937, when Elvis was two years old. This resulted in an initial sentence for Vernon Presley of three years at the infamous Parchman Farm prison (later the title of a celebrated R&B song written by Mose Allison), although Vernon probably served less than one year of his term. Gladys Presley, Elvis's mother, was thus forced to work at menial jobs to earn a pittance in her attempts to provide the necessities for her baby, especially since she actually gave birth to twins when Elvis arrived, although his brother, who was 35 minutes older than Elvis, was stillborn, which made Gladys almost unnaturally protective of her surviving child.

Elvis led a very sheltered life – for many months, his mother took him to school and met him at the school gates afterwards, and he reportedly accompanied her everywhere, which almost certainly embarrassed him as he grew older.

Then came his meteoric and totally deserved rise to fame in the mid-Fifties, when he forged a blueprint for rock 'n' roll from which the world continues to reverberate. The records Presley made before his two years in the US Army between 1958 and 1960 remain the yardstick by which everything which has subsequently occurred in rock 'n' roll is measured. By the time he went into the Forces, he had acquired a manager in the shape of the Machiavellian self-styled 'Colonel' Tom Parker, previously a carnival hustler who had earned a living in earlier times with his celebrated sideshow featuring dancing chickens –

any chicken in a cage whose floor was an electric hotplate would dance, and probably squawk!

Parker shrewdly decided when Elvis's call up papers arrived that any application for deferment might affect his meal ticket's credibility as the archetypal All American Boy, but made sure that enough recordings were available to satisfy public lust for new Elvis material during his stay with Uncle Sam, and even arranged for film footage to be shot in Germany to be used in Presley's fifth feature movie, *G.I. Blues*, his first film after a two year gap following the release of four commercial blockbusters in under two years prior to his induction as Private US53310761.

The fatal mistake, artistically speaking, was Parker's only partially successful attempt to make Elvis the hillbilly cat into Elvis the all round family entertainer, it became clear that Presley lost control over the material he was told to sing and especially over the movies in which he was obliged to appear, probably because demand for more and more Elvis was insatiable – some years later, an execrable LP of Elvis's between songs dialogue with the dubious title *Having Fun With Elvis On Stage* was released, which contained no singing. To his credit, Elvis was less than keen for this pathetically banal artefact to reach the market, but since by the time of its release, he only had three years to live, and was some distance down the road to self-inflicted oblivion, his protests were over-ruled, as they had been a year earlier, in 1973, when the rights to his back catalogue had been sold by Parker to RCA Records for a reported five and a half million dollars, of which Presley himself only netted $750,000. This must have been one of the shrewdest investments ever made by a record company, as the Presley catalogue continues to sell to the point where the company must have recouped its investment many times over.

At some point, probably around 1970, Elvis seems to have given up worrying about the quality of his output, and may even have begun to despise the fans who, lemming-like, consumed everything marketed with his name on it – dollar bills with his face in the place of that of George Washington have become very popular curios, and it is easy to purchase in gift shops in America facsimiles of Elvis' last will and testament. His marriage to the exceptionally photogenic Priscilla Beaulieu (who later appeared in a leading role in the TV soap opera, *Dallas*) ended in divorce apparently because Elvis preferred the company of the 'Memphis Mafia', a group of bodyguards and hangers-on, many of whom were reportedly prone to agreeing with Elvis, however outlandish and unreasonable his behaviour became. Accusations have been made suggesting that such people's spinelessness strongly contributed to Presley's downfall, and it is hard to deny that a rather more strong-minded approach might have prevented his self-destruct mechanisms from extracting the ultimate toll. On the other hand, he was so convinced, rather like a religious zealot, that everything he thought and did was beyond reproach that he would simply have fired anyone who dared to suggest that he might be human. Then there's the possibly apocryphal story about Elvis playing scrabble – to ensure that he had a better chance of winning, other players were restricted to five tiles (or letters) from which to construct words, while Elvis alone was allowed seven.

His drug intake, perhaps, resulting from extreme hypochondria, was said to be immense, and eventually was a major contributory factor to his death on 16 August 1977, when his heart finally gave up the unequal struggle against the weight of increasingly powerful chemicals which were, as far as can be ascertained, prescribed for him by three doctors who were prone to writing out prescriptions if Elvis asked them to. Once again, had any of these medics been sufficiently intrepid. Presley's life might have been extended, but as in the case of the Memphis

Mafia, to kill the goose which laid the golden egg would have resulted in banishment from the kingdom of plenty – Elvis was extremely generous with gifts to his close associates – and almost definitely someone else would have emerged who would be prepared to do precisely what Elvis wanted.

The subject of Presley ranks with that of The Beatles as the one about which most books have been written in the annals of rock music, simply because this popularity and influence have been surpassed. In the world of the cinema, the equivalent figure was Marilyn Monroe, and it is no accident that the legends of Monroe, The Beatles and Presley continue to make headlines decades after the death of Elvis, Marilyn and John Lennon – each of the three lived a life which was subject to microscopic scrutiny from the media. Only an extra-terrestrial might be able to survive such pressure, and Elvis Presley, sadly, was a mere mortal.

Chuck Berry

It's been the fate of many poor wretches in the music business to have hits with the one song in their repertoire which embarrasses them the most. Jeff Beck, for example, must rue the day he ever agreed to saunter his way through 'Hi Ho Silver Lining'. And David Bowie's 1967 'The Laughing Gnome', must have caused the thin white one some fearful ribbing when his callous record company re-released it in 1973. And one might wonder how Paul McCartney sleeps with the fact that his version of 'Mary Had A Little Lamb' is one of his bigger hits.

However, one man who is known to be delighted with the success of a song that appalled just about everyone else is Chuck Berry. Berry's salacious sing-song 'My Ding A Ling', ostentsibly a song about the male sexual organ that becomes more inane the closer one analyses it, was one of

1972's raves of the year. It gave Berry his only UK number one hit.

This cruel touch would embitter many performers. After all, Chuck Berry was the man who wrote 'School Days', 'Rock And Roll Music', 'Sweet Little Sixteen' and 'Johnny B. Goode' to name but four. Not all of those songs had even made it to the charts in Britain. To add to his possible misery, he had had to sit back in jail while a succession of inferior talents from both sides of the Atlantic got rich on his formula. *Surely* he would be livid that, when the great British public saw fit to recognize the genius of one of rock 'n' roll's *creators*, they did so with one of the decade's most annoying songs!

Not a bit of it. Berry is currently somewhere between seventh and eighth heaven, having negotiated clouds nine and ten, and all because the success of 'My Ding A Ling' brought in huge wads of lucre. It is as one of the meanest men in the whole business that a new generation of rock fans are hailing Chuck Berry.

When Charles Edward Berry (born 1926 in St Louis, Missouri) considered career applications in his teenage heyday, it was to the world of hairdressing that he turned. Fortunately for the rest of us he jettisoned the comb and the scissors in favour of a guitar and an amplifier. In 1955 he had his first hit with a song he had written called 'Maybellene', and thereby hangs a tale. Ignorance of record company sharp practice resulted in Berry not studying the small print, and he was horrified to learn that he had only been given a co-credit on the label. He had written the song himself, but a three-way deal was done behind his back. Two people, one of whom he had never even met, were now entitled between them to 66 per cent of his money. Chuck Berry was never ripped off again.

That incident, and repeated incidents of racism directed at Berry, hardened him into a shrewd businessman. The whites in the deep South did not like him at all because he was not the type to be in any way modest about his talent, and also because the white girls showed a tendency to be attracted to this brown-eyed handsome minstrel. Both Berry characteristics antagonized the somewhat less opulent, less confident and presumably less handsome habitués of the whites-only bars.

His song were, if not exactly sexually explicit, certainly sexually aware. He might have been singing about cars and school and rock 'n' roll music for much of the time, but there was little doubt about why he was so chuffed about 'sweet little sixteen' reaching the age of consent. Brash, brave and brilliant, he tore up the late Fifties with a series of anthems which are still staple fare for all budding rock guitarists. He also had a hand in inventing The Beatles and The Rolling Stones. Without Chuck Berry – no Keith Richards.

In late 1959 Berry was arrested and charged with transportation of a woman across state lines for immoral purposes, under the Mann Act. He had served three years in reform school for robbery and had only escaped a jail term by the skin of his teeth for trying to make it with a sheriff's daughter in Mississippi. The trial for the Mann Act charge was doomed from the moment the judge referred to 'what's his name, this Negro'. Berry's defence was poor and unconvincing, but fortunately the racism of the judge got so prejudicial that he was relieved from duty and a mistrial was announced. At the second trial Berry was found guilty as charged, and sent to prison for three years in 1962. The girl later confessed to being a prostitute.

Berry served sixteen months of the sentence and, on his release in 1964, found that the musical climate had changed. He had some more hits, probably with songs he had written before the prison term, but mostly he concentrated on business interests, setting up an amusement park complex in Missouri called Berry Park.

When he did play, it was noticeable that the famous

twinkle in the eye had all but gone, to be replaced by a bit-terly realistic level gaze. He did not even have a band. What would happen was that he would turn up at a par-ticular venue and play with a pick-up band. He wouldn't ask their names, they wouldn't know in advance what they were supposed to play, and if they were only good he would pay them. There was a strong element of 'take the money and don't look round till you're in the car and moving'.

The Seventies were a busy time for him musically. Significantly, unlike Little Richard and Jerry Lee Lewis who sometimes found it hard to whip up the same hyste-ria as they did in the Fifties. Berry has never seemed like becoming obsolete. He toured Britain to great acclaim, although interviewers were taken aback when he denied ever going to prison and said that he had never heard of The Rolling Stones.

A second prison term tainted the Seventies, when the IRS caught up with him. He had under-declared his huge earnings for 1973 by a cool $200,000. Faced with the alter-native of a hefty fine or 100 days in the slammer, Berry showed a glimpse of his character when he elected for the latter. Not many people who have served time are enthu-siastic about going back, and the decision of Berry to do just that shows what money means to him.

Every now and then a fresh rumour about the man's stinginess crops up. On his last promotional visit to England, in the wake of his film and autobiography, he amazed reporters by only granting them five minutes – or sometimes three – with the tape recorder on, and a further five with the tape recorder off. In order that they did not glean too much free information he pretended to be hard of hearing so that they only managed to ask three or four questions in the time allowed. A TV appearance on a well-known chat show was handled with almost breathtaking contempt by Berry, to the extent that he charged them according to what song they wanted, and would not go on until paid in cash. Keith Richard's involvement in the Berry tribute film could be the most unexpected display of heroism in movie history ... considering that on a previous occasion Berry had punched Richards in the mouth.

Michael Jackson

If all the peripherals had to be stripped away and all the detritus jettisoned to make way for just one surviving pop star, it would have to be Michael Jackson. This baby-faced, possibly artificially-coloured and allegedly female-hormoned young 30-year-old Peter Pan with Fred Astaire leanings, this snake-fondling llama-loving chimp-championing Howard Hughes manqué is quite simply the biggest phenomenon to hit music since Salieri's death-bed confessions. As if to prove the point he has acquired the rights to most of The Beatles' songs, with reports that he will do an album of cover versions. Paul McCartney, whom he out-bidded, is less than chuffed but is momentarily powerless – Jackson's wish is as close to a Papal Bull as makes no difference.

He had made three albums in ten years – *Off The Wall*, *Thriller* and *Bad*. The second of those, released in 1982, is the biggest-selling album of all time. Between them they have spawned fifteen hit singles.

And it is not as though stardom is a new problem for him to cope with. He was a smash hit at five years old, touring with his elder brothers. This singing group, eventually to be named The Jackson Five, may have made him a wealthy young man and an undeniable star, but it also deprived him of a childhood, something he appears to be rectifying these days.

The Jackson Five's first single, 'I Want You Back', released in 1970 on a publicity tidal wave which claimed that the boys had been discovered in Gary, Indiana, by

Diana Ross, went to number one in America. From that moment on, every move Jackson made was closely studied. While lesser beacons such as Donny Osmond and David Cassidy – and their respective families – faded from public view to do some much-needed reappraising of life, talent, the universe, etc., Jackson had no time to think.

From the embrace of The Jackson Five he went, with minimal voice-break, to The Jacksons (the same family, but minus Jermaine and plus Randy) and continued the hit-making operation. Separated from the artistic umbilical cord of Tamla Motown and the extremely paternal influence of Berry Gordy Jr. Jackson was able to make his own career decisions and he elected to go for smooth disco soul on his first major solo album *Off The Wall* in 1979. The album was a huge success, as were the unprecedented amount of singles culled from it, but so far as anyone knew, Michael Jackson, just turned 21, was still the lead singer and desperately shy focal point for The Jacksons. This was underlined when a Jacksons album, *Triumph*, came out to great acclaim in 1980. However, any remaining doubt about Michael Jackson's future role in his brothers' group, or for that matter in society, evaporated in 1982 with the release of *Thriller*.

Thriller trounced *Off The Wall* in sales in a matter of weeks and its first single, the controversial 'Billie Jean', was to be one of Jackson's finest hours. It was ostensibly a firm denial of a paternity suite – Jackson has claimed to be a virgin – but its intensity and its repetitive hook made it just another accessible pop song, and it duly scored. 'Beat It', featuring heavy metal guitar histrionics courtesy of Eddie Van Halen, followed close behind.

It was at this point that the tabloids began to take more than a friendly interest. It was well known that Jackson was reticent, even mute, when confronted with the Press. But some of his reported behaviour seemed too strange to explain away. Like, for instance, his menagerie in which he kept such prize exhibits as his pet snake Muscles and his pet llama Louie. Like his much-publicized nose job, dramatized in before-and-after shots in newspapers the world over. Like his Peter Pan existence of asceticism and sobriety. Like his courting of older women – Diana Ross, Elizabeth Taylor, even Katharine Hepburn – and the doomed relationship he had with the young actress Brooke Shields.

During the years 1984 and 1985 the myth became a legend. The early months of 1984 saw him severely burned when an advertisement he was making for Pepsi-Cola (he doesn't drink it) ended in disaster. His hair caught fire and he suffered second degree burns. A month later he cleaned up at the Grammy awards with *Thriller*. He had wept with disbelief when *Off The Wall* only received one Grammy. By March 1984 *Thriller* was the biggest-selling album of all time, its 30 million copies sold representing over 10 per cent of CBS Records' entire income during that period.

That same year he toured with his brothers on the *Victory* Tour (named after a particularly unimpressive Jacksons album) and was the indirect subject of much wrath when the exorbitant ticket prices were announced. There had been ill feeling before this – Michael was believed not to want to tour, while his brothers, angry at being overshadowed, only agreed to his being there for financial reasons. But when the ticket proviso of $28 per ticket and a maximum of four per person came to light, the flak was thrown at Michael Jackson – was he seriously worth this much? After all, Bruce Springsteen had recently toured, selling tickets half as expensive and playing for twice as long. At a press conference Jackson said he would give his share of the takings to charity. His brothers didn't.

In March 1985 his peculiar – some said suspicious – features were being duplicated for inclusion in Madame Tussaud's in London. He came to visit his replica and was the subject of much rumour – was he really bathing in

£8,000 worth of Perrier water and had he really insisted on going door-to-door for the Jehovah's Witnesses in West London? – and succeeded in blocking the approach road off with anxious fans eager to catch a glimpse.

In August, while Paul McCartney and Yoko Ono were considering a bid for the rights to old Beatles songs, Jackson nipped in and snapped up the ATV Music catalogue for a mere $40 million. This included the rights to some 5,000 songs, a hefty proportion of which were Lennon-McCartney songs. McCartney, who had collaborated with Jackson on trite but likeable tunes 'Say Say Say' and 'The Girl Is Mine', was known to the miffed, especially when stray Beatles tunes cropped up on US television advertising various products.

In September 1986 it came to light that Jackson was sleeping in a pressurized oxygen chamber. He claimed that this chamber, which had set him back £90,000, would enable him to live until he was 150. In addition he took to wearing surgical face masks on the rare occasions he ventured out into the street. And the greatest furore of all, the one his management swear is complete garbage, was that Jackson was altering his skin pigmentation, that he was actually trying to become a white man. Why? To maximize his appeal? Because he did not like being black? It all seems very unlikely.

What he did try to do, in June 1987, was to buy the remains of John Merrick, the 'Elephant Man' of Victorian times, whose tragic outcast life he believed to be similar in many ways to his own. He offered the London Medical College $1 million for the bones of Merrick, who had died in 1900. The spokesman for the LMC said that any sale would be 'morally wrong'.

Syd Barrett

The dread rock dinosaur yawns, struggles to its paws and groans. Time to lose another few pounds. Time to say au revoir to the family. Time to tune up that battered old guitar. Time to tour.

Pinkus Floydus – Latin for someone or something that has far outlived its usefulness – is a comparatively young dinosaur. It's only been around since 1965, and even then it spent the first two years hiding underground, perfecting its act. But it seems like forever. That album they made in 1973, *The Dark Side Of The Moon,* a study not so much of madness as of designer boredom, has been in the American charts ever since. Its successor, a smug diagnosis of the music scene entitled *Wish You Were Here,* qualified for a gold disc before it was even released – advance orders saw to that.

And it's been a case of irate teachers, diving bombers and recalcitrant pigs where their live show has touched down. The compact disc generation bows down in humble deference to the glory of the Floyd, for this band is just as fat, just as disillusioned and, ultimately, just as useless as they are.

Twas not ever thus. When the Pink Floyd started there was a very real case for calling them the most interesting group in the world at the time. Their songs were disarmingly innocent childhood tales, set to some of the most compulsive electronic backing heard in the Sixties. All of this – the name, the songs, the singing, the guitars – came from the strange and suspect mind of Syd Barrett.

Roger Keith Barrett was born in Cambridge in 1946. By all accounts he was an exuberant and intelligent young man, a fast sprinter who simply wanted to get on and do things, without worrying too much about what anyone else thought, or about where it would lead to. Showing

500

early talent at painting, he won a scholarship to Camberwell Art School in London, at the time a hive of activity for artistic teenagers with more than a passing interest in matters spiritual.

But 'Syd' as he was nicknamed was more of a creative brain that most of his contemporaries at art school, and he started to hang out with students from the architecture course at Regent St. Poly, among them Roger Waters, Nick Mason and Rick Wright, who completed the line-up of Pink Floyd.

In the very early days the Floyd stuck to playing cover versions of old R&B faves such as 'Roadrunner' and 'Louie Louie', although Barrett's unique guitar style and tendency to improvise on a theme until there was simply no place else to go meant that the songs bore little comparison to their vinyl originals. Gradually Barrett started to write his own songs, weird hypnotic nursery rhymes with extraordinary hooks and ultra-melodic choruses. In 1967 the band released their first single, 'Arnold Layne'.

Up to that point they had been something of an underground secret, playing at clubs like UFO and the All Saints church hall in Notting Hill, where 'light and sound workshops' were held. The audience would dutifully turn up, laden with LSD and ready to freak out to the music and roll around in great mountains of jelly. The Floyd would be singing their consciousness music, accompanied by some of the most advanced light shows of the time. Barrett would look like a pixie in his paisley shirt and cropped hair.

'Arnold Layne' catapulted them into a bigger league. In many ways it was atypical of Barrett's songwriting. For a start it was less than three minutes long; it was also an extremely contemporary song, far removed from his love of fairy tales and space stories. 'Arnold Layne' was about a man who obtained sexual gratification from stealing women's underwear from washing lines in and around the

501

Cambridge area. It was banned immediately by the pirate radio station, Radio London.

Its follow-up, 'See Emily Play', was a huge success, reaching the top five and winning the group three appearances on Top Of The Pops. A debut album, *Piper At The Gates Of Dawn*, was a triumph. Syd Barrett was, at the age of 21, one of Britain's most successful songwriters. It was ironic, given what outrageous riches later found their way into the pockets of the mark two Floyd, that one of Barrett's chief worries was what to make of even this amount of sudden fame and wealth. Unable to handle, he was driven to more and more drug excess.

Barrett, of all the members of the band, was most impressed by acid. A deeply sensitive man and an unapologetic student of the ways of the universe, he found its qualities of sound and space invaluable. Not only was he writing better and better, he was tuning in to some previously unexplored wavelengths. In a world of simplicity and decency and kaleidoscopic dreams, his songs seemed to argue, does it really matter about money, property or grown-ups?

The first real evidence that Barrett was finding it difficult to deal with the real world came at the time of 'See Emily Play'. He invited his close friend David Gilmour (who would later replace him as the Floyd's guitarist) to the recording sessions and said nothing to him all day. For the Top Of The Pops appearances he was almost wilfully uncooperative. In the rebellious manner of his hero John Lennon he dressed in rags and mimed atrociously to the words he had written. On their first American tour Barrett showed signs of being in very deep water.

On Dick Clark's Bandstand Barrett's dislike of miming reached a crisis: he did not bother at all, much to the embarrassment of the band. Then, on a teenage religious show hosted by Fifties legend and budding youth counsellor Pat Boone, Barrett posed a few problems for the wizened crooner by not answering any of his questions. He simply stared long and hard into Boone's eyes, a practice he was to adopt later with disturbing frequency Clearly Barrett was not having fun on the promotional trail.

Back in Britain, on a multi-artist tour featuring Hendrix and The Move among others, Barrett went to pieces completely. When the tour bus reached a new city he would walk off, usually not making it back in time for their appearance that night. When he did remember about the gig, he would blow it by playing the same chord all evening. On one occasion he let his right hand hang limply over the body of his guitar for the entire set while staring in mute perplexity at the people who had come along and ruined his party.

This impossible situation was at least partly rectified by the addition to the Floyd line-up of second guitarist David Gilmour. The plan was for Gilmour to take care of the live aspect of the band while Barrett wrote the songs.

'By the end of the afternoon,' says Waters. 'I thought I'd convinced him that it was a good idea, and he'd agreed, but it didn't really mean very much because he was liable to change his mind about anything totally within an hour.'

It did not work out. Too much pressure on Barrett resulted in his formal departure in April 1968. He was to pursue a solo career, with the full help and blessing of the Pink Floyd.

The recording of Barrett's first solo album, *The Madcap Laughs*, was probably one of the greatest trials in the history of rock 'n' roll. It certainly exhausted at least two men - Peter Jenner and Malcolm Jones. Eventually an album of sorts was completed, half of it an acoustic set in which Barrett's mind is seen to be on several different planes all at once. At one stage he is singing an extraordinary number called 'If It's In You'.

'Yes I'm thi-i-i-i-i-i-i-inking...' he starts, hitting a high, hysterial note somewhere up in the ether. 'Look I you know ... I'll *start again*,' he informs the studio.

'Syd', suggests someone in the control box, 'why don't you try it without guitar?

'No, it's just the fact ... of going through it ... I mean if you ... if we could cut ... hmmm...'

He starts again. This time he gets it right and the songs bursts into life. The words, however, are unlike any even heard on a rock record. Is this, as psychiatrist R.D. Laing has said, the voice of an incurable madman?

> Colonel with gloves Strauss leeches
> He isn't love on Sunday's mail
> All the fives crock Henrietta
> She's a mean go-getter
> Gotta write her a letter.

Musicians who played on the record testify to Barrett's craziness. Drummer Robert Wyatt, who had to deal with some completely unplanned time changes, as well as Barrett's inimitable tendency to drop the last beat of a bar and attach it to one further on, tells of the confusion:

'I thought the sessions were actually rehearsals. We'd say "What key is that in, Syd?" and he'd reply, "Yeah" or, "That's funny".'

Barrett's second album, eponymously titled, was if anything an even stranger affair. His voice sounds permanently on the brink of a huge scream that will never end, and the throwaway nursery rhyme at the end about the tiger eating the elephant seems plain nasty when one considers the manic character of the brain that created it.

And interviews Barrett did with *Rolling Stone* in 1971 mixes sinister aphorisms with periods of quite subterranean logic.

'I'm sorry I can't speak very coherently. But you know man I am totally together. I even think I should be. I'm full of dust and guitars.'

The interview starts to get a little said:

'That's all I wanted to do as a kid. Play a guitar properly and jump around. But too many people got in the way.
I can't find anybody [to form a band with]. That's the problem. I don't know where they are. I mean, I've got an idea
there must be someone to play with.'

He refuses to talk about the drug that led him to the
point of despair. 'There's really nothing to say. Once you're
into something ...'

Barrett was admitted into a mental hospital shortly
afterwards.

Throughout the Seventies the rumours bred and multi-
plied. The most common ones had him strolling down the
streets of Cambridge in a dress; threatening people with
guns; becoming a monk; becoming a tramp; or – best of all
– working as a roadie with Pink Floyd. Attempts to get
him back in the studio proved useless. He couldn't even
play the guitar any more.

In 1982, after years of searching, two French journalists
tracked him down to his mother's house in Cambridge.
When he opened the door he was Roger Barrett, a
paunchy, balding, peculiar man with an odd glint in his
eye as if he was saying, 'I knew this would happen'. The
journalists had a hard job convincing him that he used to
be the demon Syd.

He was looking forward to getting back to London, he
told them, but he had to wait for the rail strike to end. It
was pointed out to him that the strike had ended weeks
ago. 'Oh, thanks very much,' he said, touched. No he did-
n't play guitar, or paint, just watched TV and waited. For
what? Well, he didn't really know. Eventually the voice of
his mother was heard calling him and he went inside,
looking frightened.

It's a matter of some conjecture whether Barrett was a
fragile individual before he discovered LSD. Psychiatrists

see recognizable patterns in his condition – the sensitive youth who suddenly goes schizophrenic. LSD, they reckon, merely expedited matters. Whatever, there is little doubt that Roger 'Syd' Barrett was the victim rather than the hero of his own story. In October 1988, in a 'shock horror' story on the musical genre Acid House which was sweeping Britain at the time, the *News Of The World* ran a two-page article on Syd Barrett. Juxtaposing then-and-now photographs to admittedly devastating effect, they featured a photo of the reclusive star in his garden. He looks overweight, balding and unfriendly. Never before had he so resembled his former colleagues in The Pink Lloyd.

Keith Moon

'The production of our records has got nothing to do with sound. It's got to do with trying to keep Keith Moon on his fucking drum stool.' – Pete Townshend, The Who, 1970.

Now and again the mighty Gods of sweet serendipity smile on the beleaguered beacons of tabloid journalism and come up with a character so awesomely dangerous and dedicated to the perpetual pursuit of the offensive, the surreal and the illegal that not even the slightest degree of newshounding is necessary. The stories write themselves, arriving at the office in glorious rounded form, with a beginning, middle and end, none of which are especially believeable but all of which conspire in a recipe of prime shock-horror.

Keith Moon was such a character.

Ostensibly the drummer in a rock band, he waged a personal war against the forces of complacency and decency which saw him revered far and wide by his teenage acolytes as the all-time champion of Going A Bit Too Far. And in one of those wonderful instances where the

English language proves itself perfectly equipped to deal with its exponents, a concise, witty and irrevocable soubriquet provided itself. From the time he tore the stuffing out of his first hotel pillow until the pitiful anti-climax of his death at 32, Keith Moon was known universally as Moon The Loon.

It is said that the 15-year-old Moon passed his audition for The Who In 1962 by demolishing his drum-kit. Thereafter he embarked on a 16-year-orgy of fun and destruction that made him the scourge of hotel managers everywhere and the ultimate party guest. Listed below are a series of his exploits, in no particular order (it could hardly be argued, after all, that Moon *matured).* The authors humbly suggest that these vignettes be read aloud in order to give them their full dramatic impact.

Upon waking one night to a fierce hunger, Moon decides to treat himself to a chicken. Unfortunately the kitchens in his hotel are long since closed and his whim cannot be indulged. None too worried, Moon breaks into the hotel kitchens and raids the fridge, relieving it of its contents. He then repairs to his room, stuffs himself with chickens and finds to his chagrin that there are still some left, which he is too full to eat. There is really only one solution for him. He kicks them around the room until they are in bits, then replaces them in the fridge. Casually flipping a wad of tenners over the reception desk the next morning, he tells the management, 'By the way, this is for those chickens I had last night.'

One year The Who finds itself on a Sixties-style package tour, with Traffic and The Herd making up the numbers. The Herd, who were led by blond dreamboat Peter Frampton (who would later become an American rock 'n' roll icon), had a contemporary hit with a moody piece of nonsense called 'From The Underworld'. Onstage it was The Herd's habit to have a gong lowered behind the drummer for him to hit at the climax of the number. Bored by watching this comical stunt night after night, Moon bribes a stagehand to let him lower the gong at the appropriate moment. Sure enough this moment arrives and Moon carefully lowers the gong from the beams over the stage. The drummer of The Herd gets ready to give it a swipe when suddenly it is snatched out of his reach. The audience is then treated to the spectacle of the drummer leaping up in the air trying to strike his gong, while Keith Moon lifts it further and further out of his reach.

A Who gig in San Francisco is just about ready to start, except that there is one small problem. The drummer is in Los Angeles. Eventually located in a darkened hotel room, he proves impossible to wake. Not only that, but the lights won't come on when the switch is operated. It is a situation easily explained – both Moon and the lights are knackered because he finished off the previous evening's revelry by flinging his colour television at the chandelier.

At the same gig The Who's guitarist Pete Townshend becomes increasingly distressed at the erratic timekeeping of his drumming friend. He's slowing down by the bar, as the night's potion of drink and drugs bubbles in his system. 'Play faster!!' roars Townshend, 'play *faster*'. Moon is quite obviously in a spot of bother, so a doctor is summoned with the necessary pick-me-ups in his syringes. During a quiet section in the song Moon is given a twin boost in his ankles. He proceeds to play like a madman, flailing away at his cymbals and lashing into his drums. All the time Townshend is screaming, 'Play slower, play *slower*!!'

Driving cars is something Moon never showed a lot of skill in. Opting for the passenger seat for one particular journey, he nevertheless wishes to get involved, to help out the driver. So he elects himself operator of the gear lever. When he feels the car is going fast enough – say 120 mph (190 km/h) – he slams the car into first gear. The car, perfectly understandably, is suddenly in great pain and flees away from the road to find a quiet spot to lick its wounds. It chooses a secluded bank of a reservoir and perches there, trembling ominously.

On another occasion, having collided in a drunken stupor with meat lorry, he offers to pay the ensuing fine by American Express.

The famous incident, the one is which Moon's Rolls-Royce was driven by its owner into a swimming pool and left to drown, is not strictly factually correct. He does attempt a marriage between several thousand pounds' worth of automobile and a large amount of water, but it's his ornamental pond that ends up having a Rolls-Royce for a guest. He drives it there because he says he wants to kill himself, and he does not receive the required amount of outraged protests.

This is a trick he gets up a lot – one time he leaps off a high window sill into the sea below. Terrified, as the drummer is in no fit state to swim, the rest of the band commence a search that lasts many hours and involves coastguards, lifesavers and policemen. When Moon is sure that they have called off the search and are phoning around all the available drummers in the area, he emerges grinning, 'bet you thought I'd never do it.'

The pick-me-up trick does not work at every gig. One time Moon is playing so half-heartedly that even the audience notices it. Despite Townshend's colourful exhortations to the drummer, he clearly can't cut it and eventually he collapses into his drum-kit. Looking a little sheepish The Who carry him off.

Backstage Moon is given oxygen (always kept handy since the very nature of his percussion technique suggests that it will prove indispensable one day) and shows signs of recovery. The rioting in the hall is averted; The Who retake the stage. One song into the resumption and Moon is face down in his kit again. This time the gig's really over, and Moon is taken away to hospital – partly because everyone's intrigued to find out exactly what he's on. When his stomach is pumped out it turns out that he's been taking the exact same stuff that is used for tranquillizing gorillas

More hotel fun ensues when Moon, in a fit of anti-American hysteria, decides to booby-trap the lift. With a waterbed. But the waterbed proves impossible to lift and instead of manoeuvring it out into the hall he succeeds only in tearing it. Inevitably, its contents spill out all over the carpet of his hotel room. Unphased, he commences to swim in the liquid. Then, bored by the proceedings, he rings the management and complains in tones of outraged English righteousness that he has been given a defective waterbed and demands suitable compensation.

Complaints about Moon occur with chilling frequency during his sojourns in the world's hotels. For a man who likes his music loud (his penchant is for surf music, as practised by The Beach Boys and Jan And Dean), the apoplectic plaintiff is never too far away. The manager of one establishment buttonholes him with regard to the sonic boom emanating from his room. 'It's a noise,' he says with distaste, pointing in the general direction of the cacophony. Moon retaliates by blowing up his room with a Cherry Bomb. 'Now *that's* a noise!' he tells the manager.

Wherever The Who stay there tends to be a lot of police. There are more than usual one time when Moon picks the hotel manager's wife to blow up. Surprisingly, hotels in and around the New York area have been strangely reluctant to admit The Who and those that do – the Holiday Inn chain for example – demand a hefty sum up front.

It's the Cherry Bombs that do it. Particularly deadly fireworks, they bring Pete Townshend out in a cold sweat:

'I was in his [Moon's] room and all the paint round the door knocker was black where he had been putting these things in the key-hole. I happened to ask if I could use his bog and he just smiled like this [maniacal grin] and said, "sure". I went in and there was no toilet – just a sort of S bend coming out of the floor! "Christ, what the fuck's happened," I asked. And he said, "Well, this Cherry Bomb was about to go off in my hand, so I threw it down the bog to put it out." "Are they powerful?" I asked, and he nodded. "how many of them have you got?" I said with fear in my eyes. He said, "500", opening up a case which was full to the top with Cherry Bombs.'

One reaches, however, a plateau of destruction – everything levels out. The act of destruction becomes a bit tedious since it's the end result that counts, the sheer joy of admiring your own handiwork. Therefore, Moon starts to cut out some of the violence and concentrate on the end effect. As Townshend put it, 'he arranges it artistically'. It doesn't sound like havoc, but it sure looks it. Television sets are taken apart, cabinets unscrewed, baths filled with tomato ketchup (occasionally with a plastic leg sticking out), furniture overturned just so.

His practical jokes take on the surreal touch of an inspired clown. Once he hires six girls from a massage parlour and persuades one of them to take part in a ruse. He gets his personal assistant to telephone for help, saying, 'Come quick, Moon's gone mad, he's killed this chambermaid ...' When the door is eventually smashed in the scene to greet the intruders is priceless – one of the girls lying with a mouthful of tomato ketchup, her legs splayed all over the place, Moon weeping tears of remorse in the corner, and the rest of the party choking back hysterical laughter.

Airports are another favourite haunt. Equipping himself on one journey with a toy gun, he hides behind a pillar at an airport terminal and waits for someone to come by. He hears footsteps approaching and leaps out screaming threats. He's picked a policeman. Later the same night, having been released from police custody only on the production of a reasonable sum of money, he destroys a

511

computer terminal at the same airport. And it's back to the station, where this time the money's not good enough.

Messing with the authorities becomes a Moon hobby. Convinced – as it happens, correctly – that his cherubic charm and laddish bonhomie will rescue him from any scape, he decides to hold up a security van. So, having taken care of the first half of plan, which is to run it off the road, he contemplates the next move. Attack? Well, of course they might have guns. Sod it, he decides, and drives off. Minutes later he is surrounded by police. It transpires that the van he chose to hassle was carrying a million pounds in used notes. It takes all his crafty expertise to spring himself from the police noose this time.

One time he is not so lucky. Driving away from a gig he is besieged by hysterical fans, whom he prefers to avoid. He speeds up. The point is, he should not even be driving. Quite apart from the fact that he is drunk and does not possess a driving licence, he actually employs a chauffeur to drive for him. Moon thinks the chauffeur has run on ahead to get out of the way of the screaming fans, but he has not. Some youths have kicked him into the path of Moon's speeding car ...

Not that Moon ever uses cars for their usual purpose. Even when he uses them for transport he adds a twist to the tale. In the mood for a tincture or two. Moon orders his assistant to drive him to a nightclub, through the West End of London. The drummer stretches out on the bonnet. He is not wearing any clothes. The route they take is a fairly well-populated one and people are commencing to point and stare as they arrive at the Club. Once in the club (one wonders if he thought it was a 'members only' establishment) he spots Mick Jagger and his wife of the time, Bianca. Merrily he chats away as they consume their meals. Oddly enough, they elect not to stay for coffee.

In most of these incidents he has an accomplice, either someone he has tricked into participation, or someone who, is as wreck as he is. Never a man to use one pill where two will do, he finds himself increasingly unconscious and prostrate amid female company. However, he does have one close friend and rival, the celebrated English eccentric Viv Stanshall. Stanshall's band, The Bonzo Dog Doo Dah Band, occupies a special place in comedic/music relations thanks to his dark wit and Neil Innes' splendid tunes, and he is as daring and tasteless as Moon himself.

The apex of their high links takes place one Saturday when they raid their respective costume wardrobes and come up with a sinister Nazi look. Emerging into bright British daylight they are appalled to learn that practically nobody is shocked by their antics. Bright idea time. Why not go to Golders Green, the heart of the Jewish community? Not only will they be appalled by the sight of two high-ranking Nazis sallying forth up the High Street, but it's the Jewish holy day too.

Not even the avowed shock tactics of the punk generation phased Keith Moon. Drawing up outside the Marquee Club in his Rolls-Royce one evening, he is met by a hail of abuse. He gets out of his car, furious, slamming doors and looking dangerous. He berates the queue of punks. 'Look at you,' he sneers. 'I've never queued to get into a club in my life!' With that he barges to the head of the queue and disappears into the club. Once inside he finds himself the victim of every brash punk kid with a mate to impress. One youth gives him particular grief. 'You don't mean nothing to me,' he tells Moon, 'nothing means nothing to me.' Moon snatches the boy's drink off him and knocks it back. 'Oy, watcha doing?' howls the aggrieved wretch. 'Well, you said nothing means nothing to you.

Throughout the hectic, dangerous years Moon (it seems astonishing now) kept up a standard of rock drumming that has never been equalled. Behind his ridiculously large kit with its mountains of tom-toms and scores of cymbals, he sweated and grimaced as his extraordinary stickwork spliced through every one of Townshend's riffs. Sometimes he destroyed his kit afterwards. Sometimes he did not need to – it was hanging in bits when he finished playing on it.

Once, during a fit of the blues, he became convinced that he could improve substantially. Hearing that the great jazz drummer Philly Joe Jones was giving lessons in London, Moon trooped along. Jones did not know him from Haile Selassie. 'Beginner or advanced?'he asked. Ummm ... advanced,' shrugged Moon. 'All right, man,' said Jones. 'Show me what you can do.' Moon assumed the position behind the kit and let fly with his customary crazy armswinging hysteria, venting years and years of spleen, leaving the kit in a pulsating, shaking heap. Jones gaped at him. 'You make a living doing that?' Moon grinned. 'About 50 grand a week, actually.' 'Get out of here, man,' said Jones, 'I'd only spoil it.'

Moon died, aged 31, in September 1978. He was taking anti-alcoholism tablets at the time. One night he took 32, more than twice the recognized lethal dose.

The Who did not, as Led Zeppelin, later did, call it a day. They hired Kenny Jones, a former member of The Small Faces and in every way the antithesis of Moon, and they made a few more albums. You'll probably find them in the bargain bins at your local record store.

Malcolm McLaren, Sid Vicious and The Sex Pistols

In 1976, as people in the know now agree, things had gotten just a little stale. Well, more than just a little. Unless you were a coke fiend you couldn't keep up with the towering crass purveyors of tedious soft rock who kept their real athletics for off the field, and saw rock music as a means to owning their own pharmacy. The records they made were fun-defying exercises in fretboard contemplation. But they were snapped up by the million by spaced-out kids suckered by the handle this nowhere music had been given – progressive rock. Snails progress too, if you think about it. But not too fast.

The revolution was not planned. A chap called Wally Nightingale (a tribute to his importance is that few can recall his surname) had put together a band in school, a good times get-together that gradually got more serious as the musicians learned to play. Two of them were Steve Jones on guitar and Paul Cook on drums. Wally, after his dad objected to the racket, was ousted. A gentleman called Glen Matiock, a serious musician in comparison with the others, came in on bass.

It was these boys' habit of an afternoon to frequent a Kings Road joint called 'Sex' (Matiock worked there) which doubled as a go-ahead clothes shop and a forum for vacant teenage chat. The proprietor, one Malcolm McLaren, took an interest in the band, advising them on what songs to attempt and turning them on to The New York Dolls, whom he had managed at a particularly traumatic time in their career.

One day, when a search for a suitable lead singer had been turning up nothing, a precariously-dentured youth of speedfreak hue entered the shop, auditioned to the strains of Alice Cooper on the jukebox, and got the gig. Nobody considered for a moment that he could sing, but he had that lunatic *joie de mort* that would make him one of the great rock'n' roll howlers.

They started to play live, gatecrashing college gigs where they would last maybe three songs if they were lucky, and something about the audience reaction – the mindless violence, the beer wars, the teddy bear terrorism – told them they were on to a good thing. 1976 saw them congeal into a working unit, with real songs, a razor edge and even some vestiges of a fan club. One of their followers, a lanky youth named John Simon Ritchie, later to become famous under another name, instigated a new form of dancing. Oppressed on all sides by people just as immobile as he was, he opted for the vertical hold. A major novelty was born; the pogo, the punk movement in pure physical potency, took off.

Another fashion accessory, the safety pin, came into prominence as a patent of the singer. This recent acquisition, a highly-charged and verbal lad named John Lydon, had been re-named Johnny Rotten and he was to affront student audiences and the high hippie count thereof for the next year.

The summer of 1976 saw all sorts of bands spring up in The Sex Pistols' wake. Some were pretty good – The Damned, The Clash – some were rather dreadful – Eater, Slaughter and The Dogs. At a seedy Oxford Street venue, the 100 Club, a festival was held for all to show their colours. The violence of the crowd took a horrible twist when a glass thrown towards the front ricocheted off a pillar and shattered into a girl's eye.

The punk thing was still in the pre-media stage and everyone was bidding for territory. All the small places where the gigs took place – as well as the 100 Club there was the Nashville, Dingwalls and the Marquee – were easy to get to, and difficult to leave once you were inside.

At this point the big guns moved in. Impressed by what they took to be a rowdier, more rabid version of The Rolling Stones, EMI began negotiations with the Pistols. A contract was formally signed in October 1976 and work began on the first single, a confrontational stream of jagged one-liners called 'Anarchy In The UK.'

It was released in November 1976 but weak distribution meant that it lost momentum low in the charts. A tour of Britain was being organized and some cool publicity was needed ...

After the fuss of the Bill Grundy incident died down nobody was any the wiser: were they plied with alcohol or weren't they? The terse statement from Thames TV pointed out that no one is allowed so much as a can of lager before 5.30. But there are pubs in and around the Euston area ...

It was 1 December 1976 and in a stroke of inspired public relations one of the researchers at the 'Today' office booked The Sex Pistols and their friends to appear on the programme and explain to Bill Grundy just exactly what all this nonsense was all about.

They were the last item on the show, gathered in a malevolent giggling semicircle at Bill Grundy's feet. He laid into them right from the start. He'd heard that punks were non-materialistic chaps, anarchists and so on, and didn't this jar slightly with the news that EMI had spent £40,000 on them? Not at all, answered one of the band. The more the merrier. In fact, the more the merrier the sooner the better, since they'd spent the first lot.

Grundy then started on a totally different tack, listing some classical composers – Beethoven, Mozart, Bach and Brahms — presumably as a preamble for dismissing the Sex Pistols as musical buffoons. But he got no further. 'They're wonderful people,' chimed in a Pistol. Grundy was confused, lost for a reply. 'Well, suppose they turn other people on?' he floundered. 'That's their tough shit,' muttered Johnny Rotten. Grundy pounced on the expletive. The Pistols started to mock him, one of them suggesting that 'he's like yer Dad, inne, this geezer? Or yer grandad'.

Grundy picked on a waif-like girl at the front. 'I've always wanted to meet you,'she said. Perhaps, he suggested, they could meet afterwards. 'You dirty sod,' castigated a Pistol. And then Grundy lost the rag, altogether, forever, making TV history. Lapsing into the vernacular and desperate to regain control he said, 'Well, keep going, chief. You've got another five seconds. Say something outrageous.' 'You dirty bastard.' More, more. 'You dirty fucker.' Grundy tried sarcasm: 'What a clever boy.' The Pistols volleyed it back: 'What a fucking rotter.'

Grundy was a broken man. In his usually fluent outro-to-camera he realized what he had done and tried to make amends. 'Well, that's it for tonight. The other rocker, Eamonn, I'm saying nothing about him, will be back tomorrow. I'll be seeing you soon. I hope I'm not seeing you again (to the Pistols). From me though, goodnight.'

The Thames switchboard found itself in overload mode as the complaints reached saturation level. A Thames TV spokesman apologized on behalf of his beleaguered station and assured shocked viewers that Bill Grundy had been 'carpeted'.

It was, like the Thorpe affair and the Parkinson shenanigans, a glorious opportunity for people who have never transgressed a single law in their lives to go into a quiet studio somewhere and vent spleen. MPs were lobbied, newspapers were contacted, the IBA were notified. Bill Grundy, whose career thus far had been fairly unspectacular, became a Hitleresque villain. He provided the punchline to the affair when he was collared by a *Daily Mail* reporter. 'You'll get nothing from me,' he said, 'so you can fuck off.'

The Grundy wife and kids were dragged out to testify that Grundy senior never swore in front of them and indeed was very opposed to this sort of carry-on, although Mrs Grundy conceded that 'with the boys in the pub' her husband occasionally used some pretty strong language'.

The Sex Pistols were now stars. As Grundy was suspended and the ire of Britain aired on every available lively letters page the question of who these people were and what they wanted suddenly posed itself. There were enough defenders of their behaviour and supporters who claimed they had been provoked to keep the story running for a long time. Even arch punk terrorist Bill Haley, the scourge of suburban cinemas everywhere, was pressed for a comment. 'I'm all for entertainment,' answered the big man, 'but I've got a teenage daughter. And I wouldn't like her to listen to some of the language these fellows use.'

From this point on, every time The Sex Pistols drew breath individually or collectively – the heat was on. The press was out in force at Heathrow Airport to report on a rumpus in the VIP lounge.

They allegedly saw Pistols vomiting in corridors, spitting at other passengers and at each other, and concluded that the KLM officials gave them a VIP send-off because the other passengers on the Amsterdam flight refused to travel with them. One such plaintiff moaned, 'I think they must have been drinking and they looked as if they needed a good wash.'

The result was that EMI sacked them. Appalled by the extent of the bad publicity, and reasoning that the sale of The Sex Pistols on a worldwide basis would be a hazardous enterprise, the gentlemen of Britain's most prestigious record company baulked at the future. For one thing, there was Jubilee Year coming up, and the group had written a song that went, 'God save the Queen/Her fascist regime'.

Malcolm McLaren was rumoured to have taken EMI for £50,000 – £10,000 more than Grundy had accused them of getting. The record company's statement, while stating that a lot of the press reports had been greatly exaggerated, said that EMI felt unable to promote the group's records internationally in view of the adverse publicity.

Early 1977 saw bassist Glen Matlock sacked, allegedly for liking The Beatles. Matlock made no secret of his musicianship and the fact that he was keen for the Pistols to develop as a first-rate rock 'n' roll band. His dislike of Rotten's lyrics and his irritation at the unprofessional attitude of the singer (like when Rotten threatened to beat him up onstage for example) distanced him from the rest of the Pistols. He was replaced by an associate of Rotten's, one-time fan of the band and instigator of the pogo: John Simon Ritchie. Taking the *nom de guerre* Sid Vicious, he decided he could learn how to play the bass.

It was some comment on how McLaren saw the Pistols developing that he replaced their best musician with someone who could not even play. But Sid was an image man par excellence, a dead-end walking spike, with a chronic heroin problem and a love of beating up people smaller than himself.

On 9 March The Sex Pistols signed with A&M Records for £25,000.

On 16 March The Sex Pistols left A&M Records for £50,000.

The legend was now hysterical and cash-laden. The great rock 'n' roll swindle had taken place. A&M, it seems, had been persuaded that The Sex Pistols could be controlled, that they were merely of the order of boisterous boys, and the signing took place outside Buckingham Palace. Then came an incident in which the band were alleged to have visited their new record company to say hello and vomited all over the carpets. The staff, in a state of shock, protested, trusty A&M artist Rick Wakeman protested, and the deal was rescinded (with, of course, compensation being paid to the artists).

In May 1977 they signed with Virgin. Their second single, 'God Save The Queen', was released the same month. With newspaper outrage in Jubilee year, radio bans, and a particularly uninspiring Rod Stewart single, it failed to reach the coveted number one spot in the charts. But there seems little doubt that it was the fastest selling record of the year. In June, Virgin hired a boat and sailed a party down the Thames. Eleven people, including McLaren, were arrested on its return. The backlash had started; it would not be long before the Great British Public joined in.

In one week in June there were three savage attacks on Sex Pistols. The first incident was an assault on their art director Jamie Reid, who had a leg broken and his face smashed up. Incident number two gave Johnny Rotten a slashed face in a brutal razor attack by men who felt that the Queen was getting too hard a time from these characters, and perhaps someone ought to stick up for her. In the third attack, drummer Paul Cook was set upon by five men outside Shepherd's Bush tube station. He was stabbed several times and bludgeoned on the back of the head with an iron bar. The press expressed a wish to take photographs of the scars.

Nobody said it would be easy, but democracy's a funny old game, as The Sex Pistols found out when they released their debut LP, *Never Mind The Bollocks, Here's The Sex Pistols*. Titled after a catchphrase coined by guitarist Steve Jones, it zoomed straight to number one in the album charts and led to a dilemma for retailers up and down the country should they promote it in their windows, or hide its lurid cover in a brown paper bag, or what? Should they stock it at all? The law decided for them when a test case was brought against a Nottingham retailer, charging him with a contravention of the Indecent Advertisements Act (1889). The three magistrates found him not guilty, although they could not resist further comment: 'Much as my colleagues and I wholeheartedly deplore the vulgar exploitation of the worst instincts of human nature for the purposes of commercial profits, we must reluctantly find you not guilty.'

A newspaper article the same month, December, lambasted the group over the title of one of their new songs, 'Belsen Was A Gas'. A spokesman from the Board Of Deputies Of British Jews expressed his shock and disgust over the song, which the band had been playing on their tour of Holland: 'I can only say that theirs is a very degenerate art if they can compose songs like this with such offensive titles.'

In 1978 The Sex Pistols went on an ill-advised tour of the American South, during which all the chickens in the coop came home to roost and combustion occurred. Reports filtered through to the British papers of sporadic outbreaks of violence directed at the band, and of Sid Vicious's extraordinary behaviour on stage. At one show in Memphis he stabbed himself with a knife. The wound was dressed but he pulled the dressing off later in the show to expose the bloody gash.

Rotten got bored and headed off to New York. Vicious was admitted to hospital after a drug overdose, and the two urchin rockers, Jones and Cook, sallied off to Rio to hang out with Great Train Robber and hero of both, Ronnie Biggs. This last trio, the least likely bunch of musicians, actually continued as The Sex Pistols throughout the summer, releasing a Biggsian epic variously titled 'No-One Is Innocent' and 'Cosh The Driver' which boasted the lyrics, 'God save Martin Borman and Nazis on the run'. Johnny Rotten, when asked, claimed that The Sex Pistols had ceased operations when he left.

In October 1978 the dead body of Sid Vicious's girl-friend, Nancy Spungen, was discovered at New York's Chelsea Hotel. Vicious, who claimed not to be able to remember any of the previous evening's events, was arrested and charged with her murder. She had been stabbed repeatedly with a knife.

Five days later he was released on bail of $50,000, but he was a hopeless case by now and was back on remand in a matter of weeks, after beating up Patti Smith's brother Todd in a nightclub. In February he was released on bail again, for the same amount, and a day later he was dead. He died from heroin which his mother later claimed to have provided.

Malcolm McLaren kept the scam going a little while

longer, until the film *The Great Rock 'n' Roll Swindle* was completed. There were also assorted compilation LPs with titles like *Carri On Sex Pistols* and *Flogging A Dead Horse*. By then Jones and Cook were generally unemployed, Rotten had reverted to his real name John Lydon and was fronting an arty combo called Public Image Limited, steadfastly refusing to play Pistols songs, and McLaren was tampering with the image of one Adam Ant.

When McLaren next burst on the scene, in the early Eighties, it was with a band called Bow Wow Wow. They were fronted by a 15-year-old singer called Annabella Lwin whom McLaren had reportedly rescued from a launderette. He recreated Manet's 'Dejeuner sur l'Herbe' with Annabella naked for the cover of the band's debut album. McLaren planned to branch out into child porn and drew up a blueprint for an underage sex magazine called *Chicken*. EMI dropped the band and McLaren picked up another cool £55,000. When last seen he was making an album combining rock and opera called *Madame Butterfly*. It is highly likely that we will be hearing more from him.

Paul McCartney is Dead

One of the principal effects of The Beatles' decision not to play any more concerts after 1966 was that the public had a vital dimension to their hero worship snatched away. Sure, The Beatles were in the studio making their finest records, and could be glimpsed occasionally emerging bleary-eyed from some session or other. But it wasn't the same. The Beatles weren't visible any more. They couldn't be monitored like before. And that is how, towards the end of the Sixties, the rumour began to spread, in all its absurd, malevolent glory, that Paul McCartney was dead.

Or to be perfectly precise, that Paul McCartney had been killed in a car crash in November 1966. The implications of this were fairly obvious, such as who exactly was that playing the terrific bass lines on 'With A Little Help From My Friends' and 'Penny Lane', and how come his mysterious successor had a dead ringer of a voice?

Assuming that Paul McCartney is still very much alive, which seems like a pretty sensible assumption to make, an analysis of the so-called 'proof' of his untimely demise will give some idea of not only the frightening intensity of Beatlemania, but also the lunatic edge of the Sixties.

The story was supposedly started in America by a college paper. Pretty soon it made a local radio station, and on the basis of the no-smoke-without fire rule, spread across the States.

The car crash story started when it, was discovered that an accident of the kind described in the rumour had taken place around the time specified. One of the two fatally injured passengers was a young man with dark hair. He had been disfigured beyond all recognition.

Another fact which lent credence to the rumour was that The Beatles had held a McCartney lookalike competition in 1966. This now took on a vaguely disturbing angle – were they in fact searching, under the guise of a goodnatured contest, for a replacement for their dead bass player? It seemed plausible at the time, especially when it was discovered that no announcement had ever been made regarding any winner of the contest.

The story circulated that a young Scotsman named William Campbell had replaced McCartney and had been playing on recordings by the group since 1966. Their retirement from concert appearances meant that nobody could twig that it was a bogus Paul.

In the crazy logic of the best rumours, the treasure hunt did not end there. For the story went that The Beatles were so contrite at having duped their fans that, towards the end of the Sixties, they began to put clues on the sleeves of their albums and into their lyrics. These clues, when deciphered and compiled, added up to indisputable proof that Paul McCartney was dead. That was the theory.

The 'clues' started as far back as the song 'Yellow Submarine'. Dating from the year 1966, this song is a mildly controversial one even without shadowy undertones of possible death mentioned in the grooves – its childish ditty format is reckoned to mask one of John Lennon's most enthusiastic drug songs. As regards the Paul rumour, the story had it that at one point in the song Lennon shouts out 'Paul's a queer', the object being to instigate a smear campaign against McCartney so that fans would not feel too bad when they learned that he was actually brown bread.

Two more 'clues' in the lyrics of songs fuelled the rumours. One is fairly obvious – the line in 'A Day In The Life' which runs 'he blew his mind out in a car'. It is now widely believed that this refers to Tara Browne, the heir to the Guinness fortunes, who died in a car crash just before recording for the song commenced. The other clue is more obscure. Apparently there is a spoken line in the lengthy fade out on 'Strawberry Fields Forever' which goes 'I buried Paul'. Others have since argued that it is Lennon saying 'Cranberry sauce'. This, on the face of it, seems more likely. However, there remains the possibility that, having sung all the words to 'Strawberry Fields', he is in fact complaining to the other Beatles, 'I'm very hoarse'.

The remainder of the evidence lies in the sleeves of the LPs released by The Beatles between the years 1967 and 1969. The first one of these, *Sgt. Pepper's Lonely Hearts Club Band*, boasts an impressive pop-art mural of celebrities and statesmen, with the four Beatles at the front of the throng. Look closely and one can see a 'wreath' of flowers arranged in the shape of a bass guitar. Squint at the flowers and they appear to read PAUL? This was taken to mean a question mark hanging over McCartney's existence. The raised hand at the back of Paul's head on the front cover is supposedly an Indian death sign. But for proof positive, eager theoreticians gestured excitedly to the inner sleeve – there was the reputedly alive 'n' kicking bassist wearing a badge with the damning initials OPD. Could this mean anything other than Officially Pronounced Dead?

Yes. It could stand for Ontario Police Department, where he was given the badge.

The rumour-mongers were not deterred. All the walrus symbolism of the *Magical Mystery Tour* LP (apart from the song 'I Am The Walrus' on the record, Paul is dressed like one on the cover) was taken to mean a death obsession, for no other reason than that a walrus in *Alice In Wonderland* killed a few oysters. But, there again, was a raised hand behind McCartney's head. Twice, in the accompanying booklet.

The transitional *Yellow Submarine* soundtrack album fared no better. Yet again Paul McCartney was seen with a hand raised above his head.

However, it was the cover of *Abbey Road* that sent the really inventive scandal hunters into paroxysms of creativity. The four Beatles were crossing Abbey Road in north London in what appeared to more sensitive eyes to be a mock funeral procession. John Lennon, at the head of the procession and dressed in white, was the preacher. Ringo, lagging behind but still smartly attired, was the mourner. George, in casual clothes and languishing at the back, was the gravedigger. And Paul was the corpse. Look – not only was he quite clearly dead, he was also not wearing any shoes. And everyone knows that most countries bury their dead barefoot.

A Volkswagen car parked in the middle distance was taken as an important clue. Its registration number reads, in part, 281 F. Keen but erroneous – mathematicians calculated that McCartney's age in the year of Abbey Road's release would have been 28 IF he had lived. Actually, being of 1942 vintage, Paul would have been 27. But then it was remembered that The Beatles were heavily into Eastern mysticism, and those religions believe that everybody is born one year old. Suddenly it made sense.

Ironically, the treasure hunters missed the most blatant and irrefutable clue of all. During the fade out of 'Back In The USSR', the first song on the 'White Album', John Lennon can be heard quite clearly speaking the words, "Ere, Yoko, 'ave this bass. Paul won't need it where 'e's goin'.'

Jim Morrison

'There's the known. And there's the unknown. And what separates them is the door, and that's what I want to be. I want to be the door.' – Jim Morrison, 1967.

There is a man living in the Amazonian rainforests who has one hell of a past, should he care to own up to it.

Or, alternatively, there is a bath tub in a flat in Paris that could tell a few stories.

Nobody knows what happened on the night of 2 July 1971; nobody who is alive today saw Jim Morrison's dead body. All that is known for certain is that during his 27 years on the earth he changed forever the way rock music is presented on stage, totally redefined the concept of rock singer as messiah to a subservient generation, and completely rewrote the book on the matter of rock lyrics.

As a poet in a bluesy, gutsy rock group, as a melodramatic and dangerous performer, as a tortured artist, he appeared to be the god of several different religions, all committed to the same goal: 'the breaking away or overthrowing of established order ... revolt, chaos, especially activity that seems to have no meaning.'

James Douglas Morrison was born on 8 December 1943, in Florida, the son of a fastidiously upright highranking naval officer. A hyperactive, intelligent child, the young Jim bewildered his peers and thrilled his teachers by quoting extensively from Joyce, Kerouac and Nietzsche while still in high school. His genius IQ and craving for the classics went hand in hand with a magnetic personality. Pretty soon he was engaging in verbal duels with his English teacher.

A keen writer himself, he was a sucker for the Rimbaud legend. Rimbaud had written all his poetry by the end of his teens and vanished into a life of slave trading in Africa. He had also put forth the increasingly popular proposition that the true poet – as opposed to the would-be poet – must risk personal ruin on every level in order to stand a realistic chance of seeing the unknown, the mad, the beautiful.

Turned on to rock music by friends at UCLA, where he was studying cinematography, Morrison started to set his words to music. He met up with organist Ray Manzarek, and the latter's reaction 'Those are the greatest lyrics I've ever heard' propelled them both into a serious rock career. The whole thing gelled when guitarist Robbie Krieger and drummer John Densmore enlisted. In 1965 The Doors began to play in public.

Months of rehearsals and useful practice gigs in deserted bars helped to perfect the act. In it the hitherto-shy Morrison, skinned down to a lean, confident ten stones, was behaving increasingly dramatically, serving up his lyrics with theatrical moves and overt, sexual poses. He began to consider very seriously the role of poet/leader/visionary, and gobbled tabs of LSD to open up a few more doors. Lest the American interest in matters Vietnamese put a dampener on the exciting new proceedings, Morrison pleaded homosexuality to dodge the draft.

The blatant sexuality of his stage act in the formative months, which called for maximum friction between groin and microphone stand, was offset by the epic soundscapes that The Doors were building around his lyrics. Morrison's obsessions with potent poetic images sex, death, fire, speed, intimacy and distance, reptiles, violence and love were pretty articulate for one so possessed. What he was screaming had meaning. At this point the audience hysteria was a source of inspiration to him. Later he would be repulsed by it.

The Doors' most traumatic song at this stage was called 'The End'. It included an approximation of the Oedipal conflict, in which Morrison sang – or screamed – the following words:

And he came to a door
And he looked inside.
'Father.'
'Yes, son?'
'I want to kill you.'
'Mother!'
'I want to ffffuuuuuuuuuuuuuuuck youuuuuuuuuuuuu.'

The Doors' eponymous debut album was a mighty triumph on its release in 1967, and necessitated some sort of hackneyed biography for magazines to quote from. Bored with the usual 'favourite colour' scenario, Morrison cobbled together a few random notes along with scant biographical histories of the four Doors. He described his own attitude to being in the Doors as 'the feeling of a bow string being pulled back for 22 years and suddenly let go'. Further down the page he claimed that his parents were dead. As the focal point of the band, Morrison's life was becoming more and more complex. A natural drinker, one who drinks to drink rather than to socialize, he started to knock back greater and greater quantities of liquor, mixing it with perilous wedges of dope and frequent acid excursions. He was fairly settled into a relationship with a girlfriend, Pamela Courson, but enjoyed outbreaks of promiscuity. The faster the rollercoaster, the more he drank to stay in focus. Drink gradually usurped drugs. One night he visited Jac Hoizman, the head of his record label Elektra, and threw up all over his front porch. It was a common occurrence for him to go on stage tanked to the limit. Every night a different binge.

An incident in New Haven, Connecticut, towards the end of 1968 marked a swift decline in the quality of Doors performances. An argument backstage with a particularly unartistic cop resulted in Morrison being sprayed in the face with a can of mace. Morrison proceeded to relate the story on stage, suitably embellished, and was arrested for a breach of the peace.

Already exhibiting impatience with the mindless, stoned teenagers who he felt were desecrating the performances, he treated his audiences with more and more contempt, attempting to spur them into some kind of action, even if it had to be violent and negative.

Meanwhile his drinking had reached saturation level. His fridge had been stripped of food in order to accommodate more beer and he was banned from several bars in the Los Angeles area, where the group was based. He seemed to be drunk all the time. At a recording session for the song 'The Unknown Soldier' he needed 130 takes before he got it right.

His hatred of blanket audience conformity drove him over the edge. Being obviously drunk hadn't moved them, spitting at them hadn't moved them, and swearing at them had only excited them. He resolved to put into action a plan he had conceived many years before. He would instigate a riot, then stand back and observe at first hand the gut reactions of the rabble.

It is quite easy for a rock band to start a riot. All one has to do is play one's most provocative material very quickly, without a break, while raising personal hell up there on stage.

Therefore, one night in Chicago, Morrison deliberately

cued in the revolutionary 'The Unknown Soldier', the inflammatory 'Five To One' and the cataclysmic 'When The Music's Over'. All the while he gyrated to the music in a display of such terminal anguish that the audience charged the stage the minute he left it.

Encouraged by the toadying attentions of his entourage, he began to behave in arch poetic style – as practised years earlier by Dylan Thomas and Brendan Behan, to the detriment of both – and drank himself under every available table, emerging only to vomit or hassle some pretty waitress. His looks suffered, his weight shot up and, worst of all, his voice deteriorated.

The second riot came in New York. This time he went straight for the jugular. Right from the beginning of the set he did his epileptic contortionist's dance, clamping one fist on his crotch, the other on the microphone, writhing on the stage in a state of frenzied ecstasy. The result was a pitched battle between police and audience when the kids attempted to envelop the crazy man on stage.

He explained away the riots in playful fashion: 'We have fun. The kids have fun. The cops have fun.'

Still, the riots were becoming just another expected facet of The Doors' stage act. No longer were they a novelty. There was a depressing 'roll up, roll up, come and see the freaks' attitude in the minds of the kids.

Morrison felt that he had resolved the dilemma when he came into contact with a radical drama group called The Living Theatre. They were getting into areas of direct confrontation, using shock tactics like nudity and repetition to stun the audience and slap them out of their complacency. Morrison was starting to assimilate these ideas, wondering how to introduce them into a Doors show.

The fact that he failed miserably was put down at the time to alcohol, but it remains an extremely grey area. What he did in an effort to move a crowd was a depressing display of at worst egotistical machismo, at best

puerile petulance. Faced, in Miami, with a typically stultifying audience, he resorted as usual to some preliminary
abuse:

'You are all a bunch of fucking idiots. Your faces are
being pressed into the shit of the world. Take your fucking
friend and love him. Do you want to see my cock?'

He then, it was alleged, 'did lewdly and lasciviously
expose his penis in a vulgar or indecent manner with
intent to be observed, did place his hand on the penis and
shake it, and further . . . did simulate the acts of masturbation upon himself and oral copulation upon another.'

Although he did not know it at the time, there was a
warrant out for his arrest.

The hell-raising did not abate. A film he had an idea for
went to the rehearsal stage. One scene involved him dancing along a 17th floor ledge without a safety net. He did
this, despite the howling protests of friends, and finished
by urinating down to the street below.

The Doors were now about as popular as Henry VIII in
a singles' bar. The remaining gigs on their schedule were
cancelled by the local authorities for fear of further riots,
and they only managed to secure immediate work by
agreeing to what Morrison called a 'fuck clause' – in other
words, one hint of an unzipped fly and the cops get to join
in on the chorus.

While awaiting trial for the events in Miami, Morrison
was arrested a second time, for being drunk and disor-
derly on an airplane. In the wake of various hi-jacking
attempts, security around airports had tightened and this
was now a very serious charge. It was compounded by a
new charge, 'interfering with the flight of an aircraft'. The
offence carried ten years.

He was a wreck by now, unstable, teetering. He no
longer bothered to find a toilet when he needed to pee. Just
used the carpet. A lucky break at the 'hi-jacking' trial – the
key witness didn't recognize him – took care of one legal

matter. But the Miami affair was still outstanding and it seemed likely that no amount of hip legal rhetoric from the Morrison camp would be able to persuade the judge that Jim Morrison was actually bang in tune with the mores of the time.

In the meantime he married a witch. She was called Patricia Kennely and she edited one of Morrison's favourite American rock papers. In a formal witches' wedding, they signed their names in their own blood.

The Miami affair came to trial. Seventeen prosecution witnesses of pristine, virginal disposition took the oath and claimed to have been outraged/shocked/disgusted by Morrison's behaviour on the night of the alleged offences.

He was found guilty, to nobody's surprise, of profanity and indecent exposure. The sentence was six months in jail and a $500 fine. An appeal was lodged.

Morrison had been getting heavily into cocaine. His love of the quick high, the delirious rush, was satisfied perfectly by the effects of this drug, and he combined it with alcohol to produce a state of heightened neutralized glee.

Around this time he was approached by members of an antidrug campaign and asked to record a personalized message warning his impressionable teenage fans about the dangers of speed.

'Hello,' he began, 'this is Jim Morrison of The Doors. I just want to tell you that shooting speed ain't cool ... so snort it.'

Taking a major breather from the band, the trials, and all his worries, Morrison fled to Europe with his on-off girlfriend Pamela. He never returned.

On Monday, 5 July 1971, several calls were put through to the English offices of Elektra Records. Everybody wanted to know the same thing – was it true that Jim Morrison was dead?

The calls were shrugged off. It was perfectly in the nature of things to dodge rumours of Morrison's tragic demise. It happened every time he went on a weekend binge. The rumours, however, were gathering pace and this time there was no Morrison in the office to nullify them. So The Doors' manager called Pamela in Paris and received an oddly muted instruction to come over as soon as possible. Arriving the following day he found the flat; in it he found Pamela, a sealed coffin and a signed death certificate attributing the death of James Douglas Morrison to a heart attack. The coffin was interred the following day.

Immediately the stories began to circulate. It was pointed out that Pamela was the only one who saw the body apart from the doctor who signed the death certificate, and he couldn't be found. Suspicions were aroused that Morrison could have suffered anything so, well, mundane as a heart attack.

Jim Morrison died in a bath tub. This happens to be the common place for victims of a heroin overdose to end up (in the hope that the water will shock them back to life). Morrison had been seen hanging around notorious Parisian heroin dealers in the days leading up to his death. To this day Paris believes that Morrison died of an overdose.

The only one who could have settled the matter once and for all is now no longer in a position to do so: Pamela died in 1974.

Therefore, it is a case of whom you believe: a qualified Parisian doctor, albeit one who ran to ground and stayed there; the woman who was virtually his wife; or a few close friends who were privy to Morrison's most bitter attacks on the music business and the unspeakable evil of the dumb Pavlovian audiences. And they mention the marvellous, madcap plan he thought up one day as far back as 1967 – how, when it all got too hectic and too useless, he'd relocate to the jungle, lose his bearings in the new sensations and gradually forget the bad times. Then, when he was good and ready, he would make contact with his friends again, using the cryptic nom-de-guerre Mr Mojo Risin ... which crossword lovers will instantly recognize as an anagram of Jim Morrison.

Phil Spector

The facts about Phil Spector are easy enough to catalogue – but they make fairly astounding reading when you take into account his age and lack of experience, his small stature and his high-pitched voice. Never has such a blatantly inconsequential guy done so much. Well, at least, not since the mad heyday of Napoleon Bonaparte.

The facts are that, at age 17, he had already had a hit record. This was 'To Know Him Is To Love Him', an achingly tender love song recorded with loads of echo and credited to The Teddy Bears. Actually, apart from the sincere high school warbling of chanteuse Annette Kleinbard, the record was all Spector's. He wrote it, he sang on it, he played on it, he shared in its production. He even dreamed up the title, after reading similar words on his father's gravestone. In 1958 the 17-year-old Spector was already semi-legendary, incurring the wrath of all who met him due to his eccentricity and directness.

Three years later he was producing records regularly, with little success, but he was getting his name around. Three years after that, at the age of 23, he was the Tycoon Of Teen, producer of glorious teen laments like 'Be My Baby', 'Da Doo Ron Ron' and 'He's A Rebel', all delivered in Spector's customized 'Wall Of Sound', a studio technique whereby each record sounded as though three entire orchestras were playing on it.

The hits became longer, braver and greater. The Righteous Brothers' 'You've Lost That Lovin' Feeling' from

1965 could be called with some justification the most utterly perfect single of all time. 'Baby I Love You' was a huge hit for The Ronettes, the buxom, dark-eyed trio fashioned around Veronica Spector, Phil's wife. Then, in 1966, the industry hit back for what it saw as Spector's failure to pay his dues. All along he had played the game his way, as though rules were tiresome peripherals to be negotiated and ultimately forgotten about. He ignored the radio stations, believing (correctly) that his records were the best, so obviously they would get airplay. He was outspoken and ungrateful. Worse still, he was the very antithesis of the shy, retiring aw-shucks-it-was-nothing types much beloved of the music industry in the States at the time. After making an uncomplimentary comment about radio programmers on a TV documentary, he fell from grace with an almighty bang.

The rejection, when it arrived, came in ludicrous form. His masterwork, Ike and Tina Turner's 'River Deep, Mountain High' was not a hit. It entered the US charts at 88 and dropped straight out again. As it is now reckoned to be one of Spector's greatest achievements (as was his achievement of keeping Ike Turner off the record for fear of losing control over it), it stunned his friends. Its failure was variously laughed off, explained away with references to bad vocal mixes and so on, and most commonly justified by the assertion that Phil Spector had simply gone too far. It was, for what it's worth, a monstrous hit in Britain.

Spector retired from the music business, a crushed man, no longer interested in creating his complex 'teen symphonies'. He disappeared for more than two years, some say into the desert, and while he was gone the rumours about him started . . .

Legend had it that the reason Phil Spector was so tough and uncompromising was solely due to his height, or lack thereof. An incident from his early career brought his shortcomings sharply into focus. After a Teddy Bears show, Spector went to the lavatory and was followed in by four men who had seen the show and been less than overwhelmed. They locked the doors, opened their collective trouserage, and pissed all over the legend of Phillip Spector. He vowed, according to close friends, that this would 'never happen again'.

That is how the bodyguard obsession started – he was genuinely terrified of physical conflict.

He had been no stranger to controversy in the years before the hit flood began. Growing his hair to extraordinary lengths, even before The Beatles touched down in America and led the hirsute revolution, he also used to dress in sinister black cloaks, earning the nickname 'D'Artagnan'.

There was also the matter of the third single by his group The Crystals. They had been his first protégées, scoring reasonable hits in early 1962. Their latest single would be a song called 'He Hit Me (And It Felt Like A Kiss)'. In the song, which is in actual fact quite a happy little tune because the assailant and his hapless girlfriend make up and live to fight another day, the female singer provides a sulking commentary which was understandably mistaken for sadomasochism at the time. Listeners switched off in droves and the record was swiftly withdrawn.

After the mighty 'You've Lost That Lovin' Feeling' ('our Cilla' did a cover version of the song in Britain, cutting 40 seconds off it because she 'didn't want people to get bored'), Spector's fears and phobias took a turn for the worse. He developed a terror of airplanes, often getting off at the last minute before take-off because he was convinced it was going to crash.

Then there was the time he bought Lenny Bruce's negatives. Bruce, a risqué comedian whose persecution by the establishment turned him into first a junkie and then a corpse, died with a syringe stuck in his arm. Spector paid

$5,000 in 1966 for the police negatives.

Spector returned in early 1969 with a couple of half-hearted hits. He then began a long and fruitful association with two of The Beatles, George Harrison and John Lennon. This stemmed from his rescue- production job on The Beatles' last album, *Let It Be*, which was lambasted by, among others, Paul McCartney. Spector was the producer of Harrison's single 'My Sweet Lord', a fairly innocuous albeit uplifting record which was the subject of a court case when it was found to bear compositional similarities to a song by The Chiffons, 'He's So Fine'. (Interestingly enough, in 1976 Jonathan King, whose records tended to lampoon rather than plagiarise, included a version of 'He's So Fine' on his album *J.K. All The Way*, set to the tune of 'My Sweet Lord', complete with Harrison guitar solo impersonations and sporadic namechecks of Harrison songs such as 'Something' and 'Here Comes The Sun'.) The irony is that when Harrison lost the case, the man to whom he had to pay the damages was Allen Klein, the man whom Harrison was content to have as manager of The Beatles post-Epstein.

In April 1974 a story in the American press alleged that Phil Spector had been involved in a serious car crash travelling between Los Angeles and Phoenix. The car exploded into flames and Spector suffered multiple head injuries and severe burns. Several operations later, his press office did not seem to know exactly if he was getting better or not.

Spector recovered enough to produce Leonard Cohen's album *Death Of A Ladies' Man*, during which the story goes that he kept Cohen in the studio at gunpoint until the album was finished. That reminded the aficionados of classic Spector behaviour, like when he insisted on monitoring Veronica's calls back in the Sixties and refused to allow her to leave the grounds of the mansion in Hollywood where they lived, even threatening to kill her and keep her in a glass coffin. And the time when he pulled a gun on Stevie Wonder. And the time when he turned up at the Whisky A Go-Go and screamed so hard he had to be carried out.

If Spector stands accused of wanting the earth, all of it, right now, then he is also guilty of being a genius with malice aforethought. We don't need to know what he is up to now – every time 'Da Doo Ron Ron' comes on the radio, that's enough. His projects now are pretty insubstantial. In 1980 he produced The Ramones, a bunch of committed Spectorites from the wrong side of the tracks. One song, 'Rock'n'Roll High School' opens with a loud, effective, crashing guitar chord. It's the sort of thing Johnny Ramone plays in his sleep. Spector spent hours, days playing it back, adding to it, subtracting from it, mating it with itself until he eventually had it. Triumphantly he played it to the band. Johnny shrugged. It was okay . . . but wasn't it exactly the same as when he had played it?

The Mamas And The Papas

The pretty harmonies of The Mamas And The Papas hid a multitude of personal and narcotic sins, only really brought to the public's consciousness on the publication of John Phillips's extraordinary memoirs in the mid-Eighties. Although they were essentially a folk group, singing intricate fourpart vocal harmonies to create an often spellbinding whole, they were caught up in the superstardom channels of the mid-Sixties and they never really recovered.

The fact that the excess continued well into the Seventies and even into the Eighties is a testament both to the fact that friendships made in the Sixties are not easy to shake off, and that for a disturbingly large amount of people fame is something to be grasped at with clammy, desperate hands. Take that fame away and you are often left with a fierce drug habit.

Like many American kids of the Sixties, John Phillips was primed for performing after witnessing Elvis on the *Ed Sullivan Show*. Except that Phillips was no longer a kid. He had been in numerous vocal groups by 1956 and by the time The Mamas And The Papas had their first hit single in 1966 he would be thirty-one.

In the early Sixties he met a longhaired Californian beauty named Michelle Gilliam, whom he would later marry. She had a sweet voice, and so, together with a friend called Phil Blondheim (who would soon change his name to Scott McKenzie) they travelled the circuits as first The Journeymen and then The New Journeymen. After a minor nervous breakdown from Blondheim/McKenzie which culminated in him destroying his guitar on stage at Carnegie Hall he was edged out and Phillips met up with two Californian folkies called Denny Doherty and Cass Elliott. Doherty was a sure-footed vocalist who would eventually sing lead on several Mamas And Papas singles. Cass, or 'Mama' Cass as she was usually called, was a 20-stone kaftan-clad phenomenon with a heart made of such 18-carat gold that she had even married a casual boyfriend to enable him to dodge the draft for Vietnam.

In 1965 they practised singing together and, delighted with the results, began to travel and live as one big family. They all experimented with LSD and found it to their liking. Phillips became so dependent on it that at one stage he would not perform without it.

Barry McGuire, a fellow folkie who had had one of the biggest hits of that year with 'Eve Of Destruction', the anti-Vietnam song, advised them to see Lou Adier of Dunhill Records. They sang "California Dreamin'" and 'Monday Monday', two of their future biggest hits, and secured a record contract. Soon an album came out.

All was not happy in the Mamas And The Papas' camp however. The close personal lifestyle had inevitably led to some problems, not least the love affair that was brewing between Michelle Phillips and Denny Doherty. There was also a complex rivalry between Cass Elliott and Michelle Phillips based on the latter's good looks and the former's jealousy of same. Cass had charm, style and pizzazz but craved sexual attention, especially from Doherty. So there was a state of confusion as they faced up to stardom with the huge success of "California Dreamin'".

Of course they were acclaimed in the press nationwide. Nobody had ever seen a group like this and their image – not that they'd planned it – was a magnet for newshounds. Not only did they look great, especially Michelle, they sounded great too. And fat girls the country over were identifying with the mighty free spirit that was Cass Elliott.

Their second single, 'Monday Monday', was just as successful as 'California Dreamin'' and they should have been in a position to reap the financial rewards. However, the turbulence in the group had reached such hostile levels that John Phillips presented the others with an ultimatum: either he went or Michelle did. It was no contest and, in the summer of 1966 Michelle was fired. She was soon replaced by a girl named Jill Gibson.

The remaining Mama and the two Papas went to London where they found that they were heroes of such luminaries as The Beatles and The Rolling Stones and suddenly they gained access to a world where everything had a chemical formula. Doherty preferred to drink but the other two dived in with both feet.

Back in America things did not work out with Gibson so late 1966 saw the return of Michelle to the group. Michelle and John Phillips set up home in Bel-Air and embarked on a drug binge that lasted throughout 1967.

Phillips it was who had the original idea for the Monterey Free Festival. Mulling over the possibilities of giving something back to the beautiful children of

California he suddenly hit upon the idea of a weekend of pop music featuring such local talent as The Jefferson Airplane and Big Brother And The Holding Company, complemented by international artists like The Who and Ravi Shankar. The Mamas And The Papas would wind the whole thing up on the final day.

In order to publicize the event, he wrote a song about it which went, 'if you're going to San Francisco, be sure to wear some flowers in your hair'. He gave the song to his old friend Scott McKenzie to record and suddenly it was one of the bestselling records in the whole country. Not only had Phillips written one of the biggest hits of 1967, not only had he written the anthem for the Peace And Love generation, he has also written a song whose royalties would keep him in drugs for the next 13 years.

Phillips's role in the organization of Monterey cannot be understated. With so many dazed hippies around, it was his administration that got the whole thing going smoothly, and he even had time to throw out a few unwanted acid dealers if their supplies did not meet the required standard.

But there was one major cloud on the horizon for 1967 – Cass had discovered heroin. She was restless to forge some sort of solo career, and the rest of the group were finding it difficult to record their new album. In addition, she was having extreme weight problems. All in all, she was floundering in a sea of losers and users. Towards the end of her career in the group she was arrested in Southampton when she disembarked from HMS France for the crime of stealing two blankets and a key from a hotel.

Ironically, the group was laden with dope at the time, but it was all academic since she was found not guilty.

The next Mamas And Papas single was released in 1968. However, to the chagrin of John Phillips, it was credited to Mama Cass alone, something about which he had not been consulted. However, he did not begrudge Cass her solo glory, and when she secured a week of performances at Caesar's Palace in Las Vegas there was a convoy of well-wishers there to see her. This was unfortunate, since she was so drug-addled that she could barely stand, and the show was a disaster.

Around this time Phillips met his future third wife, the woman who would share his Seventies hell, the South African actress Genevieve Waite. He also showed a lucky streak when he narrowly avoided being one of those butchered by the Manson family. He had heard of Manson from Dennis Wilson. Wilson, the drummer with the Beach Boys, had in the beginning enthused about Manson and his liberated young protégés, but later showed fear and loathing of the crazy messiah.

Phillips did not know much about the protégés, but he'd heard the songs of the messiah, and he thought they were appalling. However, for some reason, Roman Polanski suspected Phillips of being involved in the events that had led to the death of his wife, and only after a dramatic confrontation was Phillips's innocence assured.

With the break-up of The Mamas And The Papas came solo albums. *Wolf King of L.A.*, the first effort from Phillips, died in the shops, although he was still being praised in the music press as a vital songwriter. With the failure of the record he turned to cocaine and blanked out a little of the hurt.

By 1972, when Phillips married Genevieve Waite, it had been four years since his last hit record. But the list of wedding guests proved that he was now on a plane of celebrity status where hit records don't much matter and where nobody has to prove themselves. The Jaggers, Warren Beatty, Jack Nicholson, they all kept John Phillips living in the jet set lounge.

By now his children from previous marriages were on drugs, although both of them were still in their early teens.

A flirtation with LSD gave way to a dependency on cocaine, and there was enough of it lying around the house for the kids to dip in unnoticed once in a while. Phillips himself had reached the stage where the needle does the damage.

Not even the death of Cass Elliott shocked him back to sobriety. She died in London in July 1974, after a triumphant show at the Palladium. The story that has circulated ever since is that she choked to death on a ham sandwich. Phillips later put the death down to a heroin overdose. The truth seems much more mundane. She was just too fat, and her heart gave out.

John Phillips was now mainlining heroin, shooting it straight into his veins. He had a new circle of friends, all of whom were doing exactly the same as he was. And he spent a lot of time at the London home of Keith Richards and Anita Pallenberg.

Despite the crippling effects of heroin on the creative juices Phillips still had plans to record. An album produced by Mick Jagger was mooted, but eventually the sessions descended into full-scale mayhem when Phillips refused to come out of the bathroom to sing. One day he woke up and found he did not have any veins left.

A visit to a doctor seemed to provide the answer when the medical man assured him that cocaine could cure heroin addiction if one took enough of it. But all that happened was that Phillips became addicted to that too. He was now sticking a syringe into his hand every ten minutes.

His family fell apart. His son was a heroin addict and his daughter, a successful TV actress on American networks, was arrested for possession. The network suspended her and she was forced to enter a drug-rehabilitation programme.

Phillips himself was busted in 1980. It was serious. Not only was he in possession of drugs himself, but he was accused of dealing to others. He faced a colossal forty-five years in jail if found guilty. He had only one option – to try to preach the gospel to the TV cameras and hope for leniency from the court. Therefore, he and his daughter went on anti-drug crusades for most of the following year and dealt with the inevitable jeers from cynical journalists that it was about time. Occasionally he would be given a standing ovation when he told his harrowing story, most especially if the narrative was punctuated with the odd glimpse of his scarred hands.

It looked bad. Even Michelle was against him, telling tales of drunkenness and cruelty. That, and the fact that the only obvious recourse for someone who has survived cocaine and heroin cross-addiction is to become a raving alcoholic, cast a shadow over the proceedings.

Incredibly, John Phillips was jailed for only 30 days and fined $15,000, a verdict that some resentfully attributed to his celebrity role.

He then put into action a new, though hardly improved, Mamas And Papas. The line-up was Phillips, Denny Doherty (who had had lingering problems with alcohol), Spanky McFarlane (a Cass semi-lookalike) and Phillips's daughter Laura McKenzie Phillips filling the Michelle role.

Michelle for her part was not overwhelmed by the volte face. 'I just hope John's ninth detoxification attempt is more successful than his previous eight,' she wrote to one magazine.

Fleetwood Mac

1988 saw the venerable Fleetwood Mac, originally a British R&B band but now highly regarded practitioners of what is known as AOR (album-oriented rock, or sometimes adult-oriented), celebrating its 21st anniversary with a mega-selling album, *Tango In The Night*, which, like several of its predecessors, topped the album chart in various lands, including Britain.

The years since the group's triumphant emergence at the Windsor Jazz & Blues Festival in 1967, alongside a galaxy of star names including Eric Clapton (then in Cream), Jeff Beck, Rod Stewart and Ron Wood (all part of Beck's group), and one time Rolling Stone Mick Taylor, saw ups and downs, triumphs and tragedies on a scale which would almost appear too far-fetched to be believable – except that they were true.

The group was formed by Peter Greenbaum, a guitarist from London's East End, who first found fame as replacement for Eric Clapton in John Mayall's Bluesbreakers. Calling himself Peter Green, the guitarist soon formed a bond with two other Bluesbreakers, drummer Mick Fleetwood and bass player John McVie, and with the addition of a young devotee of blues legend Elmore James named Jeremy Spencer, Fleetwood Mac Mark 1 was quickly a sensation. At first the band did not include McVie, who was hedging his bets and remaining with Mayall until Green could guarantee him a regular income. His position as bass player was temporarily filled by Bob Brunning, today Headmaster of an infants' school in South London.

When McVie finally agreed to join, the group found success at speed. By the end of 1968, they had not only achieved a chart-topping hit with 'Albatross', but had also expanded to a quintet with the arrival of a third singer/guitarist, Danny Kirwan. Things went well for a while, with several more big hits such as 'Man Of The World' and 'Oh Well'. But Green was experiencing problems in dealing with the fame, and particularly the money, which stardom brought in its wake, and in May 1970 left the band. His replacement, Christine Perfect, was a singer and keyboard player, who had enjoyed some fame as vocalist on 'I'd Rather Go Blind', a hit for the group Chicken Shack, of which she was a member. In addition, she happened to be married to John McVie.

The hits soon stopped, and not long after Christine McVie joined, Fleetwood Mac found themselves without another founder member, when Jeremy Spencer disappeared during an American tour and resurfaced as a member of a religious cult known as the Children Of God. Green was persuaded to help the band fulfil their US touring commitments, but was adamant that this was just a temporary measure.

In August, 1972, Kirwan was asked to leave the band – according to a surviving member of the band, Kirwan was a nervous wreck, which made attempts to restore the group to its former status extremely difficult. Each of the three singer/guitarists has recorded subsequently, but none of the resulting albums have achieved commercial success to compare with that of Fleetwood Mac's earlier days.

Someone claiming to be Jeremy Spencer turned up in London during the Seventies, and was booked into a large London concert hall. Bob Brunning had been asked to confirm the identity of the ersatz Spencer, which he did, later saying that the bogus Spencer seemed to know the answers to several searching questions which should have unmasked an impostor.

Green re-adopted the Jewish faith he had largely abandoned in favour of rock stardom. He was sufficiently troubled by substantial royalty payments relating to his compositions and recordings for Fleetwood Mac that he allegedly threatened an accountant with a gun in his desire to stop these payments. He subsequently spent time in a mental hospital. Kirwan periodically also finds life similarly difficult and is known to psychiatrists.

Between mid-1971 and the start of 1975, three more musicians joined and then left the band. The longest of the three to endure was the first American to join Fleetwood Mac, Bob Welch. The briefest stay was that of vocalist Dave

Walker, who was asked to leave due to his having an affair with Mick Fleetwood's wife. The group's five albums during Welch's time with the band were at best minor successes, and then only in America, where the group were now based. Stateside audiences seemed more interested in Fleetwood Mac than their British counterparts, who clearly considered the group a pale imitation of the one which had scored with 'Albatross', 'Man Of The World' and so on.

Everything changed for the better when Lindsey Buckingham, a singer/ guitarist/songwriter, and his then girlfriend, singer/songwriter Stephanie (Stevie) Nicks signed on when Welch departed. The first album by the new line up was simply titled *Fleetwood Mac*, and sold prodigiously around the world. Fleetwood Mac Mark 10 became the most successful line up thus far, and was in great demand, touring internationally for the best part of a year without a break.

This unexpected activity placed an immense strain on the group's personal relationships, and the followup album, *Rumours*, featured a collection of songs detailing the events which led to the McVies' marriage breaking up and the end of the romantic relationship between Buckingham and Nicks.

Mick Fleetwood was at the time also experiencing marital traumas (no doubt in the wake of the Dave Walker incident), and he and his wife Jenny (sister of Patti Boyd, who has at various times been married to both George Harrison and Eric Clapton) also divorced. Subsequently, Fleetwood and Jenny remarried and re-divorced.

The personal anguish which each member of Fleetwood Mac must have been feeling as they entered the recording studio to make *Rumours* appears to have made no difference to the end product which became the biggest selling album ever. Although it probably no longer holds that title it has sold an estimated 20 million copies plus at the time of writing.

More recently, after the recording of *Tango In The Night*, Lindsey Buckingham has also left Fleetwood Mac, and two newcomers have joined the band. What fresh experiences may yet accrue to this ultimately durable group can only be guessed at.

The Beach Boys

In 1988 Brian Wilson released his first solo album. If one didn't know anything about Wilson, this would not be of particular note. But to several generations of fans who continue to regard The Beach Boys as the epitome of sunshine music, it was an event akin to John Lennon's return to recording when it seemed that the exBeatle had abandoned music in favour of learning to bake bread.

Brian Wilson was the eldest of three brothers who formed the nucleus of The Beach Boys. He was the group's main songwriter, its musical heart, and his songs, arrangements, productions and clear vision had made the five-man group (completed by a cousin of the Wilsons, Mike Love, and a school friend, Al Jardine) the biggest American band during the Sixties, with classic hit after classic hit featuring in the charts. Success of this measure would be quite enough for any ordinary person, but Brian was not content to rest upon his laurels, despite the fact that his hearing in one ear was defective to the point where he was unable to listen stereophonically.

As records became more and more complex, and production values increased in sophistication, Wilson strove to keep up with the musical advances being pioneered by other artists, notably The Beatles. The difference was that the Lennon & McCartney songwriting team consisted of two equal parts, either of whom could write tunes or lyrics. With The Beach Boys, Brian was sometimes helped out with words by Mike Love, but wrote many of the group's classics by himself. The Beatles could rely on George Martin's skill as a producer and arranger, but Brian had to do all that by himself too, as well as performing live with the group on an endless round of concerts.

By the end of 1964, with a dozen US Top 40 hits to the group's credit, all masterminded by Brian, as well as seven hit albums which were largely his conception, Brian had a nervous breakdown during an Australian tour. He had recently married and almost simultaneously had experienced marijuana for the first time.

An early replacement for touring purposes was latter-day country music star Glen Campbell. A permanent sixth Beach Boy, Bruce Johnston, joined the band after Campbell left to become 'the dream of the everyday housewife', to quote the title of one of his hits.

With the burden of live work lifted apart from the mental anguish produced by overworking, the proximity to powerful amplification systems caused him hearing problems – Brian began work on the group's next album, *The Beach Boys Today*, and used the freedom from group commitments to experiment while they toured. At first this produced pop masterpieces like 'California Girls', and the album *Pet Sounds* was regarded as one of the finest albums of the Sixties. Three tracks from it, including 'Sloop John B' and the sublime 'God Only Knows' were big hits.

The only clouds on the horizon came with the release of *Sgt. Pepper* by The Beatles, which totally eclipsed *Pet Sounds* commercially. There was also growing resentment against Brian on the part of the rest of the group. Reportedly, he had virtually made the album on his own, multi-part vocals and all, while the group were out on the road, and it was presented to them as something of a *fait accompli*.

Brian may have sympathized with his group's wishes to be involved in the recordings rather than merely trying

550

to copy the hit records which bore their name, but over which they had little influence. There was greater collaboration in the next song the group released. It would become the most familiar song associated with The Beach Boys – 'Good Vibrations'. An undoubted masterpiece, it involved other group members vocally, and Mike Love wrote the lyrics, although it was recorded over a six month period and is said to have cost $50,000 to record. It topped the charts on both sides of the Atlantic, and Brian had caught up with The Beatles again – at least, in his own mind.

He was experimenting with every imaginable drug, including acid (LSD), which may explain his massive overconfidence. The next album on which he embarked, *Smile*, is still legally unreleased 20 years after it was abandoned by Brian, although substantial portions of various stages of the album have escaped into the hands of bootleggers. Although its suppression has led to it becoming something of a legend, those who are familiar with the album are unimpressed, considering it totally lacking in direction.

Brian referred to it as 'writing a teenage symphony to God', and perhaps in an attempt to reach God-like mental status, he ingested vast quantities of drugs. His collaborator as lyricist for *Smile*, Van Dyke Parks, was a charmingly eccentric child actor turned composer whose first album, *Song Cycle*, was critically praised but commercially ignored.

One song from the *Smile* sessions that was completed and released as a single was 'Heroes & Villains', a musically complex item which was substantially less of a hit than 'Good Vibes'. The rest of the album had even less to recommend it. Finally, it was removed from the record label's schedule, although about half a million sleeves had been printed; these have been circulating ever since.

Brian Wilson had apparently drugged himself into oblivion by now. Stories were circulating about how he had a sandpit constructed in his living room. The grand piano being in the sandpit allowed Brian to wiggle his toes in the sand while he composed – until the Wilson family pets found the sand very useful as a bowel-evacuation station.

One of the tracks on *Smile* is known as 'Fire' (part of 'The Elements Suit!'). An army of string players who had assembled in a large recording studio were instructed by Brian, who had hired them, to don toy fire helmets. A bucket containing burning embers was brought into the studio at Brian's instigation – he said he wanted the musicians to smell smoke. It took over 20 attempts with all the string players before Brian left the studio with the track completed to his satisfaction. Later that day, he heard that a building near the studio where he had been working had burned down, and decided that this was not a coincidence – a journalist who witnessed 'Fire' being recorded said it evoked 'roaring, windstorm flames, failing timbers, mournful sirens and sweating firemen'.

Whether or not Brian's curious behaviour had a knock-on effect on the rest of the group is difficult to decide, but other Beach Boys also began to get involved in bizarre situations. The pop royalty of the period, including The Beatles, Mick Jagger and Marianne Faithfull, Donovan and others appeared to legitimize the celebrated Maharishi Mahesh Yogi by attending the latters' classes to learn about transcendental meditation. But most of them stopped quite quickly when they discovered that the Maharishi was just as worldly as they were and was interested other than spiritually in one of the female converts from the showbiz world. John Lennon apparently became disenchanted when the 'guru' was unable to satisfactorily explain why Brian Epstein had suddenly died while The Beatles were meeting the Maharishi. Mike Love, however, was captivated by TM (even writing several forgettable songs about the subject) and has remained a disciple.

Dennis Wilson's involvement with mass killer Charles Manson was rather more dangerous than Love's belief in the Maharishi, and details of this episode can be found elsewhere in this book. Of the three Wilson brothers, Dennis was the one with the teenage heart-throb looks, plus an insatiable appetite for sex, and Manson's murderous crew included several attractive girls who would bestow their sexual favours liberally. While Mike Love's interest in TM was intellectual, Dennis's interest in Manson was sparked by lust for the latter's female followers, although he justified his friendship with Manson by claiming that the latter possessed immense songwriting talent.

At least it didn't cost The Beach Boys too much financially, which was more than could be said of the group's tour with the Maharishi, billed as 'The Most Exciting Event Of The Decade'. At the first gig of the tour at a huge New York auditorium, a witness noted that the police who were present to keep order outnumbered the audience. Even when a reasonable crowd paid to see The Beach Boys, they left in droves during the opening set by the 'guru', who tried to use the opportunity to make fresh converts to his so-called religious cause. The tour was cancelled halfway through, and lost around $500,000 and this was 20 years ago, when half a million was a vast amount to throw away.

Manson, while not being a drain on The Beach Boys as a whole, fleeced Dennis spectacularly over the period when they were 'friends', and this culminated in Manson threatening both Dennis and his son, Scott. As it happened, little resulted from the threats – Dennis would destroy himself without help from Charlie.

The majority of the records released by The Beach Boys since 'Heroes & Villains' had been musically forgettable and commercially disastrous. One possible exception was 'Surf's Up', a song written by Brian and Van Dyke Parks which was rescued from the *Smile* debacle and became the title track of a 1971 Beach Boys album. Other than that, Brian wasn't doing much apart from staying in bed, sometimes for weeks at a time. He was still ingesting copious quantities of drugs and had virtually given up writing songs – those that he did present to the group were fragmentary and useless as far as resurrecting the group's fast fading fame was concerned.

It was at this point that the decision was made that The Beach Boys should move from Los Angeles to Holland, to make a new album. No doubt the thinking was that not only would this distance Brian from his coterie of dubious drug-dealing friends, it would also restore Dennis to some kind of normality, as his paranoia about the Manson gang, many of whom were still around LA, might lessen.

Eventually, over 30 people and several dogs moved to Amsterdam, although initially Brian was not among this multitude, which not only included the group members, but also their entire families and servants and various employees plus their families and servants. Brian twice got as far as the Los Angeles airport, but then insisted that he had forgotten something and missed the plane on both occasions. A third time, everyone thought he was on his flight, but when the plane touched down in Holland, Brian's seat was empty apart from his passport and ticket. He had made an excuse to get off the plane before departure and had fallen asleep in an airport lounge. He was put on the next plane.

The entourage was deployed in various hotels, then rented houses, around Amsterdam, and reportedly there was almost constant telephonic contact between one or other of the party in Amsterdam and numerous parties in the US. Then the group decided that instead of utilizing the perfectly adequate recording facilities in Holland, they would construct their own studio in a converted barn. Such a scheme was hardly the kind of thing you might attribute to Einstein, but that wasn't all. What was to happen was that a complete studio was to be assembled in a warehouse in LA, after which it would be dismantled and rebuilt in Holland after all the constituent parts had been airfreighted across the Atlantic. Goodness knows what the eventual cost was.

After eight months in Holland, the album, which was wittily titled *Holland*, was delivered to Warner Bros, to whom The Beach Boys were signed at this point. Warners rejected it, despite the inclusion in the proposed package of a fairytale written by Brian entitled 'Mount Vernon & Fairway' which was to be pressed as a separate 7 in single and included in the album package as a bonus. Warners didn't want a fairytale, they wanted a hit single, and they couldn't hear one anywhere on the album. Van Dyke Parks came to the rescue again, with a song he and Brian had written shortly before, 'Sail On Sailor', and Warners finally agreed to release the album. It was little more than a minor hit.

Things were deteriorating. Brian was still incapable of consistent and constructive work. Dennis, while violently arguing with his wife, punched a plate glass window and was so badly injured that he was unable to use the hand for drumming for over a year. With no real prospect of a new album in the foreseeable future, both Warner Bros and Capitol, for whom they had made the vast majority of their hits, decided to embark on reissue programmes.

Warners had little to choose from, so simply reissued five previously released albums. Capitol, with more possibilities at their disposal, opted for a hits compilation with the inspired title of *Endless Summer*, and it topped the US album chart in 1974 after being advertised on television.

While this continuing interest in The Beach Boys was very gratifying to Mike Love and extremely useful in restoring the group's flagging finances, for Brian it must have been heartbreaking to realize that the great American public were considerably more interested in his group's early work, and had been virtually ignoring his newer confections. Brian was still not working on the road with the group, nor was he contributing much to their new recordings. He stayed in bed and took drugs.

On Midsummer's Day of 1975 at Wembley Stadium in London, Elton John topped a strong bill which also included The Eagles, the highly rated guitarist Joe Walsh and his band, and The Beach Boys. When Mike Love led the group into an hour-long set of their greatest hits, hardly touching on anything bar familiar singles, the sun was starting to set after a most unEnglish day of glorious sunny weather.

The group was rapturously received, and the majority of the 72,000 members of the audience considered them the highlight of a great day. When Elton came on and tried to better their remarkable performance, he made what many considered an error of judgement. He had just released a brand new album, which he wished to promote, so a large portion of his set consisted of songs which most of the audience didn't know. After lustily singing along with The Beach Boys while the sun kept everyone pleasantly warm, the crowd wanted the singing to continue. But they didn't know the tunes, let alone the words to Elton's new material, and his usually energetic performance must have been an anticlimax.

The following summer, a compilation album of most of the songs they played that day provided The Beach Boys with their first chart-topping album in Britain. This meant that The Beach Boys were forever condemned to play their old hits as opposed to their more recent output, a sad situation which continues today.

Every now and then, the announcement would be made that 'Brian Was Back', and that he would be as much involved with a new album as he had been on *Pet Sounds*. In fact, one album, *The Beach Boys Love You*, released in 1977, was almost a reversion to the days when Brian would write and record much of an album while the rest of the group were on tour, and it wasn't as bad as several of the intervening albums. Little made any difference to the public perception of The Beach Boys as perhaps the best oldies band in the world.

Brian was playing with the band again, and so was Dennis, while several hired gun session men doubled the size of the group onstage. Dennis was in poor shape, prematurely middle aged through booze, dope and frequent cheating on his wives. His voice was a croak. His latest wife – and this was unbelievable – was Mike Love's illegitimate daughter, and he had fathered a child by her, but as with most of his official and unofficial lovers, he had fallen out with her, and they were living apart. He had had five previous wives by the age of 39, and supposedly had an affair with President Reagan's daughter as well. Just after Christmas 1983, Dennis went swimming in the sea and drowned.

Brian, meanwhile, had discovered a new father figure. He had ballooned in size despite the appointment of security staff whose job it was to keep him on the straight and narrow. The arrival of Dr Eugene Landy, a psychiatrist, has been of immense and probably life-saving significance for Brian Wilson, who now looks better than for most of the past quarter of a century. Landy is also credited on Brian's songs as co-writer, and is Executive Producer of almost every record on which Brian has played recently.

His staff keep Brian under surveillance 24 hours a day, which must be costing him a fortune, but the bottom line is that Brian looks good and is more active musically than at any time since *Pet Sounds*.

At this point, he isn't even playing with The Beach Boys, whose hit-packed concerts continue to make them a major live attraction all over the world. The Beach Boys haven't made a new album in many years, and there seems little prospect of such a thing in the foreseeable future, although they actually returned to the top of the US singles chart in late 1988 with a song from a film called *Cocktail* entitled 'Kokomo'.

Brian's album qualified as one of the longest awaited in rock'n' roll history. Not because it took a long time to produce, but because he should have made it 20 years before, which in a way he had, although those records were credited to The Beach Boys. Brian Wilson is a cleverly planned album, with several of the tracks credited to 'Wilson/Landy'. There is one long track which sounds as though it has been rescued from the still unreleased Smile, and a couple of collaborations with hotshot hitmakers which are the most commercial things on the album. Sadly it dropped out of chart contention after a few weeks.

Brian came to England in September 1988, his visit coinciding with the convention of The Beach Boys Fan Club, whose fanzine, *Beach Boy Stomp*, had supported the group through thick and (mostly) thin for several years. With impressive initiative, two of Stomp's leading lights had secretly contacted Dr Landy to ask whether Brian might attend the fan convention. He arrived and the audience of 250 Beach Boys disciples behaved as if the Second Coming had taken place in that church hall in Greenford, a West London suburb. He played three songs, accompanying himself on electric piano, and then sat on the stage behind a table while every member of the audience brought him something to autograph albums, posters, anything. Attempts to engage him in meaningful conversation were mostly a failure, but he sat there for over an hour signing his name. The general consensus among those aware of Brian's precarious mental health was that Dr Landy must have thought that it would be good therapy for him, and it probably was.

John and Yoko

When Mark Chapman assassinated – somehow the word 'murdered' does not suffice – John Lennon on December 8, 1980 he unwittingly set in motion a chain of events which culminated in 1988 with the publication of the latest in a series of scabrous, dirt-dishing, ruthlessly iconoclastic biographies by the American writer Albert Goldman.

Goldman's study of Elvis Presley some years before had induced apoplexy in those Elvis fans who preferred to keep their memories pure. Not only was a highly damning portrait of a violent. Incontinent drug fiend painted, it was done in such tones of cynical glee that the over-riding feeling was that Goldman denied Elvis any talent in the first place.

His work on John Lennon had been mooted as far back as 1984. The fears of Lennon fans, and of people who simply object to the relish with which books like this are invariably greeted, were justified. Lennon, it was noted in one review, was being murdered for the second time. Ironically, the week of the book's publication saw a deeply contentious film, Martin Scorsese's *Last Temptation Of Christ*, released to choruses of vitriol from practising Christians in America. Another hero was being maltreated, and his supporters did not appreciate it. Lennon's book was not boycotted, although Paul McCartney urged people not to buy it.

It is inevitable that in a life of 40 years, including countless parties and literally thousands of mentions in the press, John Lennon's name would be linked with drugs, sleaze, alcohol and violence. The fact that Goldman should feel honour-bound to inform us of this shows that he was not really paying attention to all the other Beatle books – the Fab Four were living it up, and down and sideways, as far back as 1960 in Hamburg. There seems no reason why

John Lennon should not spend the greater part of the late Seventies in a lazy haze, worn out by too many trips on the Ferris Wheel, fed up with fame, music and people. The miracle is that in 1980 he decided that he wanted to re-enter the market place.

Up until *Double Fantasy*, the album he made that year, his career post-Beatles had been mercurial. He had actually started making solo albums before the Beatles officially broke up, much to their displeasure. His first one, a joint effort with Yoko Ono, was entitled *Two Virgins*. As a record it was an astounding flop, consisting of the same sort of meandering electronic doodling that permeated 'Revolution 9' on The Beatles 'White Album'. Yoko's role in the proceedings was unclear. However, the controversy lay with the sleeve, which featured John and Yoko totally naked, in a full-frontal shot. On the reverse, surprisingly enough, was a shot of their behinds.

On its completion in 1968 the other Beatles expressed their horror. For a start, the 'White Album' was due for release the same year, and they did not want its place usurped by this inconsequential, needlessly provocative oddity. Lennon was persuaded to shelve it until November of 1968, by which time the 'White Album' was safely in the stores. When *Two Virgins* followed it, it did so in a paper bag with a tiny shot of Lennon's and Yoko's head. It sold miserably, possibly due to poor distribution.

The month before its release, John Lennon had experienced his first drugs raid at his home in London. This was an ominous change in fortune for the Beatles and for Lennon himself, a hint that the Seventies would see the police being a lot less lenient to the band than the Sixties had. Until then The Rolling Stones had been viewed by those in authority as the real threat while The Beatles were more of a mischievous national asset. When the situation changed, it did so with a vengeance. Forty police officers turned up to arrest the waif-like twosome of Lennon and

Yoko. Even the House Of Commons thought that a little extreme. There was also speculation as to why two national newspapers had their cameras pointed before the police even showed up.

When the case came to court Lennon pleaded guilty in a gallant gesture to spare the pregnant Yoko. His guilty plea would later be used as an excuse to deny him American right of residence.

And Yoko had a miscarriage.

In March 1969 Lennon married Yoko in Gibraltar ('near Spain', as he put it in 'The Ballad Of John And Yoko') and they honeymooned in the Amsterdam Hilton. 'We're happy to be called a couple of freaks,' they announced, 'as long as we are happy and can make other people happy.' To make the honeymoon complete, they invited the world's press to photograph them in bed together. This was called a Bed-In. Or, sometimes, Hair Peace. Hair Peace was a travelling roadshow in the spring of 1969, as John and Yoko had much-publicized Bed-Ins in various capital cities. There was a prevailing feeling that the two of them had gone slightly off the rails.

Another album they released at this stage seemed to confirm this. *Unfinished Music No. 2: Life With The Lions* appeared to be nothing more than a vocal history of Yoko's miscarriage. Their next album, that same year, was called *The Wedding Album* and consisted mainly of John repeating the word 'Yoko' over and over, while Yoko returned the compliment. It was all very strange.

The Hair Peace concept – which remained throughout a vague, badly-defined idea – got even sillier. Acorns were planted in solemn ceremonies; billboard space was purchased to house huge 'War Is Over If You Want It' signs; and, in a hilarious gesture at a London gig featuring Lennon's new outfit The Plastic Ono Band, Yoko entertained the audience by handing an empty box to someone in the front row, telling him, 'There are plenty for everyone. Take one.' The box was labelled 'Smiles'.

The most ambiguous gesture made by Lennon during this period was to hand back the MBE which he had been awarded in 1966 with the other Beatles. In a note to The Queen he informed her that this was in protest against the British involvement in the Nigeria-Biafra war, against its support of America in Vietnam and 'against "Cold Turkey" (his new single) slipping down the charts'. He signed it, 'With love, John Lennon of Bag'. Bag Peace was the new gimmick. It involved lying in a bag. For peace.

'Cold Turkey' had been written about his efforts to kick heroin, which he had begun to take when The Beatles, scene got heavy. It was a frightening song, one of his best, and its harsh shrieks of pain would be echoed just over a year later with his Primal Therapy album, *John Lennon/ Plastic Ono Band*.

For the moment he contented himself with having his penis filmed in various stages of erection for Yoko Ono's provocative movie, *Erection*. In an exciting follow-up, *Number Five*, she filmed his face, concentrating on his mouth, and slowed the film down so that every time he moved his lips the audience in the cinema where it played gave a spontaneous cheer.

She announced her ambition to make a film featuring the smiling face of 'every single human being in the world'. Asked about it later, she admitted there had been 'technical difficulties'. The couple saw out 1969 by getting involved in plans for a religious rock musical based on the life of Jesus Christ. Lennon eventually refused to play the title role unless Yoko was allowed to be Mary Magdalene. Tim Rice and Andrew Lloyd Webber probably never looked back.

Lennon's behaviour throughout this period is particularly surprising given that he was always the first to prick any balloons of pretentiousness that drifted in on the Beatles' horizon. When the Maharishi Mahesh Yogi came on the scene and invited them down to Wales he was the one who tumbled that the grizzly sage was showing a less than spiritual interest in a female disciple. Hearing the telephone ring one afternoon the Maharishi wondered aloud who it could be. 'You're the bloody prophet,' replied Lennon. 'You tell us.'

Lennon later wrote a song about the trip entitled 'Sexy Sadie', scolding the protagonist, 'you made a fool of everyone', and warning him/her, 'you'll get yours yet, however big you think you are'. The consensus among cynical Lennon-watchers was that Yoko was the Maharishi in malevolent female form and that this time Lennon was being, to adopt the honest vernacular, 'strung up like a kipper'.

1970 was the year of Janov. Dr Arthur Janov's book *The Primal Scream* has become essential reading for neurotic students everywhere, with its grim diagnoses of childhood repression and parental fear. The English group Tears For Fears took their name from one of his theories which recommended crying rather than bottling up worries.

John Lennon and Yoko underwent four months of intensive therapy, from June to September 1970, and in October Lennon returned to the studio to put the Janov ideas into the grooves of his new album.

The harrowing result, *John Lennon/ Plastic Ono Band*, was released in 1971 and stands as one of his best ever records. The first track, 'Mother', featuring a chillingly basic drum pattern from Ringo Starr, dealt with the two personal traumas of Lennon's youth witnessing the death of his mother and seeing his father desert the family. The song ends in a crescendo of primal screams: 'Mama don't go/Daddy come home'.

It was similarly tense on other tracks, notably the lengthy 'God', on which he listed all the things he didn't believe in, including The Beatles. The album finished with a lo-fi recording of Lennon singing 'My Mummy's Dead', in the tentative, disbelieving voice of someone who has just heard of it.

Everything suggested that perhaps Lennon's dalliance with the distractions of Hair Peace and Yoko's cinema had been momentary aberrations. Still, one credit on the album, attributing 'wind' to Yoko Ono, stumped people who could not hear flutes on any of the songs. Lennon was quick to explain. 'She played atmosphere', he assured his fans.

His next album, *Imagine*, was released in 1971. The first thing critics noticed was a song called 'How Do You Sleep' which appeared to be a damning indictment of Paul McCartney. The end of The Beatles had been an acrimonious one, as Lennon and McCartney ridiculed each other's songs and hurried to make solo albums. But the venom of 'How Do You Sleep' took everyone by surprise, especially the line, 'Those freaks was right when they said/That you was dead'. McCartney later replied on his best-selling album *Band On The Run* with his song 'Let Me Roll It'. However, it lacked the sheer brutality of Lennon's tongue ('The sound you make is muzak to my ears indeed!)

Lennon's much-publicized retirement in 1974, after three more albums, coincided with his separation from Yoko. He took up with his secretary, May Pang, and formed a terrifying trio of carousers with singer Harry Nilsson and Keith Moon. No music was played – none of them was sober for long enough – but much merriment was had, although Lennon's enforced exit from Los Angeles' Troubador Club for wearing a sanitary towel round his head depressed those who hoped to see him in a recording studio again.

Re-united with Yoko, with a young son Sean and – at last – his American green card, Lennon claimed to be happier than ever. His retirement into what he called 'house-husbandry' had made him fat and indolent perhaps, but there was no denying the charm of his comeback album *Double Fantasy*. Actually, it was a joint effort, divided song-wise down the middle, but it's Lennon's songs that people remember. One of them, 'Woman', would be a posthumous number one single in Britain.

December 8, 1980, had been a busy day in the studio for the Lennons. They had been putting the finishing touches to a new Yoko song called 'Walking On Thin Ice'. Returning home towards midnight to their New York apartment block they were confronted by a young man named Mark David Chapman who called out Lennon's name, and then fired several shots into his turning body. He then put away his gun and stood reading a copy of J. D. Salinger's novel *The Catcher In The Rye* while John Lennon bled to death. He later pleaded guilty to murder and was sentenced to life imprisonment.

A copy of the *Double Fantasy* album was discovered by a fan propped up against the wall of the building. It transpired that this was Mark Chapman's personal copy, signed a few days previously by Lennon himself. Chapman expressed a wish from his prison cell that the record be auctioned off and the money donated to the gun control lobby in America.

Since Lennon's death a surfeit of inferior recorded material has emerged, each purporting to be positively the last work he ever made. It is irritating to listen to the half-finished ideas and nowhere-bound conversations on these records, especially since their release was not envisaged by the man who made them. Somehow they make him seem like a shoddy saint, being worshipped only until a better one comes along.

Goldman's biography took a sizeable hatchet to a few of the myths – alleging heroin abuse during the Seventies, especially by Yoko but fortunately it is a truism that the myths outlive the truth. Somewhere out there in rock 'n' roll fantasy land there are people who still believe, even after all the laughter and the denials, that Paul McCartney is dead. There are noticeably more who refuse to accept such a tragic blow happening to their hero John Lennon.

Sam Cooke

Sam Cooke's death in 1964 was one of the most violent ever suffered by a musician or singer, and was completely and tragically at odds with the gentle soulful strains of his music.

He sang melodic gospel-tinged songs for black audiences and for them he was a hero just as daunting and just as real as Elvis was for the whites. His hit songs – 'You Send Me', 'Wonderful World', 'Cupid' to name just three – perfected the style of commercial soul music. The fact that it worked spectacularly must have been a decisive factor in Berry Gordy crank-starting the Motown operation. Later singers, including Otis Redding, testified to Cooke's influence and his singles still send a lucrative shiver down the public's spine even today.

The sheer enormity of his influence suggested that his death might not have been an accident. The bizarre circumstances which led to it would seem to lend support to this argument. There are so many unanswered questions regarding the Cooke shooting that a conspiracy theory is almost inevitable.

Cooke had married his childhood sweetheart and was known as a clean living family man. So it was almost incredible to hear of his being shot while trying to rape a girl he had picked up at a party. Evidently he had persuaded this girl, Elisa Boyer, to get into his car, saying that he would give her a lift home. Instead he drove to a Los Angeles motel and, although she says she was forced into going, she seems to have stood silently by his side while he signed the register, 'Mr and Mrs Cooke'. She says that she then demanded to be taken home but, after Cooke assured her that he merely wanted to talk for a while, she followed him to the room. There he tried to undress her and she resisted. Fears that he would try to rape her made her snatch up her clothes as well as Cooke's and dash across to the motel office. Once inside she found a phone and called the police.

Cooke followed her to the office and began pounding on the door, demanding to talk to her. The motel manageress, a certain Mrs Franklin, told him that Elisa Boyer was not there. Cooke appeared to believe her and got in his car to drive away. But then he returned and resumed pounding. Mrs Franklin testified that Cooke then broke down the office door in a state of rage and proceeded to attack her. She managed to fight him off and get hold of a pistol, with which she shot him three times in the chest and abdomen. He did not die at once. Instead he leapt at her in an even greater rage whereupon she struck him with a stick. The stick broke but she kept hitting until he lay still. When the police eventually arrived he was dead.

Hearing this evidence, the inquest court ruled that the killing was justifiable homicide. Nevertheless the questions will not answer themselves. In an effort to find out what really happened that night Cooke's manager later hired a private detective to work it all out. He never came up with any satisfactory conclusions.

Sam Cooke's funeral was a tempestuous affair, with almost 200,000 people turning up to pay their respects. Many of them were hysterical, most were crying. Hundreds were crushed in the desperate attempt to take a look at his body for the last time and the local Chicago press ran stories on the pandemonium.

A week later another 5,000 people attended a funeral service for the dead singer in Los Angeles.